INTRODUCING
MICROECONOMIC
ANALYSIS

ISSUES, QUESTIONS, AND COMPETING VIEWS

EDITED BY

Hassan Bougrine
Laurentian University

Ian Parker
University of Toronto

Mario Seccareccia
University of Ottawa

2010
Emond Montgomery Publications
Toronto, Canada

Emond Montgomery Publications Limited
60 Shaftesbury Avenue
Toronto ON M4T 1A3
http://www.emp.ca/university

Printed in Canada on recycled paper.

We acknowledge the financial support of the Government of Canada through the Canada Book Fund for our publishing activities.

Acquisitions and development editor: Mike Thompson
Marketing manager: Christine Davidson
Director, sales and marketing, higher education: Kevin Smulan
Supervising editor: Jim Lyons
Copy editor: Gillian Scobie
Proofreader: Diane Gula
Typesetter: Debbie Gervais
Indexer: Paula Pike
Cover designers: Stephen Cribbin & Simon Evers
Cover photo: Courtesy of Sam Javanrouh/www.topleftpixel.com

Library and Archives Canada Cataloguing in Publication

Introducing microeconomic analysis : issues, questions, and competing views / edited by Hassan Bougrine, Ian Parker, Mario Seccareccia.

Includes index.
ISBN 978-1-55239-378-9

1. Microeconomics—Textbooks. I. Bougrine, Hassan II. Parker, Ian C. III. Seccareccia, Mario
HB172.I58 2010   338.5   C2010-901727-7

Contents

III Governments and Markets

IV Incomes and Inequality

Preface

Although economists agree on a lot more than the media generally suggest, there exist fundamental differences that at times seem completely intractable to the vast majority of students in the early stages of their study of economics. Many microeconomics textbooks reinforce this problem by systematically neglecting to cover ideas that are not from the mainstream. These books often make little effort to present theoretical and methodological differences, even though the intellectual landscape of the discipline encompasses a true rainbow of perspectives. This is especially problematic in microeconomics.

In *macro*economics, there are significant differences even *within* the mainstream approach, and so students are at least made aware of areas of contention between Keynesian, monetarist, and rational expectations camps, even if they are not exposed systematically to more heterodox approaches. In microeconomics, however, the orthodox approach has demonstrated a much greater degree of historical continuity, cohesion, stability, and standardization.

Despite heroic attempts at "product differentiation," the vast majority of microeconomics texts are remarkably similar, in terms of both what they include and what they exclude. It is therefore easier for students to remain unaware that microeconomics is not a body of revealed truths, but a contested terrain characterized by very distinct visions of the real world and very different theoretical understandings. The silence regarding such differences operates to the detriment of students, who are denied the excitement that they are part of an ongoing and unfinished intellectual enterprise, awareness of the nature and scope of the debates, and the opportunity to exercise their critical skills on both mainstream and alternative analyses. A different approach to introducing the discipline is desirable.

For a long time, we have felt the need for a book that would introduce the various perspectives at a level that would be accessible to the informed public, as well as to students at college and undergraduate levels of economics. Hence, when Emond Montgomery Publications invited us to assemble a companion volume to *Introducing Macroeconomic Analysis*, we were excited that students would have an opportunity to explore the divergent perspectives in *micro*economics as well as in macroeconomics. With the support of the publisher, with the collaboration of the authors, and also, perhaps, with the help of the current global conjuncture that has brought to light the need to rethink the nature of our economic system, we are very pleased to say that we have achieved our goal.

The 28 contributions from the authors provide an up-to-date analysis of all the major areas of college and undergraduate microeconomics. The result is a book that can be used as a main text and that is also an ideal complement for students of economics who wish to push past the current limits of understanding delineated in most existing microeconomic textbooks.

Acknowledgments

This book benefited at every stage from the insights, suggestions, questions, and encouragement of Mike Thompson, acquisitions and development editor at Emond Montgomery Publications; for his efforts we are particularly grateful. We also wish to thank Gillian Scobie, our thoughtful and meticulous copy editor, and Jim Lyons, supervisor of Emond Montgomery's editorial and production team. We are grateful for their expertise, professionalism, and good humour during the production of the volume. Several people provided helpful feedback during the development of this project, and we wish to thank them for sharing their insights: Thomas Barbiero (Ryerson University), Avi Cohen (York University), Vladimir Dvoracek (University of the Fraser Valley), Patrick Georges (University of Ottawa), and Joanne Roberts (University of Calgary).

Most of all, we thank the authors, whose excellent contributions will be invaluable for the training of a new generation of students of economics, some of whom will continue to carry forward the conversation from where the book leaves off and make their own substantive contributions to a dynamic, evolving discipline.

About the Authors

Morris Altman
Professor of Economics at Victoria University of Wellington, New Zealand and Professor of Economics at the University of Saskatchewan

Thomas Barbiero
Professor of Economics at Ryerson University

Lawrence Boland
Professor of Economics at Simon Fraser University

Hassan Bougrine
Professor of Economics at Laurentian University and Director of the International Economic Policy Institute

Michael Bradfield
Professor of Economics at Dalhousie University (retired)

Robert Chernomas
Professor of Economics at the University of Manitoba

Fanny Demers
Associate Professor of Economics at Carleton University

Michel Demers
Associate Professor of Economics at Carleton University

Gilles Grenier
Professor of Economics at the University of Ottawa

Morley Gunderson
CIBC Chair of Youth Employment and Professor, Department of Economics and Centre for Industrial Relations and Human Resources, University of Toronto

Walid Hejazi
Associate Professor of International Business at the Rotman School of Management

Richard P.F. Holt
Professor of Economics at Southern Oregon University

Ian Hudson
Associate Professor of Economics at the University of Manitoba

Derek Hum
Professor of Economics at the University of Manitoba

Peter Kriesler
Associate Professor of Economics at the University of New South Wales and Director of the Society of Heterodox Economists

Marc Lavoie
Professor of Economics at the University of Ottawa

David Leadbeater
Associate Professor of Economics at Laurentian University

Hugh Mackenzie
Research Associate at the Canadian Centre for Policy Alternatives and the Centre for Urban Studies at the University of Toronto, and Principal in Hugh Mackenzie and Associates

Brian K. MacLean
Professor of Economics at Laurentian University

Fiona MacPhail
Associate Professor of Economics at the University of Northern British Columbia

Donald McFetridge
Professor of Economics at Carleton University

Fred McMahon
Vice-President, International Research at the Fraser Institute

Ian Parker
Professor of Economics at the University of Toronto

Joseph Persky
Professor of Economics at the University of Illinois at Chicago

Robert E. Prasch
Professor of Economics at Middlebury College, Vermont

Jason L. Saving
Senior Economist at the Federal Reserve Bank of Dallas

Mario Seccareccia
Professor of Economics at the University of Ottawa and Editor of the International Journal of Political Economy

Jim Stanford
Economist at the Canadian Auto Workers Union

Niels Veldhuis
Vice-President, Research at the Fraser Institute and Economics faculty member at Kwantlen Polytechnic University

Martti Vihanto
Assistant Professor of Economics at the Turku School of Economics, Finland

William Watson
Associate Professor and Chairman of the Economics Department at McGill University

Elizabeth Wilman
Professor of Economics at the University of Calgary

Key Figures in Economics

 Adam Smith
(1723–1790)

 Karl Marx
(1818–1883)

 Alfred Marshall
(1842–1924)

 Thorstein Veblen
(1857–1929)

 Irving Fisher
(1867–1947)

 John Maynard Keynes
(1883–1946)

 Friedrich von Hayek
(1899–1992)

 Joan Robinson
(1903–1983)

 Milton Friedman
(1912–2006)

 John Kenneth Galbraith
(1908–2006)

General Introduction

Hassan Bougrine, Ian Parker, and Mario Seccareccia

Alfred Marshall defined economics as the study of "mankind in the ordinary business of life."* He went on to argue that it was above all a study of individual and social behaviour concerned with the procurement and use of "the material requisites of wellbeing." Many generations of students have been trained in microeconomic analysis—that is, the study of the behaviour of individual agents, whether households, firms, or governments, normally within a market-based economy—whose groundwork was first laid out in Marshall's *Principles* over a century ago. Marshall was well aware of the competing methodological perspectives that prevailed at the end of the 19th century. For this reason, he was very careful to address the concerns raised by the competing schools of thought of his generation, and he made an enormous effort to find ready applications of his theories to historical reality.

Between Marshall's day and the present, however, several developments have occurred within microeconomics, not all of them unqualified advances. First, the focus of the discipline has shifted. Most mainstream economists nowadays would accept Lionel Robbins's definition of the scope of economics, as a branch of the logic of choice: "Economics is the science which studies human behaviour as a relationship between ends and scarce means which have alternative uses."** The focus is on *constrained optimization*, and the working assumption is that economic behaviour is the outcome of rational, self-interested decision-making processes. A second change is that academic economics, particularly *micro*economics, has become much more professionalized, institutionalized, and standardized. A third change is that the discipline has become much more heavily mathematical, because of the usefulness of calculus in representing and solving optimization problems and the need for formal quantitative models as a basis for econometric testing. One of the costs of these developments, however, is that modern textbooks offer little of the theoretical richness and range found in Marshall's *Principles*, and generally succumb to a more narrow or monistic perspective.

Much more so than in the other social sciences, economics students are often fed enormous doses of pure theory based on the conventional representation of

---

* Alfred Marshall, *Principles of Economics*, 8th ed. (London: Macmillan, 1920), 1. The first edition was published in 1890.

** Lionel Robbins, *An Essay on the Nature and Significance of Economic Science*, 2nd ed. (London: Macmillan, 1952), 16.

the economic behaviour of a fictional rational economic agent—*homo economicus.* As students continue their studies, textbooks often show more concern with mathematical elegance than with widening students' base of theoretical knowledge through a substantive discussion of competing perspectives.

After a steady diet of the standard orthodox theoretical models of human behaviour during their undergraduate years, students of economics are then sometimes encouraged—usually after having learned some statistical techniques—to apply existing theories to the "real world." The problem, however, is that when they do engage in such statistical work, the range of models to which they have been exposed is restricted, and thus so is their capacity to develop new ways of modelling reality. Students are rarely asked to formally test an established theory against an *alternative* theoretical hypothesis. This narrow approach to economic research then finds its counterpart in the policy arena, both domestically and internationally, where policy-makers are often advised by economists that "there is no alternative" (TINA). We strongly believe that this TINA perspective is stifling and unhelpful in training students to think critically, and it is also constraining to policy-makers whose decisions sometimes rest on the advice of economists holding one point of view. We believe that this TINA perspective is largely a byproduct of how economists are educated, beginning at the undergraduate level where most introductory and intermediate level textbooks often remain within the confines of mainstream established theories.

Like its companion, *Introducing Macroeconomic Analysis: Issues, Questions and Competing Views,* this book breaks away from this academic tradition in economics and aligns itself more closely with the way other social scientists train students in their various disciplines. The book takes a modern, pluralistic perspective in assuming not only that alternative views exist but also that their proliferation is crucial to the progress of both theory and the elaboration of appropriate economic policy. Readers are asked to follow a dialogue between economists of competing perspectives in the hope that some of the differences that separate these various perspectives remain etched in their mind.

Our strong belief is that the primary objective of an economics education should not be to provide the "right" *answers,* but rather to enable students to ask the right *questions.* Do individuals in fact always behave rationally, and focus exclusively on their own self-interest? If they don't, is there still a justification for assuming in our models that individuals are self-centred rational economic agents? How effective are real-world markets in rationing and allocating scarce resources? What alternatives exist, and what are *their* capacities and limits? Why do markets fail? When markets fail, can the failures be corrected by market means alone, or are other means necessary?

Are consumers "sovereign," or are they merely pawns in the hands of corporate advertisers? Do real-life firms focus exclusively on profit maximization, or do they have other objectives? What is the role of the government in the economy? Could the market system even exist without the activities of the state? Is there really such a thing as a "free" market? Can the unconstrained private sector supply *all* goods and services more effectively than the public sector? Does the private sector need to be regulated and, if so, under what conditions? Does the ownership—domestic or foreign—of corporations matter, and what role should the government play with regard to direct foreign investment? What strategies are available to address the ecological challenges we face on Spaceship Earth, in an era when interlinked environmental crises have assumed planetary importance?

What are the mechanisms that *actually* determine the distribution of income and wealth in society? Is it possible to reconcile the goals of economic efficiency and economic justice? What is the extent of labour market discrimination, and what approaches offer the best prospects of eliminating it? Can poverty be eliminated? Would a guaranteed annual income (GAI) contribute to the elimination or reduction of poverty? Why are there substantial per capita income differences among regions? Do equalization payments and regional development programs reduce or increase inequalities?

These questions and others are posed in the chapters that follow. We have selected 14 major topics in microeconomics that generally coincide chapter by chapter with issues discussed in most textbooks, and asked leading economists to debate them in a style that is accessible to students at college and undergraduate levels. The authors not only represent different perspectives in economic theory, but come from different parts of the world, bringing with them a rich international experience. For each topic, we present the most recent thoughts and explanations from both the more established, orthodox perspective (usually the neoclassical approach) and the alternative, heterodox view (primarily the institutionalist, behavioural, post-Keynesian, and Marxian approaches).

In some chapters, the conclusions reached by the authors have some common ground; in others, their conclusions are diametrically opposed. In any given chapter, you may find yourself agreeing with one essay more than the other, or you may find that you are convinced by one author's argument, only to agree with the opposite conclusion when you read the other piece! You may find that you are convinced by an essay when you first read it, but a week later, on reflection, come to believe that the other argument is stronger. You may even find that you genuinely can't decide who is right, or that *both* are wrong and you have a better answer. If you have any or all of the above responses to the essays in the book, it will have done its job. It is our hope that the book will generate lively debate both inside and outside the classroom. The ultimate objective of this learning and exchange of ideas is to allow all participants to achieve a better understanding of how to make the world a better place to live for everyone.

PART I

Basic Economic Problems

Is Economics a Science? Is It Useful?

COMPETING VIEWS

Lawrence Boland, "Microeconomics and Methodology"

Ian Parker, "Why Economics Is—and Is Not—a Science"

Editors' Introduction

Modern economics is the child of political economy and the grandchild of moral philosophy. Its ancestral roots, however, can be traced back much further—to core religious texts (including the Bible and, much later, the *Qur'an*), to early legal systems and codes, and to the works of philosophers such as Aristotle. From as early as the 6th century BCE, the growth of trade, the development of money, and the extension of literacy and numeracy fostered systematic thought aimed at understanding the forms and processes of economic life. Subsequently, medieval scholastic thinkers, mercantilist writers during the 16th and 17th centuries (whose ideas were associated with the emergence of the nation-state and the expansion of commercial capitalism), and 18th-century physiocrats and others provided concepts that influenced the classical economists—Adam Smith, Thomas Malthus, David Ricardo, and their successors—and critics like Karl Marx in their development of political economy as a discipline.

In a capitalism increasingly transformed by the technological advances of the Industrial Revolution and the penetration of market exchange relations into all realms of society, the classical economists aimed at understanding the sources of economic growth and development, the nature of production and exchange, and the patterns and processes of distribution of society's output among the principal social-economic classes. The forerunners of modern economics were concerned with understanding both how the economic sphere *did* operate and how it *should* operate, or with what we would now call *positive* and *normative* issues. The origins of modern economics are inextricably intertwined with moral, ethical, social, and political considerations.

The 1870s saw the emergence of a new approach, a *neo*classical economics, which is the basis of most microeconomics texts to this day. From the outset, and increasingly over time, neoclassical economics was viewed as the study of optimizing decision making by rational individual economic agents—producers and consumers, firms and households, employers and workers, buyers and sellers—in a market context. Its development was marked by the increased use of abstract formal models and mathematics, the expansion of economics as an academic discipline, the amassing of quantitative data, and the growth of econometric theory and testing. The question then arises: "Is economics a science?"

In his contribution, Lawrence Boland provides a panoramic overview of the issues. He argues that the prime criterion of a science is that it can produce testable models—models yielding predictions that can be tested against empirical evidence. Since orthodox economics does produce such models, it is a science, based on this criterion. Boland then explores the question of whether scientific models have to be "true" in some sense, or just useful. Finally, he suggests that the core orthodox model encounters limits when it deals with the role of knowledge in decision making, and that this gap is particularly significant in models that focus on "equilibrium," since the models have no adequate theory of disequilibrium behaviour.

Ian Parker argues that a "science" is a way of knowing, and hence includes a wider range of forms of knowledge than those implied by the testability criterion. He provides a set of criteria of "good" models, and suggests that Milton Friedman's argument—that a model's assumptions do not have to correspond to reality, as long as the model yields good predictions—does not deal adequately with the problems of induction, and that the core orthodox model is effectively untestable. He concludes by indicating some strengths and limits of Austrian and Marxian approaches, and suggests that to be more scientific in the narrow sense, economics will have to draw on other disciplines *and* integrate the strengths of both orthodox and heterodox economics.

Microeconomics and Methodology

Lawrence Boland

Introduction

At the beginning of many economics courses, students will ask, "Is economics a science?" If this were the 18th century, asking this question might be understandable, because many philosophers of the 18th century claimed authority for science over religion. Today, many people still see science as having some sort of monopoly on truth. This image is often based on the belief that scientists employ a "scientific method" that can be used to ensure that scientific theories are true.

This common belief is based on several errors. First and foremost, there is no scientific method that, if followed, could ever guarantee that truly scientific theories will be shown to be true. Instead, scientists are always engaged in trying to see whether their theories are false—that is why they spend so much time testing them in experimental laboratories. But also, no truly scientific theory that explains some observable phenomena could ever be proven true—even if it is true! This is due to the logical nature of any explanation and, in particular, the explanation of any observable phenomena. An explanation is a logical argument consisting of explicit assumptions, which together imply that one would necessarily be observing the phenomena one is attempting to explain. To avoid begging questions, such an explanation must include at least one assumption in the form of what logicians call a "strictly universal statement." A strictly universal statement has the logical form "*all* x are y." The statement "*some* x are y" is not a strictly universal statement. The classic example of an explanation is the one that answers the question, "Why did Socrates die?" The classic explanation is in the form of what logicians call a syllogism, consisting of two "premises," or, as economists would say, two "assumptions:" (1) "All humans are mortal" and (2) "Socrates was a human." From this, it logically follows that Socrates was mortal and hence explains why he died. If instead of (1)—which is a strictly universal statement—we had assumed that "*some* humans are mortal," then we would just be begging the question of whether Socrates was one of those mortal humans or not, and thus not providing an explanation, as intended.

What then is meant by claiming that some research area in general, or an explanation in particular, is "scientific"? Today, most scholars say that for any empirical claim to be scientific it must be capable of being empirically refuted—if it is false. In short, scientific theories and explanations are "falsifiable." And since most economic theories and explanations are falsifiable, economics can be considered a science. But, of course, this is not as profound as it would have seemed in the 18th century!

Natural Sciences and Social Sciences

Another related issue is the differences between what are called natural sciences (primarily physics, chemistry, and biology) and what are called social sciences (primarily economics, sociology, anthropology, political science, cultural geography, and psychology). It is important to note that natural and social sciences have different histories. The key difference, however, is that the social sciences all involve aspects of sentient beings whereas the natural sciences, such as physics and chemistry, do not. That is, atoms and molecules don't think, but people do (we hope).

The next question is, "How is economics different from the other social sciences?" The differences were once much more distinct, but today the lines are getting blurred. And although things having to do with business and government are in the obvious domain of economics, economics can actually be extended to answer questions about almost any deliberate decision making. Why did John choose to buy a sweater rather than a shirt? Why did John choose a red sweater rather than a green sweater, since both were available? And so on. Of course, one could provide a sociological, a psychological, or even a political explanation to address these questions, but what will always be the case in economics today is that the economic explanations will involve some sort of optimization. In business, the decision-maker might be assumed to want to maximize profits, or maximize sales, or maybe to minimize costs, minimize pollution, and so on. What the decision-maker considers relevant for the choices made will usually distinguish the economic explanations from the others.

Here we will be discussing what is called microeconomics to distinguish it from what is called macroeconomics. Microeconomics focuses on explaining the decisions made by individuals whereas macroeconomics focuses on the effects of decisions made by governments, businesses, and consumers on the whole economy. If one were to read the work of economists written 150 years ago, one might not detect such differences in focus—one would be more impressed with the style of writing. Today, economic research is primarily done with heavy doses of mathematics that would be hard to find in older writings. And today, mathematical modelling is the main medium of research in both microeconomics and macroeconomics.

Researching with Models

Model building is popular primarily because it minimizes the ambiguities that plagued older economic research. With models, one must be very explicit about what one's assumptions say. But being explicit can come at a price—and too often the price is the sacrifice of realism. This is because the main characteristic of economic models is that their assumptions simplify aspects of observable reality that they are designed to represent. The simplifications can involve ignoring minor influences on the decisions being explained or simplifying the relationship between the decisions and the things that influence the decision.

The widespread use of mathematics began in the late 1930s. At the time, there were many critics of its use, in particular, its use in building mathematical models of economics. Critics claimed that mathematical models could only produce "tautologies." A tautology is a statement for which one cannot conceive of a way for it to be false. Thus, it is not testable, and hence not scientific. A simple example of a tautology is the statement, "I am here or I am not here," which is true regardless of who I am or where here is. Proponents of building mathematical models— such as the Nobel laureate Paul Samuelson—set about ensuring that, on the contrary, mathematical models can be testable and thus not tautologies. This is why, even today, testability remains a standard requirement for economic explanations in general and mathematical models in particular.

The critics then shifted to criticizing the realism of using simplified assumptions in economic models built using mathematics. For example, the typical explanation of decisions made by the management of a widget-manufacturing firm focuses on the decisions that have to be made, such as how much labour to hire or how many widgets to produce. The most common explanation of these decisions assumes that the managers wish to maximize profit. We know from the simple mathematics of ordinary calculus that if the number of widgets produced is maximizing profit, then producing one more widget would reduce profit and the firm would thus obtain less than maximum profit. Specifically, the extra revenue earned by selling the extra widget will also increase the cost, and for various known reasons that increase will be by more than the extra revenue obtained. The critics complained that this required very complicated and detailed cost and revenue assessments that few managers were capable of doing in the 1930s (long before computers or even electronic calculators). The critics conducted surveys asking managers how they made their decisions. These surveys reportedly demonstrated that, indeed, few managers made decisions using calculus to determine whether producing one more widget would reduce profit. The critics thus concluded that the process of maximization assumed by economic model-builders did not represent the real decision process. In other words, they claimed that mathematical model-builders were employing unrealistic or false assumptions and thus their explanations and models were necessarily false.

In response to such criticism, some defenders of the maximization assumption thought theorists should consider how essential perfectly true assumptions are by considering how physicists explain simple things, such as the impact speed of an apple falling from the tree. The defenders noted that physicists employ a formula based on an analogy of a ball that is falsely assumed to be falling in a vacuum. One economist in particular—the Nobel laureate Milton Friedman—claimed that false economic assumptions are not necessarily a problem *if* the economic explanation or model could be shown to still imply true predictions. For example, as we know from any high school physics textbook, physicists still accurately predict the speed of the falling apple even though the formula for calculating speed was based on a model where the existence of a perfect vacuum is assumed, even though a perfect vacuum may be impossible. After all, the formula was merely an instrument to calculate speed. Instruments are not to be judged on whether they are true or false but only on whether they produce correct predictions or are otherwise useful.

This raised a long-standing methodological question. Should we require economic explanations or models to be true or just useful? Interestingly, this too was a hot question in the early 18th century. At that time, the issue was whether Isaac Newton's laws of physics—which could be successfully used to explain the movements of planets—was a true theory of planetary movements or just a useful instrument to predict those movements. To say a theory should be considered an instrument rather than a true explanation is today called "instrumentalism" to distinguish it from what might be called "realism," which says theories are intended to be true explanations or descriptions of the observable real world.

Instrumentalism and Realism

The proponents of realism say that if you claim to understand something, such as the microeconomics of widget making, you cannot honestly say you understand it if, in constructing your explanation, you assume something that is known to be false (for instance, that the managers of the firm are making the complicated calculation needed to ensure the maximum profit). The proponents of instrumentalism respond that if you are only using an explanatory instrument because it works, the truth or falsity of the instrument is irrelevant. Amazingly, even though this is a 300-year-old debate, there are still active proponents on both sides today. After all, proponents of instrumentalism will say, when you take your broken TV to the TV repairman, you do not quiz him about his understanding of electromagnetics—for all you know, he could believe there are little green men in the transistors and one of them died. As long as he replaces the transistor with the "dead green man" and the TV works, what do you care?

Nevertheless, realism is taken for granted by many economists, so the acceptance of assumptions that have been shown to be false—like the assumption about managers in the last paragraph—is at least considered open to question. But instrumentalism is defended by claiming that conscious maximization is not necessary. Specifically, Friedman argued (like Armen Alchian before him) that only a profit-maximizer survives in a truly competitive economy. In a truly competitive economy, excess profits will eventually be driven down to zero (if not, there is an incentive for someone to go into the same business and compete by lowering the price, thus lowering profit for all). And whenever zero profit results, if a firm is not maximizing profit, then it is losing money and will thus go out of business. The issue is not whether this argument is true, but that it is a possible defence of the use of false assumptions—particularly if we take the results of the 1930s survey as evidence of what managers think they are doing and, thus, evidence that the profit-maximizing assumption isn't true.

Whether the truth status of one's theory or model matters seems to depend on the purpose of the explanation or the purpose for building the model. It also depends on two questions we might ask the model-builders. We could ask them what they think about the methodological role of theories and models or we could ask about their view of the truth status of theories and models. These are two different questions. It is easy, on one hand, to see that theories and models can be used as instruments. In that role, truth status does not matter. On the other hand, if we claim that our theory or model enables us to understand some economic phenomena, then the truth status of theories and models does matter whenever honesty matters (as it should). Nevertheless, even if we are honest, we still have the problem noted at the beginning. Every explanation or explanatory model must have at least one assumption in the form of a strictly universal statement. But, again, one can never empirically (that is, with observations alone) prove that any strictly universal statement is true even when it is true. For example, to prove the statement "all swans are white," we would have to prove that there does not exist anywhere, at any time, in the universe, a non-white swan—such a proof is, empirically, an impossible task. Note that this impossibility is not because the statement happens to be false—it would be the case even if the statement were true. Today people characterize this logical fact as the "impossibility of proving the negative." So, some think we need to employ a less strict notion of the truth status of our assumptions, theories, and models. That is, we could always ask economic theorists or model-builders how they know their assumptions are true. It could easily be claimed that our assumptions are not *known* to be absolutely true (since, in the case of the necessary strictly universal statements, that would be impossible), but we can employ some sort of minimum criteria of acceptance so that we can push on. Such a claim says that we do not claim our assumptions are true, only that they are "true" according to the current conventions of acceptance. This position concerning the truth status of theories and models is called "conventionalism." But, we should ask, will just any arbitrary conventions of acceptance do?

Conventionalism

Conventionalism—which is the most common position taken by most economists today—is also not new. At the beginning of the 20th century, Henri Poincaré, a famous physicist and philosopher of science, addressed the question of whether the laws of physics were "only arbitrary conventions." He answered, "Conventions, yes; arbitrary, no." Languages and measurement units are arbitrary conventions but conventions used for empirical acceptance need not be. Today, when it comes to empirical research, there are many statistical criteria of acceptance that can be used. When newspapers report that they have taken a poll of possible voters on a referendum, with the result that 55 percent are in favour, they may also say that the accuracy is plus or minus 4 percent. For some questions, choosing plus or minus 4 percent might be close enough. But what is sufficient for an acceptance convention may depend on the question at hand. For some questions, even 0.4 percent might not be close enough.

Model-builders today often think that, though at some point the absolute truth status of our assumptions might matter, in the short run, we should not be too quick to judge. This is because model-builders see model building as a process. That is, researchers are in the ongoing business of developing a sequence of models. The sequence starts out with very simplified assumptions, which are then, one by one, made less simple and thus more realistic in subsequent versions of the model. So, if we are too quick to judge, we may cut short a sequence that, if allowed to develop, might produce a model that comes very close to being absolutely true. In other words, the researchers say, be careful to not demand too much and thereby "throw the baby out with the bath water."

The View of the Austrian School

One persistent complaint about what is taught today in undergraduate classes comes from the older members of the so-called Austrian School of economic theorists such as Friedrich Hayek. Specifically, the complaint was that the microeconomic theory we teach in undergraduate courses fails to recognize the *process* of decision making. The term "process" raises the issue of the role of time in microeconomic theory. Decisions are not made instantaneously; they involve forming a plan and only then going about making the decision. In particular, the

Austrians often complain that one important aspect of explaining any decision is to recognize that the decision-maker must have some knowledge of the situation being faced to form a plan of action. This is especially important when considering a decision that might be made to expand one's business—that is, by investing in new machines or just expanding the capacity of one's business to produce by building a bigger factory, say. Of course, a decision-maker could expand just for the sake of expanding. But economics is more interested in the economic reasons for expanding—such as the expectation that the demand for one's product is going to be greater in the future. If the decision to expand was based on an expectation of future demand, how did the decision-maker know or think this expectation to be true? Was the expectation just a guess or were there identifiable reasons for forming it?

For many years, the Austrian School has argued that for a minimally adequate explanation based on maximization (of profit, or satisfaction, or some such objective), the decision-maker's knowledge and how it was acquired must be explained. This is because it is all too easy to dismiss a maximization-based explanation as being based on an implicit assumption of perfect knowledge. But, as Alfred Marshall argued over a hundred years ago, if everyone had perfect knowledge, there would be no need for markets! If nothing else, all members of the Austrian School think markets·do matter, so perfect knowledge is out of the question.

But, if perfect knowledge is out of the question, how do decision-makers acquire the knowledge they need? And does their method of learning or acquiring that knowledge influence their decision? Perhaps the current state of the economy affects their plans and thereby their decisions? When we see the stock markets falling, would we be likely to plan to expand our business? John Maynard Keynes raised this question when he challenged the usual notion that to stimulate business investment, all the government had to do was lower the interest rate. As Keynes argued (during the Great Depression of the 1930s), the price of borrowing for investment will never be the decisive factor when investors are pessimistic about the future. So, it seems that how microeconomics explains individuals' decisions about such things as investment or consumption (instead of saving) can even matter for macroeconomic policies.

There are two related reasons for the continued avoidance of any discussion of the knowledge or information requirements of decision making. Both involve the dominant dependence on equilibrium explanations. First, by assuming the *existence* of a market equilibrium to explain why prices are what they are, the typical model avoids explaining how that equilibrium was reached. In other words, the realism of the assumption of the existence of a market equilibrium should be open to question—not because it is false, but because its truth status has usually not been logically established. In particular, to explain fully why prices are what they are, one also needs to explain why they are not what they are not. This is because it is always possible that, conceivably, multiple possible prices exist that are consistent with the model's assumptions. The assumption thus begs the question of why the one particular price level, rather than any of the other possible equilibrium levels, is observed.

Static Balance and Dynamic Equilibrium

The other reason for avoiding the knowledge or information requirements of decision making is simply that it is all too easy to confuse an accidental static balance with a recurring dynamic equilibrium. A balance can be a static state of affairs, such as balancing a coin on its edge. A tipped-over coin does not usually pop back up and there is no reason for it to do so. Some economic theorists would say that the balanced coin is in an "unstable" equilibrium. For a balance to be in a "stable" equilibrium, there must be reasons why the balance would be restored whenever it is disturbed. If one assumes that a market equilibrium exists simply by assuming that demand equals supply, unless one explains how that equilibrium was reached, one is begging the question of why that balance between demand and supply, if disturbed, would ever be restored. Perhaps the balance is just an accident. To explain why the balance between demand and supply would be restored, the model purporting to explain a price as an equilibrium price must explain why the price is always changed back to a market-balancing price whenever the balance is disturbed. Specifically, who changes the price and why? The answer should be easy, because it involves the maximization assumption used to explain the behaviour of individual decision-makers. If market demand is not equal to supply, someone is not maximizing. For example, if demand were greater than the supply at the going price, some demanders would not be able to acquire their desired quantity. To rectify this situation, the demanders can offer a higher price to get suppliers to sell to them instead of to other competing buyers. Whether this leads back to a market equilibrium needs to be explained. The return to a market equilibrium will be assured if, for example, there are reasons why demand curves are negatively sloped and supply curves are positively sloped. Today, most microeconomic theory textbooks provide the reasons for their respective slopes, but still continue to ignore the need to explain the process of price adjustment.

Conclusion

This is where we stand today in the ongoing research in microeconomics. The question of whether the assumptions of microeconomics are true may have to be postponed. But this does not mean that the truth of our theories or models does not matter at some point if honesty matters too.

DISCUSSION QUESTIONS

1. Why can a scientific statement that is true also be empirically impossible to prove true and yet empirically easy to prove false?
2. If we know from surveys that managers of firms do not make the necessary complicated calculations to determine whether their profit is being maximized, can we still assume managers of firms are profit-maximizers?
3. If demand curves were upward sloping and supply curves were downward sloping and should the going price happen to be at the level where demand equals supply, is this an equilibrium price?

SUGGESTED READINGS

Arrow, K. 1959. Towards a theory of price adjustment. In *Allocation of economic resources*, ed. M. Abramovitz, 41–51. Stanford, CA: Stanford University Press.

Boland, L. 1986. *Methodology for a new microeconomics*. Boston: Allen & Unwin.

Boland, L. 1992. *The principles of economics: Some lies my teachers told me*. London: Routledge.

Boland, L. 2003. *The foundations of economic method: A Popperian perspective*. London: Routledge.

Clower, R. 1959. Some theory of an ignorant monopolist. *Economic Journal* 69: 705–716.

Hayek, F. 1937. Economics and knowledge. *Economica* 4 (NS): 33–54.

Richardson, G. 1959. Equilibrium, expectations and information. *Economic Journal* 69: 225–237.

Why Economics Is— and Is Not—a Science

Ian Parker

An economist is an expert who will know tomorrow why the things he predicted yesterday didn't happen today.

Laurence J. Peter

Demonology is the only exact science.

Attributed to Lawrence Durrell

All professions are conspiracies against the laity.

George Bernard Shaw

Introduction

"Is economics a science?" One of the most striking aspects of this question is how rarely it gets asked, in any serious way, in most economics programs. Why is the question of whether economics is a science so often neglected? One reason is that before we know much economics, the question can only be posed in a fairly abstract form, because we don't have the basis in experience to judge whether it is or isn't a science. Another, practical, reason is that in most economics courses, there is usually a lot of material to cover, or "content to deliver," and teachers, even those who are interested in the issue, don't have the luxury of exploring all of the implications of the question. There is a third reason: the question, when properly posed, is a difficult one to answer, and depends—among other things—on how we decide to define "science" and "economics." Fourth, it may not be clear that it *matters* whether economics is a "science" or not, *whatever* that means! After all, there are a lot of economists, doing many different types of work, and presumably producing *something* for which people are prepared to pay good money. Does it really matter whether we call what they are doing "science" or something else?

This essay first argues that whether economics is a science, and in what sense it is or is not a science, *does* matter. It then surveys some meanings of "science," indicating some of the capacities and scientific limits of orthodox, or mainstream, "neoclassical" economics. Finally, it outlines the capacities and limits of some alternative economic approaches.

How Do Economists Think About the World?

The essay is thus concerned with *economic methodology*—the study of how economists think about the world. Recalling Samuel Johnson's remark that "Patriotism is the last refuge of a scoundrel," the economic historian William N. Parker once began a lecture with the tongue-in-cheek remark that "Methodological discussion is the last refuge of the ignorant." He then launched into a brilliant methodological discussion! Parker clearly thought that methodological analysis is important, but he also recognized that it is often not given much attention or respect within the economics profession.

Why does it matter whether economics is a science? In the first place, understanding the functioning of society and the economy clearly matters, particularly in a period of rapid and dramatic technological and organizational change, growing concerns about the effects of humankind on the planet's ecological system, the continuing extension of the power and influence of transnational capital, and major geopolitical realignments. Since it has been claimed that economics aids in providing this understanding, we need to know whether the claim is justified.

Second, we are concerned not just with understanding the world but with acting in and on it. We are *all* engaged in the sphere of economic decision making, economic policy, and political–economic action. A worker will normally not use a screwdriver to hammer in a nail, nor (with the exception of television handyman Red Green) use duct tape where an arc welder is required. Similarly, we need to understand the capacities *and* the limits of our tools of *thought*—our instruments of mental production—if we are to know how much confidence to place in the conclusions we draw from using them and in the actions we take, based on those conclusions.

There is a further reason for asking the question. Not all of us are or will become professional economists. Members of the "laity," to use George Bernard Shaw's term, need to know how much trust to place in economists' conclusions, especially if laypersons are not fully informed about the methods and assumptions on which the conclusions rest. If economics is assumed to be a "science," and science is equated with "truth," rather than with the *search* for truth, then economic findings and the results of economic reasoning can acquire a certain ideological power, derived from the aura of "scientific truth" they seem to possess, *regardless of whether they merit such trust*. The danger of misplaced faith is enhanced in periods of heightened uncertainty and insecurity, when the demand for certainty tends to increase. The danger is further enhanced if the communication of economic results provides the trappings of science—impenetrable jargon, mathematical symbolism, and complex statistical estimation procedures—while at the same time constituting a "barrier to entry." The language can prevent the laity from gaining access to the palace of wisdom inhabited by those inside the charmed circle of professional economists.

This sketch is only slightly exaggerated. For reasons discussed below, the specialized languages of economics are both an essential prerequisite for communication *within* the profession and a means of preserving the "monopoly of knowledge"[1] of those within the profession in relation to those *outside* it—the laity. John Maynard Keynes (1973, 383–384) recognized both the power of such ideas and their longevity:

> [T]he ideas of economists and political philosophers, both when they are right and when they are wrong, are more powerful than is commonly understood. Indeed the world is ruled by little else. Practical men, who believe themselves to be quite exempt from any intellectual influences, are usually the slaves of some defunct economist.

Hence, a critical assessment of the scientific pretensions of economics is a form of intellectual *jiu-jitsu*—self-protection or inoculation against the ideological potential inherent in the discipline.

On Scientific Models

Although most of us have a rough-hewn idea of "what science is," the meaning of "science" has actually evolved over time. The word is derived from the Latin *scientia*, which means both "knowledge" (what is known) and "knowing" (the process of acquiring or holding knowledge in consciousness). In its original sense, then, a science is a way of knowing, as well as what is known in that way.

From at least as early as the classical Greek period, however, science or "natural philosophy" also had many of the characteristics that we associate with it today: *abstraction* from particular instances in an attempt to provide *generalized* descriptions, principles, and explanations; a related interest in *taxonomy*, the ordering of phenomena into categories; the attempt to provide *theoretical explanations* for why things behave as they do; the use of *models*—some of them, for example, in physics and astronomy, mathematical—to aid in inquiry and in organizing knowledge; and, in certain spheres, the use of *experiments and systematic observation (including measurement)* of natural phenomena as a way of verifying or quantifying the results of theoretical speculations.

By the Renaissance, the practice of science was already becoming increasingly systematized, and by the 19th century—perhaps the high point of scientific *hubris*—many felt that the scientific method could unlock all the secrets of the universe. Nowadays, notwithstanding the major scientific advances of the past few centuries, scientists themselves have tended to become more modest and circumspect about what science and scientific models can do. Rather than speaking about *immutable laws*, they tend to refer to provisional *theories* and tentative *hypotheses*. Rather than assuming that the world can be understood in terms of *deterministic mechanical processes*, they have tended—influenced by developments such as quantum theory, Heisenberg's uncertainty principle, evolutionary biology, and chaos theory—to regard many natural phenomena as *statistical* in character, with chance often playing a significant role. Rather than saying that empirical evidence consistent with a theory *confirms* or *proves* a theory, they tend to say that it does *not disprove* the theory, while evidence inconsistent with the theory *is* said to *disprove* it.

What are the characteristics of a good model? A number of candidates have been suggested:

- Prediction: The model should assist in predicting the future behaviour of the empirical entities in which we are interested.
- Generality: The model should be applicable in a wide range of situations.
- Correspondence to reality: The structure of the model should correspond to the structure of the reality it represents.
- Explanatory power: The model should provide some understanding of the empirical causal relationships that exist among the elements that it contains.
- Simplicity: The model should be as simple as possible.
- Speed and ease of testing: Testing the model should be as fast, simple, and inexpensive as possible.
- Self-referentiality: If the model is a model of human behaviour (since producing models is one of the activities engaged in by humans), the model should be able to account for or explain its own production; it should be "self-reflexive" or self-referential.

We should note several features of this catalogue. First, not all of these features are compatible with one another: greater simplicity, for example, generally implies greater abstraction, and therefore less correspondence with reality. Second, some of the characteristics partially overlap: for example, some degree of *correspondence to reality* would seem to be required for a model to have *explanatory power* in the above sense. Third, *all* of the characteristics need some qualification: the *simplest* model, for instance, would just say "Anything can happen," which is not very informative. By the same token, there are limits on how closely a model can correspond to reality: in Korzybski's dictum, "The map is not the territory." Some degree of abstraction is a necessary element of every model, and the goal is for the abstraction to be a *strategic* reduction or simplification, which retains the most significant elements of the empirical field. Fourth, not everyone would agree that all of the characteristics are equally important, and some might even question whether certain characteristics are desirable.

Milton Friedman's Position and Its Limits

Milton Friedman (1970, 3–43) argued, for example, that the capacity for *prediction*, at the lowest possible net cost, is the litmus test of an economic model, and that the *realism* of the assumptions of the model—its correspondence to reality—is unimportant. Friedman's position, despite its apparently paradoxical appearance, has been viewed as defensible. Yet it has its limits, as an example from recent history—the crisis in world financial markets that began in 2007, initiated by the collapse of the US subprime mortgage market—should illustrate. One of the principal reasons for the US collapse was the widespread diffusion in the financial sector of a model of risk assessment first published in 2000 by David X. Li, whose doctorate in statistics was completed at the University of Waterloo. The model appeared to dramatically simplify risk assessment, but its data were drawn from a period that had seen a steady rise in housing prices and low levels of mortgage defaults. When market conditions changed, many financial institutions found themselves drastically overextended and overexposed, and the crisis ensued.[2]

Three points are worth emphasizing about this episode. First, a large part of the problem was that Li's model *and its limits* were not adequately understood by those who were using it as a basis for transactions worth billions of dollars. Second, the existence of the model itself altered the behaviour of those whose behaviour it was intended to model. And third, and most relevant for assessing the soundness of Friedman's argument, the model, which performed well—that is, predicted accurately—when the structure of the economy corresponded to that required by the model, became not only ineffective but actively dangerous when the structure of the economy changed.

The Problems of Induction

In this context, one of the main problems with Friedman's basic position is that it does not deal adequately with the problems of induction. When we speak of "*the* problem of induction," we normally have in mind David Hume's critique of induction, expressed in the question, "How do we know with certainty that the sun will rise tomorrow, simply because it always has?" Hume's answer—that we *cannot* establish with certainty, by purely rational means alone, that the sun *will* rise tomorrow—is *one* of the limits of induction.[3] It can be called the problem of *set-*

extension: If we have a set composed of a number of elements all of which have the same characteristics, can the set rationally be *extended* to include a *new* element that appears to have the same characteristics as the *present* elements? This is Hume's sunrise problem.

The problem of induction, however, has a second aspect, which can be called the problem of *set-construction*: How do we establish that some entities are *sufficiently alike* that we can treat them all as elements of a designated set? The philosopher Friedrich Nietzsche (1968, 46) recognized that this problem penetrated to the heart of language itself, at the level of individual words:

> Every word immediately becomes a concept, inasmuch as it is not intended to serve as a reminder of the unique and wholly individualized original experience to which it owes its birth, but must at the same time fit innumerable, more or less similar cases—which means, strictly speaking, never equal—in other words, a lot of unequal cases. Every concept originates through our equating what is unequal. No leaf ever wholly equals another, and the concept "leaf" is formed through an arbitrary abstraction from these individual differences, through forgetting the distinctions.

As a practical matter, the concepts of economics virtually all refer to entities that are both similar to *and* different from one another in at least *some* respects. Hence the concepts are more or less precise depending on the extent and significance of the differences among the entities.

The induction problem also has a third, related, aspect, which can be called the problem of *referential stability and continuity*. Induction, practically speaking, is a temporal-spatial *process*, involving the time-consuming observation of entities separated in time and/or space. If the behaviour of elements within a set A is affected by their relations with the elements of other sets, and these relations change over time or space, then any two elements of set A will demonstrate differences in behaviour as a function of the spatial and temporal extent of separation between them. At some point, these differences in behaviour can become sufficiently significant that we can speak of *referential* and *structural discontinuity*, such as occurred in the 2007–2010 financial crisis.

Friedman's "instrumentalist" argument for predictive capacity as the primary model criterion, combined with his dismissal of the objective that assumptions correspond to reality, means that he does not adequately address the problem of induction in *any* of its three aspects.[4] Yet the foregoing argument—and Friedman's own qualification of his basic position—implies that ensuring that models have some correspondence to reality *is* important, particularly when structural change is possible, so that we have a basis for assessing the likely consequences of that change for empirical system behaviour.

To conclude this discussion, we can define "science" as characterized by formal (including mathematical) models, an emphasis on quantitatively measurable variables, and hypothesis-testing according to recognized and accepted statistical procedures. We can also, however, view science in the broader sense, as a *continuum*, ranging from such models to less formal *heuristic* models that provide guides to or ways of knowing reality. Economics is certainly a "science" in the heuristic sense, independently of whether it is a science in the narrower sense.

All of these forms of science have their own *languages*, as an economic means of facilitating communication among practitioners. These languages accelerate communication *within* the scientific community and hinder communication between members of this community and "outsiders." They have their own specialized vocabularies and stories, focused on aspects of the world that are viewed as having particular significance and importance for the science. Thus, each scientific language also has *biases*. In privileging certain aspects of reality, it necessarily encourages a relative neglect of other aspects. In analyzing the various approaches to economics, we can learn much by discovering the biases of each.

Limits of the Neoclassical Model

This section briefly outlines some capacities and limits of orthodox neoclassical economics, and the next section discusses some alternative approaches. These sections are *not* intended to provide a comprehensive analysis. Many books have been devoted to the matter, and other contributions to this volume address aspects of it in greater detail than is possible here. The purpose is rather to focus on certain aspects of these approaches that bear on the issue of the scientific status of economics.

The economic theory that dominates virtually all microeconomics textbooks is known as *neoclassical* or *marginalist* economics.[5] It focuses on the *optimizing* behaviour of economic agents who are motivated by rational self-interest—typically, *utility*-maximizing *consumers* and *profit*-maximizing *producers*. Its central canonical or "benchmark" model is that of perfectly competitive economic equilibrium—a hypothetical state in which all economic agents are price-taking perfect competitors and the quantity supplied equals the quantity demanded in all markets at the equilibrium prices. Under certain assumptions, equilibrium of supply and demand in this model has the "social welfare" property that it generates the greatest possible net benefit for society as a whole.[6] The model is a significant part of every economist's education, and is thus invaluable as a medium of communication within economics. Rather than starting from first principles, an economist can say, "Assume the basic competitive model, and in addition assume X. Then it follows that Y is true," and expect to be understood by other economists.

However, the model displays some significant limitations and biases. The assumptions on which its conclusions rest do not correspond closely to reality. A partial catalogue of its standard assumptions (excluding some that are made for technical reasons[7]) includes the following:

- Population, tastes and preferences, the number of types of goods, technology, and the initial distribution of ownership of resources among economic agents are all *given*, from *outside* the model.
- All agents have perfect information and there is no uncertainty.
- There is a complete set of costless and instantaneously functioning present and futures markets, and there are no transactions costs.
- No economic agent has market power: all agents behave as price-takers.
- Production is characterized by non-increasing returns to scale and perfect divisibility of all productive inputs, and there is no joint production.
- The utility or degree of satisfaction of each consumer depends on his or her consumption alone, and not on that of anyone else.
- There are no positive or negative "externalities" (effects of economic activity that affect parties not directly involved in a transaction) in production or consumption.

If *any* of these assumptions do not hold, then the welfare properties of the market equilibrium don't hold. But *none* of them holds in any real-world economic system. A few illustrations should clarify the implications. The assumption that no agent has market power, for example, does not correspond to a world in which many sectors of the economy have highly concentrated ownership and where transnational corporations have not only market power but also more general political–economic power. The perfect-information assumption is inconsistent with the fact that over half of measured gross domestic product (GDP) in OECD countries is accounted for by *communication* activities—the production and distribution of knowledge (plus transportation)—that would be unnecessary if people actually had perfect information. The importance of communication activities in GDP has a further consequence. While we can speak of the production function for laundry detergent, we have no corresponding production function for *knowledge*, and in fact not even an adequate unit of measurement for knowledge! Hence the neoclassical framework is inadequate for analyzing half of GDP.

The assumption that there are no transactions costs similarly takes inadequate account of the fact that over 70 percent of GDP in the OECD countries is currently accounted for by *services*, many of which are directly related to the creation, support, and maintenance of markets. It has been said that "there is no such thing as a free lunch," since it takes resources to produce the lunch. It is equally true, for the same reason, that "there is no such thing as a free market!" In an era of increased awareness of and concern with environmental pollution and global warming, the significance of *production* "externalities" goes without saying. The theoretical implications of *consumption* externalities, however, are also far-reaching. If (as a result of altruism *or* of envy) my utility is affected not only by the commodities *I* consume but also by the consumption of *others*, then competitive equilibrium is inconsistent with utility-maximization.

The above discussion of some limits of the core neoclassical model should not suggest that the model is without value as a heuristic or educational tool. Nor does it underestimate the scientific value of the vast amounts of organized quantitative data that have been gathered by economists who would describe themselves as neoclassical. What it should indicate, however, is that to the extent that some correspondence with reality is a prerequisite for empirical testing, the model is essentially untestable. Moreover, if it is used as a basis for the argument that the unaided market system will produce outcomes that are in some sense "socially optimal," then it is being used for ideological and not scientific purposes.

Alternative Approaches to Economics

The Austrian School[8] has addressed some of the gaps and shortcomings of the basic neoclassical model, notably in three spheres. First, since Menger's *Principles of Economics* (1976), the Austrians have emphasized the role of *knowledge* in economic activity, from the determination of what things are "goods" to the valuations established in the market. Second, they have recognized that economic agents operate *without* perfect information; that the production and distribution of information is not costless; and that the *market* itself is one of the most efficient media for transmitting certain kinds of information (such as the prices of goods) that enable decision-making at minimal cost. Third, they have stressed the importance of *time* in the production of goods, the significance of "roundabout" methods of production, the importance of the *structure of capital*, and the resultant necessity of prevision, planning, and provision for the future supply of the means of production ("higher-order goods").

The principal limits of the school's approach stem from its rather rigid methodological-individualist and "anti-collectivist" bias, which tends to result in a fairly uncritical and overly sanguine faith in the market, a restricted appreciation of its limits, and little consideration of situations in which hierarchical and "command" forms of social–economic organization can outperform the market, such as emergency aid missions in response to crises and natural disasters, military operations, and the internal organization of production within firms.

Marx's dialectical–materialist mode of analysis[9] also offers an alternative to the neoclassical approach. Marx focused on the conditions for the *reproduction* over time and space of political–economic systems and on the sources of historical *change.* He argued that changes in the "forces of production"—technology, population, and the means of production, including the resource base of an economic system—would generate qualitative or *structural* change in the system. He also assumed that economic systems were not simply agglomerations of individuals, but were composed of social–economic classes; that individuals were in large measure products of their class origins, class positions, class interests, and class consciousness; and that contradictions among classes with regard to political–economic control and to distribution of the surplus produced within the system would result in manifest or latent class conflict. In most of his major theoretical work, *Capital,* he used a simple two-class model of capitalism composed of capitalists and workers, but in other studies he depicted much more complex, historically informed, class structures.

Marx's reformulation of the classical economists' notion of the "subsistence wage" so that it referred not to mere biological subsistence or survival but rather incorporated a historical and moral element—so that, for example, *basic* subsistence in Canada nowadays includes computers and cellphones—provides a means of relating consumption patterns to the requirements of system reproduction rather than to abstractly conceived individual tastes. His analysis of the *causes* of political–economic power and the processes by which it is sustained provides a richer and more realistic approach to the economy than the neoclassical focus on the *effects* of narrowly defined market power. Finally, in what is not intended as an exhaustive list, his argument that the "laws of motion" of different modes of production are not identical provides an alternative to the neoclassical assumption that "one size fits all," and that *homo economicus* is equally at home in a medieval serf's cottage, a Buddhist monastery, and an IBM boardroom or cubicle.

Marxist political–economic theory has its limits. One reductionistic tendency in Marxist thought has been the *mechanistic* or *deterministic fallacy*, which assumes that the historical process is determined by immutable laws, and that individual political–economic action is therefore unnecessary. Another, opposing, tendency—manifested to some extent in the student protest movements of the 1960s—is the *voluntarist fallacy*, which assumes that armed with a "correct" understanding, it is possible to bring about significant political–economic change without regard for existing configurations of wealth and power. Yet, notwithstanding these potential biases, Marx's mode of analysis also provides avenues of insight into aspects of the real world relatively neglected within the neoclassical model.[10]

Conclusion

This essay has argued that the core neoclassical model provides a language and a distinctive way of looking at the world, and is therefore a "science" in the broader, heuristic sense. This "science," however, has certain blind spots and biases that predispose us to neglect important aspects of economic reality. The lack of correspondence between the core model (and the models that derive from it) and reality has created a gap between economic theory and empirical hypothesis-testing. Moreover, where the gaps are the greatest, the capacity for prediction—Friedman's "litmus test"—has been most compromised, and to this extent, economics has fallen short as a science in the narrower sense.

If economics is to expand its scientific capacity in ways that aid in understanding and dealing adequately with the challenges of the 21st-century global economic system, it will need to listen more closely to and incorporate the insights of other disciplines—not only anthropology, sociology, geography, history, political studies, and psychology, but also disciplines ranging from literary theory to biology. It will also, however, need to systematically integrate the insights of heterodox economics—Austrian, Marxian, institutionalist, and other approaches—and neoclassical orthodoxy.

NOTES

1. The concept of "monopolies and oligopolies of knowledge" was developed by the Canadian economic historian and communication theorist Harold Innis, in works such as *Political Economy in the Modern State* (1946) and *The Bias of Communication* (1951).
2. Illuminating non-technical discussions are found in Whitehouse (2005) and Salmon (2009).
3. Notwithstanding Hume's argument, you would still be well advised to bet someone, giving them very favourable odds, that it *will* rise, because if it *doesn't*, you are not likely going to have to pay!
4. Friedman (1970, 42) implicitly recognizes this fact in his call for an "exploration of the criteria for determining what abstract model it is best to use for particular kinds of problems, what entities in the abstract model are to be identified with which observable entities, and what features of the problem or of the circumstances have the greatest effect on the accuracy of the predictions yielded by a particular model or theory."
5. It is called "*neo*classical" to distinguish it from the *classical* economics of Adam Smith, Thomas Malthus, and David Ricardo. It is called "marginalist" because it focuses on the effects of marginal (or small incremental) changes within a given economic structure on decision-makers' total net benefit.
6. Under a restrictive set of assumptions, a competitive equilibrium is "Pareto-efficient" or "Pareto-optimal." At a Pareto-efficient point, nobody can be made better off without making somebody else worse off. Hence, for one who accepts this conservative criterion as desirable in itself without regard for other measures of social welfare, the "positive" competitive model generates a *normative* conclusion.

7. Examples of such "technical" assumptions would include the convexity and completeness assumptions for preferences and production functions, the assumption of non-increasing returns to scale in production, the assumption that no trades occur at disequilibrium prices, and the assumption that there is no bankruptcy or starvation, which are made as much for mathematical convenience as because they necessarily correspond to reality.

8. The School is known as the "Austrian" School because its founder, Carl Menger, one of the fathers of "marginalist" economics, and some of its leading exponents—figures like Eugen von Böhm-Bawerk, Friedrich Hayek, and Ludwig von Mises—were Austrian.

9. A technical note: Marx's dialectical approach owes more to Hegel's *Phenomenology* than to his *Logic*; and is not nearly as mechanical as the reductive "thesis → antithesis → synthesis" formula that has been used to describe *all* forms of dialectics might suggest.

10. Other alternative economic approaches also exist, to mention only the institutionalism of writers like Commons, Veblen, and Innis; the analyses of neo-Ricardians such as Sraffa; and the work of cultural–economic historians. There is not space here, however, to do justice to their contributions.

DISCUSSION QUESTIONS

1. In what ways does "the problem of induction" pose difficulties for Friedman's position that the realism of the assumptions of a model is unimportant, as long as it predicts well?

2. If the core neoclassical competitive market model is essentially untestable, what functions can and does it perform?

3. On which four aspects of an economy would you concentrate your analysis if it were made up of *firms* and *households*? If it were made up of *capitalists* and *workers*?

4. What in your view are the *most* significant limits and biases of the core neoclassical economic model, Austrian models, and "vulgar Marxist" models?

SUGGESTED READINGS

See also the works listed in the References section below.

Backhouse, Roger, ed. 1994. *New directions in economic methodology.* London: Routledge.

Ormerod, Paul. 1994. *The death of economics.* London: Faber and Faber.

ONLINE RESOURCES

The Library of Economics and Liberty: www.econlib.org.

Library of Marxism: www.marxists.org.

REFERENCES

Friedman, Milton. 1970. *Essays in positive economics.* Chicago: University of Chicago Press.

Innis, H.A. 1946. *Political economy in the modern state.* Toronto: Ryerson.

Innis, H.A. 1951. *The bias of communication.* Toronto: University of Toronto Press.

Keynes, J.M. 1936, 1973. *The general theory of employment, interest and money.* Cambridge: Macmillan.

Menger, Carl. *Principles of economics.* 1871, 1976. New York: New York University Press.

Nietzsche, Friedrich. 1873, 1968. *The portable Nietzsche,* ed. Walter Kaufmann. New York: Viking.

Robbins, Lionel. 1952. *An essay on the nature and significance of economic science.* London: Macmillan.

Salmon, Felix. 2009. A formula for disaster. *Wired.* March: 75–112.

Veblen, Thorstein. 1919, 1969. *The place of science in modern civilization.* New York: Capricorn.

Whitehouse, Mark. 2005. Slices of risk. *The Wall Street Journal.* September 12.

Is There Such a Thing as a Free Market?

Editors' Introduction

In 1776, during the early stages of the Industrial Revolution, in an imperial Britain whose colonial policy was still dominated by mercantilist thought, and in the same year as the outbreak of the American Revolution, Adam Smith's *Wealth of Nations* was published. In its brilliant first three chapters, Smith produced arguably the most important brief theoretical analysis in the whole of economics. He analyzed the sources of growth in per capita output and income within a nation over time. Using the example of a pin factory, he attributed most of the productivity growth to the *division of labour*.

When a production process can be divided into a number of simple, specialized tasks, each performed by a separate worker, productivity increases, as a result of the increased dexterity of the workers; the elimination of time wasted in moving from task to task; and the increased possibility of technical change—replacing human activity with that of machines. However, the vast increase in productivity enabled by specialization and the division of labour is possible only if the *surplus* production—production above the level that producers require for their own use—can be exchanged for *other* commodities that they require but have not produced. As Smith put it, "the division of labour is limited by the extent of the *market*." In a remote, self-sufficient agricultural community, all needs have to be provided for within the community. Productivity will therefore be low, because everyone has to perform a large number of tasks and the scope for the division of labour is necessarily restricted. Adam Smith's basic argument for the market, in short, was that it is an essential component of a system that enables cumulative growth in productivity. The "extent of the market" can be increased through population growth; improved, lower-cost transport and communication networks; urbanization; increased per capita income; and elimination of obstacles (such as monopolies, patents, and restrictions on labour mobility) to the market's functioning.

Smith's analysis is still relevant today, particularly in less-developed countries with large subsistence agricultural sectors. However, modern orthodox discussions of the market tend to place less emphasis on its role in economic growth and development and more on its *rationing* and *allocative* functions. In his essay, William Watson provides a spirited argument for relying on the market, unconstrained by government intervention, to ration goods and allocate resources. He acknowledges that the market may not always function in the ideal way described in basic textbook discussions, because of ignorance, externalities, public goods, asymmetric information, and monopoly. Yet Watson argues that government-backed agricultural support programs are among the most inefficient artificial monopolies; that globalization and the development of the Internet and other new media move markets closer to the textbook ideal of perfect competition; and that in a "second-best" world, the chances are slim that governments will be able to discover the appropriate combination of policies to correct market distortions.

Robert Prasch, however, argues that the image of "free" markets in opposition to the state involves a major misconception. Markets simply could not exist without the "rules of the game" provided by the state, in the form of commercial, property, and contract laws and their enforcement. He notes the importance of having the state as an impartial referee in dispute resolution, and argues that the legal framework becomes the basis of social norms and expectations that firms ignore at their peril. Prasch's conclusion is that the image of "free" markets, unencumbered by government "interference," is a myth.

Markets Are Free Enough

William Watson

What's all that got to do with the price of potatoes?

Old saying

Introduction

"Is there such a thing as a free market?" I happen to think there is—not perfectly free, perfection being rare in this world, but free enough. But let's hold off on the "positive" (or factual) question and be "normative" (or judgmental) for a moment. Why does it matter whether markets are free? As it turns out, free, competitive markets are also "efficient," both in the lay sense of not wasting inputs when producing goods and services but also in the much grander sense of the word, favoured by economists, which means producing only what really should be produced and not producing what shouldn't be. How so? Let's try to be efficient with language and see if we can't derive two fundamental propositions of microeconomics in just two paragraphs.

Why Free Markets Matter

Consider the potato. Suppose people enjoy every extra potato they eat in a given period just a little less than the one that came before. It's not that they don't appreciate the extra potatoes. They'd rather have more potatoes than fewer. More is better. They just appreciate the "marginal" potatoes, as economists would call them, somewhat less than they did earlier potatoes. More potatoes do mean more total enjoyment but the extra enjoyment is a little less with every additional potato. That seems plausible. And it might be true of many things beside potatoes. In fact, it might be true of most things: we like more of most things, but we appreciate every extra unit just a little less than the ones that came before. Assuming people do generally feel this way, how do they decide how many potatoes (or other things) to buy in a week or month or year? Presumably they do it by comparing the enjoyment they get from the extra potato with the price they must pay for it. The price is expressed in dollars but, unless you're a numismatist, dollars aren't worth anything in and of themselves. They're only valuable as indicators of the other things that must be given up in order to buy a good. If people are sensible—economists would say "rational"—they presumably stop buying potatoes when the benefit from the extra potato no longer exceeds the price of potatoes. At the margin, therefore, people value a potato at just what they have to pay for it.

That's a useful enough result in itself. It suggests rational decision-making brings about a determinate consumption of potatoes, what economists call an "equilibrium," a level of consumption that doesn't change unless either the price changes or the benefit people get from potatoes changes. But now suppose in addition that the price of potatoes represents the entire cost of growing potatoes and bringing them to market. If it does, then we've really hit on something interesting. For if people are consuming so that their benefit from potatoes equals the price of potatoes, and if the price of potatoes reflects the cost of producing potatoes, that means people only buy potatoes whose benefit to them is greater than their cost. And they stop buying when the benefit derived from the last, or "marginal," potato they purchase is just equal to what it costs them. And they don't buy at all if the marginal benefit is less than the cost. If you were assigned the task of trying to figure out the "right" or "optimal" amount of potatoes (or anything else) for a society to produce, you'd probably hit upon some formulation that it should produce everything for which benefits were greater than costs and none for which benefits were less than costs. But under the assumptions we've made, that is exactly what consumers do.

That's a result worth spending a third paragraph emphasizing. People compare the benefits they receive from a good with its price and they stop buying when the marginal benefit just equals the price. So price = marginal benefit. But it's also true that price = marginal cost. So it follows that marginal benefit = marginal cost, which is exactly what we want. In other words, the "equilibrium" this process gives rise to is also an "optimum." Where consumption ends up is where we'd want it to end up. If that's the way the world does work, then *laissez-faire*, letting people make their own decisions about what they want to buy, is the best way to reach this equilibrium/optimum. And if it's true for potatoes, it's probably true for many other things.

The first few weeks of any good microeconomics course build up this truly remarkable result: that under hospitable assumptions, decentralized decision-making all the way down to the level of the individual consumer can generate the "right" amounts and combinations of outputs and thus solve society's economic problem of exactly how much of which different goods and services to produce. But then the rest of the course focuses on what can go wrong. And lots can go wrong, though whether governments can fix these "market failures" or only make things worse is another question. If governments really are serial bunglers, then *laissez-faire* may still be the best policy. This is so even if being characterized as the least inefficient of a lot of inefficient systems of allocation is much less flattering to free markets than being thought of as the very best.

Possible Market Failures

What sorts of things can go wrong?

- People may not know what's good for them. They may not make good judgments about whether they really do benefit from a product. Many of us love French-fried potatoes, for instance, but eating too much fatty food gives us heart disease in the long run.
- Buyers and sellers may not be the only people who gain or lose as a result of a market transaction. Pollution imposes "external costs" on third parties and though these costs need to be taken into account in assessing overall benefits and costs, neither buyer nor seller has any real incentive to consider them.
- Similarly, education, vaccination, or even spraying your potato crop against disease may involve spillover benefits to people not involved in the transaction. Assuming buyers of these activities equate prices and marginal benefits, the existence of these "external," unaccounted-for benefits means that at the market equilibrium quantity, marginal benefits exceed marginal costs. More of whatever activity produces the positive spillover should be purchased, but isn't.
- Some goods, like new knowledge, everyone can consume at once without diminishing the amount available to anyone else. (Your knowing something—how to grow better potatoes, say—doesn't prevent me from knowing it, too.) In such cases, people may act as "free riders": that is, wait for other people to develop new knowledge and then take advantage of it for free. But if everyone free-rides, the new knowledge never gets developed.
- Buyers' and sellers' knowledge of a product may be "asymmetric," that is, buyers may know less than sellers. Fear of being ripped off may cause them not to buy goods they'd really benefit from. Or buyers' ignorance may allow sellers to charge prices that significantly exceed costs. Sellers make higher profits as a result, but because of the higher price, some output that should be purchased isn't.
- Markets may not be competitive. If there is only one supplier in a market (a situation economists call "monopoly") or just a few ("oligopoly"), then producers will try to keep prices above their cost of production so as to earn greater profits. But if consumers are equating benefits to prices, and prices are above costs, then "at the margin" benefits are greater than costs, which means an expansion of production would generate net benefits. The expansion doesn't take place, however, because the monopolist or cartel doesn't allow it. If, for instance, McCain's has "market power" in the

Canadian market for potatoes, Canadians may consume fewer potatoes than they should, given potatoes' true costs of production.

In these and a number of other cases of market failure, the possibility arises that government intervention can adjust output so as to bring society closer to its optimum. Governments can subsidize or themselves produce education, research, vaccines, and the like; they can tax or regulate pollution; they can regulate or even break up monopolies or oligopolies (as the United States did with the Standard Oil Company in 1911 and AT&T in 1984); or they can help consumers become better informed about products when producers have an information advantage, and so on. On the other hand, it's important to realize that government intervention may not always improve matters. Sometimes it may even make things worse. Why? Accurate information about benefits and costs can be hard to come by so even well-intentioned intervention can be difficult. And special interests may "capture" governments, with the result that policy doesn't even aim at equating benefits and costs at the margin. For example, if producers do co-opt policy, subsidies may be so extensive that marginal units of output have a benefit substantially *less* than the true economic cost of production. We then end up consuming too much of the subsidized good.

Space does not permit discussion of all the different possible types of "market failure" or the likelihood in each case that government intervention will actually improve on the failure rather than make it worse.[1] So let's focus on the last of the market failures cited, those arising from "imperfect competition": the possibility that small numbers of producers will set prices above costs. Is the market free enough, or is it in fact largely strangled by imperfect competition?

Imperfect Competition

It's called imperfect competition to contrast it with "perfect competition," which is an extreme and unlikely version of the *über*-competition that may actually characterize international financial markets, but beyond that it is very rare, if it exists at all. In perfect competition, large, maybe even infinite numbers of producers all provide essentially identical products—think of wheat farmers—and no single producer is so large that an increase in its output will affect the market price. If that's the case, the market price will end up equal to the marginal cost of production. How? Suppose one wheat farmer tries to charge a higher price, one that exceeds his or her marginal cost. If that happens, another wheat farmer will come in and undercut this higher price. With a slightly lower price this more aggressive farmer can pick up extra sales and still cover his or her costs. Seeing that, other farmers will do same thing. Downward bidding of this sort will continue until price equals cost. When it does, the undercutting will stop: prices can't go lower than costs, except temporarily.[2]

Does the world work this way? Are markets generally competitive? Or competitive "enough," so that prices generally do reflect costs? Or does the economic world consist of a maze of barriers to competition, so that prices have little relation to costs? Economists have worried about this problem almost since they began analyzing markets. And they have had detailed diagrammatic treatments of it since the 1930s, when both Joan Robinson of Cambridge and Edward Chamberlin of Harvard wrote path-breaking treatments of imperfect competition.[3] Unfortunately, the answer to such large questions likely depends more on a person's world view (or *weltanschauung*) than on a careful analysis of each and every market that exists—which would be very difficult, in any case, as there are thousands upon thousands of markets for different goods and services.

Government Discouragement of Competition

One reason some markets probably do fall well short of vigorous competition is that governments pass laws that purposely limit competition. As mentioned, one traditionally cited example of perfect competition is wheat farming. In modern-day Canada there are 15,480 wheat farmers, enough (you would think) to provide thoroughgoing competition (Statistics Canada 2010). But Canadian law doesn't allow that. It requires wheat farmers in Western Canada to sell their wheat to the Canadian Wheat Board, a marketing agency established by the federal government during the Second World War—when, arguably, the normal rules of competition did have to be suppressed—but never disbanded. Although the Board is a monopoly purchaser of Canadian wheat, it probably isn't large enough to affect the world price of wheat. Whether it gives farmers a better price for their wheat than they would get in a competitive market is therefore not clear. The Board has argued in a number of World Trade Organization and North American Free Trade Agreement cases brought against it that it neither manipulates prices nor subsidizes Canadian farmers by buying their wheat at uncompetitively high prices.

Similarly, Canada's 25,770 dairy farmers are governed by a system of "supply management," in which the overall supply of milk and other dairy products is established by provincial milk marketing boards (Statistics Canada 2010). It is actually illegal in Canada for dairy farmers to sell more milk than they have "quota"—or licences—for. Canadian dairy farmers occasionally dump excess "illegal" milk on their pastures, both in protest against this system and as a wasteful, desperate, but also legal way of getting rid of it. "Supply management" is actually a euphemism for "supply restriction," since the effect of the system is to deliberately reduce competition, restrict the supply of dairy products in Canada, and raise their price well above prices in the neighbouring US market. Because the difference in price between the two countries would normally lead to imports from the lower-price country (the US), Canada imposes tariffs on imports of dairy products, including cheese and ice cream, that in some cases exceed 200 percent.

The Canadian Wheat Board's legal monopoly in Western Canada and the nationwide system of supply management in the dairy and poultry industries are especially transparent government restrictions of competition. In many other industries, however, less obvious regulations, tariffs, and laws of one kind or another also serve to increase the market power of incumbent firms and enable them to raise prices above costs. Because incumbent firms can have undue influence on politicians and regulators, getting rid of these different government-created barriers to competition may not be easy, but in markets where there would be competition if only government stopped suppressing it, the most sensible thing would seem to be to get rid of the restrictive government regulation.[4]

The Problem of Small Numbers

A second set of competition problems arises in industries where firms are so big that the competitive ideal of cutthroat rivalry among large numbers of firms is simply not possible. In many industries, the technology of production is so complicated and demanding that firms small enough to provide the large numbers required for vigorous competition would be inefficient in the layperson's sense of that word. Unable to take advantage of the economies of large-scale production, their per-unit costs would be very high. Instead, in a lot of important industries, small numbers of very large corporations, many of them household names, may restrict supply by collusion of various sorts, whether tacit or, when national competition laws allow, overt. To make matters worse, they may also try to manage the demand for their products with widespread advertising. This critique of modern capitalism is most commonly associated with John Kenneth Galbraith (1908–2006), the Canadian-born Harvard economist who elaborated it at greatest length in *The New Industrial State* (1967). In that book, Galbraith described the goal of modern industrial price control as follows: "Prices must be low enough to facilitate the recruitment of customers and the expansion of sales and at the same time high enough to provide earnings to finance growth and keep the stockholders content" (Galbraith 1967, 189). In Galbraith's view of the world, firms do not restrict output by enough to maximize profits but neither do they compete aggressively enough to generate prices equal to the marginal cost of production. Across large swaths of the modern economy, Galbraith argued, in dozens of important industries, from autos to pharmaceuticals to tobacco to industrial inputs, electrical appliances and even foodstuffs, this was the way production and price-making took place. If he was right and firms in many important industries did not set prices equal to costs at the margin, economist's tales about efficiency could not be correct.

Was that the true state of the world in 1967, when Galbraith wrote, and is it the state of the world now?

It may have been truer in 1967. Tariffs and other barriers to international trade were higher and national markets were usually dominated by local producers. Galbraith opens *The New Industrial State* by describing the pricing, design, and promotion practices used by Ford Motor Company in introducing the Mustang sports car. At the time, auto companies were the prototypical example of the modern, dominant, "technocratic" corporation. In 1967, the "Big Three" US automakers (General Motors, Chrysler, and Ford) dominated the North American car market. Foreign producers accounted for only a small share of sales. Sightings of foreign cars, despite growing incursions by the Volkswagen Beetle, were a relatively rare thing. By early 2010, however, the North American car market had been turned almost literally upside down. The sales share of the Big Three, two of which[5] were under bankruptcy protection in the US courts, were down to just 17.7 per cent of total sales.[6] Foreign car companies had essentially taken over the North American car market. Consumers now could choose from, not three, but almost 30 Japanese, Korean, German, and Italian car brands, and in the near future will probably have Chinese and Indian alternatives as well. In much the same way, when Galbraith wrote *The New Industrial State*, the global computer market then just being born was dominated by International Business Machines. IBM is still a big and important company, 14th on the Fortune 500 list of the largest industrial corporations of 2009 with more than $100 billion in revenues, but it no longer dominates the US or world computer market. Far from it. Its Galbraithian attempt to control both the demand for and supply of computers failed utterly.

A glance at the latest Fortune 500 list suggests that modern American capitalism is hardly the staid, controlled, uncompetitive economic system Galbraith argued it looked like becoming. Many of the biggest firms of the early 21st century were either very small in 1967 or simply did not exist.[7]

The Extension of the Market

It may well be that the technology of large-scale production means there will be only a few firms of any consequence even in the largest national market. But national markets are less and less relevant. In most countries they are wide open to foreign competition. The two main reasons for this are falling transportation and communication costs, on the one hand, and on the other, a deliberate decision by the international community, acting under the auspices of the General Agreement on Tariffs and Trade (GATT) and the World Trade Organization (WTO), to pursue a long-term postwar policy of freeing up international trade and investment. Most industrial competition is no longer confined to domestic markets but takes place in a global marketplace. The United States may be big enough for only two or three major auto firms but the world market can support 25 or 30, and that seems more than enough to provide quite vigorous competition, as long as national governments keep their domestic markets open.

Communications and the Internet

Even before the Internet came along, communication satellites and other new technologies had dramatically reduced the cost of international telephone calls, thus making international trade and investment much easier than when long-distance communication was expensive. As a result, competitors that had been at a safe distance on the other side of the world were now effectively much closer. This greater proximity increased the competitive pressure on all firms, even the largest and most powerful.

The Internet has increased that competitive pressure even more. One attribute of an efficient market is that every market participant has good information about prices. In fact, some theories of economic competition depend on the existence of a mythical "auctioneer," who supposedly calls out prices so that all participants are instantly aware of them. By contrast, if participants have to spend time and money learning about prices, firms may be able to charge consumers prices that are higher than costs, thus interfering with economic efficiency. But now, in the age of the Internet, keeping track of the going price for a given good is much easier and it is correspondingly harder for producers to keep their prices artificially high. To all intents and purposes, the auctioneer of competition theory now really does exist. Firms have much more trouble selling at inflated prices when consumers can easily find out what a firm's competitors are selling for.

In sum, although there may have been a time in most national markets when big firms led a quiet, uncompetitive life, in the early 21st century that is rarely true. Because of declining shipping costs, the advent of the Internet, and continual rounds of trade liberalization since 1945, the quiet corporate life is probably gone for good. In most industries, in most countries, competition is more vigorous than it has ever been.

Second Best

Evidence about the current state of competition in most industries isn't enough to cinch the case for a general policy of *laissez-faire*, however. Those who believe that economic competition generally isn't strong enough to ensure that most industrial prices are equal to firms' marginal costs and that markets therefore aren't free enough to achieve an "efficient" solution to society's problem of what to produce have a trump card up their sleeve: "second best." The "General Theory of Second Best," propounded in the mid-1950s by the Australian Kelvin Lancaster and the Canadian Richard Lipsey, says that if the cost = price requirement isn't fulfilled *in just one market*, then it cannot be assumed that fulfilling it in all the other markets, which seems the natural thing to do, is actually second best (Lipsey and Lancaster 1956–57). For example, if supply management does keep the prices of dairy products well above their cost of production, that causes consumers to consume "too few" dairy products. Because they equate their benefits with price and because price exceeds costs, consumers' benefits are greater than costs. They really ought to consume more dairy products. How can they be encouraged to do so? With policies that raise the price of substitute goods. In theory at least, taxes on these substitute goods—another form of government intervention piled on top of dairy regulation—could do the job.

All is not lost for proponents of free markets, however. The trouble with second-best considerations of this sort is that figuring out the optimal tax for the substitute goods won't be easy: policy-makers will need good information about how producers and consumers in all affected markets will respond. And if imperfect competition is rife, so most markets can't be trusted to produce output where consumers' marginal benefits are equal to producers' marginal costs, they'll have to do second-best calculations of this sort all across the economy. The chance that policy-makers will get all these calculations right seems slight, even assuming the process isn't "captured" by political interests who have quite different goals than efficiency in mind. Once the latter are in control, efficiency goes out the door.

Little wonder, then, that many economists, even knowing they live in a "second-best" world of market-distorting interventions and imperfect competition, conclude that though markets are far from perfectly free, they're free enough that in most cases the best policy is to let the "higgling and bargaining" (Smith 1937) of producers and consumers determine what prices prevail and what outputs are produced. As so often in life, the perfect can be the enemy of the good. Dogmatically insisting on perfect competition and, if it does not materialize, replacing reasonably free and open markets with intrusive and often co-opted government controls, may end up producing a much less satisfactory "second best" than would be produced by markets that are in fact "free enough."

NOTES

1. See, for further details, Watson (2010), as well as Chapter 7 of this book.
2. If they do stay below costs longer than temporarily, farmers won't want to keep growing wheat, for anyone who sells at less than cost on a permanent basis is effectively a charity. But if farmers do sell only at cost, do they make any profit? Yes, they do, as long as "cost" is defined to include some return on both their time and their investment of capital. How big a return? Whatever is available in alternative uses of this time or capital. Make no mistake: Wheat farmers might prefer to collude and raise prices. But there are too many of them: someone will always cheat on any agreement and lower their price so as to steal market share.

3. See Robinson's *The Economics of Imperfect Competition* and Chamberlin's *The Economics of Monopolistic Competition*, both published—very competitively—in 1933.
4. Though see the discussion of "second best theory," below.
5. GM and Chrysler.
6. Source: http://online.wsj.com/mdc/public/page/2_3022-autosales.html#autosalesE.
7. Examples from the top 50 firms by revenue are: Walmart Stores (2nd on the list in 2009, incorporated in 1969), Berkshire Hathaway (13th, founded in the 19th century but taken over by investor Warren Buffet in 1962), Verizon Communications (17th, created as Bell Atlantic in the ATT breakup in 1984), Costco Wholesale (24th, founded in 1983), Home Depot (25th, founded in 1978), Target (28th, begun in 1962), Dell (33rd, founded in 1984), and Microsoft (35th, founded in 1975). See http://money.cnn.com/magazines/fortune/fortune500/2009/full_list/.

DISCUSSION QUESTIONS

1. Why does equating marginal benefit and marginal cost produce an "efficient" economic outcome? In this context, what does "efficient" mean?
2. Does the fact that over the last several decades many old firms have exited the Fortune 500 list of the largest corporations and been replaced by entirely new firms indicate vigorous competition *within* different industries?
3. If you wanted to mimic the perfectly competitive price and quantity in a market that was not at the moment competitive, how would you go about doing it? What policies or interventions would you make and what information would you need in order to be sure you had set prices and outputs right?

SUGGESTED READINGS AND ONLINE RESOURCES

Friedman, Thomas L. 2005. *The world is flat: A brief history of the 21st century.* New York: Farrar, Strauss and Giroux.

Hazlitt, Henry. 1979. *Economics in one lesson.* New York: Random House.

Ragan, Christopher, and R.G. Lipsey. 2011. Part IV: Market structure and efficiency. In *Microeconomics.* 13th Cdn. ed. Toronto: Pearson Canada.

Robson, William B.P., and Colin Busby. 2010. *Freeing up food: The ongoing cost, and potential reform, of supply management.* C.D. Howe Institute Backgrounder 128 (April). http://www.cdhowe.org/pdf/backgrounder_128.pdf.

REFERENCES

Chamberlin, Edward. 1933. *The economics of monopolistic competition*. Cambridge, MA: Harvard University Press.

Galbraith, J.K. *The new industrial state*. 1967. Boston: Houghton Mifflin.

Lipsey, R.G., and Kelvin Lancaster. 1956–57. The general theory of second best. *The Review of Economic Studies* 24 (1): 11–32.

Robinson, Joan. 1969. *The economics of imperfect competition*. 2nd ed. London: Macmillan.

Smith, Adam. 1937. *An inquiry into the nature and causes of the wealth of nations*. Book I, Chapter 5. New York: The Modern Library.

Statistics Canada. 2010. *Canada year book 2009*, Table 2.6. Ottawa: Statistics Canada.

Watson, William. 2010. Let the market work!: The market and the public sector. In *Introducing macroeconomic analysis: Issues, questions, and competing views*, eds. Hassan Bougrine and Mario Seccareccia, 9–21. Toronto: Emond Montgomery.

The Myth of a Free Market

Robert E. Prasch

Introduction

Considering the idea of a free market presupposes a coherent answer to a prior question. What, exactly, is a market? Our impulse is to conjure up a place, such as a farmers' market, where buyers and sellers periodically congregate to, as Adam Smith once famously stated, "higgle and bargain." Yet most people would agree that a farmers' market is qualitatively different from the modern North American shopping mall, where customers buy branded items at fixed prices from the entry-level employees of large national (or transnational) firms that specialize in distribution. Likewise, most people would agree that a farmers' market is qualitatively different from a modern asset market such as the NASDAQ stock exchange with no central "place" because buyers, sellers, or even their representatives or agents, rarely meet one another; they infrequently, if ever, have occasion for face-to-face interactions.

If we are to improve our understanding of markets, we need to stop thinking of them as places. Markets are no longer bound by the particulars of a given location or community. They are better understood as sets of legal institutions framed by the law of property and contract as modified by social conventions, norms of behaviour and deportment, physical infrastructure, and the underlying distribution of wealth, income, and opportunity. Analogously, let us no longer think of commodities or goods exclusively as tangible things. When we speak of "goods," we are really discussing a right of property that adheres to some "object, promise, service, or privilege" (Prasch 2008, 15). The socially structured quality of modern markets and their increasing complexity thus suggests that they can no longer, if indeed they ever could, be illustrated by the abstract vision of an idealized village fair (Commons 1924; MacEwan 1999; Prasch 2008, chap. 1; Prasch 2010).

Drawing upon this suspect analogy, economists have traditionally argued that voluntary exchanges *must* improve the lot of each and every party to the transaction. After all, if the customer does not like the quality or price of the corn on offer, she can readily trade at the next vendor, or purchase something else entirely. Likewise, if the producer does not like the offer price, she can trade with someone else or plant a different crop. Considerations of information, credit conditions, bargaining power, and the stability of the market or the system in general, play no role in this wonderfully simple (in fact, simplistic) story. Extrapolating from the idealized exchange story canonized in generations of introductory textbooks, too many economists have argued that society should accept a policy of "free markets," by which we are supposed to understand a market free of government regulation and management. Affirming his commitment to this consensus vision, President Barack Obama has proclaimed that he and his administration are also "fierce advocates" of the "free market" (Bloomberg.com 2010).[1]

The standard defence of free markets begins with a contrast between two extreme abstractions: "the free market" and "the state." It is maintained that even if a state were managed by a benevolent philosopher-king, its economy would necessarily be less efficient than if the free market were to reign. The argument is that limited information concerning what can be produced at what cost, and the clamour of competing interest groups, means that even the best of states is ill-positioned to meet the often conflicting and periodically changing demands of millions of citizens and residents.

This vision of flawed state provisioning is then contrasted with "free markets," which are said to depend exclusively upon "price signals" to adjust the economic decisions of innumerable sellers and buyers efficiently, effectively, and spontaneously. No reliance, it is said, is placed on a centralized agency to gather or act on information concerning relative scarcities, changes in demand patterns, or bottlenecks in production or delivery. We are also spared the inherently political spectacle of sorting out competing claims of priority based on relative status, presumptive merit, or any other grounds (Hayek 1945; Mises 1966, chaps. 15–16). By highlighting the complexity and pitfalls of direct provisioning by the state, we are left to suppose that "the market" (but in fact the village fair of yore) is the institution with the best capacity to understand, weigh, interpret, and adjust its programs and responses to deliver what people actually want. It follows, we are informed, that market allocations are inherently more efficient and effective than any conceivable form of state "rationing."[2]

Problems with the "Free Market" Ideal

To be sure, the argument of the previous section has a great deal of appeal. It is probable that everyone reading this essay has had one or more unhappy experiences with an obtuse government clerk or Kafkaesque bureaucracy. Nevertheless, three points substantially undermine the argument. The first is that markets are themselves creatures of the state. The second is that markets are themselves a form of rationing. The third is that the state can, and should, act as a referee to shape the parameters of the competitive process. Note that acting as a referee is not the same thing as "state provisioning," although it has profound implications for market outcomes. But the role of referee is critical to the functioning, even the existence, of markets—including competitive markets. An implication of this list is that a functioning market system requires a state.

For the first point, it is evident that market exchange must depend upon some rules concerning what can be exchanged, how it can be exchanged, who is qualified to make which exchanges, and what will occur in the event that an exchange falls through (as a result of a broken promise, bankruptcy, defective goods, and so on). Working out these issues is the purview of contract, property, and bankruptcy law. In a global economy, one would have to supplement this list with an understanding of the laws and practices governing international trade and investment flows.

The second point should be a trivial one, but it is routinely overlooked or elided in conventional presentations of the merits of markets. This is the observation that markets ration on the basis of a particular consumer's willingness *and ability* to pay. Many of us would like to own a luxury car or take a vacation at a posh resort but, not having the money, we settle for something less. This is rationing by income. (By contrast, a line to buy tickets to an important hockey game is an example of rationing by time—those unwilling or unable to wait for a ticket will be unable to attend.) An implication is that those without adequate income, savings, or credit will be denied access to goods. This system may be fine and well for the distribution of luxuries or even wants. But can it address the needs of the poor? Drawing attention to this issue, Anatole France once famously quipped that the laws granted everyone an equal right to sleep under the bridges of Paris. The problem, one that has caused great consternation for governments and political elites throughout history, is that the poor, especially the urban poor, are disinclined to suffer and die quietly.

The third essential role of the state is that of referee. Imagine a sport in which the team with the lead was empowered to reconfigure the rules of the game unilaterally. One can readily imagine that the rules would be modified in their favour, and that the losing team (and most fans) would simply turn their backs on the whole affair. The analogy to a market is clear. Some at least moderately disinterested party needs to set the "rules of the game." Moreover, a minimal standard of enforcement, or at least a compelling appearance of enforcement, must be achieved. While private parties have periodically arisen to take on this task, problems of cost, credibility, and sustainability have meant that states are almost always best positioned to play this role (Law 2003).

Economics and the Necessity of Planning

Over the past 50 years, free-market economists and allied politicians have given planning a bad name. Governments are criticized in part because it is understood that they must plan. Expenditures have to be prioritized, tax revenues anticipated, and deficits financed. Less well understood is that individual firms and private persons, even those operating in what are called free markets, must also plan.

Consider the majority of economic decisions that we make each day. They are overwhelmingly concerned with meeting some *anticipated* need, requirement, or desire. Indeed, with the exception of children and inordinately compulsive people, almost all purchasing is for the purpose of consumption at some future period. We buy wine because friends are coming for dinner, we buy a shirt because we wish to wear it later, and we buy tools because we periodically need to fix things. This point should not be controversial, because the importance of planning to individuals has long been understood by economic theorists, including those with strong predilections for market provisioning:

> Civilized men strive to ensure the satisfaction of their needs for many years to come. Indeed, they not only plan for their entire lives, but as a rule, extend their plans still further in their concern that even their descendants shall not lack means for the satisfaction of their needs. (Menger 1871, 79)

Like individuals, businesses must plan. Planning is so important to firms that each of its several elements has its own name—business strategy, liabilities management, supply-chain management, and so on. Given economies of scale and the division of labour, it has long been understood that business planning can be superior to that of private individuals (Mitchell 1912).

One of the most implausible claims of the textbooks is that business firms in competitive markets respond passively to consumer demand. However, in the "real world" of the modern economy, planning has become so important to firms that business professors, including avid proponents of "free markets," regularly teach courses and publish books on the subject. Planning on the part of firms includes thinking about how markets are likely to evolve, how to finance their operations, how to improve their advertising strategy, how to select reliable and cost-effective suppliers, and so on. They even plan for the consequences of raising or lowering their prices. The fact is, private businesses and corporations, like individuals, must plan if they are to survive, much less prosper.

These reflections suggest that a stronger argument for distributing goods through markets rather than via government is that it facilitates *decentralized* planning. The correct contrast, then, is *not* between markets and the state, but between centralized and decentralized planning. Although these subjects are related, they are clearly different.

State planning, like its business counterpart, can be centralized or decentralized. Also, like its business counterpart, it can be done well or poorly. Guidance, the zoning of land, direct or indirect subsidies, user fees, taxes, authorized monopolies, regulations, and prohibitions can be enacted at the municipal, county, provincial, or federal levels. For a variety of reasons, usually high start-up costs, excessive risk, a desire for prestige, or concerns for national defence, governments have founded and operated business enterprises. Examples of publicly sponsored enterprises near my workplace here in Vermont include the City of Burlington Electric Department (municipal), the Addison County Economic Development Corporation (county), Castleton State College and the University of Vermont (state), and the United States Postal Service and Amtrak (federal). Despite repeated assertions to the contrary, these examples and many more affirm that successful models of state planning do exist. Moreover, almost every instance of "late industrialization" has included a strong component of public planning (Chang 2007, 2002; Wade 2003).

Planning Across Firms

In addition to formulating their own plans, business leaders periodically perceive an advantage in coordinating their activities across several firms. Such planning can be formalized in a contract specifying the duties of each firm vis-à-vis the other. When a closer relationship is considered desirable, coordination can take the form of a merger. Less formally, firms can enter into a "gentleman's agreement" to coordinate their actions to their mutual advantage. Arrangements of the latter sort have long been a source of worry, one shared by Adam Smith, "We rarely hear, it has been said, of the combinations of masters, though frequently of those of workmen. But whoever imagines, upon this account, that masters rarely combine, is as ignorant of the world as of the subject" (Smith 1776, 75).

Depending upon the legal, cultural, and political situation, planning across firms can take several forms. In addition to explicitly negotiated contracts, a common method has been the formation of a cartel. One early, large-scale effort was the formation of price cartels by American railroads during the latter part of the 19th century. Railroads feared, with good reason, that unbridled competition would so reduce the tariff for shipping freight that no firm would be able to service the substantial debt incurred in the course of acquiring their expensive investments in track and rolling stock. To avoid such a consequence, rival firms, working closely with their primary debt underwriter—J.P. Morgan—formed cartels to set prices and shipping quotas. Lacking the force of law, these were effectively gentlemen's agreements. To overcome the legal and incentive-compatibility limitations of cartels, the railroads eventually turned to mergers, with some firms emerging as massive corporations. The most extensive and successful of these was the Pennsylvania Railroad. This gigantic corporation was formed to garner the substantial competitive advantage that could be achieved through centralized planning. To realize these advantages, the Pennsylvania Railroad made a number of important and lasting innovations in organizational structure and the related fields of administrative and cost accounting (Chandler 1977, chaps. 4–6). The broader lesson is clear—superseding the "free market" with a centralized planning process has been critical to the success of a number of prominent business enterprises (Galbraith 1971; Lazonick 1991; Williamson 1985, chap. 11).

Before closing this section, it should be acknowledged that some inter-firm "gentlemen's agreements" have been socially useful. Instances of the latter include agreements to improve the image of an industry or product by discouraging the sale of low-quality goods, the employment of child labour, or the use of excessively polluting production processes. The emergence of the Sunkist label for California citrus growers is an example of such coordination. Another was the decision by many firms to accept or even encourage the passage of state pure food and drug laws during the Progressive Era in the United States (Law 2003). A third was the joint decision by American and United Airlines to ground their respective fleets of aircraft on September 11, 2001—a decision only later affirmed and generalized by the US Federal Aviation Authority.

Conventions, Norms, and Social Expectations

Conventions, norms, and the consequent social expectations that shape a society's collective understanding of fair play or reasonable behaviour impose important, if informal, constraints on the plans and actions of individuals and firms. At a minimum, these norms enable us to anticipate and benefit from being able to predict the most likely responses of others—rivals, counterparties, and co-workers—to our own deportment, decisions, and actions. While norms may act as a check on market forces, and at times have even worked against some progressive social movements, these informal, often unspoken, arrangements do have the effect of reducing the time and energy that might otherwise have to be devoted to negotiating the minutiae of routine transactions and business affairs. At a trivial level, most North Americans "just know" that the workday begins sometime between eight and nine in the morning, that lunch is between noon and one, that bankers wear suits, that construction workers wear boots, and that business meetings feature coffee or tea, rather than rum or whiskey.

Conventions and norms are especially important to the success of "relational contracts." Examples might be the interactions between a firm and a career employee, a firm working with a dedicated supplier of a specialized part, or a business meeting the needs of its most long-standing and loyal customers. These long-lasting arrangements are governed by contract, but conventions and norms set the parameters for modifying them over time (Macneil 1978; Stewart 1963). In his early and classic treatment of the importance of norms to the success of society, Edward Ross observed that "If the units of a society are not reliable, the waste and leakage on the one hand, or the friction due to the checks and safeguards required to prevent such loss on the other hand, prove so burdensome as to nullify the advantages of high organization and make complicated social machinery of any kind unprofitable" (Ross 1901, 59).

While firms periodically resist or ignore widely held social norms, the smarter ones understand that such a decision can be costly. Violations of widely held norms and conventions jeopardize the goodwill of important stakeholders such as suppliers, customers, and employees, with financial implications for sharehold-ers. Sometimes this defiance promotes a socially worthy cause, such as when firms began to integrate their workforces or pay equal wages for equal work. Other times it is at the expense of the commonweal, as when a firm decides to pursue a course that is legal, yet widely perceived to be immoral or distasteful. Examples may in-clude the selling of dangerous or defective products, engaging in deceptive lending, or treating some employees unfairly or arbitrarily.

Finally, through the establishment of judicial precedents, a community's notion of "reasonable" or "prudent" behaviour can come to be written into the common law. Of course, firms (and, periodically, individuals) can contest, and have con-tested, such rulings. To this end, they have turned to the courts of appeal or the legislature to set aside the decisions of lower courts. But the point stands. Firms cannot blithely or costlessly ignore norms and conventions when making their decisions. Because a firm's leadership is itself a product of society, it is inclined to accept or even internalize these constraints, but technological innovation and market opportunities have routinely created instances when the needs of a firm and the expectations of society have come into conflict.

States and the Legal Foundations of Markets

The existence of property law, contracts, conventions, norms, and people (the latter, notoriously, have multiple sources of motivation) suggests that a complex relation can and must exist among states, private firms, and individuals. This real-ity has important implications for our understanding of markets and market societies. To put it bluntly, state rule-making provides the essential foundation for the existence, to say nothing of the success, of market systems. States define the limits of property, both what may or may not be property, and what one might do with the range of objects that may be legitimately owned. Additionally, the state decides who is eligible to own property, who may contract with others to exchange property, and the rules under which these exchanges can occur. The state also plays a formative role in the event that a contract fails by setting the rules and conditions of bankruptcy. In sum, the free market is, and must be, a myth of the textbooks (Prasch 2010; Prasch 2008, chap. 1). Contrary to the claims of "free market" pro-pagandists, the issue of interest centres on the rules governing markets, including who makes them and who has the authority to modify or change them (Baker 2006; Galbraith 2008).

The rules of property, contract, and exchange must be worked out if any economic system, or for that matter any society, is to function. Once established, these rules allow for the planning necessary for the continuance or success of a modern complex economy and society. When, for whatever reason, the administrative capacity of the state is weak or non-existent, we do not witness the emergence of a prosperous free-market utopia. On the contrary, recent history affirms that such societies may come to be ruled by a kleptocracy (Russia in the early 1990s), vicious gangs (the favelas of Brazil), or armed religious movements (the Islamic Courts of Somalia or the Taliban of 1990s Afghanistan). Moreover, weakened societies are subject to interference or even invasion by foreign forces. The choice, then, is not between states and markets. Rather, the choice is over who does or does not have the legitimate authority to manage or supervise which markets, and whether or not this can be accomplished with a greater or lesser degree of fairness, insight, and effectiveness.

NOTES

1. Such utterances have become the standard fare of those whom the media have labelled "centrist" politicians, such as Bill Clinton, Tony Blair, Al Gore, and others. I have always wondered what, exactly, are we to understand by such statements? Do these politicians believe that free markets exist? Do they believe that such markets would work in theory? In practice? If the latter, work for whom?
2. A former teacher of mine, the late Reuben Zubrow of the University of Colorado, used to illustrate the propaganda debate between the supporters of free markets and Soviet-style socialism with a 2 × 2 diagram in which one side contrasted the best of markets with the worst debacles of state provisioning, while the other contrasted the best of state provisioning with the worst forms of market predation. The inevitable consequence was, as he correctly pointed out, more heat than light.

DISCUSSION QUESTIONS

1. Why is planning necessary for the economic success of individuals, firms, and states?
2. What tasks must every state address if markets are to exist?
3. What, do you suppose, are the advantages of decentralized overcentralized planning? What are the disadvantages?

SUGGESTED READINGS

Baker, Dean. 2006. *The conservative nanny state: How the wealthy use the government to stay rich and get richer.* Washington, DC: Center for Economic and Policy Research. http://www.conservativenannystate.org.

Chang, Ha-Joon. 2007. *Bad samaritans: The myth of free trade and the secret history of capitalism.* London: Bloomsbury Press.

MacEwan, Arthur. 1999. The social construction of markets. In *Neo-liberalism or democracy? Economic strategy, markets, and alternatives for the 21st century,* chap. 4. London: Zed Books.

Prasch, Robert E. 2010. Markets, states, and exchange: An introduction to economics. In *Introducing macroeconomic analysis: Issues, questions, and competing views,* eds. Hassan Bougrine and Mario Seccareccia, 22–32. Toronto: Emond Montgomery.

REFERENCES

Baker, Dean. 2006. *The conservative nanny state: How the wealthy use the government to stay rich and get richer.* Washington, DC: Center for Economic and Policy Research. http://www.conservativenannystate.org.

Chandler, Alfred D. 1977. *The visible hand.* Cambridge, MA: Harvard University Press.

Chang, Ha-Joon. 2002. Breaking the mould: An institutionalist political economy alternative to the neo-liberal theory of the market and the state. *Cambridge Journal of Economics* 26 (5): 539–559.

Chang, Ha-Joon. 2007. *Bad samaritans: The myth of free trade and the secret history of capitalism.* London: Bloomsbury Press.

Commons, John R. 1924, 1995. *Legal foundations of capitalism.* New Brunswick, NJ: Transaction.

Galbraith, James K. 2008. *The predator state: How conservatives abandoned the free market and why liberals should too.* New York: Free Press.

Galbraith, John Kenneth. 1971. *The new industrial state.* 2nd rev. ed. Boston: Houghton Mifflin.

Hayek, Friedrich von. 1945. The use of knowledge in society. *American Economic Review* 5 (4): 519–530.

Law, Marc. 2003. The origins of state pure food regulation. *Journal of Economic History* 63 (4): 1103–1130.

Lazonick, William. 1991. *Business organization and the myth of the market economy.* New York: Cambridge University Press.

MacEwan, Arthur. 1999. The social construction of markets. In *Neo-liberalism or democracy? Economic strategy, markets, and alternatives for the 21st century,* chap. 4. London: Zed Books.

Macneil, I.R. 1978. Contracts: Adjustments of long-term economic relations under classical, neoclassical, and relational contract law. *Northwestern University Law Review* 72: 854–906.

Menger, Carl. 1871, 1994. *Principles of economics*, trans. James Dingwall and Bert F. Hoselitz. Grove City, PA: Libertarian Press.

Mises, Ludwig von. 1966. *Human action: A treatise on economics.* 3rd rev. ed. Chicago: Henry Regnery.

Mitchell, Wesley Clair. 1912. The backward art of spending money. *American Economic Review* 2 (2): 269–281.

Prasch, Robert E. 2008. *How markets work: Supply, demand and the "real world."* Northampton, MA: Edward Elgar.

Prasch, Robert E. 2010. Markets, states, and exchange: An introduction to economics. In *Introducing macroeconomic analysis: Issues, questions, and competing views*, eds. Hassan Bougrine and Mario Seccareccia, 22–32. Toronto: Emond Montgomery.

Ross, Edward. 1901, 1969. *Social control: A survey of the foundations of order.* Cleveland, OH: Case Western Reserve University Press.

Smith, Adam. 1776, 1976. *An inquiry into the nature and causes of the wealth of nations.* Chicago: University of Chicago Press.

Stewart, Macauley. 1963. Non-contractual relations in business. *American Sociological Review* 28: 55–70.

Wade, Robert. 2003. *Governing the market: Economic theory and the role of government in East Asian industrialization.* 2nd ed. Princeton, NJ: Princeton University Press.

Williamson, Oliver E. 1985. *The economic institutions of capitalism.* New York: Free Press.

PART II

Consumers and Firms

3 Is Homo Economicus an Appropriate Representation of Real-World Consumers?

COMPETING VIEWS

Joseph Persky, "The Ethology of *Homo Economicus*"

Morris Altman, "*Homo Economicus* Meets Behavioural Economics"

Editors' Introduction

Orthodox microeconomics views economic behaviour as the result of optimizing decision making under conditions of scarcity. Firms are assumed to maximize profits, while consumers are assumed to maximize their utility or satisfaction, subject to a budget constraint. The decision-makers in the core models are assumed to be guided by rational self-interest. Consumers have perfect information about the want-satisfying characteristics of all commodities; they have given tastes, preferences, and incomes; their satisfaction is determined entirely by their own consumption, not by that of others; and, faced with a set of prices for all commodities, they can instantaneously and costlessly determine which affordable bundle of commodities will give them the greatest satisfaction, and they choose it. To many students of economics, this model of the rational economic agent, also referred to as *homo economicus*, seems almost too perfect. It was satirized by Thorstein Veblen in the following terms:

> The hedonistic conception of man is that of a lightning calculator of pleasures and pains, who oscillates like a homogeneous globule of desire of happiness under the impulse of stimuli that shift him about the area, but leave him intact. ... He is an isolated, definitive human datum, in stable equilibrium except for the buffets of the impinging forces that displace him in one direction or another. .:. When the force of the impact is spent, he comes to rest, a self-contained globule of desire as before. (Thorstein Veblen, "Why Is Economics Not an Evolutionary Science?" (1898) 12 *The Quarterly Journal of Economics* 389–390.)

The two essays in this chapter provide revealing perspectives, from quite different angles, on *homo economicus*. Joseph Persky traces the history of the rational economic agent, focusing on the emergence of the concept in the works of John Stuart Mill. He argues that Mill's version of *homo economicus* is a deliberate abstraction or model, designed for use in analyzing human behaviour in the economic sphere. Mill's agent is governed not solely by the desire for riches, however, but rather by four primary motives: the desire for accumulation of wealth, for leisure, for consumption, and for procreation (including both reproduction of the species and sexual pleasure). These motives are concrete and recognizable. But as Mill's critics argued, they still involve a drastic abstraction from the full complexity of human psychology. There is little room here for patriotism, charitable acts, self-sacrifice, envy, jealousy, or the desire for social status and reputation. Persky argues, however, that much of the strength of Mill's model of the rational economic agent lies in its parsimony, its stinginess with assumptions, which gives it more predictive power than if it possessed all possible human motives.

In his essay, Morris Altman provides a guided tour of recent developments in behavioural economics and other economic subfields that cast doubt on both the realism and the usefulness of *homo economicus*. Altman points to the limits of the "perfect rationality" and "perfect information" assumptions. Not only are real-world decision-makers faced by uncertainty and imperfect information, but actually making a decision requires time, thought, and other scarce resources. Hence people's decision-making capacity is limited: they are characterized by "bounded rationality," and consequently rely on simplified decision-making techniques, rules of thumb, and "heuristics" or guides to action. They are not maximizers, but rather "satisficers," whose objective is not to make perfect, optimizing decisions, but simply to make adequate decisions. Altman also argues that moral and ethical objectives are important, and can and should be incorporated into our models of economic behaviour. He makes the case that our ability to make predictions is increased by a more realistic view of human behaviour than *homo economicus* provides.

The Ethology of *Homo Economicus*

Joseph Persky*

---

*Ethology is the science "which determines the kind of character
produced in conformity to [the] general laws [of psychology],
by any set of circumstances, physical and moral."*

John Stuart Mill (1843, 869)

The Origin of Economic Man

When browsing through the library catalogue, one might easily infer that *homo economicus* will soon appear on the endangered species list. As early as 1939, Peter Drucker warned of *The End of Economic Man.* By 1976, Harvey Leibenstein could see *Beyond Economic Man.* In 1986, David Marsden asked the perennial question: *The End of Economic Man?* And more recently, Marianne Ferber and Julie Nelson have described the territory *Beyond Economic Man: Feminist Theory and Economics.* Despite these warnings, I suspect that the majority of economists remain confident of the survival of their favourite species. In fact, many see economic man as virtually the only civilized species in all of social science. Given such conflicting assessments of his present status, a review of the origins, early character and natural history of economic man may prove useful.

While John Stuart Mill is generally identified as the creator of economic man, he never actually used this designation in his own writings. But the term did emerge in reaction to Mill's work. In its first appearances in the late 19th century, "economic man" carried a pejorative connotation reflecting the widespread hostility of the historical school toward Mill's theoretical abstractions. Economic man also raised the indignation of Victorian moralists shocked at the postulation of such blatant selfishness.[1]

For example, the earliest explicit naming of economic man that I have identified is in John Kells Ingram's *A History of Political Economy* (1888).[2] Ingram, an advocate of a broad sociology in the tradition of Auguste Comte,[3] took considerable pains to disparage John Stuart Mill's political economy, which "dealt not with

---

*   Source: Adapted from Joseph Persky, "The Ethology of *Homo Economicus.*" Originally published in (1995) *The Journal of Economic Perspectives* 9 (2): 221–231. Reprinted by permission.

real but with imaginary men—'economic men' … conceived as simply 'money-making animals'" (218). Two years later, John Neville Keynes (1890) picked up (and singularized) the phrase in his much more extensive methodological treatment.[4] Keynes's efforts, though considerably less hostile than Ingram's, still painted "an 'economic man,' whose activities are determined solely by the desire for wealth," and ascribed the origins of this tightly drawn abstraction to John Stuart Mill.

Like most caricatures, those drawn by Ingram and Keynes hardly did justice to their model. While Mill's economic man was admittedly simple, he was not trivial. To understand this economic man, we must turn to Mill's early field notes.

John Stuart Mill's Abstraction

John Stuart Mill's (1836) famous essay "On the Definition of Political Economy; and on the Method of Investigation Proper to It" described a hypothetical subject, whose narrow and well-defined motives made him a useful abstraction in economic analysis. At first glance it might seem that this economic man bears a striking resemblance to Ingram's and Keynes's caricatures. According to Mill (1836, 321), political economy

> does not treat of the whole of man's nature as modified by the social state, nor of the whole conduct of man in society. It is concerned with him solely as a being who desires to possess wealth, and who is capable of judging the comparative efficacy of means for obtaining that end.

But on the same page Mill goes on to qualify this proposition strongly:

> It [political economy] makes entire abstraction of every other human passion or motive; except those which may be regarded as perpetually antagonizing to the desire of wealth, namely, aversion to labour, and desire of the present enjoyment of costly indulgences. These it takes, to a certain extent, into its calculations, because these do not merely, like other desires, occasionally conflict with the pursuit of wealth, but accompany it always as a drag, or impediment, and are therefore inseparably mixed up in the consideration of it.

Thus economic man has a dash more character than the money-hungry monomaniac described by Ingram (1888). In addition to his underlying drive for accumulation, Mill's subject desires both luxury and leisure. And just a bit later in the essay, Mill (honest Victorian that he was) felt obligated to acknowledge that even at the level of abstract theory, we had better take account of economic man's passion for producing babies as summarized in the "principle of population."

All told, then, Mill's economic man has four distinct interests: accumulation, leisure, luxury, and procreation; more than his critics maintained, but less than they might have desired. Mill argued that this number was quite enough, since in his view economic deduction worked best when focused on well-defined and relatively simple abstractions. In his methodology, Mill did recognize a need to explore for "disturbing causes": forces not included in a theory that might be identified when discrepancies between prediction and empirical observations materialized. But no single theory could reasonably cover the full complexity of human motivation. Such efforts Mill considered both unnecessary and hopelessly indeterminate.

Mill's economic man is surely more complex than Mill's critics alleged. But we make a serious error if we read into this animal the modern identification of economic man with rationality itself. In much contemporary usage, the essence of economic man lies not in what he picks, but in his rational method for making choices.[5] Whatever the usefulness of such a "rational-man" abstraction, he hardly corresponds to Mill's insistence that the range of economic man's choices be kept quite limited. Only those motives "which may be regarded as perpetually antagonizing to the desire of wealth" are reasonable candidates. And we should note that within this narrow range of motives, Mill countenanced the likelihood that when it came to procreation, even economic man might not be all that rational.

Mill's economic man provides just enough psychological complexity to make him interesting. On the one hand, Mill argued that an expansion of economic man's range of motives risked indeterminacy. On the other, he recognized that without this modest psychological complexity, economic man would have no alternative but to work all day, regardless of incentives. Such a workaholic would behave exactly the same way in any institutional environment. But Mill recognized that a wide range of economic behaviours could be observed across industries, nations, and epochs. He reasoned that a large portion of this variation in behaviour could be traced to differing economic institutions. Indeed, Mill's central theoretical and empirical project was to use economic man, with his rudimentary but manageable psychology, to prove that institutions did matter.

Mill's Project: Economic Man and Economic Institutions

Mill (1848) began his great work, *Principles of Political Economy*, with a very Smithian discussion of the historical record of the wealth of nations. He observed that among modern societies, wide differences persisted in the level and distribution of wealth. These differences, Mill asserted, could not be traced merely to differences in physical conditions and knowledge. For Mill, the key to comparative economics lay in exploring the interactions between human nature and institutions. As soon as we recognize that economic man considers several key trade-offs in his behaviour, we can imagine a society of economic men, each with strong interests in wealth, luxury, leisure, and procreation, and attempt to determine the likely effects on them of differing institutions. Among historians of economic thought, it has often been argued that when Mill came to write the *Principles* he deserted his monotonal and abstract economic man in favour of a broader approach. This interpretation is traceable to Leslie (1879) and repeated in various forms by Marshall, John Neville Keynes, and Schumpeter. Along similar lines, several of these authors also accused Mill of deserting the deductive approach he advocated in his methodological writings in favour of an historical or inductive approach. As evidence of this inconsistency between Mill's early essay on economic man and his magnum opus on *Principles*, such critics have often pointed out the host of descriptive details on alternative land tenure structures in the latter. However, I believe that much of this material relates directly to Mill's basic project of exploring the reactions of economic man to alternative institutional regimes.

For example, when Mill discusses peasant proprietors (1848, Book II, chaps. VI–VII), his concern centres on the influence of small-scale ownership as an incentive to work effort and accumulation and a discouragement to luxury and leisure. Acknowledging that there may be economies of scale associated with large agricultural enterprises, Mill's purpose is to determine whether the incentive effects of small-scale ownership are strong enough to act as an offset and raise overall production. His conclusion, based largely on reviewing empirical (and often anecdotal) writings, is that the incentive effects in question are quite strong indeed.

Mill (1848, Book II, chaps. VIII–X) follows a similar pattern in his treatment of metayers (British and French sharecroppers) and cottiers (Irish tenant farmers). In both cases he argues that the more divided the labourer from ownership, the less industrious the labourer. Mill's strong condemnation of cottier tenancy grows directly from this analysis of economic man in differing institutional settings. In considering the situation of Irish tenants, Mill (1848, 324) argues: "What race would not be indolent and insouciant when things are so arranged, that they derive no advantage from forethought or exertion." Or again: "It speaks nothing against the capacities of industry in human beings, that they will not exert themselves without motive. No labourers work harder, in England or America, than the Irish."

Even in Mill's famous chapter on the future of the working classes (1848, Book IV, chap. VII) we find that his central concern remains the response of economic man to institutional structures. A case can be made that this chapter, with its utopian schemes of profit sharing and joint ownership, is but an exercise in political sentimentalism at sharp odds with the rest of the *Principles* and quite distant from Mill's pure theory. But even here, I believe that Mill sticks closely to his basic approach. For him the central question always concerns the interaction of economic man and economic institutions. More specifically, in this chapter, Mill is searching for the best incentive system for manufacturing workers. Consciously echoing his theme with respect to land tenancy, Mill emphasizes the effectiveness of cooperative ownership and profit sharing in raising work effort and hence output. (Mill even suggests such forms might be best for agriculture as well.) Under a wage system, Mill (1848, 761) notes, the worker's "sole endeavour is to receive as much, and return as little in the shape of service as possible." Here is a solid economic man indeed. Mill concludes that radical institutional reforms will be needed to motivate such a species.

I certainly do not hold that the *Principles* rigidly limits its purview to economic man. Mill makes more than a few forays aimed at analyzing "disturbing causes." Yet, he repeatedly emphasizes how economic man, freed from oppressive institutional forms, will produce a great deal more wealth. For Mill, the most promising institutions were *laissez-faire* in tone, but included radical reforms such as profit sharing. Far from having to make a choice between abstract *a priori* theory and the forces of historicism, sociologism, and institutionalism, Mill demonstrates that much can be learned from considering a simple, but hardly trivial, view of human nature in interaction with diverse real-world institutions. This methodology—using economic man as guinea pig in widely different institutional settings—remains an essential tool of modern economics.

Ethology and Character

While Mill often dealt with economic man as a given, he was also eager to analyze the evolution of economic man's preferences and passions. Throughout the *Principles*, Mill's discussions of incentives slipped almost seamlessly into explorations of the social psychology of tastes and character.

Strictly speaking, Mill viewed efforts to analyze the development of character as the proper task of ethology, a science he placed logically subsequent to elementary psychology. Ethology, according to Mill (1843, 869), was that science "which determines the kind of character produced in conformity to those general laws [of psychology], by any set of circumstances, physical and moral." In terms of Mill's grander scheme of sciences and arts, ethology (like political economy) produced *axiomata media*, or middle-level theory—logically precise deductions from admittedly shaky first principles that then could be applied in useful arts. Thus, the art corresponding to ethology was "education," or what today might be called "character building."

Working from the base of general ethology, Mill (1843, 905) argued that "economic ethology"[6] would then construct "a theory of the causes which determine the type of character belonging to a people or to an age." Mill thought economic ethology was still in its infancy: "The causes of national character are scarcely at all understood, and the effect of institutions or social arrangements upon the character of the people is generally that portion of their effects which is least attended to, and least comprehended."

Despite Mill's assertion that little was known of economic ethology, in the *Principles* he repeatedly attempted deductions as to the economic ethology of economic man. At any given time, economic man could be expected to respond differently to different institutions. This was political economy. Over time, continuous exposure to a particular set of institutions could be expected to influence the very tastes of economic man. This was economic ethology.

Thus Mill (1848, 286), in analyzing the character of peasant proprietors, argues that small land ownership in addition to developing mental faculties is "propitious to the moral virtues of prudence, temperance, and self-control." Or in a very different context, when discussing inheritance, Mill argues that an early life of luxury predisposes the younger children of the nobility to extravagant consumption. In many of his examples, Mill applies what might be called a Lamarckian view to the development of character: the notion that more or less rational choices made by one generation predispose the tastes of subsequent generations to reinforce similar choices.[7] The incentives facing the peasant lead to energetic effort, which becomes a way of life and even a passion. A choice of luxurious consumption by the parents becomes a taste in the children. Mill wavers on precisely how persistent an effect such acculturation has on economic man. At some points he implies that national characteristics rooted in long custom can only be changed gradually. On other occasions he suggests a change of institutional regimes will have almost instantaneous results; for example, in his discussion of Irish character quoted above, he virtually rules out an intergenerational perpetuation of lassitude once individuals are removed from oppressive institutional conditions. Closely related to this question of the cultural persistence of economic man's tastes is that of his social-historical origins. Virtually no economist in the last half of the 19th century claimed that history, or even economic history, could be understood only through the lens of economic man. A common view, championed by Walter Bagehot (1879), held that the motives and tastes typical of economic man were themselves a product of the spread of commerce. Bagehot (106) saw economic man as a product of societies where "the commercial element is the greatest element." Thus, the logic of economic man implicit in political economy could only be applied to such communities: "In so far as nations are occupied in 'buying and selling,' in so far will Political Economy, the exclusive theory of men buying and selling, come out right, and be true." Bagehot (104) thought political economy an appropriate tool for studying England where it might be "exactly true." Yet for much of the world and much of history, economic man played little role. In a military slave power like Rome or "Oriental nations" fixed in custom, Bagehot (106) wrote: "The money-getting element is a most subordinate one in their minds; its effects are very subordinate ones in their lives."

In places, Mill seemed to anticipate this more limited historical and geographic vision of economic man. In his *Logic* (1843), he had suggested: "In political economy ... empirical laws of human nature are tacitly assumed by English thinkers, which are calculated only for Great Britain and the United States." Mill did not have to go as far as Asia or back to Roman history to find the antithesis of economic man. He wrote (1843, 906) that those "who know the habits of the Continent of Europe are aware how apparently small a motive often outweighs the desire of money-getting, even in the operations which have money-getting for their direct object."

Such observations, however, remained uncharacteristic of the creator of economic man. More typically, Mill defended the basic psychological construct of economic man as primary for the purposes of political economy and argued that peculiarities of national character at odds with this psychology could be treated as secondary disturbing causes. Moreover, the trend of history was moving in economic man's favour. As Bagehot emphasized, commercial activities occupied an increasingly central position in most countries. If exposure to commerce changed tastes, then economic man might yet be universal.

Soviet Man, Feminist Economics, and Parsimonious Psychology

The science of ethology has a quaint 19th-century ring, but the questions raised by Mill are still of importance to economics. The origin and persistence of economic motives have striking implications for public policy today. The usefulness of a whole range of public and private bureaucratic reforms, including antipoverty initiatives, welfare reform, affirmative action, and foreign assistance all rest on the extent to which changing economic incentives can have rapid and predictable effects on the behaviour of the relevant population. Economists who have ventured into these areas of research are carrying out, perhaps unknowingly, Mill's ethological program. For the most part, their results support the broad usefulness of Mill's original conception of economic man.

In a basically ethological analysis, Robert Shiller, Maxim Boycko, and Vladimir Korobov (1992) focused on differences in national economic character and especially differences between the United States and Russia. Mill would easily recognize their concern with the trade-offs people make between work and leisure and between current and future consumption. In addition, they put considerable emphasis on possible national differences in attitudes toward risk taking, a dimension not emphasized in Mill's original discussion, but much discussed in his *Principles*. They also explored the trade-off between fortune and fame, finding significant minority interest in fame across all the countries studied, a finding that might give Mill pause. Their discussion guardedly concluded that situations—constraints and institutions—as opposed to attitudes accounted for the bulk of the economic lethargy of former Soviet citizens. Much of their analysis parallels Mill's own discussion of the Irish.

These scholars clearly are doing ethology. Interestingly enough, these modern-day ethologists don't seem to require a much wider universe of preferences than Mill made do with. *Homo Sovieticus* appears as a surprisingly close cousin of *homo economicus*.

In a rather different context, much of recent feminist writing can also be viewed from Mill's methodological perspective. Feminists emphasize that traditional economics puts too much weight on men's choices and too little on women's constraints. Feminists have brought attention to the long-neglected role of social and institutional constraints in limiting the economic productivity, achievements, and welfare of women. Such efforts, even as they illustrate the influences of patriarchy, draw heavily on Mill's project. Like Mill, at root they are concerned with the economic implications of oppressive or discriminatory institutional constraints.

Beyond their documentation of enforced constraints, feminist writers have also launched a broad critique of the practice of modern economics. To an extent, this work has taken Mill's ethological perspective. Like Mill, these writers show serious concern for the process of character building in the development of both women and men. Such concerns are the stuff of ethology. But unlike Mill, some of these modern feminists have generally denied the need for a parsimonious psychology. They have called for a wholesale revision of the psychology of economic persons. Like Comte, they have proposed a virtually universal social science.

The issue here is not the desirability of such a social science, but rather its feasibility. The danger arises not from well-reasoned adjustments to economic man's short list of motives, but from losing sight of Mill's methodological insistence on parsimony. Motives such as status, security, creativity, sociability, and concern for social reproduction have all been suggested by feminists as relevant to the economic behaviour of men and women. I suspect Mill himself would not have rejected out-of-hand such feminist efforts to reconsider the basic drives relevant to economics. As several of the passages above make clear, Mill at times argued the need for a broader economic ethology. Yet Mill would have counselled that any additions to the list of basic drives be winnowed to a minimum. Fundamental to Mill's methodology was his effort to limit economic reasoning to a significant but manageable set of human motives.

Many groups over the years, starting with the historical school and including institutionalist economists, have recognized that humans were a good deal more complex than the economic man Mill had suggested. Like some of today's feminists, these groups have offered a wide range of competing motives and behaviours. But their lists were so long and unwieldy that they virtually excluded tightly reasoned generalizations. Their method could perhaps generate history, but not economics.

The message to derive from Mill's *homo economicus* is not that humans are greedy, not that man is rational, but that social science works best when it ruthlessly limits its range. It is useful and serious work to explore alternative bases. But to compete successfully against economic man, a new ethology must be parsimonious; it must clearly specify the relevant psychological makeup of economic agents; and it must demonstrate that such a system yields better and/or new insights. In models where everything affects everything else, social scientists have little ability to draw inferences. Perhaps the "economic" in "economic man" relates as much to his parsimonious psychology as to his fascination with wealth.

NOTES

1. For a description of the historical school, see Leslie (1879). As to the confusion with ethical issues, see Goschen (1893). Of course, the question of the social consequences of self-interested behaviour considerably antedates economic man and formal political economy. In this respect, see the insightful essay by Milton Myers (1983), *The Soul of Modern Economic Man.*

2. The first use of the Latin *homo economicus* I turned up is in Vilfredo Pareto's *Manual* (1906, 12–14), but I haven't done a serious search of continental sources. Schumpeter (1954, 156) pointed to B. Frigerio's usage of *economo prudente*, circa 1629, as a "common sense forerunner of the Economic Man." I suspect the formal christening of economic man late in the 19th century required as a prerequisite the major change in the name of our discipline from "political economy" to "economics," which occurred about the same time Ingram wrote.

3. Comte argued for a unified social science that considered the complete range of human motives. Mill early on had been attracted to Comte's vision, but held that political economy be maintained as a separate discipline.

4. "Economic man" must have been quite the buzzword around Cambridge that year since Marshall also used it the same year in his *Principles.* See Marshall (1890, vi, 26–27).

5. Kirzner (1960) provides a clear history of the broad shift in economic theory from the classical concern with the production and distribution of wealth to Lionel Robbins's science of choice.

6. Actually Mill called this activity "political ethology," thus paralleling the field of political economy. In modern usage our discipline is called economics. Hence I think the term "economic ethology" is faithful to the spirit of the original, while being more easily understood by modern readers.

7. Late in the 19th century, J.B. de Monet Lamarck was responsible for the view, now in disrepute, that environment can cause structural changes in animals or plants that are then genetically transmitted to future generations.

DISCUSSION QUESTIONS

1. Lionel Robbins defined economics as the science of choice. What do you suspect John Stuart Mill would think of this definition? Why? What do you think of it?

2. Are four motivations for economic man just the right number? If you were going to add a fifth motivation to the four suggested by John Stuart Mill, what would it be and why? If you were going to subtract a motivation from Mill's list, which would it be and why?

3. John Stuart Mill was an early and strong supporter of women's political and economic rights. Yet he assumed that most women would choose to take on the role of homemaker and mother. Are the motives of "economic woman" different from those of "economic man?"

4. How useful is Mill's concept of *national character*? Is this just a quaint 19th-century idea or is it key to appreciating microeconomic behaviours in different societies? Put somewhat differently, if economists can give us a full description of the material incentives surrounding economic behaviour in country Z, is there anything left over for the "national character" of Z to explain?

SUGGESTED READINGS AND ONLINE RESOURCES

See the works listed in the References section below.
The Library of Economics and Liberty: http://www.econlib.org.

REFERENCES

Bagehot, Walter. 1879. The preliminaries of political economy. In *Economic studies*. Repr. 1902. London: Longmans, Green, and Co.

Drucker, Peter. 1939. *The end of economic man: A study of the new totalitarianism.* New York: John Day.

Ferber, Marianne, and Julie Nelson, eds. 1993. *Beyond economic man: Feminist theory and economics*, especially chapters by Donald McCloskey, Julie Nelson, and Diana Strassman. Chicago: University of Chicago Press.

Folbre, Nancy, and Heidi Hartmann. 1988. The rhetoric of self-interest: Ideology of gender in economic theory. In *The consequences of economic rhetoric*, eds. Arjo Klamer, Donald McCloskey, and Robert Solow, 184–203. Cambridge: Cambridge University Press.

Goschen, George. 1893. Ethics and economics. *Economic Journal*. September 3: 377–387.

Ingram, John Kells. 1888. *A history of political economy*. Repr. 1967. New York: Augustus M. Kelley.

Keynes, John Neville. 1890. *The scope and method of political economy.* Repr. 1963. New York: Augustus M. Kelley.

Kirzner, Israel. 1960. *The economic point of view: An essay in the history of economic thought.* Princeton, NJ: Van Nostrand.

Leibenstein, Harvey. 1976. *Beyond economic man: A new foundation for microeconomics.* Cambridge, MA: Harvard University Press.

Leslie, T. E. Cliffe. 1879. The love of money, On the philosophical method in political economy, and Political economy and sociology. In *Essays in political economy,* 1–18, 163–190, 191–220, respectively. Repr. 1969. New York: Augustus M. Kelley.

Marsden, David. 1986. *The end of economic man? Custom and competition in labour markets.* Brighton, UK: Wheatsheaf Books.

Marshall, Alfred. 1890. *Principles of economics.* 9th (variorum) ed. Repr. 1961. London: Macmillan.

Mill, John Stuart. 1836. On the definition of political economy; and on the method of investigation proper to it. *London and Westminster Review,* October.

Mill, John Stuart. 1843. *A system of logic, ratiocinative and inductive.* Repr. 1974. *Collected works,* vol. 8. Toronto: University of Toronto Press.

Mill, John Stuart. 1844. *Essays on some unsettled questions of political economy.* Repr. 1967. *Collected works,* vol. 4, 120–164. Toronto: University of Toronto Press.

Mill, John Stuart. 1848. *Principles of political economy with some of their applications to social philosophy.* Repr. 1929, ed. W.J. Ashley. London: Longmans, Green and Co.

Myers, Milton. 1983. *The soul of modern economic man: Ideas of self-interest, Thomas Hobbes to Adam Smith.* Chicago: University of Chicago Press.

Pareto, Vilfredo. 1906. *Manual of political economy.* Repr. 1971, trans. Ann Schwier. New York: Augustus M. Kelley. (Trans. of the 1927 French edition.)

Pujole, Michele. 1992. *Feminism and anti-feminism in early economic thought.* Hants, UK: Edward Elgar.

Reskin, Barbara, and Heidi Hartmann, eds. 1986. *Women's work, men's work.* Washington, DC: National Academy Press.

Schumpeter, Joseph. 1954. *History of economic analysis,* ed. Elizabeth Schumpeter. New York: Oxford University Press.

Shiller, Robert, Maxim Boycko, and Vladimir Korobov. 1992. Hunting for *Homo Sovieticus*: Situational versus attitudinal factors in economic behaviour. *Brookings Papers on Economic Activity* 1: 127–181.

Homo Economicus Meets Behavioural Economics

Morris Altman

Introduction

The conventional economic wisdom asserts that the representative individual or economic agent, often referred to as *homo economicus*, is characterized by a set of behavioural traits that is rational and dominates the behaviour of the typical consumer. Such rational behaviour is not only supposed to best describe typical human choice behaviour, it is also considered to be optimal behaviour: behaviour that best serves to maximize the utility or welfare of the individual. The model of *homo economicus* is considered to be both positive (descriptive and analytical) and normative (providing direction for ideal or best-practice human behaviour—how individuals ought to behave). Moreover, this model is thought to be the most effective predictor of typical human behaviour. In other words, the model of *homo economicus* stipulates not only that individuals will behave in a particular fashion but that this is how rational economic agents ought to behave.

One influential proponent of this perspective, Milton Friedman (1953), argues that how individuals actually behave (make choices) is not important at all. Rather, what is significant is that the typical individual behaves as if he or she is a practitioner of rational choice theory and that modelled behaviour yields reasonably strong and robust predictions of choice behaviour. This modelling package, often referred to as rational choice theory, is part and parcel of what is referred to as neoclassical choice theory, one component of which is the neoclassical theory of consumer behaviour. However, rational choice theory has been criticized in its various dimensions as being a poor positive and normative tool. One recent critique of rational choice theory stems from behavioural economics and builds upon a critical assessment of the micro-foundations of rational choice theory. Another important critique flows from the recent work of Gary Becker (1996), a founding father of contemporary rational choice theory.

The basic model of *homo economicus* is characterized by (1) a stable set of preferences or wants or desires that is given by a utility function; (2) a perfect knowledge of alternatives relevant to a choice problem; (3) the ability to forecast the expected consequences of particular choices made in the present into the future, even when the future is highly uncertain; (4) the ability to make use of this knowledge to maximize a person's economic well-being, given the utility function; and (5) consistency in the choices made by the economic agent. Several fundamental underlying assumptions are required for this basic model to become operational. First, it is assumed that individuals have unbounded knowledge of relevant choice alternatives and unbounded computational capacities to determine the outcomes of alternative choices. Second, individuals are assumed to make such choices independently of other individuals. They are unaffected by other peoples' choices. In other words, preferences, or utility functions, and choices derived from individuals' utility functions are said to be independent of the utility functions and choices of others.

A third assumption is that the individual has the capability and power to make the choices that he or she prefers to make. Other individuals do not, therefore, interfere with these choices. Finally, it is assumed that this rational economic agent is narrowly selfish, interested most in maximizing his or her own material well-being. It is argued that deviations from such narrowly self-interested behaviour will not be welfare-maximizing and would therefore be irrational. Smart people cannot be altruistic or self-sacrificing materially (as in charitable giving) or in terms of time (as in volunteering) unless it can be shown that such self-sacrifice provides some outweighing material benefit.

As part of this package of assumptions, it is further assumed that the behaviour of the rational individual is sensitive to the relative prices or costs associated with any possible choice and to his or her income. In the standard case, for normal goods, the higher the relative cost, the lower the quantity demanded of a good or service, and the higher the income (corrected for prices), the greater the quantity demanded. Cost and income sensitivities are typically meshed together and assumed to be dependent or contingent upon the above assumptions thought to characterize *homo economicus*. The prescribed behaviour that flows from the entire conventional economics modelling package is referred to as constrained utility- or welfare-maximization.

General Critique of *Homo Economicus*

Homo economicus has been widely criticized as simply being inconsistent with how real people engage in choice behaviour in the real world. It is also argued that often this choice model does not yield rigorous analytical predictions and that the normative narrative embodied by *homo economicus* is not consistent with economic efficiency and optimality, nor with best-practice choice behaviour. But a classic defence of *homo economicus* is that it is consistent with typical economic outcomes, such as those captured in the demand curve, which is a critical component of analyses of consumer behaviour. Because the typical demand curve is negatively sloped, price and quantity demanded are negatively related, and changes in real income tend to shift the demand curve, it is argued that this proves the validity of the *homo economicus* construct, and therefore that the demand curve flows from the core assumptions of the conventional economic agent. The standard demand curve, however, appears to be consistent with a wide variety of behaviours and decision rules that are inconsistent with *homo economicus* (Simon 1979). Experiments in economics and in economic psychology have also provided considerable evidence that in many common circumstances people do not behave in a manner consistent with *homo economicus*. Many such behaviours are not rational from this perspective. What the existence of an empirical demand curve, for example, appears to provide strong evidence for is not that humans behave or even should behave like *homo economicus*, but rather that humans are affected by economic incentives. The negatively sloped demand curve and movements in the demand curve can be better explained, at both the individual and aggregate level, using alternative models of the economic agent. This has raised the question of revising the conventional model of *homo economicus*. For example, Vernon Smith (2005, 149), Nobel laureate in economics and one of the founders of experimental economics, has argued that experimental evidence shows that profit-maximizing firms are the least likely to be market survivors. This implies that individuals who behave contrary to the conventional economic norms of rationality are rational and that the standard model is incorrect and needs significant revision.

Bounded Rationality and Fast and Frugal Heuristics

Herbert Simon, another Nobel laureate in economics and a pioneer of behavioural economics, developed the concept of *bounded rationality* as an alternative to the conventional modelling of the economic agent. Simon integrates the fact that the cognitive abilities of individuals, in terms of computational ability, knowledge, and omniscience, are limited, and prevent them from developing a better understanding of decision-making. Once these limitations are recognized, one can no longer assume that individuals know all available alternatives and all the consequences of their choices. The acquisition of such knowledge comes at too high a cost, so individuals adopt behavioural procedures or *heuristics* designed to limit such costs. Rational behaviour thus takes place within the bounds or cognitive limitations of the individual as well as within the bounds of incomplete or imperfect information. To best explain and predict consumer behaviour, then, one must understand what people are capable of doing and the environment in which they engage in decision-making.

In relation to bounded rationality, Simon introduces the concept of *satisficing* as an alternative to optimizing. A satisficer will maximize, but only given the constraints of bounded rationality. A consumer is still attempting to optimize in a loose sense of the word—attempting to do the best he or she is capable of doing given the computational and informational constraints that are imposed.

When searching for apples or cars or CDs or computers, for example, individuals will not engage in the intensive sort of searches that would characterize *homo economicus*. Nor do consumers carefully contrast and weigh the different characteristics of the products they search for to choose the product that yields the greatest increase in utility. Instead, consumers use a *stopping-rule* heuristic when shopping. For example, they stop searching when they find a particular computer that meets their basic concerns in key dimensions, such as price, functionality, and quality. This might involve going to only one or two stores, or even going to the one store that the consumer has learnt to trust. Such search behaviour, although incomplete, makes sense given the physiological and environmental constraints facing the individual. It is more consistent with lexicographic preferences, where individuals don't make choices based on trade-offs of product characteristics but rather rank-order their preferred product characteristics (like using a "ladder" of preferred characteristics) and stop searching once a sufficient number of these characteristics are met. By using a decision rule that saves scarce search and computational resources, consumers are satisficing, not maximizing.

Gerd Gigerenzer refers to this type of satisficing behaviour as a "fast and frugal" heuristic. He argues that if consumers did not use such a lexicographic decision rule they would not be maximizing their utility and *homo economicus* would be wasting her scarce resources, which could be better used in engaging in preferred utility-enhancing activities. As Vernon Smith argues, this is exactly why humans do not behave as *homo economicus*.

Another proven fast and frugal decision rule that individuals exploit is the *recognition heuristic*. Evidence suggests that individuals tend to make choices based on products that they recognize, given relative prices. If individuals recognize one alternative but not the others and choose the recognized one, they are using the recognition heuristic. This heuristic saves search and computational time and relies on readily available and trusted information. Labels and branding therefore play a critical role in the recognition heuristic. Evidence suggests that this heuristic is typically used when it makes sense, given imperfect information and costly search. However, it runs contrary to the norms of *homo economicus* for best-practice behaviour.

Fast and frugal heuristics are part of the bounded-rationality and behavioural economics research agenda that finds that rational consumers are often better off not engaging in detailed search and calculation. A key point of the fast and frugal research agenda is that "consumers do not always weigh and add when they make decisions, and that they may vary their decision processes from situation to situation, according to the perceived ecological rationality. The principle of robust decisions reminds us that less is sometimes more. Instead of trying to optimally integrate everything, good decisions in the real world need to know what information to ignore" (Kurz-Milcke and Gigerenzer 2007, 55). The bounded-rationality perspective on the economic agent suggests that modelling the consumer as *homo economicus* generates misleading narratives of actual human behaviour as well as misleading narratives of efficient and optimal behaviour. There are better ways of rendering a good and cogent understanding of decision-making in the real world.

Ethics and Human Behaviour

Individuals often make choices that involve making some sacrifice of income or time and are therefore not maximizing their income. Of course, *homo economicus* will also not always aim at maximizing her money *income*, if she can maximize her *utility* by working less and forgoing some income in order to increase her (utility-providing) leisure time. But for *homo economicus*, all of the benefits of this decision must accrue directly to her. In contrast, real-world consumers tip their servers, donate to charity, donate volunteer time, purchase at a high price products that they deem to be ethical, and return lost items to owners even if they could easily get away with keeping these items and thus increase their own material welfare. Many individuals also invest in ethical funds even when these generate lower than average rates of return. Many consumers purchase more expensive products that they know are more environmentally friendly.

These acts of self-sacrifice can be referred to as moral acts. According to the model of *homo economicus*, these are irrational behaviours. Does this mean that most people are irrational? Or that what serves to increase their welfare goes beyond material considerations? For most people, evidence suggests that money is not the only thing that matters. Individuals might still be attempting to maximize their well-being or utility or at least engaging in satisficing, but utility in the real world incorporates the supply of moral acts that is affected by education and culture and by an individual's social networks, family, affinity to particular causes or organizations, and feelings of reciprocity. It can also relate to the extent to which acts of self-sacrifice yield good feelings or a warm glow (Andreoni 1990). If a person was forced to be a *homo economicus*, maximizing wealth or income at the expense of preferred moral acts, her behaviour would be suboptimal and she would not be maximizing her utility, even though she would be doing the right thing from the perspective of conventional economic theory. This person's utility would be higher only if she behaved in a manner that generated, from her perspective, the right combination of material and moral goods (Altman 2005).

Introducing ethical or moral behaviour as part of a rational individual's utility-maximizing or satisficing objectives does not imply that the moral economic agent is not affected by incentives. Very few people would be willing to supply ethical acts that significantly reduced their level of material well-being. In other words, if the cost of being moral increases, one would expect the number of moral acts supplied to diminish. If environmentally friendly products increase in price, one would expect the quantity demanded of these products to diminish. Most people are happy to tip as long as the tipping percentage is not exorbitant. Most people are happy to donate to charity as long as these donations do not comprise too large a percentage of their income. Poor people may not engage in as much "ethical" consumption as wealthier people not because the poor are less ethical than the rich, but because they face more severe budget constraints (Altman 2006b).

Psychological Variables and Decision-Making

In the conventional economic wisdom, based on subjective expected utility (SEU) theory, what is critically important to decision-making and to a person's utility is her final state of wealth, or the net wealth an individual has at a given point in time after accounting for all gains and losses. Moreover, a dollar lost is given the same weight as a dollar gained when computing an individual's wealth. If you gain $1 and lose $1 simultaneously, there is no change in your wealth and therefore no change in utility. Individuals are assumed to maximize the *net* increase in their final state of wealth. Drawing on the results of numerous economic experiments and surveys, however, Kahneman and Tversky (2000) and Kahneman (2003) argue that this is not how individuals generally behave. They developed *prospect theory* as an alternative to SEU theory to describe aspects of individuals' choice behaviour. In prospect theory, individuals focus more on *changes* in their *initial* wealth than on their *final level* of wealth. Losses and gains are calculated separately, and losses are given more weight than gains of equal monetary value.[1] According to prospect theory, this aversion to losses (*loss aversion*) results in individuals avoiding choices that generate relatively large losses, even if those choices generate *net* increases in the final state of wealth. So, for example, if a particular prospect will increase one's net income by $200, through the combination of a loss of $1,000 and a gain of $1,200, many people will reject this prospect or choice option because the psychological pain of losing $1,000 exceeds the pleasure of gaining $1,200.

With loss aversion, consumers' decision-making is affected by pricing and product return policy. If a store introduces a "try-and-return policy," for example, its sales (even after deducting returned items) are likely to increase: once individuals have the product in hand, they are more likely to keep it, since they categorize giving it up at that point as a loss.

Kahneman and Tversky (2000) also developed the notion of the *framing effect* to help explain choice behaviour that does not correspond to that of *homo economicus*. They argue that choices are affected by how prospects are framed, even if the frame has no materially important effect on the prospect. One way the framing effect operates in choice situations relates to the "default option"—what happens if you take *no* action. Changing the default option affects choice behaviour. If donating an organ on death is the default position, most people *will* become organ donors. If this option is not the default position and one has to sign up to become a donor, most people will *not* be donors. So, in contrast to Austria, in the United States, most people are *not* donors, not because Americans are less socially motivated or altruistic than Austrians, but rather because in the United States organ donation is not the default option, whereas in Austria it is.

Also, experiments have demonstrated that whether identical options are framed negatively or positively will affect choices, whereas the conventional wisdom says that if the options are identical, the decisions should be identical. As a result of loss aversion, people are more likely to choose positively framed prospects. Some behavioural economists argue that this behaviour is quite rational in a world of uncertainty and asymmetric information. Negative frames signal that a particular choice is problematic and should be avoided.

Individuals are also characterized by what some refer to as *status quo bias*. Individuals tend to stick with what they know, even if a new product is "superior." *Homo economicus* would directly opt for the superior option but real people take more time to adjust to the new, because they need to acquire more information and experience. For some behavioural economists, a default preference for the status quo, the so-called status quo bias, is not a bias at all, but is a type of insurance against the risk and uncertainty involved in shifting from the known to the unknown.

Some critics of *homo economicus* argue that these observed phenomena— weighing losses and gains asymmetrically, loss aversion, being influenced by frames and defaults, and having a preference for the status quo—provide evidence of *irrational* behaviour (Kahneman 2003; Thaler and Sustein 2008). Others argue that such preferences are simply evidence that smart people, for *rational* reasons, don't behave according to the strictures of *homo economicus* (Gigerenzer and Todd 1999; Simon 1987). They argue, for instance, that frames can provide signals to decision-makers that affect their choice behaviour in an uncertain world, and that the status quo provides certainty in a world of uncertainty.

Capabilities and Consumption

Conventional theory assumes that individuals make choices that reflect their preferences. Individuals buy what they truly desire, given their income and relative prices. From this basic premise, it is deduced that an individual's welfare-maximizing choices are revealed by her purchases. Moreover, it is assumed that the individual knows what is in her best interest. This analytical perspective, known as methodological individualism, recommends that individual choice be respected as welfare-maximizing unless it causes harm to others (negative choice or consumption externalities). But the assumption that individuals tend to purchase and consume what they actually want is based upon very special assumptions that do not always hold in reality and are often not made explicit in discussions about welfare maximization.

Amartya Sen (1985) and Martha Nussbaum (2000) initiated an important critique of this perspective. They argue that for individuals' choices to reflect their tastes or preferences, they must be provided with the capabilities to achieve their preferences. Once this is accomplished, individuals' choices should be respected, as is the case with the conventional economic wisdom. But rational individuals deprived of adequate capabilities cannot engage in welfare-maximizing choices. Improving capabilities allows individuals to make preferred choices. Nussbaum (2000, 49) argues that it is the role of government to provide these capabilities, but not force individuals to make particular choices.

For instance, in many societies and communities, females do not have the capabilities to form or execute their preferences with regard to their consumption of goods and services (which can affect their health and overall well-being) or the number of children they wish to have. They might be deprived of the necessary information or the power to exercise their free will. In many situations, individuals do not have the information necessary to make their preferred choice of products. A person might prefer to purchase organic dairy products, but the product labels might be misleading and unreliable. A person might want to purchase healthier foods for her children but, even with an adequate income, might not have the necessary information to do so. A person might want to stop smoking cigarettes but might be addicted and not have the capabilities to realize her preference to stop smoking.

Social Context, Preferences, and Choice

Gary Becker is one of the founding fathers of contemporary economics, but he is highly critical of his colleagues who assume that an individual's preferences and choices do not depend on past experiences and social interactions, when in fact they are of critical importance. Becker (1996, 22–23) argues that "childhood and other experiences, and the attitudes and behavior of others [as well as culture and habits], frequently place more far-reaching constraints on choices than do mistakes and distortions in cognitive perceptions." In Becker's view, one cannot explain human choice behaviour solely on the basis of prices and incomes, since past experience and social variables are also critical determinants of preferences. Moreover, Becker argues, preferences are not formed independently, but are affected by the preferences and choices of other individuals. The latter point was made early on in the economics literature, first by Thorstein Veblen (1899) and later by Harvey

Leibenstein (1950). Leibenstein discussed and modelled "snob" and "bandwagon" effects. But these insights have never been integrated into the concept of *homo economicus*.

Becker (1996, 4) introduces the concept of personal capital, which "includes the relevant past consumption and other personal experiences that affect current and future utilities," and social capital, which "incorporates the influence of past actions by peers and others in an individual's social network and control system." Personal and social capital are part of an individual's human capital stock and affect individual preferences. Becker argues that our model of the economic agent needs to be revised to provide better explanations for a wide range of events. Moreover, he maintains that choice behaviour that is affected by personal and social capital is not irrational even if it does not conform to the choices that one would expect from *homo economicus*—because the only choices that rational or smart people are capable of making are choices made in a social context and influenced by their past behaviour.

As an example, when an individual's demand is influenced by the demand of her peers, that demand curve might be below or above where it would otherwise be. The demand curve for goods that improve one's relative position in society or among peers would lie above the standard demand curve. Similarly, if commodities have non-material attributes attached to them—for instance that they were produced by "ethical" means—the demand curve for such products would lie above the standard demand curve.

Conclusion

The narrow view of the economic agent conveyed by the *homo economicus* image has been criticized from many directions. A key line of defence against the critics is that people respond to incentives—this is what underlies the core of *homo economicus*. However, the most penetrating critiques of *homo economicus* allow for the reality that people respond to relative prices and income and to changes in these variables. In fact, introducing bounded rationality, satisficing, moral or altruistic behaviour, loss aversion, framing effects, capabilities, and social and personal capital into our modelling of the economic agent is perfectly consistent with individuals' responsiveness to incentives.

Enriching the conventional model of the economic agent is also consistent with individuals trying to maximize their well-being or utility. But what most people count as contributing to their utility is not what *homo economicus* prescribes. For example, being moral in consumption can be welfare-maximizing even if it is not wealth- or income-maximizing. Moreover, the evidence suggests that attempting to become "fully informed" would be a waste of scarce resources, given the physiological, psychological, and environmental realities of decision-makers. Using the recognition heuristic may be smarter and more efficient than engaging in intensive search and calculation. In its very essence, the *homo economicus* model is a recipe for *not* maximizing well-being in the real world of decision-making and consumer behaviour.

NOTE

1. In technical terms, instead of the conventional *utility-of-wealth function* (which may be concave, convex, or linear), they use a *value function*, which is *concave* in gains and *convex* in losses (relative to the individual's initial wealth position).

DISCUSSION QUESTIONS

1. Does the contemporary critique of *homo economicus* imply that individuals do not respond to incentives? Briefly discuss.
2. Why does the conventional economic wisdom consider ethical behaviour to be inconsistent with rationality? Why might behaviours such as tipping and volunteer work actually be rational?
3. What are bounded rationality and fast and frugal heuristics? Why do many economists now argue that behaviour consistent with bounded rationality and fast and frugal heuristics is most consistent with rationality?
4. What is loss aversion? How does this perspective differ from the conventional economic view of rational behaviour?

REFERENCES AND SUGGESTING READINGS

Akerlof, George A. 1970. The market for "lemons": Quality uncertainty and the market mechanism. *Quarterly Journal of Economics* 84: 488–500.

Altman, Morris. 2005. Reconciling altruistic, moralistic, and ethical behavior with the rational economic agent and competitive markets. *Journal of Economic Psychology* 26: 732–757.

Altman, Morris, ed. 2006a. *Handbook of contemporary behavioral economics: Foundations and developments.* Armonk, NY: M.E. Sharpe.

Altman, Morris. 2006b. Opening-up the objective function: Choice behavior and economic and non-economic variables—Core and marginal altruism. *Economics Bulletin* 4: 1–11. http://ideas.repec.org/a/ebl/ecbull/v4y2006i33p1-7.html.

Andreoni, James. 1990. Impure altruism and donations to public goods: A theory of warm-glow giving. *Economic Journal* 100: 464–477.

Becker, Gary. 1996. *Accounting for tastes.* Cambridge and London: Harvard University Press.

Camerer, Colin F., George Loewenstein, and Matthew Rabin, eds. 2004. *Advances in behavioral economics.* Princeton, NJ and Oxford: Princeton University Press.

Friedman, Milton. 1953. The methodology of positive economics. In *Essays in Positive Economics*, Milton Friedman, 3–43. Chicago: University of Chicago Press.

Gigerenzer, Gerd, and Peter M. Todd. 1999. *Simple heuristics that make us smart.* New York: Oxford University Press.

Kahneman, Daniel. 2003. Maps of bounded rationality: Psychology for behavioral economics. *American Economic Review* 93: 1449–1475.

Kahneman, Daniel, and Amos Tversky, eds. 2000. *Choices, values and frames.* New York: Cambridge University Press and Russell Sage Foundation.

Kurz-Milcke, Elke, and Gerd Gigerenzer. 2007. Heuristic decision making. *Marketing—Journal of Research and Management* 3 (1): 48–60.

Leibenstein, H. 1950. Bandwagon, snob, and Veblen effects in the theory of consumers' demand. *Quarterly Journal of Economics* 64: 183–207.

Lewis, Alan, Paul Webley, and Adrien Furnham. 1995. *The new economic mind.* London and New York: Pearson.

Nussbaum, Martha. 2000. *Women and human development: The capabilities approach.* New York: Cambridge University Press.

Schwartz, Hugh. 1998. *Rationality gone awry? Decision making inconsistent with economic and financial theory.* Westport, CT: Praeger.

Sen, Amartya. 1985. *Commodities and capabilities.* Oxford: Oxford University Press.

Simon, Herbert A. 1978. Rationality as a process and as a product of thought. *American Economic Review* 70: 1–16.

Simon, Herbert A. 1979. Rational decision making in business organizations. *American Economic Review* 69: 493–513.

Simon, Herbert A. 1987. Behavioral economics. In *The new Palgrave: A dictionary of economics*, eds. J. Eatwell, M. Millgate, and P. Newman. London: Macmillan.

Smith, Vernon L. 2005. Behavioral economics research and the foundations of economics. *Journal of Socio-Economics* 34: 135–150.

Thaler, Richard H. 1980. Towards a positive theory of consumer choice. *Journal of Economic Behavior and Organization* 1: 39–60.

Thaler, Richard H., and Cass R. Sustein. 2008. *Nudge: Improving decisions about health, wealth, and happiness.* New York: Penguin Books.

Tomer, John. 2007. What is behavioral economics? *Journal of Socio-Economics* 36: 463–479.

Tversky, Amos, and Daniel Kahneman. 1981. The framing of decisions and the psychology of choice. *Science* 211: 453–458.

Veblen, Thorstein B. 1899. *The theory of the leisure class. An economic study of institutions.* London: Macmillan.

Is the Consumer Sovereign? What Is the Power of Advertising?

COMPETING VIEWS

Jason L. Saving, "Consumer Sovereignty in Modern Times"

Hassan Bougrine and Martti Vihanto, "The Doctrine of Consumer Sovereignty and the Real World"

Editors' Introduction

Consumption of goods and services is an essential element of life. Our very existence depends on the hundreds of different items we use every day. However, while some of us are able to indulge in what could be labelled excessive luxurious consumption, most of the world's people face real deprivation and go through a daily struggle to satisfy even some of the most basic needs. According to the most recent data from the World Bank and the United Nations, millions of people still suffer hunger, illiteracy, and homelessness. Such inequality is also well documented in the so-called developed countries. One obvious explanation for this exclusion is the unequal distribution of income and wealth.

Mainstream economic theories dealing with the behaviour of consumers assume that individuals will always seek to maximize their satisfaction (or utility) by making rational choices—with income being their only constraint. These theories go further and elaborate quite sophisticated models to argue that consumers are in fact in a position to exercise their power by dictating to producers the types of goods and services they would like to purchase and use. Since consumers are free to spend their money on the products that appeal most to them, producers have no choice but to oblige. Hence, the argument goes, all the products we see in the economy must be the direct result of the response to consumers' wishes and dictates. This representation of the status of consumers in society is known as "consumer sovereignty" and is well defended in the essay by Jason Saving. Saving describes how, through free markets and the price mechanism, the composition of demand for the multitude of goods and services is merely an expression of consumers' tastes and preferences.

However, Hassan Bougrine and Martti Vihanto argue that this actually only reflects the competition between sellers of products that are virtually homogeneous and only minimally differentiated by packaging and labels, design and brand names, quality, or price. Since consumers have a wide variety of products from which to choose, suppliers of particular goods and services are compelled to resort to these techniques to create and secure a market share for their products. These techniques have been used successfully to encourage consumers to buy certain products and to influence people's tastes and preferences. Some firms insist on the high quality and craftsmanship of their products, appealing to consumers' desire for safety and durability, while others titillate even the most ephemeral desires consumers may have. Producers of highly substitutable products often find themselves in ferocious competitive wars. The reason is simple: private firms seek profits and to realize profits they must sell their products. To this end, they employ all possible means—and advertising is only one of them.

Bougrine and Vihanto argue further that not all consumers are the same. Those with a lot of money seek to distinguish themselves from the rest of the crowd by using expensive or unique products not available to the rest of the population. Their choices are not necessarily "rational," because they are determined within a social context and under the influence of their cultural capital. Other social classes may feel the pressure to emulate a particular lifestyle, but often find that their decisions are constrained by their relative lack of wealth. Consumers' choices tend to reflect specific positions in the social hierarchy, and as such they are interdependent and cannot be considered the result of an optimizing calculation process.

Consumer Sovereignty in Modern Times

Jason L. Saving*

Introduction

Consumer sovereignty is the idea that consumers exert ultimate control over the economy. Under consumer sovereignty, consumer preferences determine the composition of goods that are produced in the economy. Through their spending decisions, individual consumers control both the allocation of resources and the distribution of goods across the economy (Hildebrand 1951).

Three assumptions underlie the idea of consumer sovereignty. First, consumers are rational in the sense that they attempt to make optimal choices given their preferences (that is, their goals and objectives). Second, consumers are informed in the sense that they have enough knowledge to make optimal choices. Finally, consumers are able to purchase goods in a competitive marketplace. In the words of Arrow, "the consumers are in command, subject only to what they can afford to spend" (Arrow 1963a).

There is also a social welfare dimension to consumer sovereignty. Many proponents of the doctrine have asserted that the performance of an economy should be evaluated by the extent to which it satisfies consumers (Rothenberg 1962). In the words of one political economy writer, "democracy depends on a free market economic system, which in turn is based on consumer sovereignty, which is really 'voting with dollars' for our favorite products and services ... [P]olitical sovereignty is necessarily tied to the people's right to sell or buy whatever they find useful" because consumer sovereignty facilitates democratic participation—and provides an important line of defence against an overweening state (Cobb 1994).

One might expect that such a bedrock principle of both market economics and democratic politics would be uncontested in the social science literature. Instead, a large social science literature suggests that government action is needed to correct a wide variety of instances in which consumers cannot meaningfully exercise their will. Recent trends such as globalization and the New Economy (that is, the increasingly high-tech high-speed service-oriented economy of the future) have heightened these concerns, suggesting to some that consumer sovereignty is

---

* An earlier version of this article appeared in (2006) *Journal of Private Enterprise* 22 (1): 107–120. Reprinted by permission.

no longer viable in the modern age. It is the purpose of this chapter to examine these concerns and their implications.

The Calculation Debate

The first question one must answer is whether consumer sovereignty produces an economic outcome different from what government could itself provide. This question forms a major part of the so-called socialist calculation debate. In the first part of the 20th century, many economists believed that markets were no more efficient than a properly run collectivist system (Barone 1935; Taylor 1929). To the extent that government can correctly anticipate the wants of each consumer and then provide consumers with the goods they would have chosen had firms behaved efficiently and perfectly, government can produce an outcome functionally indistinguishable from what would have occurred if consumers were sovereign (Dobb 1933). All one would need is the means to write down a model of the economy and then solve for the appropriate distribution of goods across the economy.

But could government actually "get the prices right"? Mises and Hayek contended this was a theoretical and empirical impossibility (Mises 1990; Hayek 1935). But a fierce counterattack was launched by Oskar Lange, who argued that government could not only get the prices right but could also get them right in situations where markets would fail. So socialism could actually be superior to consumer sovereignty because it provides better price signals than the marketplace (Lange 1938). One would still be left with enormous technical difficulties due to the size of the optimization problem that government would have to solve, but some economists believe the advent of the computer age has made it "technologically possible" for government planners to make decisions as if they had the right prices for goods and services (Cottrell and Cockshott 1993).

Yet the fact remains that many governments have tried to solve the calculation problem and none have succeeded. Why not? Perhaps the simplest reason is that market prices do not arise in a vacuum—they are formed by market processes and are not knowable in the absence of those processes (Lavoie 1985). Further, much of the information that governs those processes is unobservable and therefore unknowable to any central planner who might seek to use them in his calculations. Certainly the fact that the centrally planned Soviet Union survived decades without advanced computing technology only to collapse as it became available suggests that technology does not play the deciding role here (Boettke 2001). Absent a computer capable not only of making a sufficient number of calculations per second but also of divining what individuals and firms would do at all points in time if free markets were to be established, the market will—even in principle— produce more efficient outcomes than would be possible under central planning.

Ignorance Is Bliss?

Having established that consumer sovereignty is in principle preferable to what one might call "government sovereignty," we turn to practical objections. The first of these objections is that consumers are simply irrational and hence would exercise their sovereignty in a way that is clearly inconsistent with utility-maximizing —that is, rational—behaviour. For example, the editors of the *Journal of Health Economics* recently signed a statement endorsing the settlement between tobacco companies and the US government. Large cigarette-price increases formed a major part of the settlement, and the editors noted that such increases might appear to violate smokers' consumer sovereignty. But because smoking is deemed to be an irrational behaviour, the higher tax would demonstrably improve the lives of American smokers, promoting consumer sovereignty by encouraging smokers to behave the way they surely would if they were capable of thinking in a more "rational" fashion.

This type of argument is not uncommon among social scientists. One noted researcher in this area concluded that "an individual's tastes, preferences, utility functions, goals, transitivity, and self-interests ... can be irrational" (Gamble 1997). To the extent that this is generally the case, he argues, consumer sovereignty becomes "irrelevant" because consumers cannot fulfill their part of the bargain. This may appear to be a compelling argument for government intervention, but if individuals are incapable of rational behaviour, why would one expect that a government composed of such individuals could behave rationally? This is the fundamental problem with which advocates of the irrationality thesis are confronted—and from which there is no obvious escape.

A similar objection is less easily dismissed: that consumers are too ignorant to make informed choices. To the extent consumers lack important information about the goods and services offered by a market economy, they will make the best choices they can with the information they have but will fail to make optimal choices due to their ignorance (Scitovsky 1962). In the limit (that is, taken to extremes), individuals are so woefully uninformed that they would with virtual certainty be better off having their decisions made by a benevolent outside arbiter, such as government. This sentiment was best expressed in Ken Arrow's seminal look at the medical profession, wherein he concluded that medical care transactions should not be governed by the market because patients don't have enough information and expertise to make sound choices (Arrow 1963b).

Two examples, both from the medical field, serve to illustrate this point. A reasonably well-known graduate program in health-care administration informs its students that "unless you know as much about medicine as your doctor, you can't evaluate the quality of the advice he gives you." The statement is demonstrably false—errors made by experts are routinely caught by others with less knowledge and training—yet it is presented as fact without any rebuttal. And a medical columnist takes even more direct aim at consumer sovereignty with his statement that "a quack is a practitioner who tries to please his customers rather than his colleagues" (Fitzpatrick 2001). This statement is not only demonstrably false but also pernicious—as George Washington, for example, discovered when he could not convince his medical team to deviate from the "sound" medical logic behind the leeches that eventually took his life.

Do people sometimes lack full information when making economic decisions? Certainly—but this is not necessarily an argument for government action. The ignorance of which researchers sometimes speak can be rational in the sense that busy individuals weigh the cost of information-gathering against the potential benefit from making the *ex post* utility-maximizing decision. But a considerable body of research has shown that consumers (by and large) behave as if they were fully informed even when only a small number of consumers actually have full information about any particular product (Teske et al. 1993). This echo of Milton Friedman's famous insight about pool players—who play *as though* they know the laws of physics, even though they cannot express them—suggests that ignorance is not enough, in and of itself, to build a persuasive case for government involvement. One can go further and apply the Austrian insight that some information is only available when entrepreneurs generate it in the marketplace (Kirzner 1997). If true, government action could actually generate more "ignorance" than it hopes to ameliorate, throwing its proper role into further question.

Corporate Control and the Need for Government

One of the ironies of the consumer sovereignty debate is that the earliest known use of the phrase was by an economist who—despite his belief that consumer sovereignty is a reasonable guideline by which to live—harboured a profound distrust of consumers' ability to exercise their sovereignty in a responsible way. "Our tastes and desires have after all," he wrote, "been almost wholly imposed upon us by the teachings, the tastes and the standards of those among whom we live" (Hutt 1936, 283). An Australian humanities course echoes this sentiment when it notes that maximizing consumer sovereignty can appear consistent with free-market principles "if you equate, as some do, voluntary transactions with market exchanges."

This theme has been echoed by the 20th century's most widely read critic of the doctrine of consumer sovereignty, John Kenneth Galbraith, who argues that corporations routinely manipulate consumer preferences through advertising (Galbraith 1958). That corporations try to make a case for their products is amply attested in the literature (Packard 1957). Galbraith, however, asserts much more than this. In his view, Americans enjoy such abundance that "a large and talented expenditure on advertising and salesmanship is needed to persuade people to want what is produced. Consumer sovereignty, once governed by the need for food and shelter, is now the highly contrived consumption of an infinite variety of goods and services" (Galbraith 1999). What is needed, he argues, is a return to the halcyon days when mankind sought to fulfill its fundamental needs rather than striving after goods that would not even exist if not for corporations' insatiable desire to invent unnecessary goods and sell them to the populace at large. And government action would be the vehicle through which consumer preferences would be reshaped into the form they "ought" to take.

Galbraith is certainly not the only one to make this argument—others have made the case in areas as diverse as arts and culture (Ridley 1983). Some have even asserted that these "unpreferred preferences," so named because of the belief that corporations have warped consumer preferences in a way that is antithetical to "true" consumer interests, are becoming ever more pervasive as the modern global economy extends the reach of the marketplace beyond what any previous generation has experienced (George 2001). But who is to say which portions of an individual's preference structure should be reshaped due to their "dependence" on corporate influence (Hayek 1961)? Who is to say which goods are valid consumer choices and which are "contrived"? The question is whether a competitive market for advertising skews consumer preferences in any particular direction—or whether it is precisely that competition gives consumers the information they need to make informed choices.

A related argument is that collective action problems necessitate government intervention because no single individual can bring about the result that everyone would like to achieve. Galbraith, for example, argues that corporations plunder natural resources despite strong protestations from the public because they recognize that no single consumer has the ability to stop them (Galbraith 1973). Another economist notes that, once one "recognizes" that the marginal utility of consumption (that is, how much happiness each dollar of additional consumption brings to consumers) quickly approaches zero, it becomes clear that any rational consumer would favour a steeply progressive income tax but have no way to implement such a tax single-handedly (Frank 1999). Both cases have the same premise—that government action can overcome the market failure that is so clear to the particular observers who are suggesting a government solution. Both cases also have the same problem: the fact that they replace the revealed preferences of consumers with what one economist believes those preferences to be.

This has occurred with particular regularity in the environmental realm, where it is suggested that individuals will not feel the proper degree of respect for the environment unless taught to do so by government (Barry 1999). A lively debate has erupted over identifying the precise environmental issues (if any) where government action is warranted and whether that "action" should take the form of new government regulations or the facilitation of private property rights (Anderson and Leal 1991). But some social scientists go further and assert that market economies drive people toward selfish behaviour—and away from the objectively knowable common good that everyone would champion if only they could be made to see the way in which their preferences have been distorted by the marketplace (Jacobs 1991). If this assertion is true, then government action is not only desirable but also imperative so that individual preferences can be transformed from what they now are into what they ought to be—the survival of the species may depend on it.

That individual preferences can be purified through government action carries with it a host of logical problems. How can we know whether the purifiers seek the common good? How can we know whether they have discovered what the common good actually is, or whether they understand the proper way to achieve it? Since ordinary individuals are by assumption unable to perceive the common good until after the proper education is received, we must simply trust that all will become clear once government raises our consciousnesses to a purified state. But if only government can enlighten individuals, by what means did the purifiers themselves become enlightened? They cannot themselves have achieved enlightenment through government action if such action is only now being initiated, after all. So it logically follows that individuals can perceive the common good without government action, undermining the intellectual foundation upon which the purifiers' claims are based.

The Death of Democracy?

A final case against consumer sovereignty is that recent trends such as globalization and the New Economy have undermined the validity of consumer choices. According to this line of argument, individuals generally choose to hear only "louder echoes of their own voices" when permitted to freely choose their sources of information, which they are now better able to do than ever before. This is said to produce a variety of negative effects including "social fragmentation, misunderstanding, and sometimes even enmity." To preserve "true" consumer sovereignty, government must subsidize speech on all sides of each issue, compel information-gathering entities to provide unbiased information about opposing points of view, and encourage self-censorship among journalists who excessively attack particular viewpoints. Only by recognizing that "unrestricted choices by individual consumers" hinder the spirit of free expression can a "well-functioning democracy" characterized by the responsible exercise of consumer sovereignty be maintained (Sunstein 2002).

If Sunstein is correct, then individuals' ability to acquire information more easily than ever before has paradoxically made them less willing than ever before to consider alternative points of view. But there is a great deal of empirical evidence to the contrary, as the worldwide convergence of values over the last few decades can attest. And even if people were less willing than ever before to hear alternative points of view, who in a world of insular consumers could be trusted to enforce ideological "balance"? Sunstein's answer seems to be that he and those like him are capable of so doing, and that for our own good we must be "forced to be free" (Rousseau 1999). And at a minimum, this has yet to be proved, despite Sunstein's sincere conviction that he has identified a deep-seated flaw in consumer behaviour that his desired set of government policies would correct.

The Final Problem

As government gains an ever-greater financial and regulatory role in private transactions and industries, consumers lose part of their influence over winners and losers in the economy. Many see this as desirable for a wide variety of reasons: consumers are irrational, or ignorant, or simply too besotted by corporatism or greed to make the proper decisions. This raises the spectre that consumer sovereignty may find itself replaced with, or at least partially supplanted by, "government sovereignty."

This chapter examines recent critiques of consumer sovereignty and concludes that consumer sovereignty is alive and well in modern times. Consumers are neither irrational nor uninformed, nor have their preferences been forcibly moved from where they "ought to be." Even if this had occurred, there would be no better doctrine for consumer well-being than the free exercise of their preferences—at least until the omniscient and impartial central planner of myth can in fact be found. And contrary to what some believe, current economic forces such as globalization will enhance rather than detract from consumer sovereignty, as consumers are presented with more options—and more opportunities—than ever before.

DISCUSSION QUESTIONS

1. What is consumer sovereignty and why does it matter?
2. Explain the difference between an irrational consumer, an uninformed consumer, and a consumer with "unpreferred preferences."
3. Some people argue that an omniscient central planner could help individuals make better choices than they currently do. If so, does this suggest government should exercise a greater role in individual lives than it currently does? Why or why not?

REFERENCES

Anderson, Terry L., and Donald R. Leal. 1991. *Free market environmentalism.* New York: Palgrave.

Arrow, Kenneth A. 1963a. *Social choice and individual values.* 2nd ed. New York: Wiley.

Arrow, Kenneth A. 1963b. Uncertainty and the welfare economics of medical care. *American Economic Review* 53 (5): 941–973.

Barone, Enrico. 1935. Ministry of production in a collectivist state. In *Collectivist economic planning,* ed. Friedrich A. von Hayek, 245–290. London: Routledge.

Barry, John. 1999. *Rethinking green politics.* London: Sage Publications.

Boettke, Peter. 2001. *Calculation and coordination.* New York: Routledge.

Cobb, Joe. 1994. The real threat to U.S. sovereignty. Heritage Foundation lecture #497 (August 1).

Cottrell, Allin, and W. Paul Cockshott. 1993. Calculation, complexity, and planning: The socialist calculation debate once again. *Review of Political Economy* 5 (1): 73–112.

Dobb, Maurice H. 1933. Economic theory and the problems of a socialist economy. *Economic Journal* 43 (172): 588–598.

Fitzpatrick, Michael. 2001. Policing the medical profession. *Spiked.* Online magazine (November 29).

Frank, Robert H. 1999. *Luxury fever: Why money fails to satisfy in an age of excess.* Princeton, NJ: Princeton University Press.

Galbraith, John K. 1958. *The affluent society.* Boston: Houghton Mifflin.

Galbraith, John K. 1973. Power and the useful economist. *American Economic Review* 63 (1): 1–11.

Galbraith, John K. 1998. Galbraith on the continuing influence of affluence. In *Human development report 1998.* New York: United Nations Development Program.

Gamble, James L. 1997. Validity, rationality definitions, and consumer sovereignty. *Atlantic Economic Journal* 25 (3): 323–324.

George, David. 2001. Unpreferred preferences: Unavoidable or a failure of the market? *Eastern Economic Journal* 27 (4): 181–194.

Hayek, Friedrich. 1935. *Collectivist economic planning.* London: Routledge.

Hayek, Friedrich. 1961. The non sequitur of the dependence effect. *Southern Economic Journal* 27 (4): 346–348.

Hildebrand, George H. 1951. Consumer sovereignty in modern times. *American Economic Review* 41 (2): 19–33.

Hutt, William H. 1936. *Economists and the public: A study of competition and opinion.* London: Jonathan Cape.

Jacobs, Michael. 1991. *The green economy.* London: Pluto Press.

Kirzner, Israel. 1997. Entrepreneurial discovery and the competitive market process. *Journal of Economic Literature* 35 (1): 60–85.

Lange, Oskar. 1938. *On the economic theory of socialism.* Minneapolis: University of Minnesota Press.

Lavoie, Don. 1985. *Rivalry and central planning.* New York: Cambridge University Press.

Mises, Ludwig. 1990. *Economic calculation in the socialist commonwealth.* Auburn: Mises Institute.

Packard, Vance. 1957. *The hidden persuaders.* New York: D. McKay Company.

Ridley, F.F. 1983. Cultural economics and the culture of economics. *Journal of Cultural Economics* 7 (1): 1–18.

Rothenberg, Jerome. 1962. Consumers' sovereignty revisited and the hospitability of freedom of choice. *American Economic Review* 52: 269–283.

Rousseau, Jean-Jacques. 1999. *The social contract.* New York: Oxford University Press.

Scitovsky, Tibor. 1962. On the principle of consumers' sovereignty. *American Economic Review* 52: 262–268.

Sunstein, Cass R. 2002. *Republic.com.* Princeton, NJ: Princeton University Press.

Taylor, Fred M. 1929. The guidance of production in a socialist state. *American Economic Review* 19 (1): 1–8.

Teske, Paul, Mark Schneider, Michael Mintrom, and Samuel Best. 1993. Establishing the micro foundations of a macro theory: Information, movers, and the competitive local market for public goods. *American Political Science Review* 87 (3): 702–713.

The Doctrine of Consumer Sovereignty and the Real World

Hassan Bougrine and Martti Vihanto

Introduction

The standard theory of consumer choice assumes that decisions made by individual consumers are rational and reflect their self-interest. The notion of "rational choice" or "rational behaviour" is a loaded one but often it is simplified to mean that consumers maximize the satisfaction they get from consuming given goods and services and minimize the cost of buying them. Indeed, the principle of maximization states that individuals acquire commodities up to the point at which the marginal (additional) utility of each commodity is equal to its price. Furthermore, rationality of choice is often associated with freedom of choice, so that consumers have the liberty to buy whatever they want—with income being the only constraint.

The underlying idea is that prices are powerful indicators of information regarding quality, availability, and so on. Consequently, changes in prices provide incentives for consumers to look for alternatives. The price system is said to guide consumers into making optimal choices that are then transmitted as orders to the producers of goods and services. In this way, consumers' preferences are reflected in the pattern of production. In fact, it is claimed that consumers' choices determine the structure of the whole economy. This is what some economists refer to as "consumer sovereignty." The aim of this chapter is to shed light on the limitations of the claim of "consumer sovereignty" by proposing alternative explanations of real-world consumers' behaviour.

Consumption Versus Production

Adam Smith (1776, IV.VIII.49), and others before him, argued that "[c]onsumption is the sole end and purpose of all production." In fact, even today many argue that our economic system seems to rely on the "produce to consume" ethic to sustain itself. The dominant culture in modern societies encourages values of work and consumption, that is, we work hard to produce goods and services so that we can satisfy our needs and desires. This seems to be quite a good decision—a rational one. Furthermore, because we want to have enough leisure so that we can enjoy "consuming" what we produce, we think it would be futile to spend time producing items that we do not need. We are disciplined and diligent when making goods and providing services but we also want to be self-indulgent when consuming them. These are conflicting sets of values, and the rational individual solves the problem by choosing the "optimal" allocation of time between work and consumption.

According to standard neoclassical economics, consumers ultimately decide what goods and services they want to consume and therefore dictate to firms what should be produced. Using this logic, whereas consumers have the freedom to choose what they want to consume, firms' choices are constrained because they are not free to produce whatever goods and services they want, for the simple reason that these may not be desired (and not purchased) by consumers. Furthermore, firms' decisions regarding what to produce affect all their suppliers so that, in the end, if consumers do not want a particular good or service, firms will not allocate any resources to its production (for example, firms will not hire any workers for that activity). Consumers seem to occupy a strategic position in this setting since the whole structure of the economy will be determined by the choices they make. In fact, the consumer emerges as a "sovereign." In the words of Ludwig von Mises (1936, 443):

> All production must bend to the consumers' will. From the moment it fails to conform to the consumers' demands it becomes unprofitable. Thus free competition compels the obedience of the producer to the consumers' will and also, in case of need, the transfer of the means of production from the hands of those unwilling or unable to achieve what the consumer demands into the hands of those better able to direct production. The lord of production is the consumer.

The questions that arise are: How do consumers make their decisions? Why do they make certain choices and not others? The underlying argument in neoclassical explanations is that individuals make choices because they consider them to be in their best interest. The pursuit of self-interest is considered to be the driving force in a market economy: producers seek to maximize their profits, workers attempt to get the highest wage for their labour services, and consumers try to maximize their utility with the lowest cost (price). To achieve their objective, private agents are assumed to have access to all relevant information regarding prices and alternative choices. They are also supposed to possess unlimited cognitive capacities for performing the calculus of maximization without interference from their emotions or moods. In this context, even though individuals are guided only by their self-interest, in the end they ensure that society as a whole attains the best possible outcome.

But why would consumers have such power to determine the allocation of resources in the economy? Orthodox economists in general tend to associate consumer sovereignty with democracy and freedom. If consumers are rational agents who are motivated by their self-interest, then they should be given the freedom to choose, that is, the freedom to demand what goods and services they think are best for them. Consumers exercise this freedom through the market, where they spend their money on items of their choice. Producers who bring unwanted products to the market are sent home empty-handed and their goods are "left to rot on the shelf." According to Mises (1936, 443), "[f]rom this point of view the capitalist society is a democracy in which every penny represents a ballot paper. It is a democracy with an imperative and immediately revocable mandate to its deputies."

Since producers (firms) do realize that their incomes (and ultimately the maximization of their profits) depend on what they are able to sell to consumers, they find it in their interest to supply *only* "that which is demanded," both in terms of quantity and quality. And so the structure of production is largely in the hands of consumers. For this reason, and since their activity is constrained to responding to signals given to them by consumers, firms are said to have a subordinate role in the market. In his review of William Hutt's work, Joseph Persky concluded that "Hutt asserted that in a market economy the sphere of freedom and power is that of the consumer, while the sphere of obedience and restriction is that of the producer" (1993, 187).

On the Consumer's Choice

The basic textbook model of consumer choice posits that information (on quality, availability, and so on) is transmitted essentially through market prices. It also states that agents have an effect on each other's choices indirectly via the price mechanism. In such a faceless society, only changes in preferences and prices alter people's decisions. In the process of making their decisions, rational individuals are supposed to gather all useful information, which is assumed to be available and accessible for everyone. In this setting, price plays a key role since it is the mechanism through which the market is brought to equilibrium and any excess (of demand or supply) is eliminated.

However, reality does not tend to conform to this imaginary world of neo-classical economics. For instance, income constitutes a fundamental constraint on consumption. Given the sometimes very large income disparities that characterize capitalist societies, it is understandable that the wealthy will have *l'embarras du choix* (that is, will be spoilt for choice) whereas the poor and low-income classes will realize that their "freedom to choose" has little or no meaning. The reason for their deprivation is obviously their lack of money, which they can acquire only in exchange for work. Freedom to choose, and consumer sovereignty, is contingent on the amount of money one has. And so consumers must work harder to get more money if they want to exercise their "freedom" to buy goods and services. Consumer sovereignty thus requires "wage slavery."

In addition, people also face a great deal of uncertainty, both regarding the availability and the interpretation of information on the price and quality of items they wish to purchase as well as regarding future events. Indeed, Robert Prasch (2010, 27) reminds us that "when we consider the markets for homes, high-tech electronic devices, fancy automobiles, and complex financial instruments, the reality that most buyers are imperfectly informed must be taken seriously." In this case, as Amy Koritz and Douglas Koritz (2001, 51) put it, "[c]onsumers, investors, and traders in all things 'real' or 'financial,' cope with that uncertainty via rules of thumb and other culturally and psychologically determined habits and behaviours." For example, consumers tend to buy certain goods or services simply because most people are buying them, not because they necessarily prefer them to all other goods and services. The need to imitate is justified not only by the fact that people want to be like the Joneses but, more important, because people feel ignorant and think that the others know better, so there is some safety in following the leaders. This situation is usually referred to in the literature as "bounded rationality," in contrast to the rational choice model discussed earlier.

A similar objection to the rational choice model was put forward by Thorstein Veblen (1899), who argued that people's preferences are interdependent. The consumption pattern of high-income classes often reflects their desire to be different and to show that they have a higher social status. They get personal gratification from the display of their wealth, such as owning a big house, driving an expensive car, or wearing the latest fashion. Since no one likes to be identified by others as a "poor" person, even the low-income classes engage in such conspicuous consumption in an attempt to seek a higher status and escape that labelling. Understandably, this type of spending behaviour leads to what many have criticized as a waste of resources. For example, Robert Frank (1985) argues that the race for status, particularly among the rich, can be counterproductive and futile since expenditures by some individuals trigger new and even higher expenditures by others, with their relative positions remaining largely the same as before. To limit such waste, Frank suggests the use of government intervention. For instance, if all education were financed by the government, the rich would not be able to use their money to pay for private education and get special advantages for their children. Frank also suggests the use of a tax on what he calls positional goods (what others have called luxury taxes). In an article in the *New York Times*, Frank (2008) proposes the abolition of income tax and its replacement by a progressive tax on consumption.

Yearning for social status may induce consumers to work more hours or to move to a better-paying job even though it may be less enjoyable and less gratifying. Social relations thus limit consumer sovereignty, both in terms of the composition and the level of consumption. Longer hours at work and less leisure may force consumers to spend the new money on something they used to produce by themselves at home. The goods and services may remain more or less the same but now they are obtained through the market. The commoditization process goes further than this, insofar as purchasing from others instead of producing oneself becomes a social standard, and a growing number of consumers are forced to substitute labour for leisure to keep up with the new way of life. Veblen (1899) argues that this behaviour is not a conscious effort but a result of cultural force.

Pierre Bourdieu's (1979) analysis of more recent consumer behaviour in capitalist societies largely complements Veblen's analysis (for a comparison between Veblen's and Bourdieu's analyses, see Trigg 2001). Indeed, Bourdieu argues that individuals' choices and actions are determined within the context of their cultural capital and under the constraint of their economic capital. People might be, in varying degrees, culturally rich but economically poor and vice versa. This analysis allows Bourdieu to identify various lifestyles, which are intended to reflect people's positions in the social hierarchy. An essential element of Bourdieu's analysis is that culture is deeply seated in people's minds, so that their actions as consumers are based on subconscious motives and do not necessarily imply rational choices that satisfy existing needs.

The rational choice model of neoclassical economics assumes that consumers make their decisions by optimizing. Imitating other people and emulating their lifestyles, as discussed above, indicates, however, that there are bounds on rationality, making optimization evidently unattainable. Experimental research suggests that human beings act in a heuristic manner and often seem to follow social conventions and habits, meaning that they tend to repeat modes of behaviour that have worked in similar cases. Heuristics can be thought of as a combination of idiosyncratic human properties, learning, and experience (something close to the cultural capital in Bourdieu's analysis). A well-known example of heuristic behaviour is what Amos Tversky and Daniel Kahneman (1974) call the anchoring effect: a consumer buys the same product at the same store for a long time simply because, through luck or advertising, she or he has purchased that item at that store some time in the past. This is clearly an arbitrary (or accidental) decision but over time the consumption of such a good or service becomes a reference point. It constitutes what some firms would call customer loyalty but which others see as a barrier to entry.

Established firms tend to reinforce these anchoring habits and exploit them to increase their profits (Hanson and Kysar 1999). Competitors can break a habit and attract potential customers (or help their own customers get rid of outdated purchasing habits) by selling a new product at a discount price to alert buyers and attract them to new alternatives. If successful, competitive efforts may give rise to new anchors and compel other firms to offer something even more alluring.

The anchoring effect is observed in people's choices of particular products, brands, or firms, but it can also mould consumers' entire lifestyle. When one group begins to spend money on the consumption of certain items and others begin to emulate that behaviour, the desire to consume, as such, may be transmitted among groups. Once a glorified lifestyle of shopping has been learned, a consumer may honestly think of it as something that he or she has always wanted. According to Edward Comor (2008), the institution of capitalist consumption shapes people's consciousness and manipulates them into believing that it works toward their best interests. The dominant ideology leads consumers to adopt the new lifestyle and makes them think that it is part of their personal development and therefore impossible to reject.

Advertising and Habit Formation

Psychologists and social scientists have noted that consumers tend to be easily persuaded by producers through advertising and direct marketing. For instance, a car salesman presents the most expensive model to customers first and then proceeds to cheaper models, rather than the other way around. Since the reference price is higher in the former case, the rest of the cars appear psychologically more affordable than they actually are. Another trick of the same sort is to put prices that no one is supposed to pay on the stickers and then give the true selling price, which is the discount off the amount on the sticker. These practices are widely used all over the world and it is well known that they actually work. That is because human behaviour is influenced by non-rational considerations (bounded rationality).

There is general agreement that consumption habits are shaped in a social setting. Recent studies of consumer behaviour have come to the conclusion that consumers' tastes and preferences are largely in the hands of marketers who, through very sophisticated techniques, are able to sell you anything from addictive high-fat/sugar/sodium foods to drugs, tobacco, alcohol, and violence. Comor (2008, 25), for instance, maintains that "consumption ... has become an important nodal point in the quest for meaning and identity," adding that "in the contemporary world, advertisers and marketers are key agents shaping these pursuits and their interests or, more generally, the interests of their clients (mostly corporations) are squarely aligned with the promotion of evermore consumption."

According to Juliet Schor (2004, 20), manufacturers and advertisers are effectively engaged in a war by which they try to shape people's tastes and convince them to buy specific products. The "targets" in this war are no longer just the adults earning the money, but, increasingly, children. Advertisers have long understood that habit formation starts at a very young age. Schor (2004, 19) has summarized this scenario in a disturbing passage, which deserves to be quoted:

> The typical American child is now immersed in the consumer marketplace to a degree that dwarfs all historical experience. At age one, she's watching *Teletubbies* and eating the food of its "promo partners" Burger King and McDonald's. Kids can recognize logos by eighteen months, and before reaching their second birthday, they are asking for products by brand name. By three or three and a half, experts say, children start to believe that brands communicate their personal qualities, for example, that they're cool, or strong, or smart … . Upon arrival at the schoolhouse steps, the typical first grader can evoke 200 brands. And he or she has already accumulated an unprecedented number of possessions, beginning with an average of seventy new toys a year. By age six and seven, girls are asking for the latest fashion … . Eight-year-old boys are enjoying Budweiser [beer] commercials (the consistent favourite ad for this age group), World Wrestling Entertainment, and graphically violent video games.

To make their strategies more effective, marketers resort to the most intrusive methods, including the exploitation of feelings of anxiety and low self-esteem, deceptive advertising, trickery, and the manipulation of both consumers and politicians (such as lobbying against regulation). The aim is to create a category of consumers who are, increasingly, shopaholics and who get a kick out of acquiring yet another commodity for which they have no obvious need. This type of consumer behaviour was criticized by John Kenneth Galbraith in his book *The Affluent Society* (1958). If Hutt (1936) thought that the producer was a servant to society, mounting evidence shows that corporations have the power to manipulate demand by transforming children and non-consumerist ordinary people who care about the lifespan of the goods in their possession, into ever more wasteful consumers who grow up attached more to brand names than to their fellow human beings (Dawson 2003). Indeed, Schor (2004, 13) thinks that "we have become a nation that places a lower priority on teaching children how to thrive socially, intellectually, even spiritually, than it does on training them to consume. The long-term consequences of this development are ominous."

Policy Implications

One implication of the doctrine of "consumer sovereignty" is that consumers' free choices should be respected and will therefore be reflected in the pattern of production. It follows then that if people want to consume dangerous drugs, if they demand firearms or even weapons of mass destruction, if they want to sell their kidneys or their bodies for sex to feed themselves or their families, then governments have no business regulating or suppressing these choices. However, no matter how liberal we might be as a society, we think these harmful choices must not be allowed. That is why we call on governments and legislators to set up rules and regulations against what we consider abusive or irrational behaviour.

Government intervention is not only warranted in extreme cases, like those mentioned above. It is necessary in practically all aspects of our daily dealings with each other. We want laws to protect consumers against fraudulent behaviour and false advertising. We want producers to honour the warranty that their products will work as advertised. We want protection against monopoly. We even want protection against uncertainty: we want to receive health care when we need it, and to have housing and food when unexpected events occur, such as when we lose our jobs. This is why we set up "the welfare state" and ask the government to pay employment insurance benefits and to provide services to the general public, such as education, health care, and so on.

From a larger perspective, the objective of economic policy is to ensure the satisfaction of consumers' needs. The efficiency of any economic system should be judged by its success or failure in achieving this objective. The underlying implication is that resources are allocated to their various uses according to economic policies set by policy-makers, not according to the wishes and whims of "sovereign" consumers. This raises the question of whether such allocation would be "inferior" compared with what would prevail in a state of perfect competition (or a free-market economy). Several economists (see, for example, Lerner 1946) have made the point that the conditions and the outcome of "perfect competition" are ideals that can best be approximated by a system of central planning, where perfect information, mobility, and so on would be the norm, thereby guaranteeing that the allocation of resources would be more in accordance with consumers' preferences.

Conclusion

The free-market economy is a social system in which the function of the government is supposed to be limited to protecting private property rights and to enforcing, when necessary, contracts voluntarily agreed upon by agents. The argument for adopting such a legal system as the foundation for social order is the doctrine of "consumer sovereignty." When consumers, who are assumed to be the experts at their subjective preferences, make free choices in the market, they provide incentives for firms to produce what consumers want. Producers reallocate resources (or factors of production) in accordance with changes in demand, and the structure of production complies to maximize consumer utility. When all this takes place in a state of perfect competition, the allocation of resources is said to be optimal. The real world, however, is characterized by all sorts of imperfections regarding the knowledge, cognition, mobility, and power of consumers to affect the market and prices. These imperfections are all indications of market failures and lack of consumer sovereignty. It is the government's responsibility to detect shortcomings in the market, remedy them through legislation, and help consumers to choose in line with their best interests.

DISCUSSION QUESTIONS

1. Do consumers have the power to impose on firms what to produce and therefore to decide the whole structure of the economy?
2. What is conspicuous consumption? Is it the same thing as Bourdieu's notion of "distinction"?
3. Does advertising provide relevant information or is it manipulation?
4. Should the government regulate the relationship between consumers and producers or should it be left to the free market?

ONLINE RESOURCES

The Association for Evolutionary Economics: http://www.afee.net.

The Association for Institutional Thought: http://www.orgs.bucknell.edu/afee/afit/.

The Progressive Economics Forum: http://www.progressive-economics.ca.

REFERENCES

Bourdieu, P. 1979, 1984. *Distinction: A social critique of the judgement of taste,* trans. Richard Nice. London: Routledge.

Comor, E.A. 2008. *Consumption and the globalization project: International hegemony and the annihilation of time.* New York: Palgrave Macmillan.

Dawson, M. 2003. *The consumer trap: Big business marketing in American life.* Champaign: University of Illinois Press.

Frank, R. 1985. *Choosing the right pond: Human behavior and the quest for status.* New York: Oxford University Press.

Frank, R. 2008. Just what this downturn demands: A consumption tax. *The New York Times,* November 9, 2008. http://www.robert-h-frank.com/PDFs/EV.11.09.08.pdf.

Galbraith, John Kenneth. 1958. *The affluent society.* London: Hamish Hamilton.

Hanson, J.D., and D.A. Kysar. 1999. Taking behavioralism seriously: Some evidence of market manipulation. *Harvard Law Review* 112 (7): 1420–1572.

Hutt, W. 1936, 1990. *Economists and the public: A study of competition and opinion.* London: Jonathan Cape.

Koritz, A., and D. Koritz. 2001. Checkmating the consumer: Passive consumption and the economic devaluation of culture. *Feminist Economics* 7 (1): 45–62.

Lerner, A.P. 1946. *The economics of control.* New York: Macmillan.

Mises, L. von. 1936. *Socialism: An economic and sociological analysis.* London: Jonathan Cape.

Persky, J. 1993. Consumer sovereignty. *Journal of Economic Perspectives* 7 (1): 183–191.

Prasch, R. 2010. Markets, states, and exchange: An introduction to economics. In *Introducing macroeconomic analysis: Issues, questions, and competing views,* eds. Hassan Bougrine and Mario Seccareccia, 22–32. Toronto: Emond Montgomery.

Schor, J. B. 2004. *Born to buy.* New York: Scribner.

Smith, A. 1776, 1976. *An inquiry into the nature and causes of the wealth of nations.* Oxford: Oxford University Press.

Trigg, Andrew B. 2001. Veblen, Bourdieu, and conspicuous consumption. *Journal of Economic Issues* 35 (1): 99–115.

Tversky, A., and D. Kahneman. 1974. Judgment under uncertainty: Heuristics and biases. *Science* 85 (4157): 1124–1131.

Veblen, Thorstein. 1899. *The theory of the leisure class: An economic study of institutions.* New York: Mentor Books.

How Do Firms Price Their Products?

Editors' Introduction

It has been said that an economist is someone who knows the price of everything and the value of nothing. Nowadays, the economist might be pardoned if he or she did *not* know the price of everything. We are faced with a weekly flood of new products, many of whose want-satisfying characteristics are unknown when they first arrive on the market, and whose initial prices may be heavily reduced to encourage consumers to try them. In addition to these new products, many existing products are made available in "improved" form. It may not always be clear whether the improvements are genuine changes that most consumers would consider improvements, or just advertising hype to expand the products' market share, or a ploy to raise the price of an essentially unchanged commodity.

The theory of product-price determination by firms has placed weight on two factors: the product's use-value or utility, which underlies the *demand* for the product, and the product's cost of production, which underlies its *supply*. But real-world price determination poses major challenges for economic theorists of both orthodox and heterodox camps. Why are prices of fashion clothing five or ten times their unit production cost ... until someone determines that it's "the end of the season," and the next day they are on sale at an 80 percent discount? If there is joint production, so that two or more commodities are produced by a single process, how are the costs of production to be allocated to each commodity, and how are their prices determined? What is the proper price for a genuine Gucci handbag, and for a "knock-off" imitation that is indistinguishable from the original? What is the real price of a "free" email account, who pays the price, and in what units is the price measured?

Thomas Barbiero provides a valuable survey of the orthodox neoclassical theory of how firms set prices. Within this framework, profit maximization by a firm requires it to set the additional *cost* of producing the last unit of output equal to the additional *revenue* obtained by selling it. He then shows that to achieve this objective, a firm's actual pricing policy depends critically on the type of *market* in which the firm operates: perfect competition, monopolistic competition, oligopoly, or monopoly. Finally, Barbiero notes a number of contemporary real-world factors that complicate the stories that emerge from these basic models, including firm objectives other than profit maximization; "principal–agent" problems when the firm's owners and managers are not the same people; the problem of defining market structure in economies that are open to international trade; and the rise of new media, such as the Internet, which have increased the volatility of price movements.

In his essay, Peter Kriesler draws on a different, heterodox tradition. Kriesler argues that the familiar U-shaped average total cost curve of orthodox theory does not correspond to the actual cost curves of most firms, for which the cost of producing an additional unit is almost constant over a wide range of output levels. He argues further that the most important market structures today are oligopolistic and characterized by uncertainty, imperfect capital markets, and interdependence between firms. Firms typically use a markup pricing policy, with price being set higher than normal unit cost by a certain percentage (the markup), and the level of the markup itself is determined by a number of factors, including the firm's competitive environment and its strategic objectives. Kriesler also provides a concise guide to some of the theoretical differences within the heterodox tradition.

Firm Pricing Policy and Market Structure

Thomas Barbiero

Introduction

One of the central questions any firm is confronted with is what price to charge for its products and services. The firm's main goal is to maximize its profit, and determining what it can charge for its products is crucial to achieving that goal.

Suppose you and a friend start a firm that produces widgets, fasteners that are used in a variety of industrial uses. Once you have the premises and the required machinery and staff, you are ready to market your product. How much will you charge for the widgets produced by your firm? Of course, you would like to be able to charge a price that will result in the highest possible profit. But how will you decide exactly how much to charge? Will you choose a price your competitors are charging? Will you charge a price that covers all your costs plus a certain percentage? Will you do it by trial and error? You will find that the price you can charge will be dictated by the general demand and supply conditions for widgets, and the market structure that characterizes the business environment your firm is operating in. The more competitors there are in the widget industry, and the more homogeneous the widgets produced, the less discretion you will have in choosing the price you charge. Conversely, the fewer the number of firms in the widget industry and the more distinctive the outputs of each firm, the more leeway you will have in setting the price.

Critics of standard economic theory argue that pricing is more complex than it first appears. For example, in some instances, firms maximize goals other than profit. International trade and costly information further complicate firms' pricing decisions.

Firm Profits and Prices

Independent of the price you will charge your clients for the widget your firm produces, you have to bear in mind the marginal cost–marginal revenue rule. This rule is essential to maximizing profit, regardless of the structure of the market in which your firm operates. The types of market structure include the two extremes of perfect competition and monopoly, and the intermediate market structures of monopolistic competition and oligopoly. Whichever market structure your firm is in, you want to make sure that it earns the maximum profit possible. To do so, it is essential that your firm's marginal cost for the last widget it produced equal the marginal revenue from its sale. When you compute your firm's costs you will want to make sure that they include both explicit and implicit costs, the latter including a normal profit. Total cost is composed of fixed and variable costs. In economics, costs always reflect alternative uses for the resources used, including entrepreneurial talent.

Firms can follow a simple strategy of "markup pricing" to arrive at their selling price. The markup could be a set amount or a percentage above the cost of production, and would represent the firm's profit margin. We will see below that usually the process of arriving at a price can be a more complex affair than simply adding a set amount to the cost of production.

In a market economy, the level of profit or loss in an industry is a signal for firms to enter or exit an industry, and thus directly influences supply conditions. In the long run, economic profits attract firms to an industry, thus increasing supply; losses lead to firms exiting an industry, thus reducing supply. The extent to which these market forces are present in any industry depends on the cost of entering and exiting the industry. Assuming a fixed demand curve, an increase in supply of any product tends to reduce its price; a fall in supply tends to increase its price. The dynamics of firms entering and exiting an industry, along with the market demand curve, affects what your widget firm can charge for its product. But the nature and the dynamics of the supply curve will depend on the market structure. Let's look more closely at the effects of each of the four market structures.

Pricing in Perfect Competition

Suppose the widgets your firm produces are indistinguishable from the widgets produced by the hundreds of other firms in the industry. In other words, the widget your firm is producing is a homogeneous product. Entry into the industry is costless, as is the exit out of the industry. An industry that has hundreds of firms producing a homogeneous product is called a perfectly competitive industry.

In a perfectly competitive industry, the firm does not worry much about what price it will charge for its products. The price is given by the market. The market supply curve is the summation of all the individual firms' short-run supply curves. The individual firm's short-run supply curve is its marginal cost curve (above the average variable cost). A change to market equilibrium generally comes from the demand side. For example, suppose that demand for your firm's widgets rises, leading to a price increase. If the increase in price leads to firms in the industry making above-normal profits, in the long run more firms will enter the widget industry, thus increasing the supply of widgets and putting downward pressure on the price of widgets. Once a price has been reached that brings profit back to a normal level, that is, a profit level that covers all explicit and implicit costs, we are back to equilibrium price for both the firm and the industry.

As you can see, demand and supply conditions dictate the price you can charge. The term "dictate" is not too strong a term when it comes to what price your firm can charge in a perfectly competitive market structure. If your firm attempts to charge a price higher than the market price, consumers will buy from other firms and your firm will sustain losses that will lead to it going out of business in the long run. Likewise, if your firm charges a price lower than the market price charged by your competitors, you will sustain losses, with the same result.

Some students have trouble with the notion of perfect competition, arguing that there are few, if any, industries that are perfectly competitive. If so, why study it? Although this line of argument is understandable, it misses an important point. The extent of competition in any given industry lies on a continuum, from perfect competition to monopoly. It would be impossible to study each shade of competition, so we take representative industry structures along the continuum. In a standard microeconomics course we focus on the four market structures: perfect competition, monopoly, monopolistic competition, and oligopoly. The important idea to take away from the perfectly competitive market model is that the closer a market structure is to such a model the more impersonal market forces will dictate the price a firm can charge.

The market price in perfect competition also has important efficiency consequences. It should be emphasized that in perfect competition, the market price dictated by the forces of supply and demand is equal to the firms' marginal cost, which results in allocative efficiency. Allocative efficiency is attained when those products most wanted by society are produced. In perfect competition, the market price also ensures that each firm achieves productive efficiency, since in the long run the market price will also equal the minimum point on each firm's average total cost curve. Productive efficiency means the firm is producing its output at the least possible cost.

It is also worth noting that the equilibrium market price in perfect competition ensures that consumer surplus and producer surplus are maximized. Consumer surplus is the difference between the market price and what the consumer is willing to pay for a particular product. Producer surplus is the difference between the market price and the price at which a firm is willing to offer its output. In no other market structure except perfect competition are consumer surplus and producer surplus maximized, or allocative and productive efficiency attained. But while competitive markets are efficient, outcomes may not be socially equitable. Equity of markets is a question that is addressed in Part IV of this book.

Pricing Strategy for a Monopolist

Suppose your firm came up with a unique widget for which there is no close substitute. You patent your new widget, so possible competitors are barred from copying it, at least legally. Given that you have a monopoly for the duration of your patent, what price should you charge? The natural inclination might be to charge the highest possible price. But such an inclination ignores the downward sloping demand curve. We know that there is an inverse relationship between price and quantity demanded; at very high prices you would not sell very many of your firm's unique widgets. Remember that you want to price your unique widget at a price that maximizes your firm's overall profit, not unit profit. So, even if you have a monopoly over your unique widget, your firm still needs to follow pricing guidelines to maximize profit. You will want to make sure that the price you charge will ensure that marginal cost equals marginal revenue. To do so, you will need to adjust the output level of your firm to ensure that you will be able to achieve that unique price.

Unlike firms in a perfectly competitive market structure, a monopolist does have a degree of discretion as to what price to charge. That discretion comes from its ability to choose the firm's output level. By increasing output, the monopolist will lower price, and vice versa. But a monopolist is not immune from changes in consumer demand. A rise in the demand for its product will make it possible for the monopolist to increase its price and thus its profits, but a large fall in the demand for its product can potentially lead to losses if the fall in demand is of a magnitude that results in a price that is lower than its average total cost.

As a monopolist, you are not very happy that the demand curve is downward sloping: if you lower the price of your unique widget, you will have to lower the price on all the widgets you sell. If it could, your firm would segment the widget market so that it can charge different prices to customers according to their willingness to pay. Such "price discrimination" is difficult to carry out, because it is practically impossible to segment clients and markets, especially where price information is easy to get. In the Internet age, price information can often be had at the click of a mouse.

At first glance, you would expect that if your widget firm were a monopolist you would not have to worry about potential competitors, since there must be barriers to entry into industry. Such expectation may be misplaced. The theory of "contestable markets" suggests that even as a monopolist you may need to behave in a manner that assumes that there are always potential entrants looming, trying to appropriate some of your economic profits. Those that make this argument sometimes cite the case of the Reynolds International Pen Company, which, in 1945, was the only seller of ballpoint pens in the United States. It was selling the pens at retail prices of $12 to $20 each, even though the marginal cost was around

80 cents per pen to produce. By 1948 there were dozens of competitors, the price of a pen had fallen to 39 cents, and the market share of Reynolds International Pen Company had fallen to zero (Srinivasan 1991).

Of course, Reynolds could have chosen to pursue a "limit price" policy and set a price lower than the monopoly price to discourage potential entrants. A limit-price strategy would, in effect, be erecting barriers to entry for potential entrants in the hope of either stopping competing firms from entering or at the very least slowing down the rate of entry. In some cases, a large dominant player in an industry may practise "predatory pricing"—selling widgets at *below* cost for a period—to drive its competitors out of business, creating a de facto monopoly, or at least fewer competitors in the industry. Significantly pushing prices down in an industry leads to losses for its competitors, which then leave the industry. A strategy of predatory pricing assumes that the dominant firm has enough resources to sustain losses for a period of time long enough to drive its competitors out of business.

Pricing Output in Monopolistic Competition

A more likely scenario than perfect competition and monopoly is that your widget firm has competitors, but that each makes a slightly different widget with different qualities, in different locations, and with different levels of services. No one firm dominates the widget industry. We refer to an industry structure with many firms, but producing genuinely (or seemingly) differentiated products, as *monopolistic competition*. The term "monopolistic" refers to the unique aspect of each firm's product. To continue with the widget example, perhaps your firm makes particularly coloured widgets, or widgets made from a particular alloy, or in unique shapes. The term "competition" refers to the many relatively small firms that populate the industry. Entry and exit into the industry is relatively easy, but not as easy as in perfect competition.

So, what pricing strategy would a firm in a monopolistically competitive market structure likely pursue? Surprisingly, the pricing strategy would be the same as that followed by a monopolist: produce a quantity resulting in a price that would ensure that marginal cost and marginal revenue are equal. Remember that the firm in monopolistic competition, like all firms in market structures that are imperfectly competitive, faces a downward sloping demand curve and a marginal revenue curve that lies below the demand curve. The firm can choose the output it wants, but the price that it can charge will be given by the demand curve. Ultimately, the firm will maximize its profit by charging a price at which marginal cost equals marginal revenue.

Unlike perfect competition and monopoly, a monopolistically competitive market structure leads to some ambiguous results. We know that in perfect competition the price charged by each firm will be equal to marginal cost and that the price equals the minimum point on the average total cost curve, at least in the long run. In the case of a monopoly, we know that the profit-maximizing firm will charge a price at which marginal cost equals marginal revenue, but since the marginal revenue curve is below the demand curve, that price is higher than in perfect competition and above the minimum point of the average total cost curve. In the case of firms in monopolistic competition, a number of outcomes are possible.

The fact that there are many firms in a monopolistically competitive market structure should ensure that, in the long run, firms charge a price that results in only normal profit. Normal profit for each firm, in the long run, is the result of firms entering and exiting the industry due to profit and loss signals. However, the degree of product differentiation may allow some firms to charge a price that will ensure earning economic profits for long periods of time. For example, some firms may have a location advantage, allowing them to charge higher prices than their competitors, even for goods that are close substitutes. Moreover, in such a situation the price will be higher than the minimum point on the average total cost curve. The fact of the matter is that firms in monopolistic competition usually have excess capacity and are thus unable to charge a price low enough to achieve productive efficiency. However, there is an upside to this relative inefficiency: product variety.

Pricing Strategy in Oligopoly

An oligopoly is a market structure with only a few dominant firms. These firms may produce either homogeneous or differentiated products. An oligopoly can consist of as few as two firms, in which case it is referred to as a duopoly. The outstanding feature of an oligopolistic market structure is firm interdependence. If your firm were one of the few dominant widget firms in the industry, you would need to keep a close eye on your competitors, since your decision on the price for your widget would depend on what your competitors are charging. This is the only market structure in which interdependence among firms dominates. An oligopolist uses two alternative pricing strategies: tacitly colluding with rivals and charging what amounts to a monopoly price, or battling head-on with competing firms in the hope of increasing profits as you take customers away from them. The latter strategy could lead to a price war that would inevitably translate into much lower profits—or even losses—for the firms in the industry.

If both you and your rivals tacitly agree on a collusive pricing approach, a number of strategies are possible. If there are a few firms in the industry and they are able to collude successfully, the pricing strategy would be similar to that of a monopolist. However, the success of the collusive effort would depend on the number of firms in the industry: the more firms in the oligopoly, the more difficult it would be to collude. The difficulty would be especially daunting if each of the firms in the industry faces different costs or, in the event of a deep recession, the survival instinct of each firm tempts some of them to cheat and increase output and lower their price.

A coordinating mechanism that can help oligopolists pursue their collusive pricing objective is the so-called leadership strategy. The largest firm in the oligopoly would communicate price changes through trade publications or speeches of major executives. Other firms in the industry would soon follow suit.

To keep out potential competitors, the price leader in the group may opt for a price that is below the short-term profit-maximizing level. Earlier, we discussed this limit-price strategy, which aims to discourage potential entrants. Oligopolists can also engage in predatory pricing to keep out or drive out competitors. It should be emphasized, however, that attempts to curtail competition by predatory pricing contravene competition policy law in virtually every country.

Since head-on price competition can be so deleterious to firm profits, oligopolists prefer non-price competition, which includes advertising and product development, to differentiate their products.

Firm Pricing in an Open Economy

All that has been said so far about firm pricing under the four main types of market structure changes somewhat when we consider an open economy, such as Canada's. We expect that, in general, competitive pressure will intensify for most firms that face import competition and that the domestic market structure may not be the dominant factor in pricing decisions. A case in point is provided by the North American automobile sector from the Second World War up until the 1980s. For the previous 30 years, we had an almost classic oligopoly market structure in North America, dominated by the "Big Three": General Motors, Ford, and Chrysler. However, by the early 1980s the Japanese (Toyota, Honda, Nissan) and German (Volkswagen) automakers had a significant percentage of the North American car market, so that market could no longer be considered a classic oligopoly. Indeed, intense competitive pressure in the automobile sector in the last decade resulted in the bankruptcy of General Motors and the disappearance of Chrysler as an independent firm.

The fall in transportation costs and tariffs has led to a steady increase in international trade, which has put competitive pressure on almost all sectors of national economies. Entire sectors have disappeared altogether in some countries, as these lost their comparative advantage. For example, the primary textile industry in the Eastern Townships of Quebec practically disappeared as production moved offshore, primarily to the Pacific Rim countries. International trade clearly complicates a firm's pricing strategy, since it has to consider both domestic and import competition.

Criticism of the Neoclassical Approach

The foregoing discussion assumes that firms always maximize profit. In the next chapter you will get another perspective on this topic. If firms do not, in fact, aim at maximizing profit, but have other goals, such as maximizing growth, then firm pricing strategies would likewise have other aims. In addition, we often treat firms as if they were run by homogeneous individuals with exactly the same goals. The larger the firms, the more likely it is that they will be run by heterogeneous agents with their own particular agendas, and that we will encounter the "principal–agent problem." Those running the firms can have interests distinct from and often counter to those of the firm's owners. For a public company, that can include thousands of stock owners. Executives and administrators of large corporations may engage in internal power struggles that lead to pricing strategies much different from those predicted by standard theory.

Critics of the mainstream view also point out that information is costly or impossible to attain, making pricing decisions and outcomes difficult to predict. For example, profits and losses are signals for firms to enter and exit an industry. But many firms, particularly smaller, privately held firms, do not disclose profit and loss data, greatly weakening profits and losses as signals to enter and exit industries, and making pricing more complex than the standard theory implies. We also noted that in imperfectly competitive markets, extensive product differentiation can complicate pricing decisions. Finally, mainstream theory is essentially a static analysis. Firms have ongoing research and development programs as well as active advertising campaigns, meaning that market structures and the extent of product differentiation are in constant flux. If we also add international trade to this dynamic situation, we can see that pricing decisions for firms become more challenging than suggested by standard theory. The growth in Internet use has added yet another layer of complication to pricing decisions. In the Internet age, firms may have to change prices practically hourly to respond to moves by competitors. A case in point is pricing in the airline industry: you can now book flights directly on the Web and prices change even within an hour!

Conclusions

A firm's pricing strategy is determined by the market structure in which it operates. In the mainstream view, firms attempt to maximize profit and their pricing strategy is designed to achieve that goal. Generally, the more competition the firm faces and the more homogeneous the product it produces, the less discretion it has in setting the price for its output: the forces of supply and demand set the market price. But even in imperfectly competitive market structures, potential competition will put pressure on firms to adopt pricing strategies that reflect market forces. We noted that costly information, international trade, and the Internet can make pricing decisions by firms more complex than suggested by the four market structure models we analyzed.

DISCUSSION QUESTIONS

1. What is the connection between market structure and the manner in which firms price their products?
2. Will a monopolist charge the highest possible price for its output? Explain.
3. Besides marginal cost pricing, what are some other ways a firm can price its products?
4. How does the theory of contestable markets relate to how firms price their products?
5. How does international trade complicate a firm's task of pricing its products?
6. What are the main criticisms of the mainstream view of the way firms price their products?

SUGGESTED READINGS AND ONLINE RESOURCES

Baumol, W.J. 1982. Contestable markets: An uprising in the theory of industry structure. *American Economic Review* 71 (1): 1–19.

Chamberlin, E.H. 1950. *The theory of monopolistic competition.* Cambridge, MA: Harvard University Press.

Coase, R.H. 1937. The nature of the firm. *Economica* 16 (4): 386–405.

Katzner, D.W. 2001. The significance, success, and failure of microeconomic theory. *Journal of Post-Keynesian Economics* 24 (1): 41–58

Lavoie, M. 2007. *An introduction to post-Keynesian economics.* London: Routledge.

Lee, F.S., and S. Keen. 2004. The incoherent emperor: A heterodox critique of neoclassical microeconomic theory. *Review of Social Economy* 62 (2): 169–199.

McGee, J.S. 1958. Predatory price cutting: The Standard Oil case. *Journal of Law and Economics* 1 (October): 137–169.

Tirole, Jean. 1988. *The theory of industrial organization.* Cambridge: MIT Press.

A good resource site for economists is http://rfe.org. For heterodox views, see http://www.economicsnetwork.ac.uk/heterodox.

REFERENCES

Lavoie, M. 1996. Mark-up pricing versus normal cost pricing in post-Keynesian models. *Review of Political Economy* 8 (1): 57–66.

McConnell, C., S. Brue, S. Flynn, and T. Barbiero. 2010. *Microeconomics*. 12th ed. Toronto: McGraw-Hill Ryerson.

Srinivasan, Kannan. 1991. Multiple market entry, cost signalling and entry deterrence. *Management Science* 37 (12): 1539–1555.

Firm Pricing, Markups, and Accumulation

Peter Kriesler

Introduction

Up until the 1870s, economists (or political economists as they were called then) were not particularly concerned with understanding how market prices were determined. Rather, the central focus of economic thought was on analyzing the forces that determined the growth of "the wealth of nations," and with the distribution of that wealth. To help analyze this, they developed the concept of "natural values," which were fundamental underlying values to which market prices would gravitate. Natural values were centres of gravity—attractors—for market prices, for which, according to the classical political economists, there was no systematic analysis. These "natural values" were the outcome of long-run systematic forces and were important in influencing the long-run development of economies.

This all changed with the so-called marginal revolution in the 1870s, when determining market price became the central concern of economics. For orthodox economists the determination of prices and outputs by supply and demand is the central question and framework for all economics.

The central problem became how to demonstrate that the market-clearing price, determined by the forces of supply and demand in a perfectly competitive market, yielded a *Pareto optimum* (at that price, nobody could be made better off without making someone else worse off). Underlying the demand curve were the decisions of utility-maximizing consumers facing budget constraints. Their optimizing strategy was to equate marginal utility with price. The supply curve, on the other hand, was derived from the actions of profit-maximizing firms, facing a constraint given by the current state of technology. Their profit-maximizing strategy was to keep producing until marginal cost = price.

From these conclusions, it is then possible to show that in a perfectly competitive market, with some further restrictions, equilibrium implied marginal cost = marginal revenue = price, which was further shown to be a Pareto-optimal outcome. Profit maximization means that firms produce an output level (Q) that maximizes the difference between current total revenue (TR) and total costs (TC), which (given certain standard assumptions) is where marginal revenue ($MR = \Delta TR/\Delta Q$) equals marginal cost ($MC = \Delta TC/\Delta Q$). Here the symbol Δ represents a quantitative change in the associated variable.

Since, in perfect competition, all firms are price-takers, this means that at the long-run profit-maximizing equilibrium, price (P) = MC = MR. This equilibrium price means that firms will produce at the lowest point on their long-run average cost curve, which can be shown to be Pareto-efficient. However, although the results are very elegant, the strong assumptions (including those necessary to generate perfect competition, as well as there being no externalities) required to generate them mean that this model has little relevance to actual behaviour.

In the 1930s, serious criticisms of the neoclassical model started to emerge at many levels. An important survey of businessmen, by the Oxford Economists Research Group, published in Hall and Hitch (1939), asking them on what basis they actually made their decisions, provided an alternative model of pricing behaviour, in which prices did not necessarily clear markets and demand played only a secondary role in how prices were determined. According to Hall and Hitch, firms determine prices mainly on the basis of either cost factors or their relations with other firms, with demand influencing the quantities transacted. Prices were determined on the basis of a markup on costs.

This is the essence of the heterodox literature on price determination, which stresses the uncertain economic environment in which firms operate and the importance of *im*perfect competition, which leads to strong interdependence of firms.

This chapter will look at the critiques of the neoclassical analysis of the determination of prices and output, before considering the heterodox alternatives.

Criticism of Neoclassical Theories of Market Structure and Pricing

Contemporary economists critical of the mainstream, often called political economists because they have returned to the interests of the original political economists, argue that neoclassical pricing theories, which are based on demand and supply comparative-static equilibrium analysis, are logically and empirically flawed, and have therefore developed alternative explanations and theories. This section will concentrate on the criticisms of the mainstream theory.

The traditional partial-equilibrium price analysis uses a U-shaped long-run cost curve to show that perfectly competitive firms will produce at the lowest point of that curve, and therefore, produce an efficient output at the lowest possible cost, where price equals marginal cost. However, Sraffa showed in 1926 that there were logical flaws in the analysis that contravened the assumptions of perfect competition and of partial equilibrium. He demonstrated that the only shape of cost curve compatible with both perfect competition and partial equilibrium was horizontal. In the neoclassical analysis, the U-shaped cost curve was important in determining the optimal size of the firm. Thus the firm should be producing at an output that corresponded to the bottom of its long-run U-shaped cost curve.

Further criticism of this idea was made by Kalecki (1937), when he argued that the two factors usually given for limiting the size of firms—diseconomies of scale and the limitations imposed by the size of the market—were not adequate. The idea that the size of firms is limited due to diseconomies of scale is unrealistic. Although it is true that each plant may have an optimal size, nevertheless firms can always replicate plants and have more than one, all operating at minimum cost. In addition, for the reasons discussed below, Kalecki rejected the view that individual cost curves were U-shaped, believing that costs were constant up to the level of full-capacity utilization. Kalecki rejected the second explanation because it could not explain why very different-sized firms exist within the same market. His explanation is discussed in the section below under the heading "Markup Pricing Models."

At about the same time, Hall and Hitch argued that firms did not operate in a competitive market, and were not price-takers, as the theory suggested. Rather, firms set price using a markup on costs, bearing in mind the actions and likely reactions of their competitors. As a result of this behaviour, Hall and Hitch showed that marginal revenue, necessary in the conventional theory for profit-maximizing behaviour, could not be defined at the prevailing market price, and even if it were, firms did not have the information about their demand curve necessary to calculate it. Firms' pricing policy was further complicated by factors relating to goodwill and the cost of perpetually changing prices, as well as to the general uncertainty about both consumers' and competitors' behaviour.

For the reasons discussed in Chapter 6, firms will not maximize profits in the narrow sense prescribed by neoclassical theory. In a world of uncertainty, and of strong interdependence of firms, they will instead rely on rules. One of the most important of these is markup pricing, discussed below.

Political Economy Approach: Basic Propositions

Kalecki's Contribution

Kalecki's contribution to price-determination theory has played an extremely influential role in the subsequent development of the analysis. Kalecki distinguished between pricing in the manufacturing sector and in the primary sector. In the former, changes in price are mainly determined by cost of production and so are cost-determined, whereas changes in prices in the primary sector are mainly determined by demand, due to the relative inelasticity of supply in the short run:

> Short-term price changes may be classified into two broad groups; those determined mainly by changes in cost of production and those determined mainly by changes in demand. Generally speaking, changes in the prices of finished goods are "cost-determined" while changes in the prices of raw materials inclusive

of primary foodstuffs are "demand-determined." The prices of finished goods are affected, of course, by any "demand-determined" changes in the prices of raw materials but it is through the channel of costs that this influence is transmitted.

It is clear that these two types of price formation arise out of different conditions of supply. The production of finished goods is elastic as a result of existing reserves of productive capacity. When demand increases it is met mainly by an increase in the volume of production while prices tend to remain stable. The price changes which do occur result mainly from changes in costs of production.

The situation with respect to raw materials is different. The increase in the supply of agricultural products requires a relatively considerable time. This is true, although not to the same extent, with respect to mining. With supply inelastic in short periods, an increase in demand causes a diminution of stocks and a consequent increase in price. This initial price movement may be enhanced by the addition of a speculative element. (Kalecki 1954, 209)

According to Kalecki, firms in the manufacturing sector of the economy face constant costs up to the level of full capacity. Supply is typically elastic, with excess capacity being the norm. As a result, price, in the oligopolistic manufacturing sector, according to Kalecki, is not determined by supply and demand, but as a markup on those constant costs. For Kalecki, the markup is determined by competitive factors within the economy, which he labelled "the degree of monopoly."

The important feature to note about Kalecki's view of pricing is that prices do not respond to changes in demand. Prices are determined on the basis of costs and competitiveness, whereas demand determines how much is actually sold. Most heterodox economists follow Kalecki's analysis in considering price to be determined as a markup over costs. However, there is much debate in the literature as to (1) what the appropriate notion of costs is, and (2) what determines the markup.

Industrial Structure

Markets are *not* "competitive" but tend to be oligopolistic in nature. Before continuing, we should say something about oligopoly. An oligopoly is defined as an industry containing a number of producers sufficiently small that the actions of any one will influence its rivals. In other words, the essential feature of oligopoly is the interdependence of producers. Related to the small numbers and the fact that producers face a downward sloping demand curve is the large influence such firms have over the setting of their price.

These factors, especially the interdependence, make oligopoly the hardest market situation to analyze. In fact, it is not analyzed at all well by orthodox economists, who tend to consider it in terms of static behavioural assumptions that assume away the interdependence that is its essential feature, emphasized in models such as those of Cournot and Stackelberg. Markup-pricing rules explicitly take into account the vast differences in the possible ranges of interdependence of oligopolistic producers, which explains why there are many different models of the markup. The dynamics of different oligopolistic industries will vary greatly, depending on a number of factors, including the industry's history, the number of domestic and international firms, and the nature of the industry's output. For this reason, no one model could capture all the possible factors influencing markups. Rather, different models capture differing factors between industries.

With oligopolistic firms, excess capacity is the "normal" situation. In other words, plant and equipment are not operating at full (potential) capacity. This enables the firm to increase output to meet unanticipated increases in demand and/or to take advantage of potential market share expansion opportunities, without incurring significantly higher average costs of production. In addition, excess capacity may help prevent the entry of new firms, who would be aware that existing firms can readily expand output.

What Is the Relevant Concept of Cost?

We can define:

Total costs (TC) = Total fixed costs (TFC) plus total variable costs (TVC).

Fixed costs are those which, in the short run, do not vary with output, so $\Delta TFC = 0$.

Average total costs (ATC) = Total costs divided by the level of output produced by the firm (Q).

$ATC = TC/Q = TFC/Q + TVC/Q$ = Average fixed costs (AFC) plus average variable costs (AVC).

Average fixed costs ($= TFC/Q$) will always decrease as output (Q) increases.

According to the political economy approach, average variable costs are constant (for given input prices) up to (or close to) full capacity utilization. In other words, productivity is assumed to be constant up to levels of output near full capacity. We can compare this with the traditional textbook explanation, which depicts average long-run cost curves as U-shaped due to the assumption of the law of diminishing marginal returns, which is rejected by political economists on both theoretical and empirical grounds. They argue that the average variable cost curve is constant until full capacity utilization is approached.

But this is not true of *AFC*, which decreases as *Q* increases. Some firms will apply the markup to the constant average variable, and set the markup at a level that also covers fixed costs. However, many firms prefer to treat all costs as the basis for applying the markup, and therefore use average total costs as the base. This leads to a further question: How can the firm calculate *ATC* if it does not know what output will be?

Actual output will vary due to both seasonal and cyclical factors: that is, short-run variations in output will cause changes in average total costs that should not influence price. As a result, most firms calculate the costs that would apply not at the actual level of output and capacity utilization, but at normal/planned/expected or "trend" levels of capacity utilization.

"Normal costs" are defined as the costs that would apply at a normal or trend level—the costs are normalized to isolate them from temporary changes in production costs or product demand which, it is argued, do not influence price. The argument for taking normal costs is that "it is absurd to imagine that firms, granted that they take costs as terms of reference in their pricing policy, are changing the price of their products in relation to the seasonal ups and downs of output: from this point of view, the use of annual data is the simple solution of the 'normalisation problem'" (Sylos-Labini 1979, 155).

Markup Pricing Models

On the basis of the discussion outlined above, prices are determined as a markup on costs:

$$P = (1 + m)U$$

where P = price, m = the "markup," and U = appropriate measure of unit costs.

Having discussed the appropriate concept of costs, we now need to consider the question of what factors determine the markup (m).

These can be divided into two distinct approaches. Some writers follow Kalecki in locating the key to determining markup in the factors that influence the competitiveness of the firm being considered. The alternative approach relates the markup decision to the firm's need for funds to finance investment, especially for additional capacity. The markup, according to this view, provides a source of internally generated funds, which can be used as part of investment financing.

Kalecki identified a number of elements that would influence the markup by influencing the degree of competitiveness faced by the firm. These include:

- the degree of industrial concentration
- the extent of sales promotion activities (product differentiation)
- trade union influence
- strategic behaviour by firms, including entry prevention and investment financing decisions

Subsequent work by Steindl and Sylos-Labini stressed the importance of the last factor, arguing that the markup was often set at a level that would deter the entry of new firms into the industry.

Longer-Period Pricing Models

Other economists link the firm's pricing decisions to questions of the survival and growth of the firm through time. To grow, firms need to invest by increasing their productive capacity. This raises the problem of how to finance investment.

Two possible sources of funds to finance investment are:

- Internally generated funds (retained earnings). An increase in internal funds can be achieved through an increase in the markup over costs;
- Externally generated funds (debt and equity).

Kalecki, in the article on "increasing returns" discussed above, uses this distinction as the basis of his discussion about why firms of very different sizes coexist in the same market. He argues that the main factor explaining the size of firms is "the amount of entrepreneurial capital, i.e. the amount of capital owned by the firm. The access of a firm to the capital market, or in other words, the amount of rentier capital it may hope to obtain, is determined to a large extent by the amount of its entrepreneurial capital" (Kalecki 1937, 276). In other words, due to imperfect capital markets, the more capital you have the more you can get, and at better terms.

This is reinforced by the principle of increasing risk, which states that the greater a firm's investment is relative to its finances, or "entrepreneurial capital," the greater the reduction in the entrepreneur's income if the investment is unsuccessful. Thus, the larger the loan, relative to internal resources, the more reluctant entrepreneurs will be to borrow money, and the capital market to lend it to them.

Kalecki argued that financial markets are imperfectly competitive because the ease of borrowing is related to the profits and wealth of the borrower. The access of a firm to capital markets for finance depends on its own entrepreneurial capital, and there is an upper limit to a firm's ability to borrow that depends on how much capital it has.

"The size of a firm thus appears to be circumscribed by the amount of its entrepreneurial capital both through its influence on the capacity to borrow capital and through its effect on the degree of risk. The variety in the size of enterprises in the same industry at a given time can be easily explained in terms of differences in entrepreneurial capital" (Kalecki 1937, 278). This is because a firm with a large entrepreneurial capital can obtain funds for a large investment whereas a firm with a small entrepreneurial capital will find it extremely difficult to do so. These differences between firms are reinforced by the fact that, below a certain size, firms may not be able to obtain access to capital markets at all.

This means that the expansion of firms depends on accumulating internal funds out of current profits. These funds will facilitate firms' ability to undertake new investment, because they increase both the ability of firms to self-finance investment and their ability to obtain external finance.

The importance of this discussion to the determination of the markup is that it demonstrates the relationship between the firm's pricing decision and its need for funds in the form of retained profits, which are used to finance investment. For economists in this tradition, the determination of the markup is closely linked to the firm's need for internally generated investment funds. They focus on an industry with a price leader, whose decision on price is followed by the other firms in the industry. The price leader is interested in growth through investment, which is financed by a combination of internal and external finance. The firm needs to decide on its desired rate of growth of capacity, as well as on the level of investment necessary to generate that growth. It also needs to decide on the division of investment funding between internal and external sources. All of these will feed into the determination of the size of the markup.

Eichner (1973) made an important original contribution to this issue. He showed how the markup was derived when firms used the funds generated by it as a source of investment financing. Eichner assumed that internal and external financing involved different costs, and showed how the markup could be determined when planned investment and finance were all part of the pricing decision. The Eichner model is developed in the analysis of Harcourt and Kenyon (1976), which extends the analysis by widening consideration of the firm's investment decision. Not only do firms, in their model, need to decide on how much investment in extra capacity they want, and on the cost and method of finance, they also need to choose which type of investment is most appropriate. This last problem arises for historical reasons related to the continual development of technology, which means that no one way of producing will always be the most appropriate.

The thing to notice about these models is that they are similar to the analysis of the classical political economists, but allow for the development, in modern capitalist economies, of monopoly and oligopoly in industry. The markup plays the role that profit did in the classical model—it is the source and motive for accumulation. The determination of price is different between the manufacturing and raw materials sectors, with the latter being more influenced by demand factors. Finally, the market imperfections of the economy are mirrored in the financial sector, where the larger and wealthier firms have access to more and cheaper finance, so that their advantages allow them to grow at faster rates, making the economy more monopolistic, and so on.

This last idea, that competitive capitalism has within it the seeds of its own destruction, was first analyzed by Marx, and later by Steindl in his excellent study, *Maturity and Stagnation in American Capitalism.* Steindl shows how competition among firms will reduce the number of firms within an industry, increasing its monopolization, until there are only a few firms left; and then stagnation sets in.

Steindl's analysis starts from cost differentials between firms within the same industry. The larger lower-cost firms will be making higher profits, and therefore generating larger internal funds. This will allow them to invest in capacity expansion using the latest technology. As long as the rate of growth of demand for the industry's output keeps pace with the increase in capacity, this will not cause a problem. However, if the rate of growth of the industry's capacity exceeds the growth in industry demand, then unplanned excess capacity will be generated. As a result, firms will attempt to expand their market share to increase the level of capacity utilization, either by a price war (reducing the markup) or by increasing expenditure on sales promotion. The smaller, higher-cost firms will have trouble matching these tactics, and the least productive may be forced to exit the market, leading to an increase in market concentration by the larger lower-cost firms. This process will continue, until the industry is dominated by a small number of large firms. At that point, price wars and increased sales promotion become increasingly risky. Under these conditions, excess capacity will increase and the industry will stagnate.

Conclusions

This chapter has examined the pricing decisions of firms. In neoclassical theory, price results from the interaction of the forces of supply and demand. Demand is the result of the optimizing decisions of utility-maximizing consumers subject to budget constraints, while supply is determined by the actions of profit-maximizing firms subject to technological constraints. However, this theory has both empirical and theoretical shortcomings. Political economists, on the other hand, reject the assumption that markets are usually competitive, arguing that they are typically oligopolistic, with price-making firms acting interdependently. In this framework, firms determine price on the basis of a markup on costs. There are two views as to how the markup is determined. According to the first view, the markup is determined by factors relating to the nature of the interdependence of firms. In the second view, there is an important link between investment and the pricing decision because financial markets are also imperfectly competitive. Internally generated funds assist the growth of firms and the markup provides an important source of these funds. Different factors will act as the dominant influence in different industries on the determination of the markup.

According to the political economy view, at normal levels of capacity utilization, prices are, therefore, cost-determined. Changes in demand will not directly influence price, but will lead to changes in output.

DISCUSSION QUESTIONS

1. Explain why, if marginal cost and, therefore, average variable costs are constant, neoclassical theory does not have a theory of the size of a firm.
2. It has been argued that the main differences between the neoclassical and the political economy theories of price determination reflect fundamentally different visions of economic society. Neoclassical economics sees the economy as being essentially resource-constrained, while political economy sees modern capitalist economies as being demand-constrained. Discuss with reference to the implications of these differences for the determination of price in both types of economic framework.
3. In what way does the political economy analysis of price represent a return to the interests of the classical economists?
4. Explain how the process of competition may lead to the emergence of oligopolies.
5. If banks decided to reduce the cost of borrowing money and, at the same time, made it much easier to borrow money, what effect would this have on prices?

SUGGESTED READINGS AND ONLINE RESOURCES

For an analysis of competing schools of thought in political economy, see
http://homepage.newschool.edu/het/.

Asimakopulos, A. 1978. *An introduction to economic theory: Microeconomics.* Don Mills, ON: Oxford University Press.

Eichner, A.S. 1973. A theory of the determination of the mark-up under oligopoly. *Economic Journal* 83: 1184–1200.

Hall, R.L., and C.J. Hitch. 1939. Price theory and business behaviour. *Oxford Economic Papers* 2: 12–33.

Harcourt, G.C., and P. Kenyon. 1976. Pricing and the investment decision. *Kyklos* 209: 449–477.

Koutsoyiannis, A. 1983. *Modern microeconomics.* New York: St. Martin's Press.

Lavoie, M. 2001. Pricing. In *A new guide to post Keynesian economics,* eds. R. Holt and S. Pressman, chap. 3, 21–31. London: Routledge.

REFERENCES

Eichner, A.S. 1973. A theory of the determination of the mark-up under oligopoly. *Economic Journal* 83: 1184–1200.

Hall, R.L., and C.J. Hitch. 1939. Price theory and business behaviour. *Oxford Economic Papers* 2: 12–33.

Harcourt, G.C., and P. Kenyon. 1976. Pricing and the investment decision. *Kyklos* 209: 449–477.

Kalecki, M. 1937. "The principle of increasing risk," reworked and reprinted as "Entrepreneurial capital and investment," reprinted in *Collected works of Michal Kalecki*, ed. J. Osiatynski, vol. II, 276–281. Oxford: Clarendon Press.

Kalecki, M. 1954. Costs and prices. In *Theory of economic dynamics*, reprinted in *Collected works of Michal Kalecki*, ed. J. Osiatynski, vol. II, 209–225. Oxford: Clarendon Press.

Osiatynski, J., ed. 1990. *Collected works of Michal Kalecki*, vol. I. Oxford: Clarendon Press.

Osiatynski, J., ed. 1991. *Collected works of Michal Kalecki*, vol. II. Oxford: Clarendon Press.

Sraffa, P. 1926. The laws of returns under competitive conditions. *Economic Journal* 36: 535–550. http://cepa.newschool.edu/het/texts/sraffa/sraffa26.htm.

Steindl, J. 1952. *Maturity and stagnation in American capitalism*. Repr. 1976. New York: Monthly Review Press.

Sylos-Labini, P. 1962. *Oligopoly and technical progress*, rev. ed. Repr. 1993. Fairfield: Augustus M. Kelley.

Sylos-Labini, P. 1979. Industrial pricing in the United Kingdom. *Cambridge Journal of Economics* 3: 153–163.

What Do Firms Try to Maximize, if Anything?

COMPETINGVIEWS

Fanny Demers and Michel Demers, "Profit Maximization and Other Goals of the Firm"

Marc Lavoie, "A Critique of Profit Maximization"

Editors' Introduction

In the "business of ordinary life" (to use Alfred Marshall's well-known expression), the vital institution engaged in the business of producing goods and services for sale to consuming households is the private firm or business enterprise. As an entrepreneurial unit, it commands human and physical resources, either through internal funds or by borrowing, to supply goods and services to the markets upon which its survival is based. Ever since economists began to recognize profit as a distinct form of income flow that was analytically separate from wages, interest, or rent, making profit has always been seen as an important objective of the firm.

With the advent of marginal analysis by the late 19th century, rational behaviour came to describe not only the entrepreneurial ability to make a profit, but also the firm's capacity to *maximize* profit—profit being defined as the difference between sale proceeds and total costs, with economists usually also including the net change in the value of the firm's assets during a given period. As a behavioural assumption, profit maximization remains prominent in practically all textbooks in economics. However, ever since its inception, there has been controversy over whether firms actually maximize profits, or even attempt to do so. For instance, do firms maximize profits in the short run, and is short-run profit maximization compatible with long-run profit maximization? Do firms seek instead to maximize sale proceeds? Or perhaps they do not maximize anything at all? Do firms merely seek to achieve a reasonable profit that would satisfy, say, the needs of the shareholders—behaviour described by Herbert A. Simon as "profit satisficing"?

A famous debate took shape during the 1940s and 1950s that pitted a wide number of mainstream neoclassical economists against a group of institutional economists, the latter armed with empirical studies conducted during the 1930s, such as those by a group of Oxford economists that questioned the assumption of profit maximization as the norm in industry. Neoclassical economists such as Fritz Machlup and Milton Friedman defended the assumption of profit maximization, and institutional economists such as Richard A. Lester and Gardner C. Means challenged its applicability to the behaviour of the firm. The original debate remains largely unsettled, with heterodox economists continuing to challenge the neoclassical view, despite its predominance in economics textbooks.

In the tradition of that debate, the essays by Fanny and Michel Demers and by Marc Lavoie take clear, yet much more guarded, positions on the question of profit maximization. The Demers offer a lucid survey of the current mainstream view and point out that, while the principle of profit maximization seems to be applicable to a world of purely competitive markets, it is less defensible as a hypothesis in an environment in which monopolistically competitive structures are prevalent.

Coming primarily from the post-Keynesian and institutionalist perspectives, Lavoie carefully reviews the criticisms of profit maximization and argues that, while this principle is inappropriate in explaining business behaviour in many industries with varying market structures, there are a number of valid heterodox perspectives that could suitably replace it. At the same time, he questions a widely held view among institutionalist economists that manager-held firms conduct their affairs differently from those run by their owners.

Profit Maximization and Other Goals of the Firm

Fanny Demers and Michel Demers

Introduction

It is often assumed in the analysis of production decisions that firms attempt to maximize profits, but in fact whether firms maximize profits or pursue other goals is a controversial topic. The importance of other goals may depend on the organizational form of business and the type of market the firm is operating in. In this essay, we will discuss the merits of profit maximization and the pursuit of other goals.

Organizational Forms for Business

There are three main legal organizational forms for businesses: proprietorship, partnership, and corporation.[1] Each of these different forms of business organization may lead to different objectives being pursued by the firm, as we will see later.

Individual proprietorship is a popular form of business organization. Although they constitute the vast majority of business firms, proprietorships only generate a small percentage of total revenues. A proprietorship typically requires only a business licence. It does not pay corporate income taxes, because all taxes are paid at the individual level. Its major drawback is the unlimited liability for business debt and the fact that the equity in the business is limited by the proprietor's wealth. Such businesses are typically owner-managed, for example, small companies offering gardening services, cleaning services, and snow removal. Start-up companies in the high-tech sector, where an inventor has a new idea or is a business consultant, may be other examples. In these cases, the person who makes management decisions that affect profits is the same person who receives the profit.

Another business form is the partnership, for which business licence fees need to be paid and a partnership agreement is usually written. In a *general partnership*, ownership and management are shared by several partners who work in the firm and each partner is responsible for the debts of the firm. In a *limited partnership*, at least one partner is a general partner, manages the business, and has unlimited liability. Limited partners do not participate in management but have limited liability. The income generated by a partnership is taxed at the individual level. Examples of partnerships include law and accounting firms, groups of doctors, and other small businesses such as convenience stores, garages, and restaurants.

The third and most important legal form of business is the corporation. As a distinct legal entity, it has an unlimited lifespan. Ownership is diffused over many individuals, called shareholders, each of whom owns a small share of the firm and is entitled to dividends. The shareholders control corporate policies and choose a board of directors. The board, in turn, selects the corporate officers who manage the corporation. Ownership is separated from management: the firm is managed by professionals who do not own a significant percentage of the firm's shares. Examples include Bombardier, Alcan, Rogers, and Bell Canada Enterprises (BCE). Shares of these companies are traded in organized stock exchanges, such as the Toronto Stock Exchange and the New York Stock Exchange. Each individual owner's liability is limited to the shares purchased. Corporate income is taxed at the corporate rate.

Accounting Profits Versus Economic Profits

Profit is defined as total revenue less total cost. However, there are different concepts of profit: accounting profit, economic profit, and monopoly profits.

Accounting profits measure a company's total earnings or net income, calculated according to generally accepted accounting principles (GAAP).[2] The calculation is based on a firm's income statement, which measures the firm's performance over a specific period of time, say a year. The accounting definition of net income is the excess of revenues over historical expenses, including financing costs (such as interest costs), taxes, research and development, and depreciation (the accountant's estimate of the use of equipment[3] during production).

Thus we have:

$$NI = EBIT - INT - T,$$

where *INT* denotes interest expenses, *T* taxes and:

$$EBIT = R - C - A - R\&D - DEP + OTHER,$$

where *R* is total operating revenues; *C* is cost of goods sold; *A* is selling, general, and administrative expenses; *R&D* is research and development; *DEP* is depreciation and amortization; and *OTHER* is other income.

Net income is a measure of the profitability of the firm. It is often reported as earnings per share (EPS), an indicator often used by investors in evaluating the performance of companies.[4]

In contrast, *economic profit* is the difference between revenue and total production costs, including the *opportunity cost* of all resources used in production. Economic profit includes the opportunity costs stemming from the use of land and buildings provided by the owner(s), the salary that the owner(s) could have earned elsewhere or in another occupation, and an appropriate return on investment. For example, if the owner of a clothing manufacturing firm decides to allocate a floor of his or her building to produce children's clothes instead of women's clothes, the opportunity cost is the profit that would have been earned had the owner decided to keep on producing women's clothes. Or instead of operating the firm, the owner could have worked as a business consultant: the forgone earnings constitute an opportunity cost. Finally, economic profit also includes a return on investment. Over the long run, if the owners of the firm do not receive a return that is sufficiently large, the firm will not stay in business.

Industrial Structure, Profit Maximization, and the Pursuit of Other Goals

We now examine the extent to which profit maximization is the main objective of the firm under various market structures.

An industry is perfectly competitive when a large number of firms sells an identical product, each firm is small and has no influence on the selling price, there is perfect information, resources are highly mobile, and there is free entry and exit of firms. In the short run, the firm operates with a fixed amount of machinery and equipment and can adjust its variable factors of production, raw materials, and labour. Its profit-maximizing choice of output occurs when its marginal cost of producing an additional unit equals the market price, provided that its average variable costs are covered. In the short run, the individual firm may earn positive economic profit.

If firms in an industry are earning positive economic profits, however, there is an incentive for *new* firms to enter the industry, increasing the industry supply to the market and leading to a decrease in the unit price of output and the economic profit of each firm in the industry. In long-run equilibrium, the individual firm makes zero economic profit but earns a normal return,[5] market supply equals demand, and there is no entry or exit of firms. In other words, excess profits disappear but the firm's opportunity costs are covered, including a normal return on investment, sometimes referred to as normal profits.

With the exception of some agricultural products, there are few real-world markets that are perfectly competitive. Thus, the profit-maximizing competitive model of the firm has few direct applications.[6]

In imperfectly competitive markets, such as those characterized by monopolistic competition, monopoly, and oligopoly, other goals may be pursued by the firm.

In monopolistic competition, a large number of profit-maximizing firms sell differentiated products. Each firm has a limited share of the market; it can adjust its selling price, although within limits, since each product has close substitutes; and there is free entry and exit. Each firm also competes with respect to product quality, service, and warranty. Finally, the firm resorts to advertising and other marketing strategies to differentiate its product. Examples of monopolistically competitive markets include tires, machine tools, wine, paints, electrical appliances, soft drinks, soaps, and dairy products. In the long run, such firms can—although they may not—earn positive economic profits.

In the case of a monopoly, a single large firm operates in the market. Monopolies can arise for a number of reasons:

- economies of scale, which result in *natural monopolies*, prime examples of which include public utilities such as Hydro Quebec and Ontario Hydro;
- patents, which give the innovator the right to prevent entry (for example, Xerox in the 1970s);
- a licence to be the exclusive seller or producer for a geographical area, or control over the supply of a key resource.

A monopolist reaps large profits whose size can be adversely affected by low demand or high costs. The monopolist may refrain from pursuing short-run profit maximization and charge a lower price to discourage entry by other firms and to deter government intervention and regulation. Profits for a regulated monopoly need to compensate shareholders for risk-bearing.

In oligopolistic markets, a few large corporations dominate the market. Each firm takes into account the actions of its rivals, there are substantial barriers to entry, and the product may be differentiated or standardized. Oligopolists compete with price adjustments in the short run while they compete in the long run with product innovation and design, product quality, customer service, and advertising. The goals pursued include maximization of industry profits (that is, through collusion, which is usually illegal), profit maximization by the price leader with the other firms acting as followers, and independent profit maximization.

Some conclusions can be drawn. When profit margins are small and competitive pressures intense, successful firms tend to be the ones that have the ability to pursue profit-maximization and those that imitate them. Firms that act otherwise will not survive and will leave the industry.

From an examination of monopolistic competition, oligopoly, and monopoly, however, we can conclude that when competitive pressures are weaker and profits large, firms may pursue goals other than maximizing short-run profits, provided that sufficient profits are generated to satisfy shareholders.

An alternative to profit maximization for oligopolistic firms where managers' decisions do not coincide with the owners' goals was proposed by Baumol (1967): revenue maximization subject to a profit constraint. Some empirical studies provide evidence that firms pursue revenue maximization.[7] Nevertheless, these firms need to attain a profit level that is high enough to satisfy shareholders and lenders to the firm.

An oligopolist may also seek a high market share so as to be able to lead the industry. Yet, typically, firms operate within self-imposed limits so as not to attract the attention of competition policy regulators.[8] Thus, a high market share may not be an alternative goal to seeking greater profits, but simply a means to a different end.

Achieving a high growth rate of sales, revenues, and profits by seeking new markets and attaining diversification of products are frequently cited corporate objectives. Growth and diversification are not incompatible with profit maximization. However, there can also be important trade-offs between these objectives, for example, when R&D projects need to be cancelled (thus lowering long-term growth and profits) to attain higher short-run profits.

Firms have to take very complex decisions requiring very complex calculations that need to be revised continuously through time as more information becomes available. These informational requirements become even more formidable under monopolistic competition, especially under oligopoly where different assumptions are made about strategic interactions. Herbert Simon (1979) has argued that managers do not attempt to maximize profits, especially in the short run. Instead, given the informational and computational costs of evaluating different courses of action, they aim at a satisfactory or "satisficing" level of profit. This satisfactory profit level may depend on the industry average or on rivals' profits and may vary through time and with the phases of the business cycle. Therefore, in the face of all these complexities, firms are likely to use rules of thumb, thereby deviating from profit maximization.

Value Maximization

In general, firms must make decisions (particularly investment decisions) today that have an impact on the firms' future profitability. They also face considerable uncertainty as to the possible outcomes of their decisions. Thus, as soon as we shift from a static framework to a dynamic one—and from certainty to uncertainty—we must enlarge our definition of the objective of the firm as being long-run expected value maximization rather than static period-by-period profit maximization.[9] If markets are complete and perfect, shareholders agree that corporations should pursue the goal of value maximization.[10]

Corporate Value Maximization, Agency Costs, and the Goals of the Manager

As the business organization becomes increasingly complex, it involves a larger number of different participants (partners, managers, employees, shareholders) who may have conflicting objectives and interests.[11] The organization also deals with other participants in the marketplace (such as its creditors, suppliers, and customers)[12] who may also have differing objectives and interests. The firm is thus a set of contracts among different individuals and groups who voluntarily enter such arrangements to undertake mutually beneficial exchanges. In this setting, questions such as "what are the objectives of the firm?" or "what does the firm maximize?" may seem problematic.

A contract will generally specify the rights and responsibilities of the participants. A "principal–agent" relationship exists whenever one person (or group), the *principal*, hires another person, the *agent*, to perform a set of tasks, and relinquishes some decision-making authority to the agent to allow him or her to perform the job. However, given the differing interests of the parties, contracts must be designed to allow the best alignment of these parties' interests.

The owners of the firm, the shareholders, through the board of directors, hire managers to run their business. The managers must take decisions that will directly affect the profitability of the firm. Yet, since ownership is separated from control (that is, managers do not own the firm), the managers may pursue their own objectives. For example, managers may want to enjoy fringe benefits such as a plush office, a private jet, and so on. Fringe benefits may, to a degree, increase the productivity of managers. However, given that managers do not bear these costs, they may excessively indulge in them.[13]

More important, though, when ownership is separated from control, managers may want to make their lives easier, for example, by choosing "safer" investment projects that have a greater probability of success, or that are easier to manage, rather than other projects that may be more advantageous for the firm; preferring to deal with suppliers with whom they entertain friendlier relations but who may not necessarily offer the most cost-effective product; or applying less effort (shirking) in managing the firm to pursue other personal objectives. These are called "agency costs" because they are specifically due to the "principal–agent" relationship that exists between the two parties.

In some cases, if shareholders were capable of monitoring the activities of the managers, they would be able to prevent these types of behaviour, which are deemed to run against the "best interests" of the shareholders. They could, for example, threaten to fire the managers if the latter are caught shirking or spending excessively on fringe benefits. However, monitoring is very costly, and thus also constitutes an agency cost. In addition, it is not always clear if shareholders have enough knowledge or expertise to determine whether, for example, one project is chosen over another only to further the managers' own interest, or whether a project fails due to lack of effort rather than unfavourable circumstances beyond the manager's control. Hence, asymmetric information and incentive problems affect the relationship between the principal and the agent.

In view of the agency and asymmetric-information problems, it is necessary to devise contracts that comprise appropriate incentive schemes to induce managers to work in the best interest of the company and to maximize the value of the firm.

Value Maximization and Stakeholder Theory

Stakeholder theory, which is grounded in sociology and organizational behaviour, is often presented as an alternative to value maximization on the part of the firm.[14] The proponents of this theory aim to take a more ethical approach to the conduct of business by having managers address the concerns of all groups that affect, or are affected by, the firm's success or failure in making their decisions. Stakeholders include not only all financial claimholders (holders of equity, debt, warrants, and so on) whose long-run interests are maximized by the value maximization approach,[15] but also employees, customers, communities, and government officials.

At first glance, stakeholder theory, with its emphasis on the social responsibility of the firm, seems to be an attractive, ethically satisfying alternative to value maximization, especially in the current economic environment, where we have recently witnessed multiple instances of corporate governance failures. However, in addressing these social issues, stakeholder theory loses sight of the main contribution of the firm to the economy and to society as a whole. The firm exists because it can most efficiently put together inputs to produce an output or service that will create welfare for the consumer, in other words, that will create social wealth. To create this social wealth, the firm's managers need to have a clear-cut objective so they can evaluate alternative courses of action and gauge performance.

As Jensen (2010) argues, how can a manager simultaneously satisfy the invariably conflicting interests of all of the stakeholders? For example, employees would want to have higher wages and salaries and better working conditions, while customers would prefer a high-quality product at a very low price with extensive product warranties. Clearly, managers will have to address the concerns of both groups, but in doing so they will have to weigh some concerns against others. The list of conflicting interests will obviously grow as more stakeholders are taken into account.

Moreover, different members of the same stakeholder group may have divergent desires: some workers may prefer higher pay whereas others may prefer shorter hours. Similarly, managers will have to make decisions favouring one investment project against another, one strategic decision against another, and so on. To decide among such alternatives, the manager will need to have a guiding principle, a single goal, a single measuring rod by which to evaluate the benefits and costs of different courses of action. This guiding principle is maximizing the long-run value of the firm. It provides a way of evaluating performance. Managers who try to satisfy a multiplicity of conflicting objectives will be unable to gauge the trade-offs involved in choosing among different alternatives, and will be plagued by ambiguity and confusion. A firm that attempts to pursue multiple objectives, as stakeholder theory advocates, will not be able to successfully compete in the marketplace and will not be able to survive.

Having long-run value maximization as the single objective of the firm does not mean being oblivious to the needs and desires of the other stakeholders. On the contrary, these needs and desires must be taken into account for the firm to be successful. For example, customer goodwill is an important element in the success of a firm. The firm would not be able to generate such goodwill if it had no concern for its customers' interests. Similarly, the firm must entertain good relations with its employees to be successful in the long run. A firm that contributes to the community in which it lives by supporting education and by sponsoring various cultural and sporting events will also generate goodwill. However, in each case, value maximization provides the necessary touchstone for weighing possibly conflicting alternatives.

Behavioural Biases

Even in the presence of optimal contracts, the separation of ownership from control leaves the door open for managers to pursue their own personal goals to some extent. By the same token, this implies that the psychological biases of managers may affect the firm's decisions. We will examine the implications of two prevalent biases, namely overconfidence[16] and herding.

Overconfident managers tend to get promoted and appointed as chief executive officers or to other senior management positions. Overconfident managers believe that they are acting in the interests of shareholders and are even willing to share in the ownership of the firm. As argued by Roll (1986), Heaton (2002), and Malmendier and Tate (2005), overconfident chief executive officers (CEOs) overestimate the returns on their corporate investment projects. Such a CEO is likely to believe that he or she can control the outcome of a project and to overestimate the probability of success. As a result, if they have sufficient internal funds and are disciplined neither by capital markets nor by corporate governance, managers will overinvest. If managers lack internal funds they will not issue new shares (since, being overconfident, they believe the stock price to be undervalued) and will instead invest less. These behavioural biases will induce investment distortions that move the firm away from value maximization.

Overconfident managers also overestimate the value they can create by taking over other firms. More acquisitions than are warranted will take place when internal funds exist, resulting in many value-reducing mergers and acquisitions.[17]

When managerial compensation is based on relative profits or value achieved, a manager may maximize the firm's value *relative* to that of its competitors, or follow what others do, even though in both cases these decisions may go against long-term profitability.

When managers are uncertain as to whether rival firms' managers are pursuing value maximization they may display "herd behaviour," that is, imitate non-rational managers.

Finally, some managers may take a special interest in their company and favour pet projects that lead to deviations from value maximization, whether the firm operates in biotechnology or runs a sports team.

Conclusions

Whether firms maximize profits in the short run or even the long run is controversial.[18] When competitive pressures are intense, successful firms are likely to pursue this strategy or imitate those that do.

Alchian and Friedman have argued that in the long run only firms whose behaviour is consistent with profit maximization will survive, since market forces will push non-rational firms into bankruptcy.

While plausible in perfectly competitive markets under certainty, it may be argued that Alchian's and Friedman's claim loses strength in imperfectly competitive markets that are shielded from competition or when firms face uncertainty and informational problems.

In markets where competitive pressures are weaker and profits large, firms may pursue goals other than maximizing short-run profits. As Simon has argued, there are many reasons to believe that firms, especially in imperfectly competitive markets, rely on rules of thumb, given high information and decision-making costs.

Furthermore, even if optimal contracts are devised, the separation of ownership from control in corporations may lead to deviations from value maximizing behaviour. This is compounded by the behavioural biases of managers, such as overconfidence and the tendency to herd.

Yet, even in oligopolistic markets (such as the US automobile industry), firms that wish to survive in the long run in today's global economy are bound to have value maximization as one of their top priorities when faced with strong international competition and demanding consumers. Thus, when competitive pressures are strong, managers' behaviour must be broadly consistent with value maximization for the firm to survive in the long run.

NOTES

1. In this essay, we abstract from government corporations and non-profit corporations. In the United States in 2004, proprietorships accounted for 72 percent of firms and 4.6 percent of revenues, partnerships amounted for 8.9 percent of firms and 4.6 percent of revenues, and corporations constituted 18.7 percent of firms and 83.2 percent of revenues. Source: www.bizstats.com.
2. GAAP are a set of rules and a standard format for companies to record and report accounting information. Although financial statements are subject to GAAP and are audited, accountants can manipulate information. In the case of the WorldCom scandal (in 2002), a fraud was conducted that classified $3.85 billion in operating expenses as long-term investment so as to artificially raise apparent profitability (net income or earnings).
3. Consider a machine whose purchase price is $1,500 with a three-year life span and no resale value. With straightline depreciation the accountant will expense the cost in three equal (depreciation) payments of $500 for each of three years.
4. That is, after dividing net income by the number of shares.
5. That is, each firm makes a normal profit but not an excess profit.
6. Some financial markets, for example, the bond market, can be viewed as perfectly competitive. However, these markets are characterized by uncertainty and imperfect information. The perfectly competitive model needs to be modified accordingly so it is applicable. See, for example, Grossman and Stiglitz (1980).
7. For an empirical study on the pursuit of this goal, see, for example, Amihud and Kamin (1979). The implications of the separation of ownership from control will be discussed in the next sections.
8. The relationship between market share and profits seems unclear. Buzzell, Gale, and Sultan (1975) argue that a higher market share leads to higher profits, while Newton (1983) puts in doubt the direction of causality.
9. First, in the case of corporations, even under certainty, it is more appropriate to consider maximization of profit per share rather than total profits, since the firm could in principle increase total profits by, say, issuing more equity and purchasing treasury bills with the obtained funds. Second, maximizing profits ("earnings") per share is no longer appropriate in a dynamic context, since it fails to take into account the value of time. Third, the concept of

(expected) earnings per share does not capture the riskiness of the projects that the firm considers. Shareholders have an optimal trade-off between expected return and risk. The capital market and the market price per share of the company reflect these trade-offs. Expected earnings per share might be higher for one project than another, but if the returns of the first project are riskier than the second, they might not be preferred by shareholders. See Van Horne (1971, 4–7). See also Copeland, Weston, and Shastry (2005, chap. 13).

10. However, when markets are incomplete, shareholders may disagree on the firm's goal. In this essay, we will abstract from this consideration.

11. Alchian and Demsetz (1972) define the firm as a contractual organization characterized by "(a) joint input production, (b) several input owners, (c) one party who is common to all the contracts of the joint inputs, (d) who has rights to renegotiate any input's contract independently of contracts with other input owners, (e) who holds the residual claim, and (f) who has the right to sell his contractual residual status." There is a very large literature on the theory of the firm, of different organizational structures, and of their *raison d'être*, starting with Marshall (1890) and Coase (1937). See also McManus (1975). For a more recent treatment, see Milgrom and Roberts (1992).

12. Jensen and Meckling (1976), while agreeing with the Alchian-Demsetz definition of the firm as a contractual organization, object to their emphasis on "joint input" or "team" production, pointing to the importance of contractual arrangements with these other groups even though they may not participate in joint production.

13. Hence, we may observe that when the sole owner-manager of a firm sells shares of the company to outside investors and stays on as part-owner-manager, the latter's consumption of fringe benefits will increase, since now, as part-owner, he or she bears only part of these costs. At the same time, however, the shareholders, anticipating this type of behaviour on the part of the former owner, will take these costs into account and will be willing to purchase the shares only at a lower price. This reduction in the value of the firm is borne by the owner. As a means of alleviating this cost, the owner may willingly submit to (and even encourage) "monitoring" activities on the part of the new shareholders.

14. For one of the first detailed accounts of stakeholder theory, see Freeman (1984). See also the "Clarkson Principles" in *Redefining the Corporation: Principles of Stakeholder Management*, and Post, Preston, and Sachs (2002). Stakeholder theory is now accepted by law in 38 American states. See Hanks (1994).

15. For a comparison of the two approaches, see Jensen (2010). The following discussion draws in part from Jensen (2010) and Post, Preston, and Sachs (2002).

16. For evidence, see Shefrin (2000, chap. 2). Overconfident individuals tend to attribute good outcomes to their actions and bad outcomes to bad luck.

17. See Roll (1986) and Malmendier and Tate (2008).

18. Unfortunately, there is little direct evidence for profit maximization. On the one hand, direct tests of profit maximization are difficult to devise as marginal costs cannot be observed and are inferred by assuming profit maximization. On the other hand, experimental studies seem to shed doubt on whether firms actually maximize profits. However, since it is impossible to replicate the complexities of the hierarchical structures of real-world organizations in the lab, this issue remains an open question. See Holt (1995). See also Romer (2006).

DISCUSSION QUESTIONS

1. What are the main legal organizational structures for business firms and what goal is each form of business organization likely to pursue?
2. Explain the difference between accounting profits and economic profits.
3. Is profit maximization always the goal of the firm regardless of the industrial market structure? Discuss.
4. What is the nature of "agency costs"? Under what circumstances do they arise? Explain.
5. What is a "principal–agent" relationship? What is the nature of an optimal "principal–agent" contract? Explain.
6. What is "stakeholder theory"?
7. How can a manager's behavioural biases affect a firm's pursuit of value maximization?
8. Herbert Simon and Milton Friedman have been major contributors to the debate on profit maximization. Analyze each economist's viewpoint.

SUGGESTED READINGS

Donaldson, Thomas, and Lee E. Preston. 1995. The stakeholder theory of the corporation: Concepts, evidence, and implications. *Academy of Management Review* 20 (1): 65–91.

Neumann-Whitman, Marina von. 1999. *New world, new rules: The changing role of the American corporation.* Boston: Harvard Business School Press.

Pendergast, C. 1999. The provision of incentives in firms. *Journal of Economic Literature* 37: 7–63.

Phillips, Robert, and R. Edward Freeman. 2003. *Stakeholder theory and organizational ethics.* San Francisco: Berrett-Koehler Publishers.

Tirole, Jean. 2006. *The theory of corporate finance.* Princeton, NJ: Princeton University Press.

Williamson, O.E. 2000. The new institutional economics: Taking stock, looking ahead. *Journal of Economic Literature* 38 (3): 595–613.

ONLINE RESOURCES

For business statistics, see http://www.bizstats.com and http://www.bizstats.com/ reports/businesses-by-structure.asp.

For the "Clarkson Principles," see: http://www.rotman.utoronto.ca/~stake/ principles.htm.

REFERENCES

Alchian, Armen A. 1950. Uncertainty, evolution, and economic theory. *Journal of Political Economy* 58 (3): 211–221.

Alchian, Armen A., and Harold Demsetz. 1972. Production, information costs and economic organization. *American Economic Review* 62: 777–795.

Amihud, Y., and J. Kamin. 1979. Revenue vs. profit maximization: Differences in behavior by the type of control and by market power. *Southern Economic Journal* 45 (3): 838–846.

Baumol, William J. 1967. *Business behaviour, value and growth.* Rev. ed. New York: Macmillan.

Buzzell, R.D., B.T. Gale, and R.G.M. Sultan. 1975. Market share—A key to profit-ability. *Harvard Business Review* 53 (1): 97–106.

"Clarkson Principles," in *Redefining the corporation: Principles of stakeholder management.* The Clarkson Centre for Ethics and Board Effectiveness, Joseph L. Rotman School of Management, University of Toronto. http://www.rotman.utoronto.ca/~stake/principles.htm.

Coase, R. 1937. The nature of the firm. *Economica* New Series IV (16): 386–405.

Copeland, Thomas E., J. Fred Weston, and Kuldeep Shastri. 2005. *Financial theory and corporate policy.* Reading, MA: Pearson Addison-Wesley.

Cyert, R.M., and J. March. 1956. Organizational factors in the theory of oligopoly. *Quarterly Journal of Economics* 70: 44–64.

Freeman, R. Edward. 1984. *Strategic management: A stakeholder approach.* Boston: Pitman.

Friedman, M. 1953. *Essays in positive economics.* Chicago: University of Chicago Press.

Grossman, Sanford, and Joseph Stiglitz. 1980. The impossibility of informationally efficient markets. *American Economic Review* (June): 393–408.

Hanks, James L. 1994. From the hustings: The role of states with takeover control laws. *Mergers & Acquisitions* 29 (2).

Heaton, J.B. 2002. Managerial optimism and corporate finance. *Financial Management* (Summer): 33–45.

Holt, C. 1995. Industrial organization: A survey of laboratory research. In *The handbook of experimental economics,* eds. John Kagel and Alvin Roth. Princeton, NJ: Princeton University Press.

Jensen, Michael. 2010. Value maximization, stakeholder theory, and the corporate objective function. *Journal of Applied Corporate Finance* 22 (1): 32–42.

Jensen, Michael, and William Meckling. 1976. Theory of the firm: Managerial behavior, agency costs and ownership structure. *Journal of Financial Economics* 3: 305–360.

Malmendier, Ulrike, and Geoffrey Tate. 2005. CEO overconfidence and corporate investment. *Journal of Finance* 60: 2661–2700.

Malmendier, Ulrike, and Geoffrey Tate. 2008. Who makes acquisitions? CEO overconfidence and the market's reactions. *Journal of Financial Economics* 89: 20–43.

Marshall, Alfred. 1890. *Principles of economics.* London: Macmillan.

McManus, John C. 1975. The costs of alternative economic organizations. *The Canadian Journal of Economics* 8 (3): 334–350.

Milgrom, Paul, and John Roberts. 1992. *Economics, organization and management.* Englewood Cliffs, NJ: Prentice Hall.

Newton, J.K. 1983. Market share key to higher profitability. *Long Range Planning* 16 (1): 37–41.

Post, J.E., L.E. Preston, and S. Sachs. 2002. *Redefining the corporation: Stakeholder management and organizational wealth.* Palo Alto, CA: Stanford University Press.

Roll, Richard. 1986. The hubris hypothesis of corporate takeovers. *Journal of Business* 59: 197–216.

Romer, David, H. 2006. Do firms maximize? Evidence from professional football. *Journal of Political Economy* 114: 340–365.

Schaffer, Mark. 1989. Are profit-maximizers the best survivors? *Journal of Economic Behavior and Organization* 12: 29–45.

Shefrin, Hersh. 2000. *Beyond greed and fear.* Boston: Harvard Business School Press.

Simon, Herbert C. 1955. A behavioral model of rational choice. *Quarterly Journal of Economics* 55: 99–118.

Simon, Herbert C. 1979. Rational decision-making in business organizations. *American Economic Review* 69: 493–513.

Van Horne, James C. 1971. *Financial management and policy.* Englewood Cliffs, NJ: Prentice Hall.

A Critique of Profit Maximization

Marc Lavoie

Introduction

Economists as diverse as John Maynard Keynes, the famous Cambridge economist who created macroeconomics, and Gary Becker, the no less famous Nobel prize-winner who extended economics to topics as varied as marriage and crime, have both claimed that a distinctive feature of economics is its method. Within mainstream economics—the kind of economics found in introductory and intermediate textbooks—this method can be summed up as the method of constrained optimization. First-year students of microeconomics get their first glimpse of this when they are told that consumers are assumed to maximize their utility (subject to their budget constraints). In a later chapter, students are told that the objective of firms is to maximize profits. There may be a sentence or two pointing out that the objective of profit maximization is somewhat controversial, that firms may have multiple goals, or that firms may not be maximizing anything. But, ultimately, textbook authors assert that the assumption of profit maximization is a useful one, and hence will be taken as the sole goal of the firm.

Convenience certainly explains the focus on profit maximization in introductory textbooks, because, at least until recently, if one attempted to briefly characterize the received view in industrial organization about the objectives of the firm, one would draw the following picture: small firms operate in competitive markets and attempt to maximize profits, while larger firms, because they operate in less competitive markets, and because their management is divorced from ownership, generally pursue goals other than profit maximization. Corporate managers are said to maximize something else, such as their own interests, or they may be said to content themselves with achieving some minimal standard of performance. But, besides convenience, what other reasons can be advanced to justify the assumption of profit maximization?

Justification and Critique of Profit Maximization

About 30 years ago, Canadian economist Lawrence Boland (1981) argued that it was futile to criticize the maximization hypothesis in general, and the assumption of profit maximization in particular. Boland claimed that there are two main arguments against this standard mainstream hypothesis. The first argument is that owners, or managers in general, lack information or don't have access to correct information, and hence are unable to maximize profits. To this, Boland replies that we do not need to assume that firms get access to lots of knowledge or to correct information; it is enough to presume that economic agents *try* to maximize profits, without assuming that managers get access to objective and true assessments of costs and revenues. The second argument against profit maximization is an empirical one: there is evidence, notably through surveys and questionnaires, that a number of firms do not achieve profit maximization. Boland questions whether we can ever be sure that firms do not maximize profits. But even if we can assert that a number of firms don't behave in this way, it cannot be concluded that no firm conducts profit maximization. Thus, Boland concludes that it is impossible to prove or to disprove whether firms are maximizing profits.

But then, if the hypothesis cannot ever be tested, isn't it some kind of tautology? Boland answers that the profit-maximizing hypothesis is useful because it is a metaphysical construct of mainstream economics that helps the research program of mainstream economics to move forward. It is a statement that is irrefutable and "deliberately put beyond question" (Boland 1981, 1034), because the purpose of the program is to see how far one can get by postulating that agents act in a certain rational way. A further related argument is that we should stick to the profit-maximizing hypothesis because that assumption leads to economic efficiency and optimality under conditions of perfect competition, and that is what most mainstream economists are concerned about (Koplin 1963, 139). Endorsing realistic assumptions is not the goal of (mainstream) economics: the goal is to find the conditions under which efficiency norms are achieved. This is Milton Friedman's defence against the lack of realism of assumptions in economics, a position known to philosophers of science as instrumentalism. For this well-known representative of the free-market school at the University of Chicago, the main purpose of economic theory is to put forth propositions that provide useful analytical tools; it is not to describe reality and attempt to reproduce it.

Needless to say, several economists disagree with this defence of profit maximization and would rather start from realistic premises. As a result, the question of the objectives of the firm or of its managers has generated a substantial amount of attention. Various maximands (the economic variables being maximized), such as sales, managers' utility, and valuation ratios, have been proposed. In addition, some economists argue that managers don't try to maximize anything, but instead try to attain an overall satisfactory performance by achieving several threshold levels simultaneously—for instance, a normal rate of return and a given market share. Faced with this profusion of possible objectives, the only rational response, it seems, is to concede that firms have multi-purpose objectives. In fact, this is the view that many empirical researchers take after admitting that the empirical evidence is unclear (Koutsoyiannis 1975, 258). Indeed, in surveys of their objectives, entrepreneurs often indicate several, rather than the standard profit-maximization hypothesis (Shipley 1981, 442). John Kenneth Galbraith, the world-renowned Canadian-born economist, claimed that it would be a serious error "to seek a single explanation of how firms behave" (1975, 124). Joan Robinson, the famous Cambridge economist, argued that firms' motivations are multi-dimensional and that as a consequence "it will never be possible to get a knock-down answer" (1977, 11).

Besides the obvious fact that there is no reason to presume that different firms will behave identically, or that the various constituents of the modern firm will pursue identical goals, the main cause of these unsatisfactory results is that the ultimate objective of the firm can only be defined in very general terms, perhaps by saying that power is the ultimate objective of firms or their upper-level management. "Power is the ability of an individual or a group to impose its purpose on others ... not being at the mercy of the market" (Galbraith 1975, 108).

Power allows firms to "control the consequences of their own decisions in order to prevent their desires being thwarted by others" (Dixon 1986, 588). The firm, whether it is a small family firm or a giant corporation, would like to exercise a degree of control over its production, financial, and sales environments. It follows that various intermediate goals that serve to fulfill this ultimate objective will be proposed, either by theoreticians or by the business world itself.

Some Empirical Data

Ever since the 1932 publication of *The Modern Corporation and Private Property* by Adolph Berle and Gardiner Means, the first author a lawyer and the second an economist, there has been a widespread belief that firms that are still under the control of their owners behave differently from those that are under the control of their managers. Roughly speaking, the authors' view is that manager-controlled firms' stock ownership is widely dispersed, which allows managers to control the board of directors and pursue goals of their own. By contrast, it is asserted that owner-controlled firms will attempt to maximize profits.

In the more modern literature, in particular in finance, where future profits and investments in new capacities are taken into consideration, the profit-maximizing hypothesis takes a slightly different twist. It is asserted that an owner-controlled firm will try to maximize the value of the firm, that is, the present value of current and future profits. When the firm is listed on the stock market, it will act in such a way as to maximize shareholder wealth, by maximizing market capitalization, that is, by taking decisions that will maximize the value of shares on the stock market. Indeed, since the 1990s, principles of corporate governance have reasserted this claim by saying that managers should act or should be constrained to act in such a way as to maximize shareholder value. Even the Organisation for Economic Co-operation and Development (OECD) has stated that "corporations should be run, first and foremost, in the interests of shareholders" (Lazonick and O'Sullivan 2000, 15), the fear being that manager-controlled firms do not follow this governance principle, or that some firms are run with the interests of other stakeholders of the firms—employees, customers, or suppliers—in mind. As a result of this fear, many incentives have been put forth to modify the behaviour of managers, so that it is aligned with the interests of the shareholders instead.

But do manager-controlled firms behave any differently than those run by their owners? Does the divorce between management and ownership truly lead to different behaviour or to different objectives? Galbraith himself, the herald of the technostructure (the set of specialists—executives, managers, engineers, scientists, lawyers—that have special knowledge and that guide corporations), believed so. But he relied on an empirical study that was an exception. As pointed out by Kania and McKean, all other studies have shown that manager-controlled and owner-controlled firms perform "equally well, or equally poorly, in regard to profit realization" (1976, 273). These two authors have looked at a large number of variables with a sample of no less than 1,800 firms. These variables included profitability variables such as earnings per share, return on equity, and dividends per share; risk variables such as cash flows and debt-equity ratios; performance variables such as the growth rate of sales and the growth rate of assets; and slack variables (expenditures over which firms have some discretionary control), such as research and development ratios, selling and advertising ratios, and labour compensation ratios. No clear difference emerged from this analysis, except for some evidence that the sales of manager-controlled firms grew faster and that retirement packages looked more generous. We may conclude from this that managers have the same goals whatever firm they work for.

What do the managers themselves say? Surveys done in the early 1980s include a most interesting study, that of Francis (1980), who first asked which objectives were most important in the long run. The top two objectives were clearly maximizing growth in total profits and maximizing the rate of return on capital. At a distant third came a variety of goals with nearly equal importance: maximizing the rewards for employees, maximizing growth in sales and in assets, maximizing growth in dividends, and the price of company shares. Way behind all of those came the objective of minimizing the risk of being taken over. Francis then asked why companies were interested in pursuing a high level of profitability (high rates of profit). Strikingly, the main reason, by far, was to provide finance for expansion. There is a circular relationship between sales growth and profitability. When managers were asked why their companies were interested in pursuing a high rate of growth in sales, the top reasons offered were because it helped secure or increase future profits and because no growth was bound to lead to eventual decline. Profitability and expansion are thus tightly related. Firms can grow because they make profits that allow them to finance their expansion. But reciprocally, the growth of firms allows them to be profitable. Clearly, it may be difficult in reality to disentangle the relative importance of the objectives of long-run profit maximization and of growth maximization, given their interdependence.

Some Alternatives to Profit Maximization

As pointed out earlier, economists have proposed various alternatives to the objective of profit maximization. Following the division proposed by Koutsoyiannis (1975), their models can be divided into two groups: managerial models of the firms and behavioural models. Managerial models assume that some variable, other than profit, is being maximized by managers. Behavioural models assume instead that managers do not try to maximize anything, being content to *satisfice*— to achieve *adequate* results—in relation to various norms.

Baumol's (1959) model of sales maximization is certainly the simplest of all these models. Like all managerial models of the firm, Baumol's model assumes that managers take their own interests into account when making decisions. Baumol argues that the salaries of upper-level managers are better correlated with sales than with profits, a claim that has been verified empirically. He also argues that managers running large firms or firms with rising sales are provided with more prestige. Saying that managers maximize sales revenue can be easily expressed with the usual textbook diagrams by saying that firms raise output until marginal revenue falls to zero, that is, until the elasticity of the demand curve that they are facing is equal to unity. A complication may be added to the model by suggesting that managers do this only as long as profits are above some minimum level, in which case sales will be limited by this profit constraint.

Whereas Baumol assumed that sales acted as a proxy for the utility that managers could derive from their jobs, Oliver Williamson (1963) introduced an explicit utility curve, which is assumed to be a positive function of the profits of the firms and of the salaries and other emoluments that the managerial staff receives. Although managerial remuneration and profits rise together initially, at some point the increase in managerial remuneration reduces profits, resulting in a trade-off between the two. Williamson got a Nobel prize in economics in 2009 for his use of the standard tools of constrained optimization to study economic institutions. He had put forth an algebraic analysis of a suggestion made ten years earlier by Andreas Papandreou (1952), who had argued that the theory of the firm had to be modified to incorporate some general preference function instead of pure profit maximization. A more dynamic version of this managerial model of the firm was put forward by Robin Marris (1964), a British economist from the University of Cambridge. In Marris's model, the trade-off is between growth and job security, the idea being that if firms grow too fast they may have to unduly increase their debt ratio and reduce their liquidity ratio, thus putting in peril the solvency of the firm or its independence from takeover raids, a feature of modern capitalism that would turn out to be highly relevant in the 1980s.

The financial requirements of the firm, which are rarely discussed in first-year textbooks, also appear in a more heterodox variant of the Marris model, the one proposed by Adrian Wood (1975). Wood assumes, as Galbraith did (1975), that managers wish to maximize sales growth, but subject to a finance constraint that depends on various acceptable financial ratios: the debt, liquidity, and retained earnings ratios. The faster firms are growing, the higher the profit rate needs to be for investment in new capacity to be financed. Indeed, Wood's model, in contrast to the previous two, does not rely on some hypothetical utility function, being based instead on financial ratios that are measurable. Wood's model incorporates the two relationships identified by Francis (1980) in the previous section. Once again the claim is that profitability and expansion are tightly related. Firms finance their growth thanks to their profits. But reciprocally, the growth of firms allows them to be profitable, at least up to a certain point. Wood (1975, 8) believes that "the basic goal of those in charge of the firm is to cause sales revenue to grow as rapidly as possible" because the urge for power is stronger than the urge for money. As a result, growth maximization is a phenomenon that can be observed in all except the smallest unincorporated firms and in closely owned companies, as well as in large quoted companies with widely dispersed ownership. Again, this is consistent with the empirical work that we examined in the previous section, which showed that the behaviour of manager-controlled firms was no different from that of owner-controlled firms.

This common behaviour may be related to the claim that neither family businesses nor corporate managers try to maximize anything, attempting instead to achieve various aspiration levels—what we denoted earlier as *satisficing*. This is the so-called behavioural model of the firm associated with the names of Cyert and March (1963) and of Nobel prizewinner Herbert Simon (1955). As summarized by Koutsoyiannis (1975, 389), "the firm in the behavioural theories seeks to *satisfice*, that is, to attain a 'satisfactory' overall performance, as defined by the set of aspiration goals, rather than maximize profits, sales or other magnitudes" (1975, 389). Aspiration goals may include a satisfactory level of production, a satisfactory level share of the market, a satisfactory level of profit, a satisfactory amount devoted to research and development, a satisfactory public image, a satisfactory amount of perks, and other "slack" payments. Satisficing occurs, first, because firms are a coalition of groups with conflicting interests, and, second, because managers must take decisions that reconcile these interests based on information that is hard to get and that can be hard to process. Managers are "people with limited time at their disposal, have limited and imperfect information and limited computational ability. Hence it is impossible for them to examine all possible alternatives open to them. ... Instead they ... choose the 'best' given their limited time, information and computational abilities" (Koutsoyannis 1975, 390). The problem is not so much a scarcity of information but rather an overload of complex information within an uncertain environment and the difficulty in assessing which information is truly relevant.

Conclusion

The modern economic and finance literature has insisted that firms both do and should maximize profits, meaning that managers ought to devote their energies to maximizing the wealth of owners or shareholder value, that is, the value of shares on the stock market. This goal came to be objectified in the form of an aspiration level, the 15 percent rate of return on equity (ROE) that has become the norm on Wall Street and other stock markets (the ROE norm). Although this norm has been achieved under exceptional macroeconomic circumstances, for instance those that arose in North America in the late 1990s, there is no way it could be achieved under normal circumstances.

Ironically, the efforts of financial markets to erase the previous stakeholder view, according to which firms belong to all those involved with the functioning and the activities of the firm, has induced a strengthening of managerial control. The incentives put in place to encourage managers to behave in the sole interest of the owners—the shareholders—have led instead to escalating remunerations for top managers. The pressures exerted by financial markets have encouraged control fraud, as top managers and their accountants cooked the books in their efforts to prop up stock market prices and generate large bonuses. Similar behaviour among bankers led to the subprime financial crisis. Pressures to maximize profits need not achieve the intended result, either at the micro or at the macro levels.

DISCUSSION QUESTIONS

1. Besides profit maximization, what other variables have economists suggested as possible maximands?
2. What critiques have been put forth against the assumption of profit maximization?
3. What responses have been proposed to these critiques?
4. Why do some economists believe that it is impossible to maximize anything?

SUGGESTED READINGS

Galbraith, James K. 2008. *The predator state.* New York: The Free Press.

Goodwin, Neva, Julie A. Nelson, Frank Akerman, and Thomas Weisskopf. 2009. *Microeconomics in context.* 2nd ed. Armonk, NY: M.E. Sharpe.

Hill, Rod, and Anthony Myatt. 2010. *The economics anti-textbook: A critical thinker's guide to microeconomics.* New York: Zed Books.

REFERENCES

Baumol, William J. 1959. *Business behaviour, value and growth.* New York: Macmillan.

Berle, Adolf A., and Gardiner C. Means. 1932. *The modern corporation and private property.* New York: Macmillan.

Boland, Lawrence. 1981. On the futility of criticizing the neoclassical maximization hypothesis. *American Economic Review* 71 (5): 1031–1036.

Cyert, Richard M., and James G. March. 1963. *A behavioral theory of the firm.* Englewood Cliffs, NJ: Prentice Hall.

Dixon, Robert. 1986. Uncertainty, unobstructedness, and power. *Journal of Post Keynesian Economics* 8 (4): 585–590.

Francis, Arthur. 1980. Company objectives, managerial motivations and the behaviour of large firms: An empirical test of the theory of managerial capitalism. *Cambridge Journal of Economics* 4 (4): 349–361.

Galbraith, John Kenneth. 1975. *Economics and the public purpose.* Harmondsworth, UK: Penguin.

Kania, John J., and John R. McKean. 1976. Ownership, control, and the contemporary corporation: A general behavior analysis. *Kyklos* 29 (2): 272–291.

Koplin, H.T. 1963. The profit maximization assumption. *Oxford Economic Papers* (July): 130–139.

Koutsoyiannis, Anna. 1975. *Modern macroeconomics.* London: Macmillan.

Lazonick, William, and Mary O'Sullivan. 2000. Maximizing shareholder value: A new ideology for corporate governance. *Economy and Society* 29 (1): 13–35.

Marris, Robin. 1964. *Theory of managerial capitalism.* London: Macmillan.

Papandreou, A. 1952. Some basic problems in the theory of the firm. In *A survey of contemporary economics,* ed. B.F. Haley, vol. II, 183–219. Homewood, IL: Richard D. Irwin.

Robinson, Joan. 1977. Michal Kalecki on the economics of capitalism. *Oxford Bulletin of Economics and Statistics* 39 (1): 7–17.

Shipley, David D. 1981. Pricing objectives in British manufacturing industry. *Journal of Industrial Economics* 29 (4): 429–443.

Simon, Herbert. 1955. A behavioural model of rational choice. *Quarterly Journal of Economics* 69 (1): 99–118.

Williamson, Oliver E. 1963. Managerial discretion and business behaviour. *American Economic Review* 53 (5): 1032–1057.

Wood, Adrian. 1975. *A theory of profits.* Cambridge: Cambridge University Press.

PART II

Governments and Markets

How Can Markets Fail? Should They Be Regulated?

Editors' Introduction

The questions of whether markets can fail and whether they should be regulated are part of a wider debate involving the nature of the economic system. Some 19th-century economists, like Karl Marx and Friedrich Engels, argued that the market system—capitalism—is doomed to fail because of its inherent contradictions: its class conflict, its "anarchic" character, and its crises. In their view, the collapse of capitalism would lead to a socialist system in which the state took control of the "commanding heights" of the economy and in which core sectors of economic activity were centrally planned. However, the recent debate over regulation versus deregulation takes place within the framework of the market system. That is to say, regulation does not aim to replace markets, but seeks to make them work to the benefit of all members of society. Those who advocate regulation do not necessarily reject the market system. Instead, they recognize that markets do fail and therefore attempt to prevent their harmful impacts on weak participants.

However, other economists, mainly from the neoclassical tradition, believe that there is no need for regulation because unfettered markets work properly to produce the optimal result, or the best social outcome. They argue that market participants engage in exchanges only when they perceive that the transactions are in their best interest. Since everyone is motivated by the pursuit of his or her self-interest, markets appear to be guided by an "invisible hand," and any intervention by an external agency would simply obstruct the functioning of the market mechanism by creating distortions and imposing unnecessary costs. For this reason, they argue that governments should be kept at bay and therefore advocate a *laissez-faire* policy.

The essay by Donald McFetridge outlines the various types of government regulations and the costs they impose on the system. He uses several examples from the Canadian context to argue that regulation has failed because of the rigidities it imposes on firms and industries in terms of competition and innovation. McFetridge argues that when the true costs and consequences of regulation are better known, and competitive alternatives have emerged as a result of changes in technology, regulation becomes unsustainable and deregulation follows. His general conclusion is that the wave of deregulation that began in the 1980s has generally increased productivity and benefited consumers.

On the other hand, Robert Chernomas and Ian Hudson take issue with the idea that self-interest and free competition make firms behave in a manner that is consistent with the wider objectives of social welfare. They give several examples of market failures and argue that such failures are too frequent—and their economic costs too high—to ignore. The examples illustrate the seriousness of the social and economic problems that arise in the absence of regulation. In conclusion, Chernomas and Hudson argue that deregulation has failed to give consumers the expected benefits it was supposed to produce and has instead benefited powerful corporations.

Economic Deregulation: Benefits and Challenges

Donald McFetridge

What Is Economic Regulation?

Businesses are subject to many different types of government regulation. Indeed, it is difficult to think of a business decision that is not constrained in some manner by government regulations. Economists sometimes distinguish between economic regulation on one hand and social and technical regulation on the other. When they speak of economic regulation of business, economists are referring to government regulation of prices, rates of return, entry, exit, and the terms, nature, and quality of service that businesses are permitted to offer. Most of the examples of regulation discussed here refer to economic regulation.

The term "social regulation of business" is often used to refer to health, safety, and environmental regulation. Technical regulation refers to the adoption of common technical standards so that products can be used interchangeably (for example, so that electrical appliances can use the same wall plug). Some types of regulation do not fit neatly into the "economic," "social," or "technical" boxes. It is important to understand, however, that all regulations are economic in the sense that they have both direct and indirect economic costs and benefits. Defining a regulation as "social" or "technical" does not mean that it should not be subject to economic analysis of its costs and benefits.

A reasonable public policy goal is for governments to impose only regulations yielding economic benefits that exceed costs. While it might seem self-evident that government regulations should yield a net economic benefit, this is not always the case (Weimer and Vining 2005, 156–191). Government regulations are the result of a political process that is often more concerned with transferring wealth than creating it. This is called rent-seeking. Rent-seeking enriches one group in society at the expense of others and reduces the size of the economic pie rather than increasing it. It is a source of market failure rather than a remedy for it. In some cases, government regulation is redundant in that it attempts to remedy a perceived market failure that market participants themselves have already addressed (see for example, Cheung 1973 and Coase 1974). In other cases, government regulation remedies an actual market failure but the benefits of doing so are not commensurate with the direct and indirect costs of the regulations involved.

Much of the traditional economic regulation of business is intended to remedy problems arising from natural monopoly. A natural monopoly occurs when the advantages of large-scale production (economies of scale) are such that production is most efficient when there is either only one firm in the market or one firm dominates the market. In this case, the traditional view has been that price or rate of return regulation allows the realization of economies of large-scale production while protecting customers from monopoly or dominant firm pricing. There have, however, been many instances in which economic regulation has been imposed on industries that are not natural monopolies.

Costs of Economic Regulation

Government regulation of business has both direct and indirect costs. The direct costs of regulation are compliance and enforcement costs. Government regulation has numerous indirect costs. These include:

- Reducing competition or potential competition;
- Inducing wasteful competition;
- Reducing incentives to operate efficiently or to innovate;
- Facilitating market distorting cross-subsidization.

Economic regulation reduces competition by restricting the entry of new competitors into regulated markets, setting price floors or otherwise preventing price competition in regulated industries, and by preventing interindustry competition. By restricting price competition, economic regulation also induces wasteful non-price competition among regulated firms. Customers derive some benefit from this type of competition but it is less than they would get from simply paying a lower price.

Economic regulation reduces the incentive of regulated firms to operate efficiently or to innovate. It has been found that countries with less extensive and less intrusive economic regulation have higher rates of productivity growth and adjust more rapidly to economic shocks than countries with more heavily regulated markets (Conway et al. 2006).

Traditional economic regulation allows a firm to earn enough revenue to cover its costs plus a "fair" return on its investment. Rate of return regulation is costly in itself. It is often characterized by lengthy disputes about what the rate base (the amount a regulated firm has invested in its operations) is, how costs should be measured, and what a fair rate of return is. Firms subject to rate of return regulation also have little or no incentive to control their operating costs or to introduce innovations that reduce cost or improve service. If operating costs go up, the regulator allows firms to raise their prices until revenues are sufficient to cover them while any cost savings must be given back in the form of price reductions.

Cross-subsidization is the use of excess profits earned on one product to cover losses on another. A cross-subsidized product does not yield enough revenue to cover its costs. Normally, a profit-maximizing firm would not offer a loss-making product or product line because that reduces its overall profits. Cross-subsidization is common, however, in regulated markets.

Regulatory cross-subsidization typically involves protecting a regulated industry from competition and allowing the firms in it to charge supra-competitive prices for some products so that they earn excess profits that can then be used to subsidize loss-making services specified by the regulator. Regulatory cross-subsidization is costly and inefficient because it distorts market price signals. Supra-competitive prices are charged for some products while resources are diverted to supply other products that cost more to supply than their users are willing to pay for them.

Regulatory cross-subsidization has often been described as relying on "hidden taxes." This makes it a politically attractive way of catering to special interest groups. Although many of the activities that regulators cross-subsidize might be deemed worthy social goals by voters if they were consulted, it is usually neither fair nor efficient to force some or all of the customers of the regulated firms involved to pay for them.

Economic Deregulation

It is now widely recognized that economic regulation rarely yields net economic benefits and that even very imperfect competition is preferable to regulation. This has led some analysts to conclude that economic deregulation should be the default option for public policy if the market concerned isn't unavoidably dominated or monopolized by a single firm (Telecommunications Policy Review Panel 2006, 3-11–3-12).

The major instances of economic deregulation, some of which are described below, have usually involved the elimination of rate of return or price regulation and restrictions on entry and exit. These industries continue to be subject to a myriad of other government technical and social regulations. Many of these regulations would also fail a cost-benefit test and there are ongoing efforts to "cut red tape" and "regulate smarter" (External Advisory Committee on Smart Regulation 2004).

Traditional economic regulation often imposed two tests on potential entrants. One was a "fit, willing, and able" test. The other was a "public convenience and necessity" test. The fitness test assessed the competence of the business concerned to offer a proposed service. The public convenience and necessity test assessed whether there was a demand for the services proposed by the new entrant. With deregulation, the fitness test remains in place whereas the public convenience and necessity test is either limited in its application or has been eliminated entirely. The rationale is that market participants are better judges of whether there is a market for their products, and customers are better judges of the products they prefer than government regulators are.

The process of economic deregulation has often been very slow. Regulators are often reluctant to give up their ability to "micromanage" the industries over which they have jurisdiction. The process of deregulation sometimes stalls at the stage of "managed competition" rather than open competition. Regulators often retain the power to intervene when they think prices are either "too high" or "too low." They do this in part to protect new competitors from predatory pricing, a role that they are poorly equipped to play (Iacobucci and Trebilcock 2007). After they finally do stop intervening in this manner, regulatory agencies may neverthe-less continue to impose new "social" obligations on firms under their jurisdiction (for an example, see Discussion Question 2 at the end of this essay).

Drivers of Economic Deregulation

Deregulation occurs for a variety of reasons. These include:

- the emergence of competitive alternatives to the product of a regulated industry;
- changes in technology that reduce economies of scale so that a regulated industry is no longer a natural monopoly;
- new learning about the consequences of government regulation and changes in interest group pressures.

THE EMERGENCE OF COMPETITIVE ALTERNATIVES

Sometimes, the emergence of competitive alternatives renders unsustainable a regulatory regime that raises prices and cross-subsidizes uneconomic services. For example, one of the factors leading to the deregulation of long-distance telephone rates in Canada was that major customers were bypassing Canada's high-priced, regulated system by routing their calls through the United States. In turn, the advent of competition in the long-distance market made the continued cross-subsidization of local telephone service from excess long-distance profits impos-sible (Telecommunications Policy Review Panel 2006, 3–7).

Another example of new competitive alternatives undermining an existing regulatory regime is the threat posed by competition from the Internet ("new media") to both Canadian content regulations imposed by the regulator (the Can-adian Radio-television and Telecommunications Commission [CRTC]) on broad-casters and the means the CRTC now uses to cross-subsidize the production of

Canadian content. Some lobby groups advocate that the CRTC impose similar Canadian content restrictions on the Internet. The question is how the CRTC would go about preventing Canadians from visiting foreign websites and downloading foreign videos, music, or books, or watching foreign videos on YouTube. Others argue that subsidies to the production of Canadian content may have to be financed by explicit and more broadly based taxes in the future (Hunter et al. 2010).

Elimination of Natural Monopoly by Technological Change or Diffusion

Natural monopolies may be deregulated when technological changes make competition possible. Some argue that, generally, as technologies mature, competition becomes possible (Shepherd 1991, 348–350). In other cases, it is the emergence of new technologies that makes competition possible, for example, wireless, fibre optics, and Internet Protocol in the telecommunications industry, which has resulted in the elimination of at least some aspects of economic regulation of telecommunications markets in most developed countries.

In some industries, competition is possible at some stages of production but not others. In that case, it may be feasible to separate out the potentially competitive stages of production and deregulate them while continuing to regulate the natural monopoly stages of production. This is called vertical separation or vertical de-integration. Examples of this are discussed below in connection with the deregulation of the railway and electric power industries.

Effects of Shifts in the Balance of Power Among Special Interests

Industries that have been subject to special-interest regulation may be deregulated as a result of shifts in the balance of power between contending political interest groups. This could be the result of new information on the magnitude and incidence of the costs and benefits of a particular regulatory regime. For example, research by economists showed that airline price and entry regulation in the United States resulted in higher fares and that the airlines dissipated the resulting excess profits in various forms of non-price competition. This led to congressional hearings and ultimately to deregulation legislation in 1978 (Joskow 2005).

Special interests may stop lobbying for regulation if the regulator can no longer guarantee them excess profits. Similarly, regulatory cross-subsidization may collapse when it is no longer possible for the regulator to guarantee the excess profits required to finance cross-subsidies. Railway regulation reduced competition among railways in the United States, but as truck competition grew stronger, rail regulation no longer enhanced railway profitability and the railways stopped supporting it. In Canada, truck competition reduced railway profitability and made it impossible for regulators to continue to force railways to use part of their profits to cross-subsidize uneconomic passenger services and branch lines.

Economic deregulation of telecommunications, airlines, railways, and trucking came later in Canada than in the United States. Observing the benefits realized in the United States may have provided additional impetus to the deregulation movement in Canada. This may have been reinforced in some cases by Canadian customers migrating to lower-priced, deregulated alternatives in the United States.

Some Examples of Economic Deregulation

AIRLINES

The elimination of economic regulation of passenger airlines in the United States was rapidly phased in, beginning with the passage of the *Airline Deregulation Act* of 1978. This gave airlines the freedom to set fares and to serve any domestic route. The benefits of this deregulation included lower fares and better utilization of capacity (higher load factors) and innovation in the form of discount carriers and hub and spoke operations. One study estimated the annual benefits to passengers to be in the order of $20 billion (Morrison and Winston 2000). Greater benefits would have been realized except for capacity limitations at airports and in air navigation, both of which remain under government control.

Airlines were formally deregulated in Canada in 1988, although regulation was retained in the north until 1996. Deregulation freed up entry by domestically owned airlines into domestic routes by eliminating the public convenience and necessity test. Foreign-owned airlines continue to be barred from serving domestic routes.

Deregulation resulted in increased operating efficiency and benefits to passengers in the form of lower fares, although bankruptcies and mergers among carriers resulted in a market that was dominated at times by one carrier. Competition could be increased by allowing foreign-owned airlines to serve domestic routes, a practice called cabotage. Instead, the federal government has chosen to protect domestic airlines on domestic routes and to intervene sporadically in instances in which the regulator (the Canadian Transportation Agency [CTA]) deems fares to be either too low or too high. Despite some liberalization under bilateral "Open Skies" agreements with other countries, competitive entry on international and transborder routes remains restricted.

RAILWAYS

In Britain, Australia, and some European countries, deregulation has taken the form of opening up the government-owned monopoly rail infrastructure to competing operating companies. In both Canada and the United States, regulatory reform has focused on increasing the extent to which existing vertically integrated railways compete with each other (intra-modal competition) and with other modes of transport (inter-modal competition).

In the United States, economic deregulation occurred in 1980. It gave the railways freedom to enter and exit markets and to set rates, with some ceilings to protect shippers that were captive to a single railway. The results were higher productivity, lower freight rates, and innovation in the form of increased inter-modal capabilities. Railways stopped losing market share to trucks as well. Despite continuing concerns among captive shippers, deregulation has been described in general as being a "win–win" for shippers and railways (Grimm and Winston 2000).

In Canada, the *National Transportation Act*, which came into effect in January, 1988, deregulated the two major railways (Canadian National and Canadian Pacific), enabling them to set freight rates (except for grain). The Act attempted to encourage intra-modal competition by eliminating the railways' previous ability to set rates jointly and by allowing for confidential contracts between shippers and railways.

To protect captive customers, the Act contained measures that increased the access of these customers to competing railways and also provided for arbitration of freight rate disputes. The access provisions allow captive shippers to seek a regulated rate at which they can ship their goods to an interchange point with the nearest competing railway, and also allow a railway to apply to the regulator (the CTA) for the right to operate on the track of another railway (running rights).

These access provisions, especially running rights, have not been widely used. Debate continues regarding the most effective means of providing captive shippers access to competition.

The intensity of intra-modal competition has also been increased as a result of the privatization of Canadian National Railway in 1995. Its shares are now publicly traded and widely held. Privatization turned a moribund government enterprise into one of the most efficient railways in North America, generating efficiency gains of as much as $15 billion (Boardman et al. 2009).

The 1996 *Canada Transportation Act* eased the regulatory restrictions on the disposal of uneconomic branch lines. This has resulted in greater utilization of remaining capacity (increased traffic density) and increased productivity.

The general assessment of this sequence of regulatory changes is that it has resulted in a more competitive and more efficient railway industry in Canada. Although there are still complaints from captive shippers, few favour a return to the old regulatory regime (Canada Transportation Act Review Panel 2001, 39–57).

TELECOMMUNICATIONS

There are many different types of telecommunications services and thus many different telecommunications services markets. Most are well on their way to economic deregulation and some are fully deregulated, but the process has been slow.

The process of deregulation has often begun by allowing new entrants to compete with the regulated incumbent monopoly telecommunications carrier. Some of these competitors, called facilities-based competitors, used their own equipment and infrastructure. Other competitors, called resellers, purchased access to the facilities of the incumbent, which they used to provide telecommunications service to business and residential customers. Though facing competition, the incumbent typically remained subject to maximum and minimum retail price regulation as well as regulation of the wholesale or access prices it charged resellers. The rationale was that this regulation was required to prevent the incumbent from setting retail prices too high (hurting consumers) or too low (hurting its competitors). For this reason, the intermediate stage was called "managed" or "regulated" competition. When it was satisfied that competition was sufficiently well-established, the regulator (the CRTC in Canada) stopped regulating the incumbent's prices. This is called regulatory forbearance.

In the United States, the process of deregulation of telecommunications began with a 1984 antitrust judgement that broke up the incumbent monopoly telephone company, American Telephone and Telegraph (AT&T) into seven regional Bell operating companies (RBOCS or "Baby Bells"), leaving the remainder of AT&T to continue to compete in the market for long-distance service. The RBOCs were not allowed to compete in the long-distance market and state regulators controlled rates and limited competitive entry into markets for local telephone service. Dissatisfaction with the slow progress toward deregulation led to federal legislation in 1996, which opened up markets for local telephone service to competition and allowed the RBOCs to compete in the long-distance market.

In Canada, the market for long-distance telephone services was opened up to competition from resellers in 1990 and to facilities-based competition in 1992. Long-distance rates were deregulated in 1998. Pricing of retail Internet access was deregulated in 1997 for telephone companies and in 1998 for cable companies.

Mobile wireless telephone service has never been subject to price or rate of return regulation in Canada. Prior to 1996, however, the radio frequency spectrum required for the transmission of wireless signals was assigned to carriers by the federal government on the basis of bureaucratic and political assessments of the merits of their requests. Beginning in 1996, spectrum has been auctioned by the government to the highest qualified bidder. This increased the likelihood that the spectrum would be put to its highest valued use. In its 2008 wireless spectrum auction, however, the government set aside 40 percent of the spectrum for new entrants in the hope that this would increase the number of facilities-based wireless carriers competing in Canada.

The most recent example of regulatory forbearance by the CRTC involved local telephone service. Local telephone service was opened up to competition effective January 1, 1998. At that time the CRTC switched from rate of return regulation to price-cap regulation of incumbent local telephone service providers (such as Bell and Telus).[1] There is now competition from cable (Voice over Internet Protocol [VoIP]) and wireless in most areas of the country. The CRTC has eliminated (forborne) price-cap regulation of local residential and business telephone service in geographic areas (called local exchanges) in which it deems this competition to be strong enough. By mid-2009, economic regulation of 77 percent of residential lines and 68 percent of the business lines in the country had been forborne (Canadian Radio-television and Telecommunications Commission 2009, 41).

Electric Power

In much of the world (including Ontario and Alberta in Canada), the electric power industry has been separated into a generation industry that is not subject to economic regulation and regulated transmission and distribution utilities. In Ontario, this partially deregulated market replaced Ontario Hydro, a vertically integrated, government-owned monopoly.

Deregulation of the electric power industry has meant that, subject to compliance with environmental, health and safety, and related regulations, a firm can build a natural gas-fired or hydro-generating station or a wind farm, produce electric power, and sell it into the transmission grid at a price that is determined in a competitive wholesale market. This market is generally operated by a non-profit market operator often referred to as the "independent system operator" or "ISO." The transmission grid may be government-owned or investor-owned and subject to rate regulation.

The hourly prices in the competitive wholesale market reflect the marginal cost of electricity generation. This price signal is available for both consumers and generators to see. In high-demand periods, generators with higher marginal costs are called to market (dispatched) and the market price is higher. In low-demand periods, only the lower-cost generators are needed and the wholesale price is lower. Thus, the competitive market makes efficient use of existing generating capacity. In addition, the competitive, investor-owned electric power generators have performed better (both with respect to operating efficiency and investment decisions) than the government-owned monopolies they replaced (Fabrizio et al. 2007).

Markets for electric power differ from markets for other goods and services. Demand is highly inelastic (insensitive to price changes) in the short term and electric power cannot readily be stored. As a consequence, there can be price spikes in times of high demand, which has often resulted in various forms of government intervention to suppress them. This can have two adverse effects. It blunts the incentive for consumers to conserve and it leaves generators with insufficient incentive to invest in new capacity. This has been the case in Ontario where the government has felt it necessary to offer price guarantees to new entrants into generation and to set a regulated retail price to consumers that is largely detached from variations in the wholesale price.

In jurisdictions that do not suppress market price signals, the advent of smart meters will expose consumers to the true cost of electric power on an hour by hour basis and enable them to shift their consumption to periods in which generation costs are lower.

Conclusions

Economic deregulation has generally increased productivity and benefited consumers, but progress has not been smooth and serious issues remain. These include: (1) determining the prices that resellers or, more generally, non-integrated competitors, should pay for access to the facilities (called essential facilities) they require to compete; and (2) finding a substitute for regulatory cross-subsidization as a means of achieving social goals. The industries that have been subject to economic deregulation are highly visible and interest group pressures for various forms of regulatory intervention (including reregulation) will continue (Waters and Stanbury 1999).

Government regulation that is truly in the public interest should help the market to allocate resources more efficiently. Proponents of government regulation should answer three questions:

- Is there a market failure?
- Is government regulation the best remedy for this market failure?
- Do the benefits of eliminating this market failure exceed the direct and indirect cost of regulation?

In the increasingly rare instances in which it might be required, economic regulation of an industry should adopt the following principles:

- Rely on the forces of competition and potential competition wherever possible.
- Do not attempt to manage competition or protect individual competitors.
- Allow firms flexibility in achieving regulatory objectives.

NOTE

1. Price-cap regulation imposes a ceiling on the annual rate at which a firm can increase the average price of a "basket" of its products. The allowed annual rate of increase can be negative, implying annual price reductions. Price-cap regulation is also called incentive regulation because, unlike rate of return regulation, it allows a regulated firm to keep any profits it earns when it reduces its costs below the price cap. Although a properly designed price-cap regime provides an incentive for innovation and efficiency, it remains costly and complex to administer. For a discussion of price caps and other forms of incentive regulation, see Lyon (1994).

DISCUSSION QUESTIONS

1. Most Canadian cities restrict the number of taxi cab licences they issue. As a consequence, these licences have a scarcity value in excess of $100,000 in some cities. Is this restriction of entry of new competitors an example of successful rent-seeking by the holders of taxi licences or is it intended to remedy a market failure? If it is the latter, what is the nature of this market failure and are there remedies other than the restriction of entry?

2. The Canadian Transportation Agency has ruled that obese and disabled persons requiring two seats on a passenger airliner should only have to pay for one seat and the Supreme Court of Canada upheld that decision. If an obese or disabled person does not pay for their second seat (even if they have the means to do so), who should pay (other airline passengers? airline shareholders? taxpayers at large?) and how should this be determined?

3. Some Canadian provinces restrict competition among gasoline stations by setting minimum retail prices or margins. For example, Nova Scotia sets a minimum retail markup of 4¢/litre. The expressed intent of this regulation is to stabilize the retail price of gasoline and to allow stations to earn sufficient profits to remain in the market. What are the likely effects of this type of regulation on: (a) the price of gasoline, (b) the quality of retail service, and (c) the efficiency of the retail distribution network?

SUGGESTED READINGS

Brander, James. 2000. *Government policy toward business.* 3rd ed. Toronto: Wiley.
Iacobucci, Edward, Michael Trebilcock, and Ralph Winter. 2006. The Canadian experience with deregulation. *University of Toronto Law Journal* 56: 1–74.
Weidenbaum, Murray. 2004. *Business and government in the global marketplace.* 7th ed. Upper Saddle River, NJ: Pearson Prentice Hall.

REFERENCES

Boardman, Anthony, Claude Laurin, Mark Moore, and Aidan Vining. 2009. A cost-benefit analysis of the privatization of Canadian National Railway. *Canadian Public Policy* 35 (March): 59–83.

Canada Transportation Act Review Panel. 2001. *Vision and balance: Report of the Canada Transportation Act Review Panel.* Ottawa: Minister of Public Works and Government Services Canada. http://www.reviewcta-examenltc.gc.ca/ english/pages/final/pdfe.htm

Canadian Radio-television and Telecommunications Commission (CRTC). 2009. *Communications Monitoring Report 2009.* http://www.crtc.gc.ca/eng/publications/ reports/policymonitoring/2009/2009MonitoringReportFinalEn.pdf.

Cheung, Steven. 1973. The fable of the bees. *Journal of Law and Economics* 16: 11–33.

Coase, Ronald. 1974. The lighthouse in economics. *Journal of Law and Economics* 17: 357–376.

Conway, Paul, Donato de Rosa, Giuseppe Nicoletti, and Faye Steiner. 2006. *Product market regulation and productivity convergence.* OECD Economic Studies No. 43, 2006/2.

External Advisory Committee on Smart Regulation. 2004. *Smart regulation: A regulatory strategy for Canada* (September). http://dsp-psd.pwgsc.gc.ca/ Collection/CP22-78-2004E.pdf.

Fabrizio, Kira, Nancy Rose, and Catherine Wolfram. 2007. Do markets reduce costs? Assessing the impact of regulatory restructuring on U.S. electric generation efficiency. *American Economic Review* 97 (September): 1250–1277.

Grimm, Curtis, and Clifford Winston. 2000. Competition in the deregulated railroad industry: Sources, effects and policy issues. In *Deregulation of network industries,* eds. Sam Peltzman and Clifford Morrison, 41–71. Washington, DC: AEI Brookings Joint Center for Regulatory Studies.

Hunter, Lawson, Edward Iacobucci, and Michael Trebilcock. 2010. *Scrambled signals: Canadian content policy in a world of technological abundance.* C.D. Howe Institute Commentary No. 301 (January). Toronto: C.D. Howe Institute.

Iacobucci, Edward, and Michael Trebilcock. 2007. The design of regulatory institutions for the Canadian telecommunications sector. *Canadian Public Policy* 33 (June): 127–146.

Joskow, Paul. 2005. Regulation and deregulation after 25 years: Lessons learned for research in industrial organization. *Review of Industrial Organization* 26: 169–193.

Lyon, Thomas. 1994. Incentive regulation in theory and practice. In *Incentive regulation for public utilities,* ed. Michael Crew, 1–26. Boston: Kluwer Academic.

Morrison, Steven, and Clifford Winston. 2000. The remaining role for government policy in the deregulated airline industry. In *Deregulation of network industries*, eds. Sam Peltzman and Clifford Morrison, 1–40. Washington, DC: AEI Brookings Joint Center for Regulatory Studies.

Shepherd, William. 1991. *Public policies toward business.* 8th ed. Homewood, IL: Richard D. Irwin.

Telecommunications Policy Review Panel. 2006. *Final report 2006.* http://www.telecomreview.ca/eic/site/tprp-gecrt.nsf/eng/rx00101.html.

Viscusi, W. Kip, Joseph Harrington, and John Vernon. 2005. *Economics of regulation and antitrust.* 4th ed. Cambridge: MIT Press.

Waters, W.G., and W.T. Stanbury. 1999. Deregulation, pressures for re-regulation and regulatory shifts: The case of telecommunications and transportation. In *Changing the rules: Canadian regulatory regimes and institutions,* eds. G. Bruce Doern, Margaret Hill, Michael Prince, and Richard Schultz., 143–173. Toronto: University of Toronto Press.

Weimer, David, and Aidan Vining. 2005. *Policy analysis: Concepts and practice.* 4th ed. Upper Saddle River, NJ: Pearson Prentice Hall.

Market Failure: The Regulatory Solution and the Costs of Deregulation

Robert Chernomas and Ian Hudson

Introduction

Free-market economists argue that competition among firms will protect people from costly, dangerous, unhealthy, or shoddy commodities because firms need to produce quality fare at attractive prices to attract customers. Firms are not benevolent organizations. They are not particularly interested in the well-being of their customers except insofar as it can help them earn a profit. Fortunately, according to the opponents of government intervention, the profit motive can protect consumers and automatically lead to a socially desirable relationship between producers and consumers. As Adam Smith so memorably stated, it is not from the benevolence of the butcher that you get your meat, but from appealing to his self-interest (Smith, 1976, 26–27). According to Smith and the economists who claim his legacy, even if he abhors you, it is in the butcher's best interest to provide quality cuts of meat at a reasonable price, because that is how customers are attracted and maintained in a competitive environment. Similarly, it would be business suicide to offer up meat that made customers sick, because word would soon get around and the butcher would have no more clients. Thus, driven by competition and self-interest, firms must be innovative, safety-conscious, quality-focused, price-minimizing organizations. Although there will always be a very few underhanded firms that attempt to mislead the public or cut corners on safety, opponents of government intervention argue that the market works to minimize this sort of behaviour, both because firms will prosper by protecting their customers and because firms that do not do so will soon find themselves out of business. If regulation is largely unnecessary in a functioning market economy, then the costs it imposes on firms must inevitably be wasteful.

History has not been kind to this free-market position. The problem with this theory is that it rests on a number of assumptions that are frequently violated, resulting in what are called "market failures." Over the years, economists have identified numerous types of these failures, any one of which will prevent the market from fulfilling its supposedly beneficial role. Monopoly power exists when there are too few firms in the market to create proper competition. Information asymmetry occurs when selling firms have more knowledge than the consumer, rendering the purchaser unable to properly assess the quality of the good or service being exchanged. Externalities are present if a third party is positively or negatively affected by the production or consumption of a product. Allowing income to be determined by the market can create undesirable levels of inequality in society. Public goods, like street lamps and a clean environment, benefit everyone simultaneously rather than just one person at a time (as would be the case with a pair of pants), creating an incentive for people to "free ride" on others by not paying for the public good but still getting to enjoy it. Markets also fail when one party can exercise power over another—a common occurrence when massive corporations dominate the economy and the political system that is supposed to be overseeing it.

These failures occur with a frequency that free-market advocates should find disturbing. From the many sources of market failure and the numerous examples that could be easily found in each category, we will focus on a few cases. The problems of political and economic power will be illustrated with the catastrophic deregulation of the banking industry, although corporate power also plays a central role in the cancer and drug industry cases. Cancer and innovation will highlight the problems of positive and negative externalities. Finally, the drug industry will demonstrate how information asymmetry can create deadly results in the free market. The examples in this chapter are not small mishaps caused by a few rogue firms affecting a tiny fraction of the citizenry but system-wide breakdowns causing enormous economic loss.

Too Big to Fail: Banking

One of the main lessons from the Great Depression was that banking failure is likely to cause widespread economic collapse. In the run-up to the 1929 failure, overly optimistic banks had engaged in risky investments during what appeared to be good economic times. When these investments failed, the banks went under, curtailing the availability of loans and swallowing many people's hard-earned life savings. This greatly exacerbated the economic crisis of the 1930s. In an effort to avoid a repeat of this collapse, the United States passed the *Glass-Steagall Act* (or *Banking Act*) of 1933, which prevented commercial banks that collected deposits and made loans from also dealing in securities. The *Banking Act* was designed to prevent banks from undertaking speculative investments that might cause a banking collapse, in a deliberate attempt to create a very conservative industry. The logic behind this move was that banks were so crucial to the smooth functioning of the economy that, should they fail, the onus would be on the government to bail them out to avoid a repeat of the Great Depression.

The banking industry was never happy with the legislated separation of commercial banking and investment. In the 25 years between 1975 and 1999, the banking industry unsuccessfully attempted 12 times to get Glass-Steagall overturned (Barth et al. 2000). The industry lobby finally paid off in 1999, when the Act was repealed and replaced with the *Gramm-Leach-Blilely Act* (GLBA). The general thrust of the GLBA was to allow banks to engage in a wider range of activities, including the previously forbidden roles of selling securities and insurance. It also eliminated many federal and state restrictions on affiliations between banks and investment and insurance firms. The new regulations were enacted in spite of a prescient warning by the Congressional Research Service: "Securities activities can be risky, leading to enormous losses. Such losses could threaten the integrity of deposits. In turn, the Government insures deposits and could be required to pay large sums if depository institutions were to collapse as the result of securities losses" (Jackson 1987, CRS-3).

The elimination of Glass-Steagall was not the result of a groundswell of popular anger against unjust and archaic legislation. The pressure for regulatory change came directly from the banking and finance industry, which could count on some sympathetic figures in high-profile places when pressing its case for deregulation. The former chairman of the Federal Reserve, Alan Greenspan, had been a director of investment giant J.P. Morgan. The secretary of the treasury under the Clinton presidency from 1995 to 1999, Robert Rubin, was a former co-chair of Goldman Sachs, a securities firm. Perhaps more tellingly, only days after the Clinton administration (and his treasury department) agreed to support the GBLA, Rubin took one of the top jobs at Citigroup, where he went on to support its increasing exposure in the debt market.

To grease the political wheels before the 1999 passage of GLBA, the banking and finance industry spent heavily on donations and lobbyists. Over the two-year period of 1997 and 1998, the finance, insurance, and real estate sector, known as FIRE, spent over $200 million on lobbying and $150 million on political contributions (PBS 2008). The financial push paid off when the GBLA finally received approval from the House, the Senate, and President Clinton.

Despite the promises of free-market advocates and the banking industry that regulation was unnecessary, the result of the deregulation was exactly what the *Glass-Steagall Act* was designed to prevent. Banks made risky investments in fancy financial instruments that depended on the overheated US housing market. When the housing market collapsed, so did the banks, forcing the government to spend trillions of dollars of taxpayers' money to prop up the financial sector to avoid an even worse economic crisis.

Negative Externalities: Cancer

A negative externality exists when a third party (neither the producer nor the consumer) is adversely affected by an economic activity. The most commonly cited negative externality is pollution, because its damage is felt by those who do not produce or consume the product. Negative externalities create a cost to society that is over and above the private cost to the company.

One particularly deadly example of the externality problem is the increase in cancer in modern society. It is hard to imagine someone living in Canada today who has not lost someone important to them from cancer. One hundred years ago, knowing anyone who had cancer would have been unusual. Cancer now kills 27 percent of men and 23 percent of women in Canada (Canadian Cancer Society 2003, 56). The increased incidence of cancer is not due primarily to our increased longevity. From 1970 to 1998, after controlling for aging, the incidence of cancer in Canada increased by 35 percent for men and 27 percent for women (Nagnur et al. 1987). What happened?

The World Health Organization estimates that 20 percent of cancers are genetic in origin and that 80 percent are environmentally based. Each year, medium- and large-sized Canadian companies are required to report emissions of carcinogens to the National Pollutant Release Inventory (NPRI). In 2001, Canadian industries reported the release of 18,455,237 kilograms of known carcinogens (cancer-causing agents) into our air, soil, and water (Pollution Watch 2005). In the neutral language of economics, the increased cancer rates caused by firms dumping carcinogens into the environment are a negative externality.

Cancer is primarily a result, not of individual lifestyle choices, but of involuntary exposure to carcinogens at work, in the environment, and at home. This is demonstrated by a recent study led by researchers at the Mount Sinai School of Medicine in New York, in collaboration with the Environmental Working Group and Commonweal. Nine volunteers, including PBS journalist Bill Moyers, were tested for the presence of chemicals, pollutants, and pesticides in their blood and urine. None of the volunteers worked with chemicals on the job, yet their bodies contained an average of 91 compounds, most of which did not exist 75 years ago. Each of the nine subjects carried, on average, 53 chemicals linked to cancer in humans or animals (Environmental Working Group 2003).

The increased incidence of cancer creates a case for some form of regulation that would reduce the number of carcinogens to which the population is unknowingly exposed. The problem with this seemingly rational solution is that it shifts the costs from the public (in the form of health-care costs and illness) to the private realm (in the form of reducing emissions or finding alternative production practices). Individual businesses, which compete with other capitalists in other countries, must be preoccupied with minimizing their costs, which means avoiding this kind of regulated solution.

Dr. Samuel Epstein, author of *The Politics of Cancer Revisited*, gave a very clear example of how this system works in a 1999 speech in Hamilton:

> I remember having got DDT off the market in 1969 as a key expert against USDA and then proceeded to work with the EPA (Environmental Protection Agency) in getting its replacement, chlordane … off the market. But that took eighteen months of work in which the industry hired its consultants and so called experts from all over the world and you're faced with a barrier of 20 or 30 people and a barrier of attorneys going at you day and night. But I remember one evening … sitting and having a drink with the chief Shell attorney, and I said, "You know, why in the devil do you proceed with this nonsense because you know you're going to lose?" He said, "My dear chap, you really don't know what you're talking about. Let me explain the realities to you." He said, "Do you know how much it costs for us to litigate and play games with you in court per annum?" I said no, and he said, "Well, about two and a half million, bringing everybody and all our experts to court … ." He said, "Do you know how much money we make by selling our product [the pesticide chlordane] while we're in court with you? About $65 million. It's time you grew up, Sam." (Quoted in Canadian Labour Congress 2005.)

Positive Externalities: Innovation

The government can't pick winners, but losers pick government.
Canadian Deputy Industry Minister V. Peter Harder,
cited in *The New York Times*, August 28, 2001

As the name implies, positive externalities occur when a third party benefits from an economic activity. In this case, society benefits more than the producer or consumer, so the product will be "underproduced" in the free market because the private producer cannot capture all of the benefits when it sells its product. This creates a case for government regulation to foster industries that feature positive externalities, contradicting free-market claims that government should let the market determine the survival of firms, such as the one at the beginning of this section. One of the most important positive externalities is scientific research.

What do maxipads, Deet bug repellent, permanent-press cotton, shrink-proof wool, the soybean ink used in *USA Today*, disposable diapers, frozen foods, and lactose-free milk have in common? None of them were invented by the corporations that currently profit from them. These and many other products we associate with corporate brands were actually invented by the Agricultural Research Service of the US government (Rawe 2004, 68). On the off chance that the previous list of food, cloths, and dyes was not suitably impressive, US federal funding was also directly responsible for the cross-country railroad, the exploration of space, atomic energy, the Internet, the Global Positioning System (GPS), lasers, computers, magnetic resonance imaging (MRI), teflon and other advanced materials and composites, communications satellites, jet aircraft, microwave ovens, solar-electric cells, modems, semiconductors, storm windows, genetic medicine, and biotechnology (Office of Science and Technology Policy 2000).

We are told that we owe our present affluent lifestyles to the innovations in both production techniques and products brought about by the dynamism of private business and that competitive, profit-maximizing firms need to innovate continuously if they are to lower costs and provide new products to their customers. While this is undeniably true, what is often neglected in this standard tale is the crucial role played by the state in our dynamic economy. The preceding examples are only a few of the countless major inventions brought to you, not by the benefits of profit-maximizing and competitiveness, but by the public ownership of the state. As we shall see, this is no coincidence. There are crucial reasons why profit-maximizing firms will not invest sufficiently in many areas of research and development (*R&D*), necessitating state intervention. The idea that the private sector is dynamic and innovative whereas the state sector is stagnant and moribund does not stand up to either good economic theory or historical evidence.

A major theme in much of Lester Thurow's work has been the need to recognize capitalism's failure to make long-term investments (Thurow 1999, 57). In *The Future of Capitalism* (1996), he argues that in addition to the problem of the differential between private and social return, private firms will not invest in R&D because they tend to have short-term time horizons. Corporations that must maintain shareholders' rates of return in a competitive environment cannot afford to undertake costly current investments for long-run payoffs. Since the return to basic, as opposed to applied, science is both longer term and more uncertain, it is extremely unlikely that private firms could afford to undertake this type of research. Because government tends to be less concerned with who reaps the benefits from investments in R&D and is not focused on its own profits, it plays an essential role in long-term investment in capitalist economies.

According to Thurow, the claim that innovation occurs due to intense competition in a profit-maximizing corporate system is very misleading. In fact, he argues that competition limits firms' willingness to engage in basic research. The private sector will only engage in this type of long-run, uncertain activity when shielded in some manner from competitors. "The only private labs that have ever focused on anything other than short-run results are those such as Bell Labs and the IBM labs that were run by quasi-monopolies" (Thurow 1996, 291). Tellingly, since AT&T and IBM have been forced into a more competitive environment, both have ended their commitment to more basic, longer-term research.

The World Economic Forum (WEF) is a Geneva-based foundation whose annual meeting of chief executives and political leaders, held in Davos, Switzerland, is a gathering of the truly rich and powerful. The WEF is a think tank funded by 1,000 corporations. Member companies must have annual revenues of more than $1 billion. Every year the WEF produces its Global Competitiveness Report, which ranks the competitiveness of the world's economies. It is the product of work by, among others, Harvard professors such as Michael Porter and Jeffrey Sachs.

The top-ten countries of World Economic Forum Growth Competitiveness Index Rankings for 2005 in rank order are: United States, Finland, Sweden, Denmark, Taiwan, Singapore, Iceland, Switzerland, Norway, Australia, Netherlands, Japan, United Kingdom, Canada, Germany (Lopez-Carlos et al. 2006). The countries that dominate the top-ten list are the so-called Nordic countries, which deliberately eschew the free-market model in favour of an active government. It seems the quality of their public institutions, with their high taxes, strict regulatory framework, and high degree of technological innovation create "excellent macroeconomic management overall," according to Augusto Lopez-Carlos (2005), chief economist at the WEF:

> Integrity and efficiency in the use of public resources means there is money for investing in education, in public health, in state-of-the-art infrastructure, all of which contribute to boost productivity. Highly trained labour forces, in turn, adopt new technologies with enthusiasm or, as happens often in the Nordics, are themselves in the forefront of technological innovations. In many ways the Nordics have entered virtuous circles where various factors reinforce one another to make them among the most competitive economies in the world, with world class institutions and some of the highest levels of per capita income in the world.

Information Asymmetry: Prescription Drugs

Information asymmetry occurs when one of the parties in a market transaction has much more knowledge about the exchange than the other. This information problem is particularly problematic in the world of prescription drugs. Drug companies obviously have a much better idea about the health benefits, and potentially harmful side effects, of their products than those who purchase their drugs. Few people are able to accurately evaluate the costs and benefits of taking a particular drug. This creates a case for independent government testing of both the safety and effectiveness of new drugs brought to the market, a role that was at one time taken seriously by the Canadian and US governments. But in recent years they have been abandoning this regulatory role. As a result, the research on both the effectiveness and harm done by prescription drugs is most often carried out by the drug companies themselves, leading to results that are, predictably, biased in favour of the drugs in which companies have invested so much to bring to market.

In 1997, the Canadian Health Coalition reported, the entire Bureau of Drug Research was quietly dismantled and the facilities for independent lab investigations of pharmaceutical products destroyed. The Bureau's scientists were recognized internationally for their independent research on drug quality, toxicity, bioequivalence, and clinical application of drugs. The dismantling of the Bureau caused the head of the pediatrics branch, Dr. Michelle Brill-Edwards, to resign because she could no longer assure the Canadian public of the efficacy of new drugs now that pharmaceutical companies were doing their own safety studies.

The Health Protection Branch drug reviewers were also instructed by the government that their client was no longer the general public, but the drug companies they were supposed to be overseeing. "By adopting a client focus and service orientation, regulatory organizations can help those seeking approval to comply with regulations as easily as possible, promote voluntary compliance, earn goodwill from the regulated community… and improve the working atmosphere." The bulletin also says: "there is no conflict of interest between delivering a service to a client and functioning in a regulatory environment" (Canadian Health Coalition 1998).

In the United States, the Food and Drug Administration (FDA) has also been abandoning its regulatory role. Dr. David Graham is the associate director for science and medicine in the FDA Office of Drug Safety. Despite his rigorous background—he received his medical, epidemiological, and biostatistics training from Johns Hopkins, Yale, and the University of Pennsylvania—his ability as a researcher was called into question when he blew the whistle on Vioxx, a drug that has caused some 100,000 heart attacks and 50,000 deaths in the United States.

According to Graham, the FDA "reacted violently" when he announced he was going to submit his research for peer review. His supervisors described his work as "scientific rumour" and his director called the study "junk science." The day after his supervisor's remarks, Graham's study was the lead article in the *Journal of the American Medical Association*, and was accompanied by a call for a complete restructuring of the FDA. After Graham's study was published, the FDA contacted a key senator, who accused Graham of being a "liar, cheat, bully, a demagogue and untrustworthy." The FDA also contacted the Government Accountability Project with the same line of character assassination. Graham's director contacted the editor of the *Lancet* and accused Graham of scientific misconduct, the highest crime a scientist can commit.

According to Graham, the FDA's angry response is due to its willingness to sacrifice safety for its own revenue. In 2002, the FDA collected fees of $143.3 million from the pharmaceutical industry, under the *Prescription Drug User Fee Act*, most of the $209.8 million in total operating costs for reviewing drugs. Graham goes on to argue that the FDA approach is to virtually disregard safety as something to be managed "in the post-marketing setting." The effect is that "our parents, and grandparents, our children get to be the guinea pigs in the grand experiment while drug companies continue to make profits." Graham is not alone. Two-thirds of FDA scientists are not confident that products approved by the FDA are safe. Eighteen say they have been pressured to change their own conclusions. Graham's policy prescription is that industry cannot be the client. Public health must be funded by the public for an institution run by and for the public.

If we do not wish to be guinea pigs, a proper study on drugs like Vioxx would take longer and need to be much larger than those that serve only industry interests. "If you are making $3 billion a year selling a drug, every day of clinical trials is another day you are not making $10 million" (Graham 2004, 25). Deregulation of the drug industry resulted in Vioxx hitting the market, and staying on it, despite the fact that it was killing people.

Conclusion

Market failure is not an occasional anomaly or deviation from the usual proper functioning of the market. Market failures are ubiquitous. Yet in recent years, policies to address these failures have rarely been implemented despite the fact that deregulation has been disastrous in cases such as those presented here. Even the massive banking failure in the United States seems to have produced little in the way of stronger regulation. The reason for this might be the identity of the winners and losers in many regulatory situations. In the banking, cancer, and drug examples, inevitably it is the politically powerful firms in the industry that would be harmed by regulation and citizens that would benefit.

What if we ignore market failures that contribute to financial disaster, cancer, and deadly products and just focus on what conservatives argue deregulated markets do best—provide high-quality, low-cost goods and services? *Consumer Reports* evaluated deregulation in several US industries. Predictably for a magazine dedicated to customer satisfaction, its evaluation was based solely on criteria that would matter to consumers, such as prices, consumer rights, safety, choice, and innovation. Its conclusion was that, on balance, consumers have lost ground since deregulation began in the telephone, banking, electricity, television, and airline industries. Consumer choices decreased, prices fell at a slower rate, the quality of services declined, and taxpayers had to pay for failing banks. Lack of industry-specific regulation has proved to be a problem even within the narrowly defined world of consumers, supposedly the ultimate beneficiaries of deregulation. If we extend our perspective to include the decline in protective regulation that has led to pollution problems like global warming, occupational disease, and injury, the accounting becomes even grimmer.

DISCUSSION QUESTIONS

1. What makes the banking and finance industry different from many other industries and how does this difference create a justification for regulation?
2. Why might profit-maximizing firms be reluctant to invest in research and development?
3. What is wrong with the usual "lifestyle" explanation of the causes of cancer?
4. Identify and explain the market failure that plagues the drug industry.

SUGGESTED READINGS

Chernomas, R., and I. Hudson. 2007. *Social murder and other shortcomings of conservative economics.* Winnipeg: Arbeiter Ring.

Friedman, M., and R. Friedman. 1990. *Free to choose.* San Diego: Harcourt Brace Jovanovich.

Krugman, P. 2007. *The conscience of a liberal.* New York: W.W. Norton & Company.

Polanyi, K. 1944, 2001. *The great transformation: The political and economic origins of our time.* Boston: Beacon Press.

ONLINE RESOURCES

The Becker-Posner Blog: http://uchicagolaw.typepad.com/beckerposner.

The Post-Autistic Economics Network: http://www.paecon.net.

REFERENCES

Barth, J., R. Brumbaugh, and J. Wilcox. 2000. Policy watch: The repeal of Glass-Steagall and the advent of broad banking. *Journal of Economic Perspectives* 14 (2): 191–204.

Canadian Cancer Society, National Cancer Institute and Statistics Canada. 2003. Canadian cancer statistics 2003. http://www.cancer.ca/Canada-wide/About%20cancer/Cancer%20statistics/Canadian%20Cancer%20Statistics. aspx?sc_lang=en.

Canadian Health Coalition. 1998. A citizens' guide to the Health Protection Branch (HPB) transition consultations. http://www.healthcoalition.ca/abdication.html.

Canadian Labour Congress. 2005. Preventing cancer: A campaign for workers. Health Safety and Environment Series: 21. http://www3.canadianlabour.ca/images/hseimages/cancer2005-e.pdf.

Center for Responsible Politics. 2009. *Influence and lobbying.*
http://www.opensecrets.org/influence/index.php.

Consumer Reports. 2002. Deregulated. *Consumer Reports* (July): 30–35.

Environmental Working Group. 2003. Body burden: The pollution in people.
http://www.ewg.org/reports/bodyburden1/es.php.

Graham, D. 2004. Blowing the whistle on the FDA: An interview with Dr. David
Graham. *Multinational Monitor* 25 (12): 22–25.

Jackson, W. 1987. *Glass-Steagall Act: Commercial vs. investment banking.* Washington,
DC: Economics Division Congressional Research Service.

Kroszner, R., and J. Rajan. 1994. Is the Glass-Steagall Act justified? *American
Economic Review* 84 (4): 810–832.

Lopez-Carlos, A. 2005. The global competitiveness report 2005–2006: Video inter-
views. http://www2.weforum.org/site/homepublic.nsf/Content/The+Global+
Competitiveness+Report+2005-2006_+Video+Interviews.html.

Lopez-Carlos, A., K. Schwab, and M.E. Porter. 2006. *The global competitiveness
report 2005–2006.* London: Palgrave Macmillan.

Nagnur, D., and M. Nagrodski. 1987. *Cause-deleted life tables for Canada (1921 to
1981): An approach toward analyzing epidemiologic transition.* Ottawa:
Statistics Canada.

Office of Science and Technology Policy. 2000. Fact sheet on federal R&D investments. The White House, June 15. http://www.clintonfoundation.org/
legacy/061500-fact-sheet-on-federal-r-d-investments.htm.

Pollution Watch. 2005. Pollution timeline. http://pollutionwatch.org/timeline.do.

Public Broadcasting Service (PBS). 2008. The long decline of Glass-Steagall.
http://www.pbs.org/wgbh/pages/frontline/shows/wallstreet/weill/demise.html.

Rawe, J. 2004. Where the best ideas take wing. *Time Magazine.* October 11: 68.

Smith, A. 1976. *An inquiry into the nature and causes of the wealth of nations.*
Oxford: Oxford University Press.

Toronto Cancer Prevention Coalition. 2001. Preventing occupational and environmental cancer: A strategy for Toronto. http://www.city.toronto.on.ca/health/
resources/tcpc/pdf/tcpc_occupational_enviro_carcinogens.pdf.

Thurow, L. 1996. *The future of capitalism.* New York: Penguin Books USA Inc.

Thurow, L. 1999. Building wealth. *The Atlantic Monthly* 283 (6): 57–69.

Is the Private Sector Better Than the Public Sector in Providing Goods and Services to the Public?

8

COMPETING VIEWS

Niels Veldhuis, "The Power of the Private Sector"

Hugh Mackenzie, "Microeconomic Issues Raised by Public Services"

Editors' Introduction

During the 40 years or so that followed the Great Depression of 1929, governments assumed a greater role in the management of the economy. They enacted rules and regulations to govern virtually all markets, from finance to labour. They created Crown corporations to provide certain goods and services, and even monopolized or dominated some key sectors such as natural resources, postal services and communications, and water and electricity supply. During this era, which became known as the "golden age" of capitalism, governments also built public infrastructure and provided universal health care and education. Such government intervention was widely accepted and a general consensus emerged that "we are all Keynesians now"—a reference to John Maynard Keynes, who advocated this type of policy.

However, other economists, such as Friedrich Hayek, advocated a free-market economy and were staunchly opposed to government regulations because they believed that these would only create market distortions and inefficiencies. In addition, they argued that the public sector is inherently inefficient because of the government's inability to run a business. Some even argue that a large public sector is a source of slow economic growth, and they therefore recommend a smaller, leaner public sector and a greater role for market incentives. Consequently, public sector downsizing and privatization of public services became a significant objective of economic policy.

In his essay, Niels Veldhuis follows this line of thought. He maintains that the public sector typically fails to provide high-quality goods and services to the public because it is not focused on the pursuit of profits and is not guided solely by the price system. Relying on the "invisible hand" of the market is a better option, he argues, because the pursuit of self-interest by private sector firms ensures that consumers will get the goods and services they want. His argument that the public sector is inefficient and fails to provide high-quality products is linked to the idea that policy-makers care only about improving their chances of being re-elected and not about the welfare of society. Decisions made in the public sector are, therefore, considered biased and less efficient, and often result in a waste of resources. The conclusion that follows from this point of view is that government activities should be restricted to the provision of basic services such as defence, law and order, and public goods, and that the private sector should be allowed to take care of the rest.

By contrast, in the second essay, Hugh Mackenzie argues that when markets are left to their own devices, they often fail to generate socially acceptable outcomes. To avoid such undesirable outcomes, governments intervene either as direct providers of goods and services or as regulators and facilitators. These last two forms of government involvement give rise to different channels through which goods and services are delivered to the public, such as concessions, contracting out and public–private partnerships. When comparing the public and the private sectors as providers of goods and services, Mackenzie finds that the public sector has many cost advantages, which allow it to deliver products at a price that is accessible to all citizens.

The Power of the Private Sector

Niels Veldhuis

Introduction

During the course of a day, Canadians use thousands of different goods and services. If you are like me, most of your days start with the annoying buzzer of an alarm clock. Once I'm up and at it, it's into the shower with soap, shampoo, and conditioner. By the time I finish breakfast, read the morning news on my Black-Berry, and drive to work, I have used hundreds of different products. Whether it is the alarm clock, toast, BlackBerry, or gas, most of us never think about who made these goods and services, how many people contributed to producing them, and why most are readily available when we want either more, a newer version, or a substitute.

While most of the goods and services we buy are produced by the private sector, some are provided by the public sector. This essay highlights key differences between how the private and public sectors operate, and argues that forces at work in the private sector lead it to satisfy our needs and wants better than governments can. Of course, some goods are best left for the government to provide. We will discuss these goods and why the private sector has a difficult time providing them.

The Price System and the Pursuit of Profit

As the terms are used in this essay, the "*private* sector" includes privately owned and operated business firms, from single proprietorships to partnerships and large corporations, whereas the "*public* sector" includes federal, provincial and territorial, and municipal levels of government, and Crown corporations.[1] Some economic activities are also carried out by public–private partnerships, and some activities funded by public expenditures are contracted out to the private sector.

Perhaps the essential difference between the public and private sector as producers of goods and services is the mechanism by which decisions about what, where, when, and how much to produce are made. The private sector uses the price system and the pursuit of profit to make these decisions. Prices and profits coordinate the spontaneous actions of millions of people and businesses without a central body directing their actions. In the public sector, prices play a much smaller role in decision making. Instead of relying on prices and aiming to maximize profits, the public sector's objectives are political and social, and it is politicians and bureaucrats, influenced by voters and special-interest groups, who make the decisions on production and on who consumes the goods and services produced by the government. This essay argues that the private sector's reliance on prices and profits is a primary reason why the private sector is better at providing goods and services to the public.

To demonstrate the ability of prices and profits to coordinate activity in the private sector, consider the market for gasoline.[2] When most of us fill up our cars, we never wonder why we have numerous different gas stations to choose from, why gas always seems to be available, and how many people contributed to making sure the gas is available when we want to purchase it.

Since gas is produced from crude oil, companies and individuals around the world continuously search for new deposits beneath the earth's surface. Thousands of petroleum geologists are involved in studying geological maps and doing aerial and seismic surveys. Once a potential new oil reservoir is discovered, exploratory drilling is needed to confirm whether or not it exists. If an oil reservoir is actually present, an appraisal must be done to determine whether or not it is economically feasible to develop the newly found deposits. If it is, the oil must then be extracted, shipped to oil refineries, stored, and converted into different fuels, including gasoline and diesel. The gasoline must then be transported by pipelines, ships, and trucks to gas stations across the country.

While this is a simplified chain of production, think about the millions of people involved in this process, from those who produce the equipment and machinery needed at each stage, to those who educate the geologists, engineers, managers, pipefitters, and the countless other skilled workers involved. At the retail stage alone, gas stations must be constructed, stocked, maintained, and serviced by employees. We can even go so far as to consider all the untold millions of people who provide clothing, food, and shelter to each person involved in the production of gas. After all, each contributed, directly or indirectly, to ensuring that gasoline is available when we want to purchase it.

It is amazing to think that no central office, committee, or mastermind gave all these people orders to do what they did. No centralized decision-maker directed all the actions of the millions of people who help get gas into our vehicles. All of these individuals and businesses acted voluntarily. Furthermore, they did not contribute to the production of gas because they necessarily wanted gas themselves. Many might not even have realized that they were contributing to the market for gas; they span the globe, speak different languages, hold different beliefs, and most do not know each other.

That is the power of the private sector.

Why did all of these people voluntarily decide to contribute to the production of gas? The folks involved do not provide their goods and services because they like us and want to ensure that we are able to fuel our cars. They provide their goods and services because they *all* benefited. That is, they cooperated and contributed by exchanging their services and goods at a "profit," which allows them to buy the many goods and services they want (which may or may not include gas).

Indeed, this is one of the great insights of Adam Smith, the 18th-century philosopher and father of modern economics, who observed, "It is not from the benevolence of the butcher, the brewer, or the baker, that we can expect our dinner, but from their regard to their own interest" (Smith 1981, 26–27). In other words, people act out of self-interest, which causes them to do things that benefit other people. We get our gasoline by making all of the people engaged in the production process better off. It is a voluntary exchange, which benefits all parties.

But if no central mastermind directs all of these self-interested people, what coordinates their decisions and actions? Smith noted that we are "led by an invisible hand" (Smith 1981, 456). The invisible hand is the price system and the pursuit of profit.

Unfortunately, the word "profit" is a dirty word to many Canadians, because they believe that profit is equivalent to "ill-gotten gains." We say, for example, that someone profited by taking advantage of someone else. However, as Smith highlights, that is tragically wrong. Profits, in the *general* sense of "net benefits," are simply the difference between the value of what we give up to get something and the value of the item we want. Workers give up free time and other opportunities to do their jobs—the difference between their wages and what they gave up to earn them is profit. The reality is that in a market, consumers profit, workers profit, and businesses profit. They all trade because they all benefit (profit), not because one party is exploiting the other.

One of the central roles of profits and prices is that they provide and transmit critical information, or signals. For example, a significant increase in profits is a signal for entrepreneurs and businesses to invest capital and resources in that area of the economy. Since increased profits are usually the result of an increased demand for goods and services, or a shortage of supply, the signal typically comes about through changes in price.[3]

Suppose, for example, that consumer demand for gasoline in Canada increases. The increased demand raises the price of gas and induces gas stations to put in more orders for gas. Increased orders for gas lead oil refineries to increase their output, motivating trucking companies to increase the number of loads they carry. Increased demand for workers throughout the process leads to an increase in wages. Increased production in oil refineries also increases the demand for crude oil and brings about increased oil exploration.

This increased demand for gas by Canadian consumers affects prices in many different markets all over the world. People and businesses spring into action because they see a personal benefit, that is, they profit from their activities. All of them work toward meeting the increased demand for gas, even though most may not even know they are doing so.

Prices not only send signals from the consumers to the producers, but they also work the other way. Suppose the supply of crude oil drops sharply because of a war in the Middle East, a region of the world that provides much of the world's oil. The reduction in oil supply means that it becomes difficult for oil refineries to obtain crude oil and produce gas. The decreased supply of gas leads to an increase in its price, sending a signal to consumers to use less gas, leading them to reduce the amount of time they drive, by car pooling and/or switching to mass transit. They do not need to know *why* the price of gas has increased to change their behaviour. The simple fact that it *has* increased provides the needed incentive.

As Nobel-prizewinning economist Milton Friedman notes, "One of the beauties of a free price system is that the prices that bring the information also provide both an incentive to react to the information and the means to do so" (Friedman and Friedman 1980, 18). That is, higher prices for a good or service spur its producers into action. It enables them to hire more workers and increase output. It provides businesses with information about where their goods and services are most wanted—that is, where prices are highest. Since prices indicate the relative value of goods and services, higher prices discourage waste. If production becomes more expensive because of a scarcity of skilled workers, businesses will increase their use of machinery.

Allowing prices to fluctuate freely efficiently coordinates the billions of decentralized decisions of people to do what is in their own self-interest. Relying on the "invisible hand" of the private sector ensures that the products and services consumers want are in the right place at the right time.

The Pursuit of Votes and Bigger Budgets

However, if the public sector were managing the economy, politicians and bureaucrats would decide what to produce, where to produce it, how much to produce, and who ultimately gets to buy or use the goods and services. Most decisions would be centrally made; prices, if they existed, would be centrally determined and would not freely adjust; and the pursuit of economic profit would not exist. Such a public sector would generally fail to efficiently provide high-quality goods and services to the public in the right amounts, at the right place, and at the right time.

In some respects, Canadians do choose the kinds of goods and services their governments provide, since we are fortunate enough to elect our governments democratically. However, as voters we have only one vote to make decisions about a whole range of goods and services (health care, education, taxes, defence, environment, policing), unlike goods in the private sector, on which we decide item by item.

In addition, many people, including many economists and political scientists, assume a benevolent, selfless public sector in which politicians and bureaucrats are looking out for the best interests of society. Do politicians and bureaucrats really decide which goods and services to provide by doing what is best for society? A branch of economics known as public choice theory has developed in an attempt to better understand the government sector and how it operates. Public choice scholars make assumptions about the motivations of the participants in the public sector, and assume that rather than maximizing the public interest, politicians and bureaucrats, like folks in the private sector, act in their own self-interest.[4]

Politicians want to win elections, and will therefore provide goods and services that maximize their chances of getting elected or re-elected. Because taxes rather than prices typically fund the goods and services produced in the public sector, a separation between the costs and benefits of these goods exists. Politicians use the separation of costs and benefits to provide benefits to specific groups that helped them get elected while spreading the costs among the rest of us.

Similarly, bureaucrats are compensated, by the size of their budget and staff, according to the extent of their responsibilities and thus have an incentive to seek more power and influence. It is often in their interest to make problems they are tasked with solving appear worse than they truly are to get their budgets increased. For example, Canada's auditor general found that the Department of Transportation had given the government the impression that road conditions needed to be improved and would require billions of dollars of expenditure. However, an internal departmental study revealed that pavement surfaces were acceptably smooth. In addition, public choice theory implies that efficient choices aimed at reducing costs will often be rejected because of the incentives that encourage bureaucrats to increase, not decrease, spending on the goods and services they produce.

These problematic incentives for politicians and bureaucrats are exacerbated by special-interest groups who try to extract benefits from government at the expense of the general public. For example, farmers in Canada have successfully lobbied Canadian governments for subsidies and quotas that provide benefits to farmers through artificially high prices that average Canadians must pay. The types of goods and services the public sector provides will therefore often reflect the desires of the best-organized and -funded interest groups, rather than the best interests of society.

Finally, the price system does not operate freely in determining public sector provision of goods and services, and prices are often determined by governments. As discussed above, one of the central roles of prices is to provide and transmit information to millions of dispersed individuals who then use the price signals to determine what actions to take: what to produce, how to produce, how much to produce, and to whom to sell. As Nobel prizewinner Friedrich Hayek (1945) argued in his seminal paper, "The Use of Knowledge in Society," politicians, bureaucrats, and central planners cannot aggregate all of the information in society to design a functioning and prosperous economy. Hayek also argued that the information on what, where, and how much to produce emerges from the rise and fall of prices in the market system. Distort or eliminate prices and the power of the "invisible hand" disappears.

Private Sector Competition Versus Government Monopolies

Another critical difference between the private and public sectors is that government businesses, programs, and departments typically operate in monopoly environments. That is, governments often become the sole provider of a particular good or service, and competition is prohibited by law, for example, basic car insurance, in many provinces. On the other hand, in the private sector most businesses face stiff competition. Competition from other businesses means that each one must continuously cater to the needs and preferences of its customers. If they can't appeal to customers, businesses lose out to competitors and their profits decrease or disappear altogether.

Competition leads to many positive outcomes for customers. When businesses make profits, other businesses try to emulate the profit-making company. When they do so, the output in the market increases and prices decrease. Businesses may also focus on reducing their costs through improvements in production processes, enabling them to undercut the prices of their competitors.

Businesses also engage in non-price competition. For instance, many businesses try to increase the quality of their goods and services to gain an advantage over their competitors. In addition, businesses might offer generous warranties and free future servicing of their product. Competition also motivates businesses to innovate, providing new products and services.

Price and non-price competition force businesses in the private sector to remain squarely focused on their consumers. Government monopolies are shielded from this competitive discipline. When goods are produced in the public sector, the monopoly environment can lead to higher prices, increased cost, lower-quality products, less innovation, and lower levels of customer service.

Although private sector monopolies are possible, they face different pressures than a government monopoly. Many people wrongly think that the level of competition in the private sector is directly related to the number of businesses in a market, yet often markets with two or three business are extremely competitive. For example, the market for soft drinks is dominated by two firms, the Coca-Cola

Company and PepsiCo, but that market is extremely competitive. Even a market in which there is only one business (a monopoly) can exhibit competitive behaviour (lower costs and prices, innovation, and improved customer service) as long as there are no barriers for other firms to enter into the market and eliminate the monopoly power. As renowned economist Joseph Schumpeter noted, competition "disciplines before it attacks" (Schumpeter 1983, 85). The only monopolies that tend to persist over time are those in which the government forcefully excludes competitors, for example Canada Post.

Should Any Goods and Services Be Provided By the Public Sector?

If the private sector is better at providing many goods and services because it makes better use of dispersed knowledge, provides incentives through prices and profits, contains competitive pressures, and promotes innovation and entrepreneurship, then which goods and services should be produced by the public sector?

Most economists believe that governments ought to provide some "public goods." However, it is important to note that there is a difference between "public goods" and goods provided by the public sector. For example, if the public sector started to produce iPods, that does not make iPods a public good. "Public goods" are typically thought to have two defining characteristics: non-excludability and non-rivalrous consumption. Non-excludability means that no one can be excluded from consuming the good or service, or at least that it would be extremely costly to exclude anyone from consuming it. Since public goods are non-excludable, it is difficult to get people to pay for them voluntarily. And if someone does not pay for a public good, there is no cost-effective way to exclude him or her from using it. That is why markets tend to underproduce public goods and why we rely on government to finance these goods through taxes. Non-rivalrous consumption means that one person's use of a good does not reduce the ability of another person to use it. Non-excludability is the more important characteristic, because if people can be excluded, then businesses can charge people for the good or service.

Perhaps the best example of a truly "public good" is national defence. National defence is non-excludable. Canada's army provides national defence and protects us all from foreign attacks. It would be almost impossible to exclude some Canadians from this protection. In addition, my "consumption" of national defence does not reduce your ability to be protected.

Other public goods include law and order—the police force, legislative bodies, and the judicial system. It would be extremely difficult to exclude non-payers from the benefits of police protection and the punishment of criminals. Similarly, having an unbiased and uniform system of laws and courts in place provides substantial benefits to people regardless of whether or not they pay.

Roads can also be thought of as a public good. If all streets, roads, and sidewalks were owned and operated by the private sector, the costs of collecting tolls would be extremely high and the roads would be undersupplied. Of course, with significant improvements in tolling mechanisms through electronic transponders, the financing, construction, and maintenance of an increasing number of highways and bridges could be left to the private sector. However, it is unlikely that we would enjoy our current road system without government involvement.

The answer to the question of which goods the government should provide has not changed much since Adam Smith described the three main duties of government: to protect society from other societies, to protect members in the society from each other, and to establish and maintain certain public works, which would not be privately supplied.

While governments are needed to provide some public goods, the government will only provide them imperfectly in the absence of competitive forces in the public sector to ensure low costs, good customer service, and continuous innovation. For that reason, the activities of the government should be strictly constrained, leaving as many things as possible to the private sector and the forces of competition.[5]

Conclusion

Most of the goods and services Canadians buy are produced by the private sector. The essay has argued that the private sector is better at providing goods and services because it makes better use of dispersed knowledge; provides incentives, through prices and profits, for people to act on their knowledge; and contains competitive pressures that ultimately lead to lower costs, lower prices, improved quality, increased innovation, and better customer service.

Despite the power of the private sector, governments are needed to provide some public goods such as national defence, police protection, and the judicial system. While governments will imperfectly provide these public goods, as noted earlier, the private sector would likely undersupply them.

Except for these rare public goods, it would be in our best interest to leave as many things as possible to the private sector and the forces of competition.

NOTES

1. While the private sector includes not-for-profit and charitable organizations, and the public sector includes government-established regulatory and licensing bodies, these organizations and bodies are not discussed in this essay.

2. A powerful short essay about how millions of voluntary exchanges contribute to producing a single product is *I, Pencil: My Family Tree as Told to Leonard E. Read*, available at http://www.econlib.org/library/Essays/rdPncl1.html. The essay is written in the first person through the point of view of a lead pencil.
3. In microeconomics, we model the price system through supply and demand. See Heyne et al. (2005) for a detailed explanation and presentation of the supply and demand model.
4. See Mitchell and Simmons (1994) for an excellent overview of public choice economics.
5. While a full analysis of health care is beyond the scope of this essay, students are encouraged to read Esmail and Walker (2008) and Skinner (2009).

DISCUSSION QUESTIONS

1. How are the actions of participants in the private sector coordinated? How are the actions of those in the public sector coordinated? Explain the key differences between how the private and public sectors operate.
2. Many Canadians think that some goods and services should be provided by the public sector because they assume that politicians and bureaucrats are guided by doing what is in the best interest of society rather than doing whatever leads to the highest profit. Is this assumption correct? Discuss.
3. Are public goods the same as goods provided by the public sector? Explain.

SUGGESTED READINGS

Friedman, Milton, and Rose D. Friedman. 1980. *Free to choose: A personal statement.* New York: Harcourt.

Henderson, David R. 2008. *The concise encyclopedia of economics.* Indianapolis, IN: Liberty Fund.

Heyne, Paul, Peter J. Boettke, and David L. Prychitko. 2005. *The economic way of thinking.* 11th ed. Upper Saddle River, NJ: Prentice Hall.

Mitchell, William C., and Randy T. Simmons. 1994. *Beyond politics: Markets, welfare and the failure of bureaucracy.* Boulder, CO: The Independent Institute.

Read, Leonard E. 1958. *I, pencil: My family tree as told to Leonard E. Read.* Irvington-on-Hudson, NY: The Foundation for Economic Education. Available at http://www.econlib.org/library/Essays/rdPncl1.html.

ONLINE RESOURCES

Cafe Hayek: http://cafehayek.com.

Fraser Institute, Key Economic Concepts: http://www.fraserinstitute.org/
researchandpublications/researchtopics/key-economic-concepts.htm.

The Library of Economics and Liberty: http://www.econlib.org.

REFERENCES

Boardman, Anthony E., Claude Laurin, and Aidan R. Vining. 2002. Privatization in Canada: Operating and stock price performance with international comparisons. *Canadian Journal of Administrative Sciences* 19 (2): 137–154.

Clemens, Jason, Charles Lammam, Milagros Palacios, and Niels Veldhuis. 2007. *Government failure in Canada, 2007 report: A review of the auditor general's reports, 1992–2006.* Vancouver: The Fraser Institute.

Esmail, Nadeem, and Michael Walker. *How good is Canadian health care?* 2008 ed. Vancouver: The Fraser Institute. http://www.fraserinstitute.org/commerce. web/product_files/HowGoodisCanadianHealthCare2008.pdf.

Fraser, Brett. 2009. *Canadian health policy failures: What's wrong? Who gets hurt? Why nothing changes.* Vancouver: The Fraser Institute.

Fraser Forum, November 2008. Vancouver: The Fraser Institute. http://www.fraserinstitute.org/commerce.web/product_files/FraserForum_November2008.pdf.

Friedman, Milton, and Rose D. Friedman. 1980. *Free to choose: A personal statement.* New York: Harcourt.

Hayek, F.A. 1945. The use of knowledge in society. *American Economic Review* 35 (4): 519–530.

Lammam, Charles, and Niels Veldhuis. 2009. It's time to privatize Crown corporations. *Fraser Forum*, May. Vancouver: The Fraser Institute.

Megginson, William L., and Jeffry M. Netter. 2001. From state to market: A survey of empirical studies on privatization. *Journal of Economic Literature* 39 (2): 321–389.

Organisation for Economic Co-operation and Development (OECD). 2009. *Economic outlook 86*, annex tables at http://www.oecd.org.

Schumpeter, Joseph A. 1983. *Capitalism, socialism and democracy*. New York: HarperCollins.

Skinner, Brett J. 2009. *Canadian health policy failures: What's wrong, who gets hurt, and why nothing changes.* Vancouver: The Fraser Institute.

Smith, Adam. 1981. *An inquiry into the nature and causes of the wealth of nations.* Vol. 1. Indianapolis, IN: Liberty Fund.

Microeconomic Issues Raised by Public Services

Hugh Mackenzie

A Framework for Thinking About the Provision of Public Goods and Services

Although the economic theories identified with John Maynard Keynes address the functioning of what economists classify as the macro economy, the underlying messages of Keynesianism—that markets are not self-regulating; that the ordinary functioning of markets can be a potent source of instability; and that at the aggregate level, markets cannot be expected to produce a balance between demand and supply in the short-to-medium term—translated into a healthy skepticism about the functioning of markets at the micro level.

For the first quarter-century after the Second World War—before the ascendancy of the Chicago School's free market approach—the Keynesian view of the role of governments in economic stabilization, in income redistribution, in the regulation of markets that were structurally unable to function, and as significant producers of goods and services, was broadly accepted. The idea of "market failure" was acknowledged to be an appropriate basis for government involvement in the goods and services sector, either as a direct provider of goods and services or as a regulator of goods and services markets. Market failure could arise for one of two broad reasons: because pricing was heavily influenced by the exercise of monopoly (limited number of sellers) or monopsony (limited number of buyers) power by players in the market or because the production of a good or service gave rise to "externalities"—external benefits or costs accruing to people or institutions other than the buyer or seller—that could not be captured in the price.

The ascent and 30-year reign of the hands-off approach to macroeconomic management built around the approach of the Chicago School had a corresponding spill-over effect on mainstream thinking about the role of government in the micro economy. The idea that "the market is always right" at the macroeconomic level translated directly into a view of the micro economy that was at odds with anything more than an extremely limited view of the role of government. If markets are always right, it follows that anything that either interferes with the functioning of the market or doesn't behave the way a market behaves must be wrong.

This thinking had a profound impact on the political–economic view of the role of government. The theory of rational expectations told orthodox economists that governments should not intervene at the macro level because the risk that governments would get it wrong outweighed any losses that might be incurred as markets adjusted. Thus the previously accepted role for governments in economic stabilization was rejected. Whereas even the most zealous of the rational expectations theorists were forced to accept a role for government in income redistribution, mainstream microeconomists became preoccupied with the trade-off between efficiency and equity in income redistribution policies. Millions of trees were sacrificed to the study of efficiency losses—that is, the differences between an outcome affected by income redistribution policies and a "pure" market outcome—to be set against income distribution benefits.

This theoretical trade-off formed the foundation for a debate over income redistribution, and the form, if any, that government intervention should take. Adherents of the pro-market Chicago view argued for an income redistribution mechanism that would have the least "distorting" effect on markets. They settled on the "negative income tax" or guaranteed annual income as the form least likely to distort the consumption choices of recipients, with a threshold level of support low enough to minimize its impact on the labour market because, for the rational expectations theorists, delivering income redistribution through the direct provision of goods and services was anathema.

The negative view of government as a producer of goods and services was predicated on the assumption that either market failure did not exist or that once the most obvious candidates for public production of goods and services, such as national defence and international relations, were dealt with, the remaining examples would be too rare to be of any interest.

It is now obvious that this view of the primacy of markets was wrong. At the macroeconomic level, it is plain that markets are not self-clearing. Market outcomes generate income distribution outcomes that are beyond the range of what is politically acceptable. And although the public policy challenges of the next decades—climate change, escalating health care costs, deteriorating public infrastructure, the aging population, growing income inequality—differ in many respects, each is a textbook example of market failure.

Despite the pervasive evidence that the market-centric view of the role of government has failed, the political–economic momentum against the role of government in the delivery of goods and services engendered by the Chicago model continues.

Redrawing the Line on the Role of Government

The ideological battle over the role of government in the delivery of goods and services has taken two broad forms: the outright removal of the provision of certain goods and services from the public sphere to private interests and the redrawing of the line between what is public and what is private.

The first of these forms—the shifting of goods and services production from the public sector to the private sector—is closely identified with the government of Margaret Thatcher in the United Kingdom. Substantial segments of goods and services production that had been public were simply auctioned off to private sector buyers and left to operate as private businesses, with varying degrees of regulatory oversight. Thus the public railway system was auctioned off and much of the local sewer and water system was sold off to private operators.

The second of these forms—the redrawing of the line between what is public and what is private—is most closely identified with Thatcher's successor plus one, Tony Blair. Blair extended the distinction between provision for and delivery of specific public goods and services by establishing mechanisms through which broad areas of public policy could be funded from public money but actually be managed and delivered by private businesses through public–private partnerships (known as "P3s"). Although public–private partnerships are represented publicly as easily identifiable projects like toll roads or hospitals, they actually encompass a wide variety of different incursions of private sector businesses into the provision of public services. Services that even the most hardened conservative would concede are the purview of government are being privatized through this mechanism. For example, the United States Army now contracts out logistical support and security for its troops in war zones.

Although these two mechanisms appear to be quite different, in practical terms they are simply points on a continuum that has atomized private production at one end and purely public provision at the other. For example, there is no practical difference between selling a public asset like a highway and granting a 50-year concession to operate the highway as a toll road.

Analyzing Public Services

From a political–economic perspective, the definition of "public service" is, appropriately, perfectly circular. Since what governments do is provide public services, anything that is provided by government is by definition a public service. While this definition raises the interesting question of how societies decide what their governments should do, it is not particularly helpful in evaluating the relative strengths and weakness of the public and private sectors in providing goods and services to the public, and therefore not particularly helpful in thinking through the issues raised by the erosion of the role of the public sector in the delivery of goods and services.

To get at the microeconomic issues behind the delivery of goods and services to the public, it is helpful to focus on two key questions:

- What is it about a good or service that makes it subject to public interest?
- What are the strengths and weaknesses of the public and private sectors as providers of goods and services?

What Gives Rise to a Public Interest in the Provision of Public Services?

Generally speaking, the public interest in the provision of a good or service arises from market failure, broadly defined. What is meant by market failure in this case is that the private market, left to its own devices, will produce one or more of the following outcomes:

- production of too little of the good or service (because external benefits cannot be captured in its price)—for example, basic research and development, postsecondary education, immunization from infectious diseases;
- production of too much of the good or service (because negative externalities cannot be captured in its cost of production)—for example, production that involves the burning of fossil fuels, leading to greenhouse gas emissions, leading to global warming;
- a pattern of production that may meet the needs of the immediate buyer and seller but conflicts with the broader public interest—for example, development of large, single-family homes on large lots located on farmland distant from urban areas;
- a distribution of the good or service, access to which is considered essential or a basic human right, that denies or restricts access by certain individuals or groups; or
- production of the good or service by a natural monopoly or by a firm, which, through the operation of the market, becomes a natural monopoly.

In other words, the role of government in the production or distribution of goods and services may be defined economically as a response to the failure of the market to produce a socially acceptable outcome. In turn, public policy responses to market failure may be divided into three categories:

- the establishment of regulatory regimes designed to force the market to produce outcomes that are consistent with the public interest (telecommunications services, for example);

- provision for the production of services in the public interest that are actually produced and delivered by the private sector (most physicians' services in the Canadian health-care system or rent-geared-to-income housing in the private sector, for example); or
- direct production of services in the public interest (national parks, most local sewer and water services, public housing, public elementary and secondary education, for example).

Both the definition and the expression of the public interest are dependent on context: current and historical, and social, political, and economic. Context explains why some jurisdictions express public interest in the provision of a public service and other jurisdictions do not. For example, in Canada there is a broadly accepted consensus of public interest in the availability of health-care services to every individual, regardless of economic circumstances. In the United States, there is no such consensus.

Context also explains why the same good or service may be produced in the public sector in one jurisdiction and in the private sector under regulation in otherwise similar jurisdictions. For example, electricity production and distribution is public in some parts of Canada and private in other parts of Canada.

The importance of social and political context means that even when it is determined that there is a public interest in the production of a good or service, the decision of whether to choose from among regulation, funding, and direct provision as an expression of the public interest is never going to be determined exclusively by economic factors. As a consequence, an analysis of the strengths and weaknesses of the public and private sectors in the production and delivery of services to the public will inevitably be an "other things being equal" exercise.

Public Sector Versus Private Sector: Strengths and Weaknesses

The question of whether a particular good or service should be delivered privately under regulation, privately with public funding, or directly publicly almost never arises in an analysis from first principles. Rather, the question inevitably arises in connection with specific political decisions. For example, how do we provide for access to electricity in rural areas? Jurisdictions across North America confronted this question between the 1920s and 1940s and answered it in many different ways. In the rural mid-south of the United States, for example, access was delivered publicly through the creation of the Tennessee Valley Authority. In other areas, public subsidies were provided for rural electrification. And in others, cross-subsidies to permit the servicing of high-cost areas were built into regulated rate structures.

In a different context, the regulation/funding/direct provision debate repeats itself in connection with every proposed privatization or public–private partnership, or every time a public service is contracted out.

PUBLIC SECTOR ADVANTAGES

In these debates, both the public and the private sectors bring a range of strengths and weaknesses to the table. The advantages of the public sector in the provision of goods and services in the public interest arise from four basic characteristics: scale; time horizon; the power to tax; and, in a functioning democracy, the existence of a direct, continuous, and flexible connection between the provision of a public service and the public interest that mandates its provision.

Scale matters for a number of reasons. Unit costs of providing for many services decline as scale increases. The natural capacity of the public sector to provide aggregate service delivery on a society-wide scale provides a potential cost advantage. The question of scale can, however, cut both ways, particularly where a service is specialized and/or the jurisdiction is small. As a result, there are services or components of services in which the ability of the private sector to provide the same service in a number of different jurisdictions shifts the scale advantage to private-sector providers.

The public sector will generally have a much longer time horizon than a private-sector corporation. A government can undertake a long-term project with the confidence that it will continue to be around to manage it until its completion. A government can establish long-term economic relationships at a more reasonable cost because the parties with whom it deals can be confident of its longevity. A government's longer time horizon means that it can afford to be a much more patient investor than a private corporation whose shareholders are preoccupied with quarterly profit and loss statements.

However, it is in the combination of scale, time horizon, and the power to tax that the advantages of public sector provision in comparison with the private sector are most apparent.

The most important of these advantages are found in governments' ability to borrow money and to pool and bear risk. Time horizon, scale, and taxation power give governments a substantial cost advantage in borrowing funds in investment markets. Governments at all levels will typically be able to borrow funds at a rate 100 basis points (1 percent/year) or more lower than the rate charged to even the most credit-worthy corporate borrowers. Compared with the borrowing costs of the typical stand-alone operator of a P3 project, a government's cost-of-borrowing advantage over the private sector will be a minimum of 200 to 300 basis points (2–3 percent/year) and can rise to as much as 400 to 600 basis points or more.[1]

What appear to be relatively small differences in borrowing costs—1 percent to 2 percent per year—actually make a substantial difference in the financing costs embedded in the costs of large capital projects. For example, in a project with an economic life of 30 years, a 1 percent difference in the cost of borrowing translates to a difference of 20 percent in the present value of financing costs. This difference in the cost of access to capital is the economic reality behind the fact that, in general, it makes no economic sense for governments to finance public capital projects through P3s. Governments can always borrow money more cheaply than private corporations.

RISK MANAGEMENT

These three differences also mean that governments have a substantial advantage over the private sector in risk management. For example, whereas in a private-sector P3 the risk associated with adverse economic events must be absorbed by a single project, for a government risk can be pooled across all projects and multiple time periods. For a private operator, the ability to absorb risk is limited by the capital that its shareholders and lenders have provided. For a government, the ability to absorb risk is backed up by its access to the tax base.[2]

In some aspects of risk management, however, the private sector has a distinct advantage over government. This advantage arises from institutional differences between governments and private sector corporations.

In general, one would expect a private corporation to underweight downside risk relative to upside risk. That asymmetry arises from the fact that while there is no effective limit on the ability of a corporation to profit from risk on the upside, the concept of limited liability puts a floor under the corporation's downside risk. The downside is limited by the amount invested in the company by its shareholders and lenders. In the private sector, there is a walk-away right. There is no corresponding right in the public sector.

The opposite problem arises in the public sector. Our collective obsession with financial accountability, value-for-money auditing, and the constant quest for examples of waste and inefficiency in the public sector has a direct impact on attitudes toward risk in the public sector. The penalty for taking a risk and losing out is extreme; the reward for taking a risk and succeeding is much more limited. As a result, one would expect the public sector to attach relatively more weight to downside risk than to upside risk—exactly the opposite of the private sector.

The factors discussed above go to the issue of whether the public sector or the private sector is more cost-effective in the delivery of public services. Indeed, much of the debate over the role of the private sector in the delivery of public services revolves around the cost advantages claimed for private delivery.

THE DEMOCRATIC FACTOR

As mentioned above, the fourth significant advantage enjoyed by the public sector in the delivery of public services is the direct, continuous, and flexible connection in a functioning democracy linking the delivery of the service to the public policy considerations that govern its delivery.

Public services are not delivered on the basis of a business rationale. They are delivered based on a political rationale. The decisions that determine our consumption of goods and services in common rather than individually are the most fundamental political decisions we make as a society. They are central to the way we define our society. As such, those decisions also define much of the field of political debate in every election campaign at every level of government. And it is the ability of different governments to offer and act on different answers to those fundamental questions that makes a functioning democracy meaningful.

In more colloquial terms, as a society we have to be able to change our mind about what public services we want to deliver and how we want to deliver them, and our governments have to be able to act on that change.

But that is not how the private sector works. Whereas the public sector operates based on political direction that is subject to change, the private sector operates based on contractual rights and a legal framework that protects those rights.

The significance of this distinction is that, generally speaking, when a government contracts with a private business to deliver a public service, it gives up the right to change its mind. In effect, private sector delivery locks in the political preferences of the government that arranges for that private sector delivery.

Examples of the kinds of problems one can encounter with private sector delivery of services abound. In Ontario, in the late 1990s, the Mike Harris Conservative government decided to sell off the right to operate and collect tolls on Highway 407, a then newly built expressway intended to relieve pressure on a freeway, Highway 401. Under the terms of the sale, the Harris government granted the concession holder the right to set toll rates and other fees. The concession holder was also granted the same right as municipalities to use the provincial vehicle licensing system as a collection enforcement mechanism.

When the government changed, and toll inflation, late payment fees, and aggressive use of licence denial as a collection tool became political issues, it turned out that the new government was powerless to change the terms of the deal. The Harris government's decision in the late 1990s on the terms of the concession sale effectively prevented any change in public policy for the 99-year term of the concession.

Furthermore, because the sale had established the contractual right of the concession holder to operate the highway within the terms of the concession, a change in the overall policy framework would have required the government to compensate the concession holder.

Another example concerns a decision by the government of Alberta to use the P3 framework for the construction of new schools in Calgary and Edmonton. Shortly after the contracts were awarded, the Calgary school board decided that it wanted to provide in-school child care in all schools serving primary school age children. Because the P3 contract had not specified the inclusion of facilities for early childhood education, however, the child-care policy could not be implemented in the P3 schools.

In the case of the highway, a publicly operated toll road would have been subject to political pressure to justify its toll rate increases and to moderate its collection procedures. The private operator is immune to those pressures. In the case of the school facilities, had the facilities been provided in the normal manner—constructed by private builders on contract with and operated by the school board—the construction contract could have been amended to provide for the necessary facilities. That was not possible with the P3 contract.

In addition, for a combination of legal and economic reasons, privatization of public services or their delivery tends to be difficult to reverse. Legally, once a service is contracted for private provision, it is difficult to bring it back within the public domain, regardless of changing political preferences. As a practical matter, an end to contracting out of a service depends on synchronizing a political cycle— the political preferences of the government of the day with the contractual cycle for the service.

A specific case in point: curbside garbage collection in the city of Toronto was primarily being provided publicly, but for historical reasons in two geographic areas it was contracted out. In the mid-2000s, a city council was elected that favoured delivering all garbage pickup services in-house. However, only one of the two contracts expired during the council's term in office. That contract was not renewed, at a saving of $4 million per year. The other contract will expire after a new council is elected, and may be renewed by that council.

There are also provisions of the North American Free Trade Agreement (NAFTA) that give US and Mexican corporations rights to bid for any work that has been contracted out in the past. Although the proposition has not been tested in the courts—there are not a lot of precedents in Canada for major public services that have been contracted out being brought back into the public sector—the NAFTA can be read as giving US and Mexican corporations access to the courts to claim compensation for the loss of the opportunity to bid to provide a service that had previously been contracted out.

The economic factors that make contracting out difficult to reverse are more subtle. Many contracted-out services involve specialized knowledge as well as equipment that is both specialized and costly. Once a service has been shifted from public provision to private provision, the public sector will no longer own the specialized equipment and will likely lose the specialized knowledge required to provide the service. This phenomenon will also tend to push up the price of private provision over time, as the initially successful bidder acquires a significant advantage over other bidders when it comes to contract renewal. In effect, the initial bidder acquires a limited monopoly on the provision of the service, regardless of the term of the contract.

In effect, the essence of private sector delivery arrangements—contractual certainty—is inconsistent with the essence of political decision making: the freedom to change.

NOTES

1. For a more detailed analysis of impact of borrowing cost differentials on P3 costs, see Hugh Mackenzie, *Doing the math: Why P3s for Alberta schools don't add up* (Edmonton: CUPE Alberta, December 2007).
2. Pam Edwards, Jean Shaoul, Anne Stafford, and Lorna Arblaster, *Evaluating the operation of PFI in roads and hospitals*, Research Report No. 84 (Toronto: Association of Chartered Certified Accountants, Certified Accountants Educational Trust, 2004).

DISCUSSION QUESTIONS

1. What key economic factors should be considered in determining whether or not a particular good or service should be produced in the public sector or the private sector?
2. What characteristics of governments make it possible for them to borrow money more cheaply than private corporations?
3. Discuss the difference between providing public services publicly and providing those services through contractual arrangements with private businesses.
4. What non-economic factors affect the public versus private provision decision? Why do those factors matter?

SUGGESTED READINGS

Goodwin, Neva, Julie A. Nelson, Frank Ackerman, and Thomas Weisskopf. 2008. *Microeconomics in context.* 2nd ed. Armonk, NY: M.E. Sharpe.

Mackenzie, Hugh. 2009. *Bad before, worse now: The financial crisis and the skyrocketing costs of public private partnerships (P3s).* Toronto: CUPE Ontario.

Rosen, Harvey, Beverly George Dahlby, Roger Smith, and Jean-François Wen. 2008. *Public finance in Canada.* 3rd Canadian ed. Toronto: McGraw-Hill Ryerson.

Does Foreign Ownership of Corporations Matter?

COMPETING VIEWS

Walid Hejazi, "Foreign Control in the Canadian Economy"

David Leadbeater, " Foreign Ownership: Context and Issues"

Editors' Introduction

Since the end of the Second World War in 1945, the world's nations have become much more economically interdependent. World trade in goods and services has grown much faster than gross world product (GWP), and as a result the openness of most countries has risen significantly. Nowadays, the average ratio of countries' imports plus exports to their gross domestic product—a good measure of openness—is about 45 percent, and Canada's ratio is over 60 percent!

International capital flows—both equity and debt instruments, direct and portfolio investment*—have also increased over the same period more rapidly than GWP. As a result, the ownership of countries' capital has become more diversified and international in character. The rapid growth of transnational corporations (TNCs) since 1945 has been an important cause and effect of these changes. TNCs, as their name suggests, operate in more than one country. In a given country, they may establish wholly owned subsidiaries of the parent corporation, they may purchase a controlling interest in a pre-existing company, or they may simply purchase a non-controlling interest in a firm for marketing or other purposes. TNCs have been important actors on the world stage since the late 19th century. Since 1945, however, their role in global development has become more and more significant, and the possibility of any one state's exercising political control over their operations has become increasingly remote.

---

* "Equity" refers to ownership (stocks or claims on profits), while debt instruments are government and private loans, including bonds (which yield interest). Direct investment relates to ownership or control of a company, while portfolio investment (which can involve the purchase of both bonds and stocks) is undertaken to receive interest and dividends and/or capital gains if the market value of a security appreciates (increases).

Throughout most of its history, Canada relied on net inflows of foreign capital to finance a portion of its development investment. Initially, most of the foreign capital inflows were in *portfolio* form, principally from Britain, but during the 20th century, foreign *direct* investment rose in importance, the United States became the most important foreign investor, and a number of important sectors of the Canadian economy were dominated by subsidiaries of US firms. From the early 1970s onward, however, Canadian direct investment abroad grew faster than foreign direct investment flows into Canada, and by the late 1990s Canada's direct ownership of foreign companies exceeded foreign ownership of Canadian companies.

Recently, two arguments have been put forward, sometimes both by a single commentator: first, the nation-state is on its way to becoming obsolete; and second, concerns about the extent of foreign ownership or control of a country's industry and resources are misplaced. The late Canadian neoclassical economist Harry Johnson said, in a deliberately provocative remark that echoes the argument of a certain strain of Marxist thought, "Capital is capital. If the workers are going to be exploited by the capitalists, they might as well be exploited by *efficient* capitalists!"

The two contributions in this chapter should likely both be read *twice*. Working from many of the same statistical sources, and agreeing on many of the overall trends in foreign investment and ownership, Walid Hejazi and David Leadbeater come to diametrically opposite conclusions, and both offer rich and persuasive arguments in support of their conclusions. Hejazi argues that rather than having too much foreign investment, Canada runs the risk of having too little. He shows that Canadian ownership of foreign firms now exceeds foreign ownership of Canadian firms, and argues that foreign ownership provides an important channel for technological change and productivity growth. Leadbeater argues, in contrast, that the concerns which were expressed about foreign ownership in the 1972 Gray Report are still valid, that aggregate data mask significant differences between sectors in the importance of foreign ownership, and that foreign ownership inhibits Canadian-based research and development expenditures and renders Canada more vulnerable, both economically and politically.

Foreign Control in the Canadian Economy

Walid Hejazi

Introduction

The Canadian economy is heavily dependent on international trade and foreign direct investment (FDI). Although the benefits of international trade are clear to many Canadians, there is less of a consensus on foreign investment. Often, take-overs of iconic Canadian companies, such as steelmaker Dofasco, Hudson's Bay Company, Inco, and Alcan, result in emotional discussions regarding the "hollow-ing out" of the Canadian economy, that is, moving all the high-value decision-making functions out of Canada, the corollary being that only lower value-added functions are left in Canada. The implication of such discussions is that foreign investment into the Canadian economy is bad, at least when that investment is accompanied by foreign control of Canadian assets.

These public debates are often too narrow and often inconsistent with the facts. This essay will put the discussion of foreign ownership of the Canadian economy into broader perspective. The data on Canada's experience with foreign ownership will be reviewed,[1] as will the discussion on the pros and cons of foreign ownership. Policy recommendations will also be provided.

Definitions

Portfolio Versus Direct Investment

When a foreign investor buys the bonds of or a few shares in a Canadian company, the investments are referred to as foreign portfolio investment into Canada. These investments are passive: the investor has no effective influence, or control, over the actions of the underlying corporation. In contrast, when a foreign investor opens a new business or buys in full an existing business in Canada, these invest-ments are referred to as foreign direct investment (FDI).

The distinction between portfolio and direct investments is one of control. When an investment is not accompanied by control of the underlying assets, it is referred to as portfolio investment. When the investment is accompanied by con-trol of the underlying assets, it is referred to as direct investment.

In the above examples, the distinction between portfolio and direct investment is clear but in many situations, the distinction would not be as clear-cut. For example, suppose that an investor begins with portfolio investment and increases his holdings in a company. At what point will that investment change from portfolio to direct investment? Of course, to have absolute control, the investor would need 50 percent plus 1 share of all voting shares. In reality, however, a single investor does not require such a majority stake in an organization to exert effective control over the corporation. The rule of thumb in Canada and in the United States is 10 percent, meaning that if a foreign investor holds 10 percent in a publicly traded company, that investment is said to be direct investment.

Stocks Versus Flows

Flows of foreign investment represent the new investments that take place in a particular year. In contrast, the stock of foreign investment represents the accumulated flows of foreign investment, plus retained earnings, plus an adjustment for appreciation/depreciation.[2] The stock of foreign investment therefore provides a clear picture of the extent of foreign capital that has been invested in Canada. These data are often reported on a historical cost basis.

Ownership Versus Control

An important distinction must be made between foreign ownership of the Canadian economy and foreign control. Although only a fraction of a company may be owned by the foreign interest, all of its assets would be foreign controlled.

Canada's Experience with Inward FDI and Foreign Ownership

The Ratio of Canada's Outward to Inward FDI

Canada has had a long history with FDI. Figure 1 plots the ratio of Canada's outward FDI stock to inward FDI stock since 1930. Outward FDI represents direct investments by Canadians into foreign countries, and inward FDI represents FDI into Canada by foreigners. Between 1930 and 1974, the ratio of Canada's outward to inward FDI stocks was between 0.20 and 0.30. This means that for every dollar of Canadian direct investment abroad, there were between 3 and 5 dollars of foreign investment in Canada. That is, Canada was more of a host economy.

However, in the early 1970s, Canada's FDI abroad began growing more rapidly than foreign direct investment in Canada, and as a result the ratio of Canada's FDI abroad to foreign investment in Canada began to rise. By 1997, Canada had more investment abroad than there was foreign investment in Canada.

FIGURE 1   Ratio of FDI Abroad to FDI in Canada

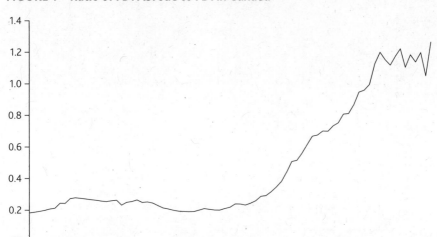

Sources: Data underlying this figure are from Statistics Canada: Foreign direct investment stock in Canada (CANSIM V235412) and Canadian direct investment stock abroad (CANSIM V235396). The series plotted in the figure is outward divided by inward investment.

Underlying the ratio of outward to inward FDI in Figure 1, above, however, are stocks of outward and inward FDI in Canada, which continue to grow at quite rapid rates, as shown in Figure 2, below. In 2008, Canada's outward FDI reached over $637 billion, whereas inward FDI reached over $500 billion. Over the past two decades, the stocks of both outward and inward FDI have grown more rapidly than GDP or trade.

It is also interesting to note that in the early 1970s, Canada brought in the Foreign Investment Review Agency (FIRA) to protect Canadian companies from foreign investors. At that time, Canada had four times more inward investment than outward—that is, Canada was very much a host economy. Today, Canada has more outward than inward FDI. As a result, if Canada were to restrict foreign investment into the Canadian economy, the sizable Canadian investments abroad might be exposed to retaliation by foreign countries that host Canadian investments. Also, Canada's obligations under NAFTA limit to some extent its ability to implement restrictions on foreign investment.

Canada Losing Its Attractiveness as a Destination for FDI

Figure 2 clearly shows that Canadian companies are expanding abroad at a faster rate than foreign companies are expanding in Canada. Nevertheless, Canada is

FIGURE 2   Inward and Outward FDI

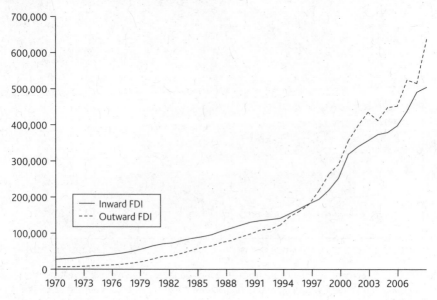

Sources: See Figure 1.

losing its attractiveness as a destination for global FDI. Figure 3 clearly shows this to be the case. In 1970, Canada received 15 percent of the world's stock of FDI. This share has fallen continuously: in 2007, Canada received only about 3.5 percent.

Some may argue that it is obvious that Canada's share of global FDI should fall as emerging economies such as China, India, and Brazil grow rapidly and attract more FDI. However, when we benchmark Canada against the G7, the NAFTA countries, or just the United States, Canada's share is still falling. That is, regardless of whether the emerging economies are included in the comparison or not, Canada has become less attractive to FDI.

At the same time that Canada has seen its share of FDI on the inward side fall, the figure indicates that, at a minimum, its share on the outward side has remained stable, or perhaps even increased (see Figure 4). That is, Canadian multinationals are keeping pace with the rapidly growing stocks of world outward FDI.

Foreign Control

Figure 5 demonstrates foreign control in the Canadian economy over the period 1965 to 2006. Foreign control in the Canadian economy was highest in the early 1970s, when 35 percent of Canadian assets and 37 percent of revenues were controlled by foreigners. Over the 1970s and early 1980s the extent of foreign ownership in Canada fell, with foreign control over Canadian assets reaching its

FIGURE 3   Canada's Share of Inward FDI Stocks: 1970–2007

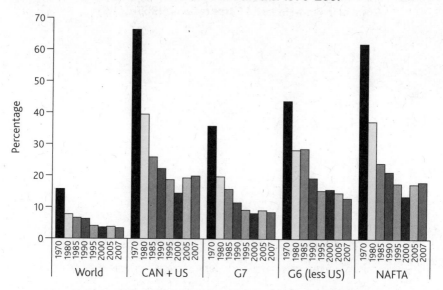

Source: The United Nations Conference on Trade and Development (UNCTAD) Foreign Direct Investment database. http://www.unctad.org/Templates/Page.asp?intItemID=1923&lang=1.

FIGURE 4   Canada's Share of Outward FDI Stocks: 1970–2007

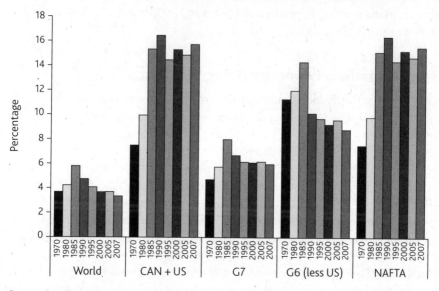

Source: See Figure 3.

FIGURE 5   Percentage of Assets and Revenues Under Foreign Control in Non-Financial Corporations (1965–2006)

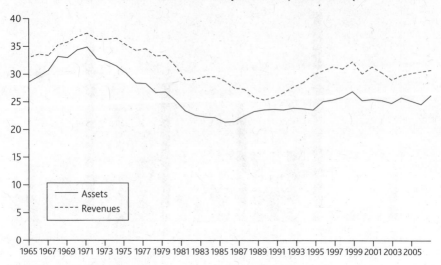

Sources: The data for the period 2000–2006 are from Statistics Canada CANSIM labels v6168923 for assets and v6168939 for revenues. The data for the period 1965–2000 are from Baldwin and Gellatly (2005).

minimum in 1985 at 21.4 percent and foreign-controlled revenues in 1989 at 25.4 percent. Control over revenues increased through 1997 and has fallen slightly since then. In 2006, foreign control over Canadian revenues stood at 30.8 percent. Control over assets increased over the late 1980s and 1990s, but has remained roughly constant since 2000 at about 25 percent.

Is the Canadian Economy Being "Hollowed Out"?

Many would argue that foreign investment into the Canadian economy is, on balance, negative for Canada. It is argued that Canada's most prominent and successful corporations are being bought out by foreigners and that when a Canadian company is taken over by a foreign company, the headquarter (high-value) functions are all moved out of Canada. These assertions will be reviewed below.

The data presented above do not indicate any obvious "takeover" of the Canadian economy. We have seen that, although it is true that the amount of foreign investment into the Canadian economy in dollar terms is growing rapidly, the amount of Canadian investment abroad is growing more rapidly. Since 1997, Canada has had more investment abroad than there is foreign investment in Canada. In addition, Canada has been losing its attractiveness as a destination for foreign investment relative to global trends, as is seen in the reduction in the share of FDI locating in Canada, again whether emerging economies are included in the calculation or not. These facts are not consistent with the assertion that the Canadian economy is being taken over by foreigners.

There is more evidence that indicates that the Canadian economy is not being hollowed out. According to a study on global leaders undertaken by the Institute for Prosperity and Competitiveness, there is no evidence to conclude that a foreign takeover of a Canadian company has a negative impact on Canada's prosperity.[3] On the contrary, the study finds that such foreign investment in Canada contributes to our productivity and prosperity.

Research by the institute uses the following criteria to identify Canada's global leaders: (1) public or private Canadian-controlled companies listed in *The Report on Business* Top 1,000 or *Financial Post* 500; (2) revenues exceeding $100 million in 2007; and (3) one of the five largest by revenue globally in a specific market segment—in some cases where global competition is precluded (for example, rail service and CN Rail), or only North America was used, and in other cases where revenue was not the factor used (for example, market capitalization and Manulife). Using these criteria, the institute identified 33 global leaders in 1985, 86 in 2003, 84 in 2008, and 86 as of April 2009. In other words, the number of Canadian global leaders is actually increasing, not decreasing. To quote from the institute's website, "While these takeovers have been highly visible, the Institute's research shows that, over the past two decades, the number of global leaders in Canada has actually increased. ... These global leaders, like McCain, Open Text, and Research in Motion, have competed on the basis of innovation, globally significant capabilities, and global expansion to generate prosperity." What this evidence shows is that Canada's leading organizations are increasing and are not being taken over by foreigners. More important, they reveal dynamism in the Canadian economy, which has allowed Canada to create an increasing number of global leaders.

As for the discussion about head office functions, research by Statistics Canada directly addresses this point. The following quotation from a Statistics Canada study is instructive:

> Much of the dynamism in Canada's head office sector actually comes from foreign-controlled firms. The head offices of foreign-controlled firms contributed to all of the gains in the number of head offices over the past 6 years and accounted for 6 out of 10 new jobs created. The effect of foreign takeovers has not been to reduce the number of head offices in Canada or head office employment. As a result of foreign takeovers, more new head offices were created than lost and employment in head offices was as high after the takeovers had occurred than before. (Beckstead and Brown 2006, 15)

The available research therefore is not consistent with the conclusion that the Canadian economy is being hollowed out. The public debate that often follows a high-profile takeover of a Canadian company is typically emotional and is not supported empirically.

Foreign Investment and Control in the Canadian Economy

Are There Any Benefits to Foreign Ownership in Canada?

One question that is often raised concerns the benefits of foreign ownership. Are the Canadian economy and Canadians better off as a result of foreign ownership, and if so, how? As an article in the *National Post* (November 14, 2007) explains:

> A disproportionately large share of the contribution to labour productivity growth is due to foreign-controlled firms closing less productive plants and opening more productive plants. ... More broadly, foreign-controlled firms make more use of technology and scale, have higher labour productivity, pay higher wages because their workforces are more skilled, hire more white-collar workers to oversee complex processes, and innovate more.

So the question becomes, why are foreign firms more productive than domestic firms, not just in Canada, but generally? International business theory states that foreign companies must be more productive than domestic companies, otherwise the foreign company could not overcome the additional costs associated with working in foreign markets and still remain profitable. Those additional costs are known as the liability of foreignness and are well documented in the literature.

The foreign firm must have developed some firm-specific advantages that it is now exploiting in foreign markets, such as patents, brands, managerial know-how, supply chain flexibility, or some other advantage that allows the firm to be profitable in a foreign market—just think about Microsoft, Apple, PWC, Deloitte, McDonald's, Starbucks, or Walmart.

Often, the advantages held by foreign companies are driven by research and development (R&D) efforts on the part of the foreign affiliate's parent in the foreign jurisdiction. This is especially true in the Canadian context, where it is well known that Canada lags the G7 countries in R&D efforts, despite the fact that the Canadian government is among the most generous developed nations when it comes to incentives to undertake R&D.

An important area of policy research helps to better understand why Canadians undertake significantly less R&D than other nations. One hypothesis is based on concepts known as domestic and foreign R&D efforts. Domestic R&D efforts are those undertaken within Canada. Foreign R&D efforts are the R&D embedded in Canada's imports of goods and services as well as in Canada's inward FDI. That is, both international trade and FDI are important channels for international technology diffusion.

Empirical evidence for the Organisation for Economic Co-operation and Development (OECD) in general and for Canada in particular shows that FDI is the dominant channel, accounting for twice the spillovers attributed to trade. What this means is that the Canadian economy is accessing pools of international R&D (that is, knowledge) through its trade and FDI linkages into the global economy.

Foreign ownership in the Canadian economy therefore brings great benefit. As foreign multinationals come into the Canadian economy, they bring with them knowledge and technology. This allows them to be more productive. By competing and interacting with foreign firms, Canadian firms "absorb" the knowledge and technology from the foreign companies—known as knowledge spillovers—as a result also enhancing the productivity of Canadian companies (Coe and Helpman 1995; Hejazi and Safarian 1999).

Do Canadian Companies Need to Be Protected from Takeover by Large Global Companies?

Financial markets are important for any modern economy. If operating efficiently, financial markets will allocate resources to their most productive uses. When managers of publicly traded companies do a poor job, shareholders express their disapproval by selling shares, resulting in a fall in share prices, which makes it more difficult for those companies to get access to credit. On the other hand, if managers do a good job, they are rewarded by higher stock prices, the result of increased demand by investors for their company's shares.

One of the disciplines imposed by the market is the threat of takeover. When managers do a poor job and their company's stock price falls as a result, someone may attempt to buy the "underpriced" shares and replace the management team. In a market like Canada, where there may often not be a corporation large enough to take over a viable organization with poor management, foreign companies can fill the void. When the threat of takeover by foreign companies is reduced or eliminated through regulation (in this case, restricting foreign investment), the discipline imposed by the market on domestic managers by way of actual or potential takeover can no longer operate, and Canadian economic prosperity suffers. Foreign ownership thus forces Canadian managers to operate up to global standards.

Conclusions

Foreign ownership of the Canadian economy is an important area of public policy in Canada. Each time there is a takeover of an iconic Canadian company, such as Hudson's Bay or even Tim Hortons, many Canadians respond emotionally. They often feel as though such sales of Canadian assets represent a loss. The analysis presented in this essay should indicate that this is not the case. First, it is important to note that Canadians are expanding their investments globally at a faster pace than foreigners are expanding into Canada. Second, Canada continues to create global leaders, and this number is increasing, not decreasing. Third, and perhaps most important, foreign ownership in the Canadian economy brings with it many benefits—enhanced technology, competition, and managerial discipline—all of which make Canadian companies more competitive. This translates into higher incomes and prosperity for Canadians. Indeed, the fact that Canada is not getting *more* foreign investment has been linked to lagging prosperity for Canada.

The policy recommendations from this discussion are clear. The best way for the Canadian government to protect domestic firms from takeover by foreign companies is not by protecting them through legislation. Such an approach would result in the Canadian economy being less competitive, and would hurt Canadian employment and incomes. Rather, the best way to protect Canadian firms is to ensure that they operate in an environment that allows them to be globally competitive. As a result, Canadian companies will be able to compete with global companies and at the same time create the maximum amount of prosperity for Canadians. In such an environment, we have nothing to fear from foreign investment.

NOTES

1. The data on foreign control in Canadian industry are not available on a timely basis. For example, the CANSIM series with data for December 2006 was released in April 2009. Foreign control data are based on information obtained under the *Corporations Returns Act*, combined with information from the annual Financial and Taxation Statistics program.

2. FDI stocks are defined as follows:

$$FDI_t = FDI_{t-1} + \text{Retained earnings} + \text{Net flows of FDI} + \text{Price appreciation/depreciation on } FDI_{t-1}$$

The stock of FDI at any point in time is defined as the level of FDI in the previous period, plus retained earnings, plus net new flows of FDI, plus price appreciation (or less depreciation). This is the balance of payments definition of FDI.

3. For information on the Institute's research on global leaders, see its website: http://www.competeprosper.ca/index.php/canada_global_leaders.

DISCUSSION QUESTIONS

1. Do Canadian companies need to be protected through regulations restricting foreign entry?

2. What explains Canada's changing FDI patterns? Think about the role of Canada's free trade agreements with the United States and Mexico and the benefits of locating in Canada and gaining market access.

3. What explains differences in foreign ownership across sectors? More specifically, why do you think financial services and telecommunications have the lowest foreign ownership stakes whereas industries such as mining have the highest?
4. Should the Canadian government encourage more foreign investment?
5. What impact did the entry of Walmart have on the Canadian economy? Or to ask this differently, would Canadian consumers be better or worse off if Walmart had not been allowed to enter the Canadian economy? Would Walmart's competitors be better or worse off if Walmart had not been allowed to enter the Canadian market? In light of your answer, is it consumers or Canadian businesses that are driving government policy on foreign investment?
6. If the exchange rate were to depreciate, as Canada's did during the 1980s and 1990s, would you expect Canada to become more or less attractive to FDI? Did Canada become more or less attractive to FDI during this period?

REFERENCES AND SUGGESTED READINGS

Baldwin, John R., and Guy Gellatly. 2005. *Global links: Long-term trends in foreign investment and foreign control in Canada, 1960 to 2000.* The Canadian economy in transition series, 11-622-MIE, No. 008. Ottawa: Statistics Canada. http://www.statcan.gc.ca/bsolc/olc-cel/ olc-cel?lang=eng&catno=11-622-M2005008.

Baldwin, John R., and Guy Gellatly. 2007. *Global links: Multinationals in Canada: An overview of research at Statistics Canada.* The Canadian economy in transition series, 11-622-MIE, No. 14. Ottawa: Minister of Industry. http://www.statcan.gc.ca/ bsolc/olc-cel/olc-cel?lang=eng&catno=11-622-M2007014.

Beckstead, Desmond, and W. Mark Brown. 2006. Statistics Canada 11-624-MIE No. 014. http://www.statcan.gc.ca/pub/11-624-m/11-624-m2006014-eng.pdf.

Coe, David T., and Elhanan Helpman. 1995. International R&D spillovers. *European Economic Review* 39: 859–887.

Hejazi, W. 2010. *Dispelling Canadian myths about foreign direct investment.* Institute for Research on Public Policy (January 26).

Hejazi, W., and A.E. Safarian. 1999. Trade, foreign direct investment, and R&D spillovers. *Journal of International Business Studies* 30 (3): 491–511.

Foreign Ownership: Context and Issues

David Leadbeater

---

*If the free-traders cannot understand how one nation can grow rich
at the expense of another, we need not wonder, since these same
gentlemen also refuse to understand how within one country one class
can enrich itself at the expense of another.*

Karl Marx, 1848

Introduction

Foreign ownership and, more broadly, economic and political independence from
outside domination has been the subject of intense debate in Canada since colonial rule. The debate reflects not only historically rooted concerns about outside
exploitation of labour and resources and about the limiting of economic opportunity to being "hewers of wood and drawers of water," but also aspirations about
political sovereignty and democracy—to be "*maîtres chez nous*, masters in our own
house." As with many economic issues, the economic analysis of foreign ownership
is inevitably tied to political–economic views concerning the role of the state and
democracy, income and wealth distribution, the goals of economic development,
and globalization, particularly US power in the world and pressures in Canada
toward integration into the United States.

Foreign Ownership, Influence, and Control

This essay focuses on the two main modern forms of foreign ownership: foreign
portfolio investment and, especially, foreign direct investment, given the latter's
greater control and permanence. Both foreign portfolio and foreign direct investment in Canada entail external financial claims and thus obligations to foreign
corporations, individuals, or governments. They also involve different types and
degrees of external control or influence. With *foreign portfolio investment*, the
foreign investors who own Canadian debt or equity securities are taken to have
"no significant influence" in the management or operations of their investment.[1]
Historically, the largest type of foreign portfolio investment in Canada has been
in government and corporate bonds (debt), though the value of foreign portfolio

ownership of Canadian stocks (equity) now exceeds that of bonds. A significant difference between bonds and stocks is that bonds usually have a maturity date and can be paid off, while stocks can be an enduring financial claim.

In contrast, the official definition of *foreign direct investment* requires that an investor have "a significant voice in the management of an enterprise operating outside his own economy" (International Money Fund, cited in Lajule 2001). For the foreign (equity) ownership to be considered *direct* investment, Statistics Canada uses a threshold of 10 percent for a single investor. But to have a *controlling interest*, the threshold is 50 percent. A firm with 50 or more percent ownership is a *foreign subsidiary* while the former (10 up to 50 percent ownership) is a "foreign associate." Statistics Canada's foreign-control statistics also provide that "if control is acknowledged by a corporation" then there is deemed to be effective foreign control.[2]

The issue of influence or control goes well beyond simply the capacity of individual foreign investors to control appointments in subsidiaries, determine investments, repatriate profits, or control research, patents, and other, narrower, financial matters. Larger sectional and class interests also exist, today particularly those of multinational corporations, behind major political directions such as free trade and other neoliberal policy measures (including privatization, deregulation, subcontracting, and reducing social program standards). The Gray Report (Canada 1972, chap. 18) discussed this "foreign corporate influence" in the Canadian political process and noted the role of foreign corporate pressures, such as through the Canadian Chamber of Commerce, the Canadian Manufacturers' Association, and, one could add today, the Canadian Council of Chief Executives. Foreign ownership has also been associated with empire and modern imperialism. It is difficult to appreciate the depth of the foreign ownership issue without understanding the evolution of corporate power and the class structure of Canada. Indeed, there is a significant social science literature that attempts to explain the ultimate causes of the high level of foreign ownership and economic subordination in Canada by examining the evolving class and sectional interests and struggles in Canada, particularly the role of natural resource or "staple" export dependence (see, for example, Laxer 1991). Uneven development and unequal structures of national and class ownership, as Marx's comment over 160 years ago illustrates, have long been with us and continue to be major defining issues in economic development and policy.[3]

Canada's Historically High Level of Foreign Ownership

The historical context of the high level of foreign ownership in Canada is crucial to understanding present conditions, particularly three patterns. First, foreign investment in Canada was dominated overwhelmingly by the world's two leading capitalist countries, Britain and then the United States, which had much higher levels of capital accumulation and technological development than Canada, levels that allowed major capital exporting. Second, that initial dominance was later extended into Canada mainly through foreign direct investment and in the more rapidly growing and technologically dynamic industries. Third, once established, foreign sectoral dominance tended to continue and even to be extended by market forces, including financing by Canadian banks. Foreign dominance was limited and substantially reversed in only a few sectors, largely due to government actions that restricted or nationalized foreign direct investment.

During the 19th century, most foreign investment was portfolio investment from Britain, tied to large infrastructure projects, particularly canals and railways, in the form of bonds, typically guaranteed by the colonial and later Canadian governments. As European settlement and industrialism spread, capital accumulated, and corporations grew in number and size, there was a generally increased demand for capital not satisfied by domestic savings, hence capital was borrowed from London finance. One such project, the Canadian Pacific Railway (CPR), completed in 1885, depended on such foreign borrowing but ownership and control remained in Canada.

Capital accumulation and industrialization in Canada occurred later than in Britain and on a much smaller scale, but it was nonetheless substantial, stimulated in part by major government-supported infrastructure investments and portfolio borrowing. For manufacturing, estimates placed Canada as eighth in the world in 1870 and seventh in 1900 (Laxer 1989, 11). But the United States had an earlier start as well as conditions that permitted rapid expansion largely independent of Britain, especially after the Civil War. By the early 1900s, large-scale industrial and financial "big business" such as Standard Oil (Rockefeller) and US Steel (Carnegie) had appeared and were expanding internationally. It was during this period, up to the First World War, that several leading Canadian industries fell under US foreign ownership—automobiles, chemicals, electrical manufacturing, oil, and non-ferrous mining. These were industries associated with the second industrial revolution and included DuPont (later including part of C-I-L, 1877), Inco (formed in 1886 as the Canadian Copper Company), Imperial Oil (taken over by Standard Oil in 1898), Ford Canada (1904), Union Carbide (1914), IBM (1917), GM Canada (took over McLaughlin Motor Car in 1918). Most of these corporations still occupy dominant positions in production and technology, particularly in manufacturing and natural resource industries in Canada.

As Table 1 shows, the amount of foreign investment in Canada continued to expand between the world wars at a faster rate than gross domestic product (GDP). The dramatic increase in Canada's GDP during the Second World War reduced the relative importance of foreign capital. However, in the nearly three decades of relatively high growth after the war, Canada witnessed a second major wave of foreign investment. This was largely US direct foreign investment, but the US also replaced Britain as the world's leading capitalist power and Canada's major foreign investor: foreign direct investment expanded from 27.6 to 35.7 percent relative to GDP. During this period—as later—most of the expansion of direct investment was from profits made in Canada (retained earnings) plus Canadian finance, and the proportion of new foreign capital inflows as the source of expansion actually declined. The Gray Report commented that "if new direct investment were to be entirely excluded from Canada, foreign control would continue to grow in absolute terms."[4]

By 1970, non-residents controlled 36 percent of non-financial capital (Laliberté 1993) and manufacturing was over 60 percent foreign-controlled (Canada 1972). Canada had so many branch plants that it was characterized by some as a "branch plant economy." In 1981, in manufacturing, Canada had 37 percent of employment in foreign-controlled firms compared with 7 percent in the US; among the OECD countries, Canada's level was exceeded only by Belgium (at 38 percent) and equalled by Ireland (Safarian 1993, 32). However, political resistance was also growing against US domination, culminating with the Gray Report (Canada 1972). In 1973, the federal government established the Foreign Investment Review Agency (FIRA) to screen foreign acquisitions of Canadian firms and the establishment of new foreign firms. Further, on the heels of the 1974–75 oil crisis, the Liberal federal government established Petro-Canada as a fully government-owned Crown corporation.

These federal government initiatives led to a decline in foreign control, particularly in the petroleum industry.[5] They were historically short-lived. Only a decade later, in 1985, leading the rightward shift to neoliberal policies, the then-Progressive Conservative government renamed FIRA Investment Canada, changing its mandate largely to promoting foreign investment. But the reduced level of foreign control did continue in the petroleum industry, even after the privatization of Petro-Canada (beginning in 1991), because Petro-Canada was protected from foreign takeover by a maximum 25 percent foreign-ownership limit.

Overall, however, by 2000, the level of foreign control of Canadian industry had returned to the peak levels of the 1960s and continued to grow. Indeed, in the decade since, there has been a third wave of increased foreign ownership and control, though one diversified beyond the United States, as more major manufacturing industries, such as steel and beer, and resource industries, particularly mining, came under majority foreign control.

TABLE 1   Foreign Investment in Canada, 1926–2006 ($ million current)

	1926	1939	1946	1956	1966	1966	1966	1976	1986	1996	2006
Total foreign investment in Canada	6,403	7,388	8,288	17,899	40,232	40,232	40,232	114,582	598,610	819,392	1,272,727
% foreign direct investment	27.8	32.7	35.7	52.0	48.6	48.6	48.6	36.3	16.0	22.2	34.5
% portfolio investment	61.8	59.7	50.5	34.9	29.7	29.7	29.7	34.0	28.0	54.1	41.9
% other investment	10.4	7.6	13.8	13.1	21.7	21.7	21.7	29.7	22.6	23.8	23.7
Total Canadian investment abroad	1,296	1,880	4,236	7,582	16,520	16,520	16,520	53,275	201,794	509,132	1,188,105
% Canadian direct investment abroad	30.6	35.7	18.1	26.3	23.7	23.7	23.7	22.7	32.1	35.6	44.2
% Canadian portfolio investment abroad	38.0	38.2	13.0	13.3	13.5	13.5	13.5	8.7	11.0	21.3	31.3
% Canadian other investment abroad	31.3	26.1	68.9	60.4	62.8	62.8	62.8	68.6	56.8	43.1	24.6
Canadian investment abroad as % of foreign investment in Canada	20.2	25.4	51.1	42.4	41.1	41.1	41.1	46.5	33.7	62.1	93.4
Canadian direct as % of foreign	22.3	27.8	25.9	21.4	20.0	20.0	20.0	29.1	67.5	99.5	119.6
Canadian portfolio as % of foreign	12.5	16.3	13.2	16.1	18.7	18.7	18.7	11.8	13.3	24.4	69.7
Canadian other as % of foreign	61.1	86.9	255.5	196.2	118.7	118.7	118.7	107.5	85.0	112.6	96.9
Net international investment position	−5,107	−5,508	−4,052	−10,317	−23,712	−23,712	−23,712	−61,307	−196,816	−311,370	−84,623

(Table 1 is continued on the next page.)

TABLE 1 Continued

	1926	1939	1946	1956	1966	1966	1976	1986	1996	2006
Gross domestic product (GDP)	4,866	5,102	10,716	28,658	54,764	64,818	199,994	512,541	836,864	1,449,215
Total foreign investment in Canada as % of GDP	131.6	144.8	77.3	62.5	73.5	62.1	57.3	116.8	97.9	87.8
Foreign direct investment % of GDP	36.6	47.3	27.6	32.5	35.7	30.2	20.8	18.7	21.8	30.3
Foreign portfolio investment % of GDP	81.3	86.4	39.1	21.8	21.8	18.4	19.5	32.7	53.0	36.8
Total Canadian investment abroad as % of GDP	26.6	36.8	39.5	26.5	30.2	25.5	26.6	39.4	60.8	82.0

Sources: Statistics Canada: for investment position data 1926–1986, *Canada's Balance of International Payments and International Investment Position* (cat. no. 67-506-XIE), appendix table 2; for 1996–2006, *Canada's International Investment Position* (cat. no. 67-202-X). For GDP data 1926–1966, *Historical Statistics of Canada* (cat. no. 11-516-X), series F71; for 1966–2006, *Canadian Economic Observer: Historical Statistical Supplement* (cat. no. 11-201-X), table 1.1. The series is broken in 1966 due to revised concept of GDP.

Canadian Direct Investment Abroad, Concentration, and the Balance of Payments

In recent decades Canada has also seen a substantial growth in Canadian investment abroad, especially direct investment. While this has changed the character of foreign-ownership-related balance of payments issues, the growth of Canadian direct investment abroad has not altered the long-standing domestic structural problems of foreign dominance. Since the early 1900s, there have been relatively small amounts of Canadian direct investment abroad, particularly in banking and utilities. By 1970 it was still less than a quarter of foreign direct investment in Canada, but from the 1970s on, Canadian direct investment abroad increased rapidly, still heavily in finance. In 1996, Canadian direct investment abroad surpassed foreign direct investment in Canada.

Table 2 shows that from 2006–2008, Canadian direct investment abroad exceeded foreign direct investment in Canada while Canada's net international

TABLE 2   Foreign Ownership in Canada's International Economic Accounts, 2006–2008 ($ million Canadian)

	2006	2007	2008
Canada's international investment position			
Total assets	*1,188,105*	*1,198,644*	*1,486,171*
Canadian direct investments abroad	524,749	515,445	637,281
Canadian portfolio investments (foreign bonds, stocks)	371,311	369,509	424,335
Other Canadian investments (loans, allowances, deposits, official international reserves, other assets)	292,045	313,689	424,555
Total liabilities	*−1,272,727*	*−1,324,359*	*−1,479,450*
Foreign direct investments in Canada	−438,648	−491,287	−504,864
Foreign portfolio investments (Canadian bonds, stocks, other)	−532,732	−502,418	−584,958
Other foreign investments (loans, deposits, other)	−301,348	−330,653	−389,628
Canada's net international investment position	*−84,623*	*−125,716*	*6,721*
Canada's balance of international payments			
Current account receipts			
Goods and services	522,620	532,763	560,334
Goods	453,951	463,127	489,857
Services	68,669	69,637	70,478
Royalties and licence fees	3,599	3,745	3,643

(Table 2 is continued on the next page.)

TABLE 2   Continued

	2006	2007	2008
Investment income	66,086	76,546	71,668
Direct investment income	36,646	41,884	37,590
Portfolio investment income	17,308	22,066	22,197
Other investment income	12,131	12,596	11,880
Current transfers	9,559	9,489	10,321
Total current account receipts	***598,265***	***618,798***	***642,324***
Current account payments			
Goods and services	−486,952	−503,840	−535,965
Goods	−404,345	−415,229	−442,988
Services	−82,607	−88,611	−92,977
Royalties and licence fees	−7,914	−8,769	−9,363
Investment income	−79,993	−87,880	−86,891
Direct investment income	−36,479	−39,830	−40,002
Portfolio investment income	−29,074	−30,999	−31,982
Other investment income	−14,440	−17,051	−14,908
Current transfers	−10,987	−11,473	−11,352
Total current account payments	***−577,932***	***−603,192***	***−634,209***
Current account balances			
Goods and services	35,668	28,924	24,370
Goods	49,606	47,898	46,869
Services	−13,937	−18,974	−22,499
Royalties and licence fees	−4,315	−5,024	−5,720
Investment income	−13,907	−11,334	−15,224
Direct investment income	167	2,054	−2,412
Portfolio investment income	−11,765	−8,933	−9,784
Other investment income	−2,309	−4,455	−3,029
Current transfers	−1,429	−1,984	−1,031
Total current account balance	***20,333***	***15,606***	***8,115***

Sources: Statistics Canada, *Canada's International Investment Position* (cat. no. 67-202-X); Statistics Canada, *Canada's Balance of International Payments* (cat. no. 67-001-X).

investment position in 2008 nearly reached a balance. Part of the large 2008 increase in Canadian direct investment abroad, which is denominated in foreign currencies, reflected the depreciation of the Canadian dollar. But there has been a definite shift in the last decade, which has reduced the balance of payments impact of the high level of foreign investment in Canada. In decades past, high levels of net international indebtedness were a common pattern. Large outflows of interest and profit from foreign investment in Canada were covered by current account goods exports, particularly natural resource exports; by increased capital inflows; and by a lower Canadian dollar. However, despite a narrowing gap between the current account receipts and payments for direct investment income, there is still a major deficit in overall investment income and, in addition, a telling gap in royalties and licence fees. In this context, royalties and licence fees are generally payments made by companies or institutions for the use of particular technologies, usually patented and copyrighted materials ("intellectual property"); the gap is one indicator of Canada's technological dependency.

The main source of Canadian direct investment growth abroad is finance. In Table 3, one can see that in 2008 the finance and insurance industry accounted for nearly 50 percent of all Canadian direct investment abroad, up from about 32 percent in 1996. A significant part of the increase was in "Offshore Financial Centres"—tax havens.[6] This major expansion of the financial sector relative to the real sector of the economy is part of a bigger pattern that has been characterized as financialization.[7] In 2007, Canada's highly concentrated finance, insurance, and real estate industries absorbed over 35 percent of the county's operating profits, despite productivity growth below the average for the business sector. It is significant that the banking sector has long had federal protection against foreign takeover (federal regulation last limited foreign ownership to 25 percent). Arguably, this greater independence from the US financial system was a significant factor behind the greater stability of the Canadian banking system during the 2008–2009 financial crisis. But it also means that the new balance of payments situation now depends on financialization, and hence on maintaining a monopolistic, oversized, low-productivity industry and tolerating large capital exports to overseas tax havens.

Since the 1970s, particularly with the weakening of the US economic position in the world, there has also been some overall diversification of the country source of foreign investment. However, the United States still remains overwhelmingly dominant, particularly in the context of continuing pressures to continental integration. Those who assume that a weakening of the US position might automatically reduce foreign ownership domestically in Canada should examine the persistence and form of foreign control. There is little need for new external investment once dominant direct ownership positions are established and expanded. As Mel Hurtig (2005), a long-time critic of foreign investment in Canada, observed of published data for 1985 to 2005 from Investment Canada: "In that period of just over 20 years, there were 11,380 companies in Canada taken over by non-resident-controlled corporations. The total value of the takeovers was just over $548.49 billion. During the same years, new foreign investment for new businesses in this country was just over $18.04 billion. So it was just over 96.8 percent foreign investment for takeovers, and a pathetic less than 3.2 percent for new business investment."[8]

Development Critiques of Foreign Direct Investment

The most common postwar critiques of foreign direct ownership emphasized, particularly for manufacturing, that the operations of Canadian branch plants of foreign multinationals were "truncated." The Gray Report (Canada 1972, chap. 3) argued that such foreign-controlled branch plants meant "fewer export opportunities, fewer supporting services, less training of local personnel in various skills, less specialized product development aimed at Canadian needs or tastes, and less spillover economic activity." Truncation also meant a parent-subsidiary relationship of dependence "for technology, components and services." The branch-plant subsidiary structure, moreover, permitted foreign corporations to use their control of internal pricing ("transfer prices") between the subsidiary and parent, which enabled foreign corporations to repatriate profits and charge the subsidiary for components at prices above incremental cost, thus reducing taxes and other benefits to Canada. The report also argued that foreign direct investment favoured large firms with the necessary resources to establish a global market position: "To the extent that foreign investment is pre-emptive, preventing a potential Canadian competitor from developing, it will further reduce competition in the Canadian economy" (Canada 1972, 43).

In addition, the report stated that foreign corporations responded more to foreign than domestic demands, which led to natural resources being overdeveloped relative to manufacturing. Foreign direct investment and backward vertical integration[9] in resource industries also reduced further processing and fabrication in Canada and the development of supporting industries, and it made entry of Canadian firms more difficult in extraction and in processing. The report noted that large capital inflows associated with a resource boom could push up the Canadian dollar exchange rate and, in turn, inhibit the development of manufacturing by increasing export prices. Not least, the report raised the problem of "extraterritoriality," particularly the application of US laws and policy to US corporations doing business in Canada, for example, the US *Trading with the Enemy Act*, export controls, or antitrust decrees. It also stressed the impacts of these issues on Canada's culture, political process, and foreign policy (Canada 1972, chaps. 16–19).

Most of these economic development and sovereignty issues continue today in one form or another. Manufacturing is majority foreign-controlled and leading parts of it continue to be dominated by relatively concentrated—oligopolistic and monopolistic—foreign firms. The manufacturing share of employment is not only declining, it remains below that of such relatively small open economies such as Sweden and the Netherlands, and with a relatively low and declining contribution in high-tech manufacturing (Pilat 2006). Canada's research and development

TABLE 3 Foreign Direct Investment in Canada and Canadian Direct Investment Abroad, by Industry, 1996–2008

	1996	1997	1998	1999	2000	2001	2002	2003	2004	2005	2006	2007	2008p
Wood and paper industry													
Abroad	4,710	6,154	7,053	7,636	7,050	8,814	9,597	8,490	10,787	9,562	10,738	10,418	12,965
In Canada	10,206	12,595	13,487	15,345	16,384	14,898	15,066	15,113	13,095	14,122	15,481	16,756	16,420
Net FDI	−5,496	−6,441	−6,434	−7,709	−9,334	−6,084	−5,469	−6,623	−2,308	−4,560	−4,743	−6,338	−3,455
Energy and metallic minerals industry													
Abroad	44,703	53,079	58,700	60,444	67,625	76,743	83,627	85,273	99,836	113,165	127,661	124,779	144,792
In Canada	31,799	33,923	38,651	42,884	56,305	75,402	83,821	85,367	85,097	98,504	121,444	161,334	171,899
Net	12,904	19,156	20,049	17,560	11,320	1,341	−194	−94	14,739	14,661	6,217	−36,555	−27,107
Machinery and transportation equipment industry													
Abroad	5,867	7,715	11,752	10,036	21,064	25,603	24,610	23,774	27,252	20,955	23,364	20,853	23,289
In Canada	25,366	28,043	30,029	30,563	43,647	46,460	49,825	47,498	47,926	43,497	51,013	55,037	48,450
Net	−19,499	−20,328	−18,277	−20,527	−22,583	−20,857	−25,215	−23,724	−20,674	−22,542	−27,649	−34,184	−25,161
Finance and insurance industry													
Abroad	58,098	73,714	85,562	104,111	120,483	150,258	188,448	179,236	194,456	205,067	240,437	245,263	318,079
In Canada	33,506	35,781	40,787	52,755	53,965	67,725	65,318	89,756	90,870	92,045	90,208	92,205	94,506
Net	24,592	37,933	44,775	51,356	66,518	82,533	123,130	89,480	103,586	113,022	150,229	153,058	223,573
Services and retailing industry													
Abroad	19,724	21,760	31,643	30,130	48,259	56,989	59,773	53,178	51,372	49,018	62,899	54,951	69,372
In Canada	18,852	19,460	21,642	23,462	25,367	25,245	28,873	32,557	36,280	38,458	46,391	50,786	51,695
Net	872	2,300	10,001	6,668	22,892	31,744	30,900	20,621	15,092	10,560	16,508	4,165	17,677

(Table 3 is continued on the next page.)

TABLE 3 Continued

	1996	1997	1998	1999	2000	2001	2002	2003	2004	2005	2006	2007	2008p
All other industries													
Abroad	48,138	56,184	68,199	78,373	92,027	80,845	69,439	62,267	64,843	54,429	59,650	59,181	68,783
In Canada	62,399	64,476	74,793	87,555	123,447	110,698	113,917	103,393	106,182	111,202	114,110	115,170	121,895
Net	−14,261	−8,292	−6,594	−9,182	−31,420	−29,853	−44,478	−41,126	−41,339	−56,773	−54,460	−55,989	−53,112
All industries													
Abroad	181,238	218,607	262,909	290,730	356,506	399,253	435,494	412,217	448,546	452,195	524,749	515,445	637,281
In Canada	182,126	194,277	219,389	252,563	319,116	340,429	356,819	373,685	379,450	397,828	438,648	491,287	504,864
Net	−888	24,330	43,520	38,167	37,390	58,824	78,675	38,532	69,096	54,367	86,101	24,158	132,417

Note: 2008p indicates preliminary data for 2008.
Source: Statistics Canada, *Canada's International Investment Position* (cat. no. 67-202-X).

225

(R&D) activity continues to be among the lowest of OECD countries (ab Iorwerth 2005) and depends heavily on imported technology; as noted earlier, the balance of payments for royalties and licence fees (Table 2) is substantially negative. There still remains a high level of concentration: large enterprises are foreign-owned to a much greater extent than medium or small enterprises (Taylor 2001). Monopoly power is consistent with data indicating that the profit rates of foreign direct investment in Canada have been generally higher than the profit rates of Canadian foreign direct investment abroad (Lajule 2001, 19).

The Canadian economy has remained skewed toward natural resource exports. This bias increased during the latest resource boom that began in 2002, to the point where natural resource exports were nearly 65 percent of goods exports in 2008. The proportion of natural resource shares in the Toronto stock market rose to over half the value of all shares; foreign investment and takeover in resources industries also increased sharply (to over half of all gross long-term direct investment flows); and now over half of mining is foreign-controlled (Cross 2008). Also, as expected, the rising value of the Canadian dollar, driven largely by increased resource exports and investment, negatively affected manufacturing: non-resource exports, notably automotive products, fell during the resource boom. However, the resource boom did not have an important effect on employment growth, since resource production is heavily capital- rather than labour-intensive.

Firm-Level Arguments About Multinationals

There are several common arguments or disputes about the effects of multinational (or transnational) corporations that recur in debates about foreign ownership in the firm-level or microeconomic literature relating to foreign ownership. Today these arguments are dominated by proponents of globalization and the multinational corporation. It is useful to review some key observations as they apply to Canada.[10]

Productivity. It is often argued by advocates of foreign investment that foreign-controlled firms tend to have higher levels of labour productivity. It turns out, however, that this has less to do with whether a firm is foreign than with capital-intensity, scale, and proprietary firm-specific assets (such as patented technology). Much study for Canada centres on the manufacturing industry, which in 2008 provided about 11.5 percent of employment and 14.0 percent of GDP in Canada. Using 1993 data, Baldwin and Gu (2005) found that foreign multinationals have higher labour and multifactor productivity than Canadian domestic firms but that there was no significant difference between Canadian multinationals and foreign multinationals (whether US or other). They suggest that the difference with domestic firms is due partly to the higher capital-intensity of multinationals. For an earlier period, using foreign direct investment and a wider range of industries,

Gera et al. (1999) found much less effect on productivity from foreign direct investment, with the maximum productivity gains being in the energy industry.

Wages. Another common view is that foreign-controlled corporations pay higher wages. Again, the picture is not so simple. In manufacturing, Baldwin and Gu (2005) found that average wages at Canadian, US, and other foreign multinationals were similar, about 12 percent higher than in domestic plants: wages were about 15 percent higher for production workers and only 7 percent higher for non-production workers. However, the study did not examine unionization or bargaining power issues, especially for production workers, as a determining factor, so it cannot be concluded that foreign ownership leads somehow automatically to higher wages and improved labour conditions in the absence of countervailing union power or labour regulations.

Worker bargaining power and economic inequality. A growing literature argues that the growth of multinationals and their economic power has adversely affected worker bargaining power and social inequality. The effect of increasing foreign investment on workers is important because labour incomes make up about 54 percent of GDP. This issue is part of the debate on globalization, which is treated in Chapter 13 of *Introducing Macroeconomic Analysis*, the companion volume to this one. However, the issue must also be raised here, given the numerous cases of multinational behaviour adverse to higher wages and union rights in Canada. For instance, one of the largest multinationals in the world, Walmart, has pursued a virulent anti-labour strategy that is widely seen by unions as *reducing* established labour rights and wages and that has been found to have violated established norms. Well-known are the cases in Quebec, in Jonquière and Gatineau, where Walmart refused to recognize unions and closed stores to prevent collective agreements. The fast-food sector, led by the multinational McDonald's model, is dominated by low-wage, low-skill, non-unionized employment.

Even in unionized workplaces, such as mining, increased multinationalization has had substantial adverse effects on labour. To illustrate, in the 1950s, in collective bargaining at Inco, one of the largest mining corporations in Canada, the union local bargained for nearly all Inco's employees; today, as part of a wholly owned subsidiary of Vale corporation of Brazil, the local accounts for about 3,200 of Vale's employment of 100,000 worldwide.[11] At an aggregate level, the trend of multinationalization and multinational corporate pressures for privatization, deregulation, subcontracting, and reduced social program standards have been increasingly associated with growing social inequality, stagnant wages, and a decline in the benefits to labour of productivity increases.[12] It is highly misleading to suggest that the growth of foreign multinational investment and their neoliberal policies *in general* raise wages or improve social equality.

Employment. Foreign direct investment has not been found in general to increase employment relative to Canadian firms. In a study for the years 1973–1992,

Gera et al. (1999, 17–19) find that foreign direct investment actually lowered the demand for capital, labour, and intermediate goods at a given output level. The study by Baldwin and Gu (2005, 18–19) finds little difference in the employment per plant between Canadian and foreign multinationals in manufacturing. It also finds that foreign multinationals, compared with Canadian multinationals, have a larger share of non-production workers: "When MNEs establish foreign subsidiaries to exploit proprietary [knowledge] assets, they make use of more white collar workers to handle the complex tasks related to management and marketing."

Considerable public attention has been given to head office employment and concerns about "hollowing out," that is, that multinationals were causing head offices in Canada to be closed. Proponents of foreign investment have been encouraged by Statistics Canada studies (Baldwin et al. 2003 and Brown and Beckstead 2006) for the years following 1999 that indicate some annual growth in head office employment, although the rate has been less than the average for business employment growth. Also significant, as mentioned in passing in the earlier study, "the data here do not capture the hollowing out of the senior management function, which involves relatively few individuals" (17).

R&D. Research and development has been central to the foreign ownership debate, notably for its association with higher productivity and higher quality jobs. As reported in Baldwin and Gu (2005), manufacturing plants introducing innovations had higher productivity increases than plants that did not. Since R&D stimulates innovation, firms having higher levels of R&D or access to others' R&D tend to gain higher productivity. Baldwin and Gu find that Canadian-controlled multinationals are significantly more likely (by 10 percentage points) than foreign-controlled multinationals to perform ongoing R&D. Domestic firms are less likely than foreign-controlled multinationals to perform ongoing R&D, though part of this stems from the smaller size of domestically controlled plants. In terms of innovation rates, the highest rates are among Canadian multinationals, followed by foreign multinationals, then by exclusively domestic firms. The innovation measures include product innovation, process innovation, and world-first innovation. In the adoption of advanced technologies, Canadian domestic firms with international operations have results similar to those of foreign multinationals.

Overall, the results of recent studies of firm performance are not surprising given the historically dominant position of foreign capital, especially in Canada's manufacturing development. The central element of the debate on the role of foreign multinationals, particularly in terms of productivity, typically comes down to the need for multinationals to provide technology and related managerial expertise. The role of technology in economic development is a major question, which is beyond the scope of the present essay, but three points deserve mention.

First, in contrast to earlier periods of Canadian development, the main constraints on economic development now are not from lack of capital or labour. This is evident in the massive export of capital from Canada, particularly by Canadian banks and financial interests, and in the relatively high levels of unemployment, notwithstanding Canada's relatively high levels of education and highly developed education and training institutions.

Second, much of the world's technological development and related managerial capacity is under the control of the multinational firms, which often have a monopolistic character. Intellectual property rights (particularly patents and copyright) are being claimed in an increasing range of areas, and, given the scale of the markets, economic rents, and the centrality of technology to economic development today, the limits and distribution of such rights are not only contentious but carry even greater economic and social consequences, including among multinationals themselves.[13] It has been argued that the root of the historically low R&D activity in Canada is branch plant control itself. Laxer (1989, chap. 1) refers, for example, to the pattern whereby early Canadian manufacturers imported technology through licensing agreements that limited applications to the Canadian and sometimes British Empire markets, and where US branch plants were allowed to dominate the most dynamic manufacturing sectors, "often by taking over the Canadian firms that had started out by licensing American technology."

Third, while one might agree that technology is central in economic development, it is not at all clear that the best vehicle for its development and diffusion is the capitalist multinational corporation. The conclusions of the broader literature on multinational technology transfer are actually mixed, particularly when indirect effects ("spillovers") are taken into account. This is not a surprise, as direct investment is actually a means of monopolizing and controlling the diffusion of proprietary technology, so the economic and political context is crucial. Generally, the higher the level of existing education and technological capacity, the greater the capacity for transfer and diffusion, while the sharing of benefits and costs across countries and sectors remains an issue of bargaining power (Vaitsos 1974).

However, transfer is not the only issue. Technologies are developed in a socioeconomic context and reflect particular needs; and choices of technology often entail not simply an independent, single element but a technological system that implies a chain of commitments. Hence, economic and social independence and differentiation also require the development of an independent scientific, research, and development capacity. At this time it is not clear what alternatives to the multinational corporate control of technology might emerge. The example of the "open source" movement in computer software development is seen by some as one alternative; another is stronger governmental action to reduce the range and duration of intellectual property rights; another, a larger role for public universities and research institutions in the social provision and free international exchange of basic as well as applied research. Such actions could reduce the dominance of multinationals and provide alternatives to the claimed need for multinationals—as a means of obtaining technology and managerial expertise.

Conclusion

Economic development occurs in a situation of great economic and political inequality and diversity, not with a blank or equal slate. The political–economic structures of Canada's development, such as colonialism, class, and national interest, and inequality-increasing aspects of capitalist development, are still significant in the concerns and analyses of the present, and render suspect recommendations that simply reinforce existing patterns. Many of the criticisms of globalization and multinationals, such as their labour and environmental records, their effects on the food system, the dollarization of human culture, and, above all, their effects on issues of war and peace, do interact with the issue of foreign ownership. The present argument is not about nationalism or any Canadian superiority or inferiority, but ultimately about independence, democracy, and allowing different paths in economic development. Advocates of globalization who trivialize such concerns as "nationalism" or who ignore deep issues of empire and inequality in the world today do a serious disservice to the debate at hand.

NOTES

1. The definitions noted here are taken from Statistics Canada's publications directly relevant to foreign ownership data: *Canada's International Investment Position* (cat. no. 67-202-X), *Corporations Returns Act* (cat. no. 61-220-X), and *Canada's International Balance of Payments* (cat. no. 67-001-X). These and other Statistics Canada publications are available without charge on Statistics Canada's website: http://www.statcan.gc.ca/start-debut-eng.html.
2. The data provided by Statistics Canada on foreign ownership and control measures only the value or percentage (incidence) of foreign ownership for any given period; Statistics Canada does not provide data on the duration of ownership or the cumulative flows of profits and capital gains associated with particular forms of foreign investment. Unfortunately, the part of the debate about foreign ownership and its distributional impacts is weakened by this lack of transparency.
3. Students who study historic events, such as the pipeline debate (1956), the Petro-Canada debate (1973), or the Canada–US Free Trade Agreement debate (1988), will find a range of larger foreign ownership concerns about the long-term direction of economic and political development. The analysis of empire goes beyond the discussion of this essay. Those interested can read such contemporary critics of empire and neoliberal policy as William Blum (http://killinghope.org), Michel Chossudovsky (http://www.globalresearch.ca),

Yves Engler (http://en.wikipedia.org/wiki/Yves_Engler), Susan George (http://www.tni.org/george), and Michael Parenti (http://www.michaelparenti.org).

4. For the period 1946–1967, a Dominion Bureau of Statistics (DBS) study found that for the source of expansion funds only around 22 percent came from outside Canada, while the rest was largely from retained earnings of foreign-controlled firms and Canadian finance (Canada 1972, 24–26).

5. Baldwin and Gellatly (2005) show that increased regulation did reduce foreign control levels, while deregulation led to a rebound in foreign control levels, particularly for manufacturing industries.

6. Lavoie (2005) reports that between 1990 and 2003 Canadian assets invested in Offshore Financial Centres (the largest growth in Canadian direct investment was to Barabados, Ireland, Bermuda, the Cayman Islands, and the Bahamas) expanded eightfold, and in 2003 amounted to over 20 percent of all Canadian direct investment abroad.

7. On financialization, see Palley (2007) and Baragar and Seccareccia (2008). In Canada's monopolistic banking industry, the Big Six banks control more than 90 percent of assets in the banking system (Allen and Liu 2007, 1). For evidence on the relatively low productivity growth in the banking industry see, for example, Baldwin et al. (2001, Figures 1.5, 1.6, and 1.10).

8. On Canada's international position as a recipient of takeovers, see data by Hejazi (2010).

9. This occurs when a corporation, usually with monopolistic power, owns or controls parts or all of the supply chain—or inputs—for its resource commodity production.

10. Those interested in more critical views of the theory of multinational corporations, such as their supply-side orientation, might consider Pitelis and Sugden (1991) as well as references to the economist Stephen Hymer (Cohen et al. 1979).

11. A critique of multinational-dominated development in hinterland communities is Leadbeater (2008).

12. See, for example, Fortin and Lemieux (1997), Sharpe et al. (2008), and Osberg (2008).

13. For example, the issue of patented natural products. Students can search for information on the Percy Schmeiser case or Kem Ralph cases or consider DuPont's recent claim that the US Departments of Justice and Agriculture should curb Monsanto's alleged seed monopoly.

DISCUSSION QUESTIONS

1. Given that Canada has a much higher level of foreign ownership than the United States and many other countries, should Canadian governments encourage more (or less) foreign investment in Canada? Is it a significant factor in public policy on foreign ownership that most finance for new expansion of foreign-controlled firms in Canada is derived within Canada?

2. Do different policy approaches or rules about foreign ownership need to apply to different industries or activities in the economy, such as natural resources, telecommunications, culture, banking, manufacturing, newspapers, transportation, or health services?

3. Have high levels of US foreign direct investment in Canada increased the likelihood of the economic and political integration of Canada into the US? What sustainable alternatives, if any, can you foresee to continental economic integration?

SUGGESTED READINGS

DeMartino, George. 2000. *Global economy, global justice: Theoretical objections and policy alternatives to neoliberalism.* London: Routledge.

Godfrey, Dave, with Mel Watkins, ed. 1970. *Gordon to Watkins to you, documentary: The battle for control of our economy.* Toronto: New Press.

Laxer, Gordon, ed. 1991. *Perspectives on Canadian economic development: Class, staples, gender and elites.* Toronto: Oxford University Press.

Pitelis, Christos, and Roger Sugden, eds. 1991. *The nature of the transnational firm.* London: Routledge.

Safarian, A.E. 1993. *Multinational enterprises and public policy: A study of the industrial countries.* Aldershot, UK: Edward Elgar.

Vaitsos, Constantine. 1974. *Intercountry income distribution and transnational enterprises.* Oxford: Clarendon Press.

ONLINE RESOURCES

Centre for Research on Globalization (Montréal): http://www.globalresearch.ca.

Global Policy Forum (New York): http://www.globalpolicy.org/home.html.

Mining Watch Canada (Ottawa): http://www.miningwatch.ca.

Multinational Monitor (US): http://www.multinationalmonitor.org.

Transnational Institute (Amsterdam): http://www.tni.org.

United Nations Conference on Trade and Development (UNCTAD), Division of Investment and Enterprise (includes *World Investment Report*) (Geneva): http://www.unctad.org/Templates/StartPage.asp?intItemID=2983&lang=1.

REFERENCES

(* = available online)

*ab Iorwerth, Aled. 2005. *Canada's low business R&D intensity: The role of industry composition.* Working Paper 2005-03. Ottawa: Canada Department of Finance.

*Allen, Jason, and Ying Liu. 2007. *A note on contestability in the Canadian banking industry.* Discussion Paper 2007-7. Ottawa: Bank of Canada.

Baldwin, John, et al. 2001. *Productivity growth in Canada.* Cat. no. 15-204-XPE. Ottawa: Statistics Canada.

*Baldwin, John, et al. 2003. *Hollowing-out, trimming-down or scaling-up? An analysis of head offices in Canada, 1999–2002.* Research Paper, cat. no. 11F0027MIE No.019. Ottawa: Statistics Canada.

*Baldwin, John, and Guy Gellatly. 2005. *Global links: Long-term trends in foreign investment and foreign control in Canada, 1960 to 2000.* Research Paper, cat. no. 11-622-MIE No.008. Ottawa: Statistics Canada.

*Baldwin, John, and Wulong Gu. 2005. *Global links: Multinationals, foreign ownership and productivity growth in Canadian manufacturing.* Research Paper, cat. no. 11-622-MIE No.009. Ottawa: Statistics Canada.

Baragar, Fletcher, and Mario Seccareccia. 2008. Financial restructuring: Implications of recent Canadian macroeconomic developments. *Studies in Political Economy* 82 (Autumn): 61–83.

*Brown, Mark, and Desmond Beckstead. 2006. Head office employment in Canada, 1999 to 2005. *Canadian Economic Observer* (cat. no. 11-010-XIB), July. Ottawa: Statistics Canada.

Canada. Privy Council Office. 1972. *Foreign direct investment in Canada* (the Gray Report). Ottawa: Information Canada.

Cohen, Robert, et al., eds. 1979. *The multinational corporation: A radical approach: Papers by Stephen Herbert Hymer.* Cambridge, MA: Cambridge University Press.

*Cross, P. 2008. The role of natural resources in Canada's economy. *Canadian Economic Observer* (cat. no. 11-010-XIB), November. Ottawa: Statistics Canada.

Fortin, Nicole, and Thomas Lemieux. 1997. Institutional changes and rising wage inequality: Is there a linkage? *Journal of Economic Perspectives* 11 (2): 75–96.

*Gera, Surendra, et al. 1999. *Foreign direct investment and productivity growth: The Canadian host-country experience.* Working Paper No. 30. Ottawa: Industry Canada.

*Hejazi, Walid. 2010. *Dispelling Canadian myths about foreign direct investment.* IRPP Study. Montreal: Institute for Research on Public Policy.

Hurtig, Mel. 2005. Letter to Industry Canada, reprinted in *Vive le Canada*, October 18. Accessed May 2010 at: http://www.vivelecanada.ca.

*Lajule, Christian. 2001. *Foreign direct investment: A driving force in economic globalization.* Research Paper, cat. no. 67F0001MIB01020. Ottawa: Statistics Canada.

Laliberté, Lucie. 1993. *Globalisation and Canada's international investment position, 1950 to 1992.* Research Paper No. 6, cat. no. 67F0001MIB1997006. Ottawa: Statistics Canada.

*Lavoie, François. 2005. *Canadian direct investment in "offshore financial centres."* Analytical Paper, cat. no. 11-621-MIE No.021.

Laxer, Gordon. 1989. *Open for business: The roots of foreign ownership in Canada.* Toronto: Oxford University Press.

Leadbeater, David, ed. 2008. *Mining town crisis: Globalization, labour and resistance in Sudbury.* Halifax: Fernwood.

*Marx, Karl. 1848. *On the question of free trade.* In *Marx–Engels Collected Works,* vol. 6. New York: International Publishers.

*Osberg, Lars. 2008. *A quarter century of economic inequality in Canada, 1981–2006.* Report. Toronto: Canadian Centre for Policy Alternatives.

*Palley, Thomas. 2007. *Financialization: What it is and why it matters.* Working Paper No. 525. Annandale-on-Hudson, NY: The Levy Institute.

*Pilat, Dirk. 2006. *The changing nature of manufacturing in OECD economies.* STI Working Paper 2006/9. Paris: Organisation for Economic Co-operation and Development.

Sharpe, Andrew, Jean-François Arsenault, and Peter Harrison. 2008. Why have real wages lagged labour productivity growth in Canada? *International Productivity Monitor* (Fall): 16–27. [Ottawa: Centre for the Study of Living Standards.]

Taylor, S. 2001. Foreign control and corporate concentration. *Canadian Economic Observer* (cat. no. 11-010-XIB), June. Ottawa: Statistics Canada.

*United Nations Conference on Trade and Develpment. 2009. *World Investment Report 2009.* New York and Geneva: United Nations.

Addressing Environmental Problems: Is There a Market Solution?

Editors' Introduction

As a subfield of economics, environmental economics is an area of study that, almost by its nature, is transdisciplinary in scope, since it interconnects with so many other disciplines in both the social and the natural sciences. The recognition within economics that human productive activity is set in and depends on the natural environment was evident by the 18th century, as land and its natural products were conceived of as the fundamental inputs to the human economy. Concern with how the environment affects human activity is not new; it is an important theme in the writings of economists such as Thomas R. Malthus (1766–1834). These economists recognized that there were limits to the growth of the human economy, since nature could eventually impose physical constraints on production. John Stuart Mill noted, however, that human activities could also do significant damage to our natural environment—damage that later economists referred to as detrimental or negative externalities.

Environmental economics really started to take shape during the 1960s as celebrated economists such as Kenneth Boulding began to conceive of the ecological system as a closed system or, to use his expression, as "Spaceship Earth." Boulding asked economists to abandon the image of the "cowboy economy," in which the frontier environment appears boundless, in favour of the "spaceman economy," where limited natural resources and environmental damage could endanger the very existence of the human economy.

Nowadays there exists substantial agreement that our production and consumption activities can wreak serious havoc in the natural environment, and that the feedback effects from the environment on human activity can also be very significant. Although researchers dispute the magnitude and severity of the damage to our environment (for example, the impact of air pollution on world climate and on human health), few economists would question the existence of these ubiquitous externalities. Similarly, economists generally recognize that pollution highlights an important market failure that ought to be addressed by policy-makers. However, there is much debate as to what role market-based policies should play in addressing pollution and environmental degradation by way of market incentives offered by taxes, subsidies, or an organized market for emission permits. The idea of establishing markets for pollution emissions permits through a formal cap-and-trade system has achieved prominence and greater popularity, especially as a result of the political support that it garnered at the United Nations Climatic Change Conference in Copenhagen at the end of 2009, but there is still much debate among economists on the appropriate role of markets in solving environmental problems.

Elizabeth Wilman's essay is supportive of the supply/demand analytics and provides a comprehensive list of available market incentives to deal with environmental matters. She takes the position that the market-based framework can be appropriately used to address environmental problems. Although the traditional regulatory approach may continue to be present, the increasing popularity of the market-based approach in dealing with traditional environmental issues such as air and water pollution suggests that the latter's domain of application can only expand.

Richard Holt's contribution to this chapter, in contrast, takes a somewhat broader systems perspective. Holt's analysis is inspired by ecological economics, which is grounded in an understanding of how the human economy is embedded in nature and the wider social environment. Ecological economics offers what Holt describes as a pluralistic approach that incorporates stronger concepts of environmental *sustainability*. Holt argues that the market-based approach may be inappropriate, severely circumscribed, and inadequate in dealing with environmental problems. In his view, successful environmental policy must be based on the broader ecological-economic perspective.

Addressing Environmental Problems with Market-Based Incentives

Elizabeth Wilman

Introduction

At first blush, markets would seem to be the cause of environmental problems, not the solution. Contemporary awareness of the seriousness of the ecological problems caused by market activities was first heightened by the publication of Rachel Carson's *Silent Spring* in 1962. Chemicals, which were big business and important in improving agricultural productivity, came with a hitherto unrecognized cost to the ecological system. Another prescient scholar was Kenneth Boulding, one of the founders of the field of ecological economics, whose 1966 essay, *The Economics of the Coming Spaceship Earth*, pointed out that our historical, cowboy view of our relationship with the economy, which worked fine when our numbers and technological capabilities limited the ecological damage humans could cause, would have to be replaced with a view of the earth as a single spaceship. Markets served us well in the cowboy economy. The question is whether they can continue to serve as well in the spaceship economy. The answer is a "yes," as long as we recognize that markets exist within an institutional structure of laws and customs, which can be modified to reflect our transition from the wild west to the spaceship.

The Market System

Perhaps the best known depiction of the market system is Adam Smith's invisible hand, which characterizes the self-interested actions of buyers and sellers as frequently and unintentionally promoting the interest of society (Smith 1776). However, Adam Smith was not promoting completely unrestrained markets; he recognized that considerable institutional structure was required in society for the invisible hand to work its magic. For example, property rights must be strong, and there must be widespread adherence to moral norms. Later, economic thinkers such as A.C. Pigou (1920) introduced the concepts of externalities and market failures. These can be negative effects, like pollution damage, caused by actors within a market system. But the market fails to capture the costs associated with

237

pollution damage, and no payment is extracted from these actors. This leaves the pollution damages as costs that are external to the market, which are borne, not by the actors who caused them, but by the broader community in their role as users of the ecological system damaged by the pollution: those who breathe the air and drink the water. Although externalities were initially thought of as fairly minor, Carson's book, and Boulding's work, as well as that of others such as Allen Kneese and his colleagues (1970), drove home the growing pervasiveness of environmental externalities.

Since economic activities generate excessive negative ecological consequences, and since the source of this excess is market failure, the question becomes one of how to correct the market failure and limit the negative ecological consequences. The proposed solutions run the gamut from getting rid of the market to arguing that if the problem is sufficiently serious, the market will find a way to ensure that economic actors pay for the negative ecological consequences of their actions. Getting rid of the market is clearly an unworkable proposal. The market isn't something that can be created or destroyed; it is simply the consequence of humans, with their natural characteristic of self-interest, interacting in the business of life. Trying to eliminate the market only stifles the self-interest motivation, and the desirable, as well as the undesirable, outcomes of a market economy are lost. Putting one's faith in the unfettered market is not workable either. As Adam Smith pointed out, if market forces are to promote human welfare rather than hinder it, they have to operate within a set of constraints. The problem for society is choosing the manner in which to constrain the market so that ecological damage is limited but the desirable aspects of the market are maintained. This makes the matter of government intervention in the market a rather delicate matter. Ronald Coase (1960) recognized this and pointed out the benefit of taking advantage of market transactions whenever possible, specifically when private property rights can be clearly specified and there are no obstacles to negotiation between the parties causing and experiencing the externality. However, as Coase himself recognized, property rights are often ill specified, and the obstacles to bargaining can be substantial.

The fact that there are benefits and costs of restraining the market is what is behind the rise of what are called market mechanisms in environmental regulation. If ecological damages are caused by market failures, then let us fix that market failure by making the regulations as market-like as possible, using the fact that humans respond to incentives to our advantage rather than our detriment. This is what the field of environmental economics is about. It identifies the failures in the market system, which are the source of too much pollution and other forms of environmental degradation, and devises environmentally and cost-effective ways to correct those failures.

Property Rights

Market mechanisms include such things as pollution taxes, subsidies, and markets for emissions permits. To investigate market mechanisms, it is necessary to look at how a market works. Markets need the key institution of strong property rights to function. These are a set of rights and obligations that are part and parcel of the ownership of property. Property rights can be privately held by individuals or companies, or they can be held by the state. If property rights are to be effective they must exhibit at least three characteristics:

- *Excludability:* the owner can exclude others from the enjoyment of the property.
- *Transferability:* all property rights should be transferable from one owner to another. The transferability of property is what ensures that it is used in its most valued way. When effective property rights exist and can be transferred, the market exhibits prices that reflect the true value of the property to the buyer and the seller.
- *Enforceability:* property rights should be sanctioned by the society within which they exist, and should be free from involuntary seizure or encroachment.

Many environmental assets, such as the atmosphere, and aquatic and terrestrial ecosystems, cannot be covered by private property rights. They cannot be neatly divided into units of ownership, from which non-owners can be excluded unless they pay the price. Such resources may be owned by the state or they may be *res nullius* (owned by no one). Even if they are owned by the state, excludability is not necessarily enforced. In other words, they may be effectively *res nullius*.

Consider the case of ozone. Near the earth's surface, ozone is considered a "bad." Motor vehicle exhaust and industrial emissions contain nitrous oxides and volatile organic compounds that help form ozone. Ozone is the primary constituent of smog, which can be a serious problem in the summertime in urban areas.[1] For the most part, smog is a localized problem, and amenable to being dealt with within one political jurisdiction. That jurisdiction can effectively exercise its property rights to limit smog-causing emissions.[2] At the other end of the spectrum, ozone in the stratosphere is considered a "good," because it forms a layer that protects life on earth from the sun's harmful rays. However, ozone-depleting chemicals, such as chlorofluorocarbons and halons, which are emitted into the lower atmosphere, travel into the upper atmosphere and act as catalysts in chemical reactions that destroy ozone. Although ozone depletion is concentrated in the polar areas, the source of the ozone-depleting emissions can be any place on the globe. The fact that they travel to a part of the atmosphere from which they can negatively influence another part of the planet is what justifies the term global. Because there is no effective global government, dealing with global pollution problems requires many countries to agree to act collectively to reduce emissions. The Montreal Protocol is the agreement for ozone-depleting substances. While the Montreal Protocol has been largely successful in limiting global production of ozone-depleting substances, countries around the world are still struggling to reach a global agreement to reduce greenhouse gas emissions.[3]

Market Mechanisms

When an environmental resource, such as a portion of the atmosphere, cannot be privately owned, but can be owned by government, it is possible for government to regulate the use of that resource for its citizens, for example by creating the benefits of a less smoggy environment. A less smoggy environment may mean fewer hospital visits, fewer sick days, and fewer deaths, as well as greater enjoyment of the outdoors, for citizens. However, such regulation will be costly because it will restrict activities occurring within the market economy. The government's job is to decide, on behalf of the citizenry, how much less smoggy the air should be, and to ensure that smog is reduced in a manner that imposes the least cost on the economy. Market mechanisms are designed to achieve a given level of environmental quality improvement in the most cost-effective, or least-cost, way. They do this because, like the market itself, they use the self-interest incentive to achieve their result. The self-interest incentive motivates individuals or firms to look for the cheapest available option to abate their pollution and to invest in new technologies that will further reduce abatement costs. Since the emphasis is on indirect, rather than direct, regulation of behaviour, emission levels do not need to be specified for every emitter. To some extent, regulators can simply get out of the way and let the market work. Market mechanisms come in a number of forms. The main ones are emission taxes, subsidies, and cap-and-trade systems that create a market for emissions permits.

Emissions Taxes

Emissions taxes work on the theory that the government regulator owns the resource into which polluters put their emissions. The tax is the price that the regulator charges for the right to dispose of emissions in that resource. A tax on sulfur dioxide emissions is a tax on disposing of these emissions in the atmosphere. The company that wishes to dispose of its emissions must pay the price in the form of the tax. The tax minimizes the cost of emission reduction because each emitter responds to it by equating the marginal cost of abating its emissions with the marginal cost of disposing of them in the atmosphere (the tax). This can be seen most easily by comparing the tax with a regulation that requires all emitters to reduce their emissions by x tonnes. Not all emitters will have the same marginal abatement costs, so, in meeting the regulation, some will end up with higher marginal abatement costs than others. The overall cost of cutting aggregate emissions would be reduced if emitters with lower marginal abatement costs increased their abatement and those with higher marginal abatement costs decreased their abatement. A tax automatically equalizes emitters' marginal abatement costs. Of course, the regulator needs to monitor emitters to ensure that they are not emitting more than they are paying for. Nor is the government as free as a private market entrepreneur might be in setting the price. Governments typically have to enact legislation to put a tax into effect. Both polluting companies and consumers who buy their products have an interest in the level of the tax, because companies may well be able to pass the tax on to consumers.[4] It may be difficult to set the tax at the level required to improve air quality to the desired level, and it may be even more difficult to raise the tax when the number of emitters in the area grows and creates an increased demand to dispose of emissions in the atmosphere.

Subsidies

There are various kinds of subsidies: subsidies for the installation of pollution control equipment, subsidies for the development of new technologies, and payments to reduce emissions. The first two types are aimed at making it cheaper for companies to reduce their emissions. The third, and the one we will focus on here, has some similarity to the tax on emissions, except that the companies are paid for reducing the extent to which they dispose of their emissions in the atmosphere, rather than paying for such disposal.

The key difference between a tax on emissions and a subsidy for reducing them is the implied-use right. With a tax, the government is the implied owner of the resource, and sells the right to use the resource to companies. With a subsidy, the government still owns the resource, but has made an implied *gratis* allocation of use rights to emitters. The use rights are obtained via the rule of capture, that is, by emitting or threatening to emit, and there is no upper limit on their quantity. To reduce emissions the government must buy back some of these use rights. This creates the incentive for companies to pollute, or threaten to pollute, in order to be paid not to pollute. This problem is typically called the baseline problem, and shows up in offsets programs, where companies are paid for sequestering carbon in trees or soils, or in programs like the Clean Development Mechanism (CDM), where companies in developed countries pay for reductions in greenhouse gas emissions in developing countries. Recently proposed Chinese wind farm projects provide an example of the baseline problem. These projects are controversial because it is argued that China would have gone ahead with them even in the absence of CDM (Murray 2009). Some consider the baseline problems so bad that they would abolish CDM. In general, the existence of baseline problems makes subsidies less desirable market mechanisms. If they are used, steps should be taken to ensure that the baseline problem is manageable.

An Emissions Cap with a Market for Emissions Permits

Programs that entail an emissions cap with a market for emissions permits are typically called cap-and-trade programs. Like an emissions tax, cap-and-trade programs initially give governments property rights over the environmental resource. The government regulator decides on the cap, or how much use of that resource will be made available to emitters. The regulator then transfers use rights (emissions permits) in the amount of the cap to potential emitters. The transfer could be via sale or auction, or the permits could be given *gratis* to emitters according to some formula. Once permits have been transferred to emitters, they can then be traded among the emitters.

A Canadian economist, John Dales (1968), originated the idea of setting up a market in pollution rights. This system is similar to an emissions tax in the sense that government holds the property rights to the atmosphere. It transfers a limited amount of use rights to emitters and allows them to trade among themselves. With a tax, the regulator sets the price at which the right to emit will be sold. With a cap-and-trade system, she sets the aggregate quantity of emissions that will be allowed. If the regulator is perfectly informed about the demand for disposal of emissions in the environment, the tax will be set to produce aggregate emissions equivalent to the cap, and the cap will be set to generate a permit price equivalent to the tax.

Just as it can be politically difficult to set the level of the tax, it can be politically difficult to set the cap. When a cap is used, the permit price is influenced by the stringency of the cap. Even if permits are initially allocated *gratis*, the fewer permits that are available, the higher their price will be and the greater the amount of costly abatement polluters will have to undertake. This can mean political pressure for a lax cap. The recently introduced European Union Emission Trading System allocated so many permits in its first phase that the permit price dropped to close to zero (Ellerman and Joskow 2008). At such a low price polluters have little incentive to reduce their emissions. However, the over-allocation problem has been recognized, and in the second and later phases the number of allowances is being reduced and some are being auctioned rather than allocated *gratis*.

Perhaps the most successful cap-and-trade system is the US system for emissions of sulfur dioxide (SO_2). With this system, there is a national emissions cap, and emitters receive a limited number of emissions permits/allowances for a given period, which they may trade. The history of the SO_2 trading system provides evidence of the cost-effectiveness of cap-and-trade systems. In the early 1970s, before any trading systems were in place, the US *Clean Air Act* specified allowable ambient SO_2 concentrations. But many locales become non-attainment areas:

areas whose actual concentrations equal or exceed allowable ones. New emitters were not allowed to locate in non-attainment areas, and this restricted economic growth. In response to the pressure created by this restriction, the US Environmental Protection Agency designed an offset system that allowed new emitters to pay existing emitters to sufficiently reduce their emissions to offset any increase in emissions. The success of the offset program was a motivation for the cap-and-trade system for SO_2 emissions introduced in Title IV of the 1990 US *Clean Air Act* amendments.

The effectiveness of the SO_2 trading program can be gauged by the extent to which it reduces emissions and the extent to which it encourages cost effectiveness in reducing emissions. The emission-reduction goals of the SO_2 cap-and-trade system have been met, and there is compelling evidence that this has resulted in substantial cost saving compared with a uniform standard that would have regulated the emissions of each emitter. Burtraw and Szambelan (2009) summarize studies of the cost savings, and report cost savings of 43 to 55 percent or larger, depending on the exact comparison.

Other Market Mechanisms

Taxes, subsidies, and cap-and-trade systems are not the only market mechanisms that can be used to internalize externalities. Two others are deposit refund systems and reverse auctions.

The deposit refund system (DRS) is an upfront charge/deposit payable upon purchase of a product, with the refund paid upon proper/safe disposal of the product. The goal is to avoid a high cost for unsafe/improper disposal. DRSs are used widely for beverage containers, where the goal is to reduce litter, but they are also used for pesticide containers, lead batteries, electronic equipment, and used-car hulks. If the deposit and the refund are equal, the DRS is simply a tax on unsafe disposal. A variant on the DRS is the assurance bond. When undertaking a potentially environmentally damaging economic activity, such as oil sands extraction, the company undertaking the activity would be required to post a bond sufficient to cover the largest estimate of environmental damages. If the damages did occur, the bond would be used to rehabilitate the environment and/or compensate injured parties. All, or a portion, of that bond would be returned if less than the maximum amount of damage occurs. The bond shifts the burden of proof from the public to the company undertaking the activity, so there is an incentive for the company to limit the damage caused (Costanza and Perrings 1990).

Reverse auctions are a form of subsidy. They are used when it is impossible, or at least extremely difficult, for the regulator to enforce property rights over the resource. An example is non-point source water pollution from agricultural run-off. Because it is difficult to identify the source of the pollution, it is difficult to tax it or cap it. However, it is possible to identify projects (for example, better manure storage) that would reduce it. The regulator, who will always have a limited budget, can take bids for pollution-reducing projects and allocate the funds so as to produce the most bang for the buck. Reverse auctions have been used to improve water quality (Rolfe and Windle 2009) and as a way to encourage private landowners to preserve biodiversity (Whitten et al. 2007).

Innovation

The successful development of low-carbon technologies is often cited as the only way to make substantial reductions in greenhouse gas emissions. Without such technologies, an excessively high carbon tax, or permit price, would be required to yield significant carbon dioxide (CO_2) reductions. Such technologies will require substantial new investments in research, and the incentives provided by emission-reduction regulatory tools play an important part in encouraging these investments.

An example comes from the Title IV amendments. Title IV allowed abatement options other than scrubbers. What resulted was a greater reliance on blending low-sulfur and high-sulfur coal, which prior to 1990 was thought to be unfeasible (Torrens et al. 1992). Carlson et al. (2000) assert that the flexibility of using low-sulfur coal was responsible for about 80 percent of the decline in marginal abatement costs. Another example is Norway's Sleipner project, which began in 1996 and has stored 8 million tonnes of CO_2 in a saline aquifer under the North Sea. The project was stimulated by a CO_2 tax of about €40 per ton of CO_2 instituted by Norway in 1991 (Parliamentary Office of Science and Technology 2005). In a recent article in the *Economists' Voice*, Islegen and Reichelstein (2009) argue that carbon capture and storage (CCS) is a technology that could significantly reduce the marginal abatement cost for CO_2 emissions from coal-fired electric power plants. A price on carbon of at least $25 per tonne, instituted through a carbon tax or a cap-and-trade system, would provide the incentive for operators of coal-fired power plants to reduce their abatement cost by investing in new coal-fired plants with CCS capabilities.

Another Revenue Grab?

One of the criticisms of some market mechanisms, such as an emissions tax or emission permits that are auctioned off, is that they are just a way of collecting more tax revenue. This need not be the case. Revenue raised from a tax, or the auctioning of permits, can be used to reduce other taxes that are more distortion-ary. As it is sometimes put, the welfare of society can be improved by shifting taxation from goods to bads. The carbon tax recently imposed in British Columbia follows this tax-shifting principle. All the revenue collected through the carbon tax must be returned through reductions in personal income taxes or corporate taxes. Another approach is the one followed by Quebec, which puts its carbon tax revenues into a green fund that will invest in initiatives like commuter rail networks and energy efficiency (Duff 2008).

Market Mechanisms with Incomplete Global Agreements

In the case of global pollutants like CO_2, the ideal is to have a global agreement using market mechanisms to limit climate change. However, as proven by the absence of any meaningful post-Kyoto climate change agreement, global agreements can be very slow to materialize. This means that if individual countries pursue policies to limit their own emissions, they must be concerned about international competitiveness or leakage, that is, shifting carbon-intensive production to countries in which emissions are free. There are a number of approaches to this. One is to tie the allocation of free allowances to output in trade-sensitive sectors. Another, which has been used in Alberta, is to use an intensity cap, rather than an aggregate emissions cap.[5] However, both of these approaches inevitably work at cross-purposes with respect to pollution, subsidizing output while pricing emissions (Fisher and Fox 2007). The better solution is to eliminate leakage through complete global agreements.

Conclusion

Although they do not yet dominate other regulatory approaches, market mechanisms are gaining acceptance in policy circles. While they have been long recognized as applicable to air and water pollution, more recently they have been recommended for biodiversity and habitat (Weber and Adamowicz 2002; Goldstein 1991). Of course, no one policy instrument is appropriate for all environmental problems. But economic market mechanisms are now part of the policy portfolio, and are likely to be used frequently in the years ahead.

NOTES

1. Sunlight and hot weather cause ground-level ozone to form in harmful concentrations in the air. As a result, ozone is known as a summertime air pollutant.
2. In some cases, smog problems extend over large enough areas to involve multiple jurisdictions. In the northeastern United States, a number of states have formed the Northeastern States for Coordinated Air Use Management (NESCAUM), which enables them to better coordinate their regulatory efforts and institute regional programs such as emissions trading. See http://www.nescaum.org.

3. For a full discussion of international environmental treaties see Scott Barrett (2003).
4. When Quebec announced its plans to levy a carbon tax on all fossil fuel sold in bulk to retailers, there was considerable concern about who would end up paying the tax. See CBC News, June 7, 2007. http://www.cbc.ca/canada/montreal/story/2007/06/07/carbon-tax.html.
5. An intensity cap is a limit on emissions per unit of output. It can be imposed simultaneously at the aggregate level and the firm level.

DISCUSSION QUESTIONS

1. What is cost-effectiveness and what makes environmental regulation that uses market mechanisms cost-effective?
2. How would a carbon tax promote investments in technologies like carbon capture and storage?
3. An emissions tax regulates the emissions price, a cap-and-trade system regulates the quantity. How do these two types of regulation compare in a growing economy in which the demand to be able to create emissions is increasing?

SUGGESTED READINGS AND ONLINE RESOURCES

Boulding, K.E. 1966. The economics of the coming spaceship earth. In H. Jarrett, ed., *Environmental quality in a growing economy*, 3–14. Baltimore, MD: Johns Hopkins University Press. http://www.eoearth.org/article/The_Economics_of_the_Coming_Spaceship_Earth_(historical).

Ellerman, A.D., and P.L. Joskow. 2008. *The European Union's emissions trading system in perspective.* Prepared for the Pew Center on Global Climate Change. http://pewclimate.org/eu-ets.

Parliamentary Office of Science and Technology. 2005. *Postnote* 238. March 2. http://www.parliament.uk/parliamentary_offices/post/pubs2005.cfm.

Rolfe, J., and J. Windle. 2009. Costing water quality improvements with auction mechanisms: Case studies for the Great Barrier Reef in Australia. *Environmental Economics Research Hub Report* 35, Crawford School of Economics and Government, Australian National University, Canberra, Australia. http://www.crawford.anu.edu.au/research_units/eerh/pdf/EERH_RR35.pdf.

Smith, A. 1776. *An inquiry into the nature and causes of the wealth of nations.* http://www.econlib.org/library/Smith/smWN.html.

Tietenberg, T., E. Wilman, and P. Tracey. 2009. *Environmental economics and policy.* Toronto: Pearson Education Canada.

REFERENCES

Barrett, S. 2003. *Environment and statecraft: The strategy of environmental treaty-making.* Oxford: Oxford University Press.

Burtraw, D., and S.J. Szambelen. 2009. Trading markets for SO_2 and NOx. *Resources for the future discussion paper.* RFF-DP 09-40.

Carlson, C.P., D. Burtraw, M. Cropper, and K. Palmer. 2000. SO_2 control by electric utilities: What are the gains from trade? *Journal of Political Economy* 108: 1292–1326.

Carson, R. 1962. *Silent spring.* Boston: Houghton Mifflin.

Coase, R.H. 1960. The problem of social cost. *The Journal of Law and Economics* 3 (1): 1–44.

Costanza, R., and C. Perrings. 1990. A flexible assurance bonding system for improved environmental management. *Ecological Economics* 2: 57–75.

Dales, J.H. 1968. *Pollution, property and prices.* Toronto: University of Toronto Press.

Duff, D.G. 2008. Carbon taxation in British Columbia. *Vermont Journal of Environmental Law* 10: 87–107.

Fischer, C., and A.K. Fox. 2007. Output-based allocation of emission permits for mitigating tax and trade interactions. *Land Economics* 83: 575–599.

Goldstein, J.G. 1991. The prospects for using market incentives to conserve biodiversity. *Environmental Law* 21 (3): 985–1014.

Islegen, O., and S.J. Reichelstein. 2009. The economics of carbon capture. *The Economists' Voice* 6 (12). http://www.bepress.com/ev/vol6/iss12/art5.

Kneese, A.V., R.U. Ayres, and R.C. d'Arge. 1970. *Economics and the environment: A materials balance approach.* Baltimore, MD: Johns Hopkins University Press.

Murray, J. 2009. Carbon traders demand Copenhagen CDM reforms. *Business Green.* December 7. http://www.businessgreen.com/business-green/news/2254538/carbon-traders-demand.

Pigou, A.C. 1920. *The economics of welfare.* London: Macmillan. http://www.econlib.org/library/NPDBooks/Pigou/pgEW.html.

Torrens, I.M., J.E. Cichanowicz, and J.B. Platt. 1992. The 1990 Clean Air Act amendments: Overview, utility industry response, and strategic implications. *Annual Review of Energy and the Environment* 17: 211–233.

Weber, M., and W. Adamowicz. 2002. Tradable land-use rights for cumulative environmental effects management. *Canadian Public Policy* 28 (4): 581–595.

Whitten, S., R. Goddard, A. Knight, A. Reeson, and D. Stevens. 2007. Designing and testing an outcome focused conservation auction: Evidence from a field trial targeting ground nesting birds. Presented at the Tenth Annual BioEcon Conference. http://bioecon.www.ucl.ac.uk/10th_2008/13.Whitten.pdf.

Traditional Economic Development Versus Sustainable Economic Development

Richard P.F. Holt

Introduction

Many environmental economics textbooks are now feeling more comfortable approaching environmental problems from two different perspectives. The first approach, and still the dominant one, uses standard neoclassical economic analysis, a method that is based on price theory—relying on the market forces of supply and demand to determine the relative prices of goods and natural resources—to address environmental problems, now and in the future. Neoclassical economics uses such concepts as competitive markets, utility, diminishing returns, private versus public goods, substitution, externalities, marginal benefits, and costs to analyze and evaluate environmental issues in economics.

The second approach comes from ecological economics. This approach takes a much broader perspective by looking at the economic system as a subset of our ecosystem. Ecological economists also insist that to adequately deal with environmental problems we need to incorporate the laws of natural science in our economic analysis. For example, besides the constraint of scarce resources that consumers and firms face in making economic decisions, we need to recognize the physical constraints of energy use and the carrying capacity of our environment.

These two approaches are not necessarily exclusive, but ecological economists argue that neoclassical economics, with its price theory, cannot capture the complexity of environmental problems, and needs to be supplemented by other methods of analysis that bring in the constraints of natural and physical laws. Let us now explore in greater detail how the two methods differ in their approaches to environmental problems.

Neoclassical and Ecological Economics: Views on Capital Stocks

A good place to start in understanding the differences between neoclassical and ecological approaches is by looking at the scope of capital in their analysis.[1] In neoclassical economics, *capital* refers to manufactured equipment owned by private businesses that can produce future output, in other words, private ownership of the means of production. The term *human capital* is used to describe investment decisions in skills and education for the labour market (which is also private). For ecological economists, these are just two types of capital used in the production process. They insist that *all capital stocks* that are used in production need to be recognized and their interdependence in economic production and consumption understood. Some capital produces a profit when goods are sold in the marketplace, and that is where private businesses invest their dollars. But other kinds of capital are provided outside the market by nature, by government, or informally by family and community. Along with manufactured equipment, stocks of human skills and talents are necessary for economic output and income; public infrastructure produces services that do not necessarily yield a profit, but are equally needed for economic production and growth. There is also the non-market value of civic participation and neighbourliness, sometimes called *social capital*. Finally, there is *natural capital*, which is unique in that some elements are non-renewable. All of these capital stocks are necessary for economic development.

Besides understanding the interrelationship and interdependence of the different capital stocks, we need to be aware that some of these stocks are held privately and others in common. Some natural resources are private property, such as a ranch or farm or a large corporation like Exxon having property rights over a large reserve of oil, while others, such as the oceans or the atmosphere, are common property. Businesses own manufactured equipment privately, but rely on infrastructure, which is a shared common resource. What we call human capital is privately held, but social capital is a common resource developed and shared by people. In the ecological capital-stocks framework, new technologies are embodied in new skills (human capital), new equipment (private business capital or public infrastructure), and community and work places (social capital), and use natural resources (natural capital). In addition to maintaining economic production, all of these capital stocks also support future quality of life and sustainability. Parks (public capital) provide beauty and wildlife habitats as well as recreation (quality of life) and CO_2 conversion, which supports natural capital (sustainability).

This view is very different from the neoclassical perspective, which looks at the environment more or less as an extension of the economy.[2] For mainstream economics, not all types of capital are needed for a sustainable economy as long as there are substitution opportunities between the different capital stocks. If one type of capital runs out, price changes are expected to stimulate new technologies and find new resources to replace that capital. Neoclassical economists such as Solow (1991, 1992) have argued that any depletion of natural resources can be matched by increases in another form of capital. This potential capacity of human capital to substitute for declining natural capital has led to a discussion between neoclassical and ecological economists about what sustainable development means. The debate has led to two definitions. The first is a *weak* definition: the losses of a non-renewable or renewable resource (natural capital) can be compensated for by a substitution—that is, of man-made capital—of equal value. The second is a *strong* definition: natural capital and other types of capital stocks must be kept intact, given their unique and complementary quality.

An example of the use of the "weak" definition of sustainable development can be found in the work of Hartwick (1977, 2001) and Solow (1974, 1986), which looks at the extraction of a non-renewable resource over an infinite time horizon to see if it can be sustained. Whether it can be sustained or not depends upon the substitutions that exist. If substitutes do exist, then the optimum extraction and substitution rate can be calculated to sustain the resource over time. It seems that at the heart of the neoclassical analysis of sustainable development lies the assumption that adequate substitutes exist. This story might be a plausible one, but does it represent the reality we face? Neoclassical economists deal with environmental management only as an optimization problem. This assumes fixed tastes, adequate information, and rational individuals making decisions in a static world, driven by the goal of allocating limited resources in the most efficient way. But this approach does not ask whether efficiency should be our only goal when faced with environmental problems. Ecological economists point out that social welfare needs to be put in a broader context that looks at institutional, social, and—in this case—environmental welfare. This context can be found in the writings of one of the first environmentalists, John Stuart Mill (1848), who stated that efficiency is not an end in itself, but a means to an end. Efficiency has meaning only when the goals that society and individuals want to achieve are clarified. That means that we need to be concerned with the sustainability of *all* capital stocks, since all are necessary.

To explain how sustainability can be achieved with its theories, the neoclassical story typically refers to a unique equilibrium point representing efficiency, which in the Hartwick-Solow model is the same as sustainability. Market forces will lead naturally to that point. Prices do it all by allocating resources and choices in the most efficient way. This, of course, is not how ecologists define sustainability—it means more than just reaching a determined equilibrium point. Ecological economists and other heterodox economists feel uncomfortable with the assumption that market forces will inevitably lead to a particular equilibrium outcome at some future time. Instead they talk about multiple equilibria, where many outcomes are possible. Once the possibility of multiple equilibria exists, we need to adopt more powerful and flexible tools, such as path-dependency theory, which looks at economic outcomes that are determined not just by present decisions but also by events that took place in the past; complex systems, economic models that take into account dynamic interactions of consumers and firms, where these economic actors have less than full information and face bounded or limited rationality; and game theory, which is concerned with how individuals make decisions when they are mutually interdependent. These additional methods and tools provide us with new ways to understand the dynamics of the economy.

Environment, Society, and the Economy

Another difference between these two approaches is how they look at the interconnection of the environment, society, and the economy.[2] In ecological economics, it is important not to lose sight of how the environment supports and encompasses both the economy and society, and how neoclassical economics focuses primarily on the economy. The neoclassical model of the relationships between the environment, society, and the economy is illustrated in Figure 1. All areas are important in this model, but investments of private capital in the market economy are seen as the primary catalyst for wealth creation. Private capital also dominates other capital stocks: other forms of capital are secondary except when they are used to meet economic needs. This model usually ignores the long-term effects of the economy on the environment, because neoclassical economists believe that market forces can quickly deal with environmental problems. If there are adequate incentives for technological development, small government, and limited regulation, then property rights, substitution effects, and price signals will take care of environmental issues. Environmental values can only be determined within

FIGURE 1

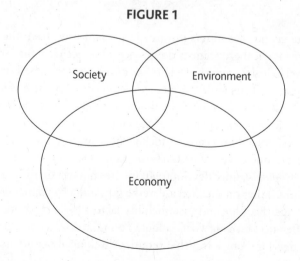

the utilitarian framework of the market. Every value—the value of the existence of life, environmental amenities, and biodiversity—is determined solely by market forces.

The emphasis here is on accommodating the needs of private capital (business), so that it can create growth and jobs. Benefits from economic growth are then expected to trickle down to the other kinds of capital (human, natural, and infrastructure) that are needed for production.

Ecological economists believe a more accurate representation shows the economy as a subset of society and the environment (see Figure 2). Viewed this way, the synergies between investment in the economy, the environment, and society are easier to see, and the inevitable trade-offs will be approached differently. In this model, economic growth and investment in private capital are not the sole requirements for economic development.

FIGURE 2

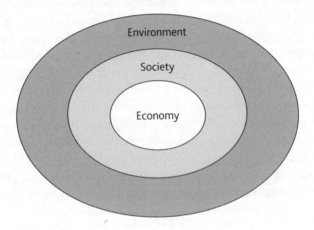

Ecological economics differs in three important ways from the neoclassical model. First, ecological economists do not accept as accurate the "trickle-down" model of neoclassical economics, where economic growth based on investment in private capital will sustain *all* capital stocks needed for the economy, society, and environment. Second, they believe that *all* capital stocks need to be protected and have intrinsic value, independent of the market. Society needs to make investments in all of them, and no capital stock is more important than the others for sustainable economic development. Third, economic *growth* is not the same as economic *development*, since development focuses not just on the output of goods and services, but rather on the increase in the per capita *standard of living*, a value that includes quality of life and sustainability factors besides economic growth.

These differences provide what ecological economists call a true understanding of economic development, a way that requires thinking about goods and services from a full cost perspective. Economic development has tended to be defined in terms of the more limited target—economic growth—and the impact of quality of life and sustainability issues on economic activity has been recognized only later on in the process. For ecological economists, these factors should be recognized up front, along with growth of output. Neoclassical economists argue that economic growth is actually good for the environment. They cite empirical evidence suggesting a correlation between per capita income and environmental quality, that is, when per capita income grows to a certain point, people put a higher value on environmental quality. If we look closely at this argument, what we find is that the correlation between economic growth and environmental quality is limited at best and not sufficient for overall environmental improvement. For example, studies show that economic growth can improve the environmental quality of a specific group of pollutants associated with poor sanitation and impure water supplies, but can make global warming worse (Shafik and Bandyopadhyay 1992). Different economic growth paths can also have different outcomes on environmental quality, depending on the capital used and its depreciation. For example, natural capital is not static. It is based on technology, consumer preferences, and a dynamic relation between abiotic resources, which are non-living and non-renewable, such as fossil fuels, minerals, and land, and biotic resources, which are living, such as trees and fish. Ecological resilience can decrease abruptly and irreversibly. To develop adequate signals to protect ecological resilience and natural capital, we need to look at the dynamic effects of changes in the ecosystem, its buffering capacity, and the thresholds that are required for sustainability.

The uncertainty about the resilience of our environmental resources has led ecologists to call for the wise management and conservation of these resources, and to look at natural resources as a stock and a complement to other forms of capital, not as a substitute. Ecological economists recognize that the effects of the level of economic activity on environmental resilience are still often unknown. Hence they place a high priority on developing policies that improve their understanding of the early-warning signs of our impact on natural capital and the environment.

Many neoclassical economists would agree with much of what ecological economists are saying, but insist that the market system is the best way to achieve sustainable economic growth. We now look in more detail at the market approach to sustainable economic development.

Neoclassical Approach: The Market System

In a market system, both the private and public sectors use prices as signals of scarcity. If labour is scarce and low-cost energy is abundant, it is better to use technologies that use energy but economize on labour. Once energy becomes more expensive, the way to be efficient also changes. This leads to optimally allocating limited resources that require competitive market conditions. Moreover, all benefits and costs are known, property rights are clearly defined, and individual agents are assumed to face small transaction costs. These are strong assumptions and some question their realism, but let's explore how the model works.

Neoclassical economics deals with environmental problems through efficiency analysis. The model starts out with full competition, where there are many firms that are all price-takers. Pollution is considered an "external" event to the activities of the market and is usually described as coming from one stationary point, such as a power plant. An externality occurs when one individual or group causes a third party an unintended loss or gain, and the market price does not show all the costs and benefits. Now there is an "external" benefit or cost that needs to be taken into consideration and brought back into the market so that the market price represents all true costs and benefits. For this method of dealing with externalities to work, it must be assumed that all costs and benefits are known and expressed in monetary value and in discrete units of measurement. To "internalize" these external costs, four types of policy are generally used: (1) Coase's theorem, (2) taxes or subsidies, (3) command and control, and (4) market for emissions permits. Let's look at each one.

Coase's theorem (1960) states that if there are zero transaction costs, an efficient outcome will occur if property rights are clearly defined, regardless of who has legal entitlement to the property. If there are externalities associated with pollution, market failure will not occur because the party that has the property rights can force a negotiated solution. This allows the true costs of the externality to be "internalized" and brought back into the market calculation. There are primarily two problems here: a wealth effect and transaction costs. If one party is forced to go out of business to compensate the other party, the new property rights that result can cause a shift in distribution, creating a "wealth effect" that will typically favour one party over the other.

The second problem is with transaction costs. Transaction costs—including legal fees, gathering information, and negotiating—are hardly ever zero, as assumed by Coase's theorem, and can be very substantial. But more important, externalities typically affect more than just one party; they can affect a large number of individuals and groups. With so many parties involved, it becomes very difficult, if not impossible, to coordinate actions to cover so many people and interests. While Coase's theorem might suggest the possibility that private negotiations alone can increase social efficiency in the use of certain resources or reduce certain kinds of pollutants, such measures are not well suited to deal with large-scale problems where different parties have difficulty coming together (Stiglitz 2000).

Related to transaction costs is the "free-rider" problem. If others pay to reduce the quantity of a pollutant to a level at which I feel comfortable, then I may not have the incentive to participate in sharing the cost. Ecological economics extends this argument by saying that *all* economic production creates "externalities," because there is a link between production and waste emission. Trying to "internalize" all these social costs is prohibitively expensive. The most cost-effective method is to change the production and consumption behaviour of consumers and firms. This can be of particular importance for externalities that affect future generations, where lack of information and uncertainty regarding the long-term impact of some pollutants on the environment make it almost impossible to estimate the magnitude of their cost.

Another policy method of dealing with pollution externalities is to set a tax equal to the marginal external cost of the externality, forcing a readjustment. The tax would require the firm or individual to pay a fee equal to the marginal damage caused by the pollutant. One problem with using taxes, however, is the difficulty of knowing by exactly how much the firm will reduce its level of pollution in response to the tax. Hence, policy-makers might need to adjust the tax frequently to attain the appropriate level of pollution reduction. Such frequent adjustments could result in uncertainty, inability to plan, and additional costs for the firms affected by the tax.

Another option is a subsidy, with the government or a third party paying a certain amount to the firm per unit of pollution that it eliminates. A problem here is that the subsidy can actually provide an incentive to *increase* pollution, by increasing the profit margin, which, in a competitive market, gives an incentive for more firms to enter the market. Each firm pollutes less, but more firms create greater total pollution to the environment. In addition, paying someone *not* to impose a cost on others may raise ethical and political concerns, although one can see how the subsidy might work to restore environmental amenities, for example paying someone to plant trees on their land. But again, the problem with subsidies is that if individuals are compensated for eliminating externalities, they may produce more, not less.

Besides taxes, subsidies, and property rights adjustments based on Coase's theorem, we can have command and control policies, strict regulations that limit the amount of pollution to what is considered an acceptable level. The disadvantage is that such restrictions may not meet the neoclassical standard of cost-effectiveness for pollution control, since total pollution abatement costs are minimized when the largest share of pollution reduction is carried out by the firms that can reduce their emissions at lowest cost.

Tradeable permits offer another option that is a mixture of command and control and fees. Here you determine the optimum amount of pollution, where the marginal damage of the last unit of pollutant is equal to its marginal abatement cost, and issue a number of "pollution permits" equal to that amount. This sets a cap on the amount of the pollution that goes into the environment. What creates economic efficiency is not the number of permits but their tradeability. Polluters have a choice of cutting back on their emissions to the level given by the number of permits they have or of going out onto the open market to buy more permits. Polluters with high marginal costs in reducing the pollutant will go out to the market and buy more permits. Those that have low costs will sell the permits for a profit.

Again, however, this mechanism assumes a perfectly competitive market, where polluters know the exact costs of controlling their emissions, the transaction and information costs of trading the permits are negligible, and no party has the power to affect the price. These are strong assumptions. Finally, according to neoclassical economics, each individual, given their preferences, puts a *different cost* to the effect of the pollutant on them. To achieve efficiency in the neoclassical model those individual costs need to be known, but that is not realistic. Tradeable permits, taxes, subsidies, and control and command policies are better at capturing total damage costs of pollutants to a community than individual costs. The consequence is that it is very difficult for these policies to achieve the neoclassical standard of efficiency. Ecological economists recognize this problem and focus more on policies that will prevent costs of pollution from occurring rather than compensating individuals and society for health and environmental damage.

Concerns with the Neoclassical Model and Environmental Problems

A main problem that ecological economists and others see with neoclassical economics is a lack of realism. One example is treating market and political power as an exception instead of the rule in energy and other environmental markets. The mainstream view is that markets are perfectly competitive, with firms being price-takers that limit their power. In reality, most industries, particularly in the energy sector, are not perfectly competitive but highly concentrated, which allows for markup and price discrimination. This means that using market prices to determine the social costs of pollution is difficult. In the oil market, where imperfect competition dominates, it is impossible to determine an appropriate price, because so many market structures and institutional factors affect price determination.

The distribution of wealth and power is not central to the neoclassical model. However, as Galbraith points out (1985), when power enters the picture, one group can control the use of resources to the exclusion or detriment of another. This asymmetry cannot be dealt with unless the vulnerable group also has access to political or economic power. Galbraith discusses how industries often consist of two sectors, one that is competitive and lacks power and another that is large and has a professional managerial team he calls the "technostructure." This structure has close ties to politicians and regulators, and there is usually a revolving door between the industry and government. Since the energy, oil, and automotive industries are all found in the concentrated sector, not the competitive industrial sector, the technostructure has tremendous lobbying ability. This power and influence can affect the type of public policy or regulation that is put into place to deal with an environmental problem. For example, a policy of allocating tradeable permits of pollutants based on emissions intensity would protect the status quo of the industry, since larger polluters would be compensated more than smaller firms.

Industrial concentration hence leads to what has been called "government or political failure," where regulatory instruments are influenced by politics and special interest groups (Colander 2009). Good examples are the Kyoto and Copenhagen agreements, which assume that the best way to deal with climate change is by using tradeable carbon permits. But there are concerns that the permits will be manipulated by international financial and banking organizations. The Stern review (2007, 377–379) on the economics of climate change emphasized that without perfect competition, banks and other financial outlets could make substantial "windfall profits" on carbon permits by converting them to financial instruments. The reality is that not only is the energy industry not competitive, but the financial institutions that would play an important part in the buying and selling of the permits are also not competitive. Instead of focusing on the goal of creating stable carbon prices, players in the market would be engaged in speculation that would affect the price of the permits. Firms deal with price speculation by using forward contracts and hedging. The probable result would be the development of a complicated, multi-billion dollar new financial and commodity market based on new financial instruments that are difficult to regulate.

Conclusion

Ecological economists believe that the best way to deal with environmental issues is to develop models that take a pluralistic approach that incorporates the effects of power, institutions, and distribution. Given the power structure in both the energy and financial markets, it might be better to use a carbon tax, rather than tradeable permits that could be financially manipulated. Given their concern for long-term economic and social stability, ecological economists would embrace a "strong" definition of sustainability and carry out policies that recognize the vulnerability of the environment and human institutions. On a theoretical level, they would embrace the new paradigm of complexity economics over neoclassical economics. This allows them to focus on policies that would deal with environmental complexities in a global ecological-economic framework that takes into consideration critical boundaries and threshold levels to protect *all* capital stocks for sustainable economic development.

NOTES

1. Part of this section is based on parts of my book, *Local Economic Development for the 21st Century: Quality of Life and Sustainability* with Daphne Greenwood (New York and London: M.E. Sharpe, 2010).
2. Material here comes partly from my article "Post-Keynesian Economics and Sustainable Development" (2005) *International Journal of Environment, Workplace and Employment* 1 (2): 174–186.
3. The figures and material are based on chapters 1 and 4 in my book, *Local Economic Development for the 21st Century: Quality of Life and Sustainability* with Daphne Greenwood (New York and London: M.E. Sharpe, 2010).

DISCUSSION QUESTIONS

1. Which goal do you think should come first, efficiency or sustainability?
2. While neoclassical economists see creating private property rights as the best way to look after the environment, ecological economists disagree. What do you think? Can you give examples showing that private property rights would protect the environment and other examples when it would not?
3. Many neoclassical economists would argue that the five capital stocks mentioned in the chapter are important for social and ecological well-being, but should not be the focus of economists who are concerned about efficiency and economic growth. Do you agree?

SUGGESTED READINGS

Common, M. 1995. *Sustainability and policy.* Cambridge: Cambridge University Press.

Daly, H.E., ed. 1973. *Toward a steady state economy.* San Francisco: W.H. Freeman.

De Steiguer, J. 1997. *The age of environmentalism.* New York: WCB/McGraw-Hill.

Georgescu-Roegen, N. 1971. *The entropy law and the economic process.* Cambridge, MA: Harvard University Press.

Greenwood, D.T., and R.P.F. Holt. 2010. *Local economic development in the 21st century: Quality of life and sustainability.* New York and London: M.E. Sharpe.

Holt, R.P.F. 2009. The relevance of post-Keynesian economics to sustainable development. In Philip Lawn, ed., *Environment and employment: A reconciliation,* 146–160. London and New York: Routledge.

Holt, R.P.F., Steven Pressman, and Clive Spash. 2009. *Post-Keynesian and ecological economics: Confronting environmental issues.* Cheltenham, UK and Northhampton, MA: Edward Elgar.

Meadows, D.H., D.L. Meadows, J. Randers, and W. Behrens III, eds. 1972. *The limits to growth.* New York: Universe Books.

Mill, J.S. 1848. *Principles of political economy with some of their applications to social philosophy*. Reprints of economic classics. Repr. 1965. New York: Augustus M. Kelley.

Solow, R. 1991. Sustainability: An economist's perspective. Paper presented at the eighteenth J. Seward Johnson lecture to the Marine Policy Center, Woods Hole Oceanographic Institution, at Woods Hole, MA, on June 14. Reprinted in R. Stavins, ed. 2000. *Economics of the environment*, 4th ed., 131–138. New York: W.W. Norton & Co.

REFERENCES

Coase, R. 1960. The problem of social cost. *Journal of Law and Economics* 3 (October): 1–44.

Colander, D. 2009. *Economics*, 485–504. Boston: McGraw-Hill-Irwin.

DeGregori, T.R. 1974. Power and illusion in the marketplace: Institutions and technology. *Journal of Economic Issues* 8 (4): 759–770.

Galbraith, J.K. 1985 (1967). *The new industrial state*. Boston: Houghton Mifflin Co.

Greenwood, D.T., and R.P.F. Holt. 2008. Institutional and ecological economics: The role of technology and institutions in economic development. *Journal of Economic Issues* 42 (2): 445–452.

Greenwood, D.T., and R.P.F. Holt. 2010. *Local economic development in the 21st century: Quality of life and sustainability*. New York and London: M.E. Sharpe.

Hartwick, J.M. 1977. Intergenerational equity and the investing of rents from exhaustible resources. *American Economic Review* 66: 972–974.

Hartwick, J.M. 2001. *Non-renewable resources extraction programs and markets*. London and New York: Routledge.

Holt, R.P.F. 2005. Post-Keynesian economics and sustainable development. *International Journal of Environment, Workplace and Employment* 1 (2): 174–186.

Holt, R.P.F. 2009. The relevance of post Keynesian economics to sustainable development. In Philip Lawn, ed., *Environment and employment: A reconciliation*, 146–160. London and New York: Routledge.

Holt, R.P.F., Steven Pressman, and Clive Spash. 2009. *Post Keynesian and ecological economics: Confronting environmental issues*. Cheltenham, UK and Northampton, MA: Edward Elgar.

Mill, J.S. 1848. *Principles of political economy with some of their applications to social philosophy*. Reprints of economic classics. Repr. 1965. New York: Augustus M. Kelley.

Shafik, N., and S. Bandyopadhay. 1992. Economic growth and environmental quality: Time series and cross country evidence. Background paper for the *World Development Report*. Washington, DC: World Bank.

Solow, R. 1974. Intergenerational equity and exhaustible resources. *Review of Economic Studies* (Symposium): 29–45.

Solow, R. 1986. On the intergenerational allocation of natural resources. *Scandinavian Journal of Economics* 88: 141–149.

Solow, R. 1991. Sustainability: An economist's perspective. Paper presented at the eighteenth J. Seward Johnson lecture to the Marine Policy Center, Woods Hole Oceanographic Institution, at Woods Hole, MA, on June 14. Reprinted in R. Stavins, ed. 2000. *Economics of the environment*, 4th ed., 131–138. New York: W.W. Norton & Co., 2000.

Solow, R. 1992. *An almost practical step toward sustainability*. Washington, DC: Resources for the Future.

Splash, Clive L. 2010. The brave new world of carbon trading. *New Political Economy* 15 (2).

Stern, N. 2007. *The economics of climate change: The Stern review*, 377–379. Cambridge: Cambridge University Press.

Stigliz, J. 2000. *Economics of the public sector*. 3rd ed. New York: W.W. Norton & Co.

PART IV
Incomes and Inequality

How Does the Market Determine the Distribution of Incomes Among Economic Agents?

Editors' Introduction

When social scientists in the emerging industrial economies of the late 18th and early 19th centuries began to analyze production, a widespread agreement developed among classical economists that the fundamental problems of economics had to do with how the net product of a society is generated, valued in the market context, and, above all, distributed among the various social classes that interacted to produce it. For David Ricardo, at the beginning of the 19th century, economics (or "political economy") was ultimately all about how this "net produce" is divided among the three major social classes of his era: the workers (being paid wages), the capitalists (receiving profits), and the landlords (receiving rent). The owners of landed property have seen their importance wane over the last two centuries, and they have been replaced as an important income group by owners of financial assets (or interest income earners). The question of what determines the various shares of the economic pie, however, continues to generate much controversy among economists and other social scientists.

In the modern context, economists would all agree that incomes, such as wages, profits, or interest, are not somehow randomly distributed across individuals, but are the result of the working of both economic and institutional forces. Economists fiercely disagree, however, on the relative importance of the various market and non-market mechanisms that generate these various income flows. Most mainstream neoclassical economists would subscribe to a productivity-based theory of incomes, usually referred to as the *marginal productivity theory of distribution*. In a competitive market for productive inputs, such as the market for labour, income differences ought to reflect primarily differences in productivity, say, across the different qualities of labour services. Only institutional barriers and monopolistic practices would prevent relative earnings from mirroring those differences in the productive contribution of each input.

The contribution by Gilles Grenier follows this general approach to explaining income distribution. Tracing these ideas back to Adam Smith, he analyzes how differences in abilities, skills, education and training (or human capital), and job conditions are often the most important variables that account for differences in relative earnings among individuals. While recognizing the significance of discriminatory practices, as well as institutional features such as minimum wages and degrees of union density that can affect earnings and prevent markets from clearing, he points to the importance of the market mechanism in providing higher earnings as a reward for higher productivity.

Jim Stanford's essay offers a more radical perspective, one that draws on the classical and Marxian "surplus" tradition. Instead of seeing the division of the economic product as the result of market forces that reward individuals according to their respective productivities, he points to the underlying institutional and political forces that affect the relative bargaining position of certain social groups. For him, the forces of supply and demand are much less important in the determination of *individual* rewards across the earnings scale and of *overall* factor (wage and profit) shares. The share of profits, according to Stanford, has little to do with "the productivity of capital." Hence, from the heterodox standpoint, incomes are not the outcome of an impersonal market process but the result of institutional forces that are themselves market-determining.

Why Some People Earn More Than Others

Gilles Grenier

Introduction

When we look around us, we see different kinds of people: old and young, male and female, a mixture of ethnic origins with various educational backgrounds and occupations. And there are huge differences in the amount of money those people earn. Some are millionaires while others have barely enough to survive.

Under the eyes of the law, all human beings are equal, but it does not seem to be true when we consider incomes. Do the disparities reflect the fact that some people are more productive or work harder than others? Or are they the result of an intrinsically unequal access to economic resources? Those are not easy questions to answer because the factors that determine earnings are complex. In this essay, economic analysis is used to investigate the causes of inequality among economic agents.

I will start by sketching the economic position of a subset of Canadians, looking at their earnings and at some related characteristics. I will then consider the various explanations offered by economic theory for the differences in income. A distinction will be made between factors that we may think of as acceptable, because they are related to what people contribute to society, and those that are unacceptable because they have nothing to do with how much people produce. Another distinction will be between what is easily observed and what is not. To the extent that some disparities are unacceptable, it is important to discuss policies aimed at reducing them. This will be done in a further section of this chapter. The last section will conclude the essay.

The Economic Position of Some Prominent and Some Ordinary Canadians

To get an idea of how incomes vary, let us look at real people who work for a living. In Table 1, I have gathered information on four prominent Canadians whose incomes are higher than those of ordinary people. They are, from the highest to the lowest income: Céline Dion (the well-known singer), Gordon Nixon (president of the Royal Bank of Canada), Allan Rock (president of the University of Ottawa),

TABLE 1   Earnings and Characteristics of Some Prominent Canadians

Name and age	Occupation and place of residence	Education	Province of birth	Annual earnings
Céline Dion, 41	Singer, Las Vegas, USA	High school equivalent	Quebec	$100,000,000
Gordon Nixon, 52	President, Royal Bank of Canada, Toronto, Ontario	Bachelor of Commerce	Quebec	$9,500,000
Allan Rock, 62	President, University of Ottawa, Ottawa, Ontario	Bachelor of Laws	Ontario	$365,000
Stephen Harper, 52	Prime Minister of Canada, Ottawa, Ontario	MA in Economics	Ontario	$315,500

Sources: Wikipedia, the Free Encyclopedia; *Forbes* (2009); *National Post* (2009); University of Ottawa website (2009); *MoneySense* (2009).

and Stephen Harper (prime minister of Canada). Their salaries are in the public domain and can be freely obtained. In Table 2, I did the same for five anonymous ordinary Canadians, with information taken from census microdata. The names are fictitious and details have been changed to preserve confidentiality, but the data are real. Though not a random sample, these people represent a microcosm of Canada.

The two tables show the annual earnings and some individual characteristics: age, occupation, place of residence, education, and place of birth. Those characteristics may help explain the earnings differences. As can be seen, there are large discrepancies. The highest paid person in the group, Céline Dion, earned $100 million in 2008 according to *Forbes*, which is about seven thousand times more than the lowest paid individual, Sandra C., a Filipina woman with a university education, but who works as a clerk, at an annual salary of only $14,400.

Of course, superstars are not representative of the population. Among the ordinary people in Table 2, the ratio between the highest and the lowest paid is a bit more than four. At the top, we have Paul M., a middle-aged, well-educated man, who appears to have had a respectable career as a teacher. Like most members of his profession, he probably belongs to a union. Next, there is Mary B., who is also doing well as an office administrator, despite her low education. Like many women her age, she may have interrupted her career earlier in her life to raise her children. And then there is Leslie B., still young, with a college education in management, who works in a restaurant. It looks like a decent job, but Leslie will probably not follow a career in that same occupation. Promotions, or changes in employer, will eventually come.

Not surprisingly, the two lowest paid people in the group are immigrants. Arun H., from India, works in the retail trade business, a job that does not seem to be related to his MA degree in political science. If his education was received

TABLE 2 Earnings and Characteristics of Some Anonymous Canadians

Name (fictitious) and age	Occupation and place of residence	Education	Province or country of birth	Annual earnings in 2008 dollars
Paul M., 51	Teacher, Sherbrooke, Quebec	MA in history	Quebec	$62,200
Mary B., 57	Office administrator, Calgary, Alberta	Incomplete high school	Saskatchewan	$39,200
Leslie B., 23	Restaurant worker, Montreal, Quebec	College certificate in management	Quebec	$29,900
Arun H., 51	Retail trade supervisor, Vancouver, BC	MA in political science	India	$26,300
Sandra C., 40	Office clerk, Toronto, Ontario	Baccalaureate in finance	Philippines	$14,400

Source: Canadian Census, Public Use Microdata File of 2001 for individuals. The information is based on real records, but the names are fictitious and some details are changed to preserve confidentiality. The income values are adjusted to 2008 dollars using the Consumer Price Index for Canada.

abroad, it may not be valued as much as a Canadian education. And finally, there is Sandra C., whom I already mentioned, who is also not benefiting much from her education. Her very low income may be due to the fact that she worked part time or was without a job for part of the year.

Coming back to Table 1, there are important discrepancies among the well-known Canadians. The prime minister of Canada earns the least in the group. Because of high visibility and public scrutiny, politicians usually earn less serving their country than they would in other jobs. However, having been in politics can be a good stepping stone to a further career. Allan Rock, the president of the University of Ottawa and a former federal cabinet minister, is a good example of that. Yet his earnings are less than 4 percent of those of the president of the Royal Bank of Canada. The huge amounts of money made by bank executives provoke a lot of public controversy and anger, especially in hard economic times. Many believe that these incomes are not justified. But by far the highest paid person is Céline Dion. Some famous artists and athletes make enormous salaries. Interestingly, this does not lead to as much outrage as the incomes of the bank executives, perhaps because those celebrated performers are widely admired by the public.

The earnings discrepancies can be explained in part by the characteristics that are shown. For example, the more educated and the older tend to earn more, but the relationship is not clear-cut. A lot of other factors seem to enter into consideration. For a deeper understanding of those factors, economic analysis is needed.

What Are the Causes of These Differences in Earnings?

Economists have tried for a long time to explain income disparities and numerous hypotheses have been proposed. Most of the time, no single theory can explain everything in a given situation, and it is difficult to quantify the role of each factor. In this section, I will briefly go over some of those theories.

Table 3 shows a number of explanatory factors. They are organized around two dimensions: *acceptable* versus *unacceptable*, and *observable* versus *unobservable*. The first distinction depends on values. Different people have different values, but there is probably a consensus that some disparities are warranted if they reflect differences in productivity. On the other hand, most people would consider vast differences in earnings among equally productive people unacceptable.

The other distinction is between observable and unobservable factors. Some explanatory factors can be seen without difficulty by the employer or by the social scientist, while others are hard to perceive unless one knows a person well. The observable characteristics, such as a diploma and past experience, can be easily put on a person's curriculum vitae, but other features, such as enthusiasm and motivation, are much more difficult to demonstrate. The presence of those unobservable characteristics makes it difficult to fully grasp the causes of earnings differentials.

Human Capital

One important acceptable and observable factor shown in Table 3 is *education*. To explain its role in the determination of earnings, economists have developed the theory of human capital (Becker 1964; Mincer 1974). People's skills are a kind of capital that determines how productive they are. Education is an investment that increases the value of that capital. For education to be profitable, the benefits must outweigh the costs. The costs of education include books, tuition fees, and the forgone income that students would have received if they had worked instead of studying. It is generally accepted that individuals with higher education must earn more to compensate those costs.

Work experience is another aspect of human capital theory. Investment does not take place only in school, but also on the job where workers learn new skills that make them more productive. The longer a person has been working, the more skills he or she would have acquired.

Compensating Wage Differentials

Type of job and level of responsibility can be significant factors in earnings determination. Workers with the same education and experience can receive different

TABLE 3   Factors Related to Earnings Differences

	Observable	Unobservable
Acceptable	Education Work experience Type of job, level of responsibility	Work effort Innate talent
Unacceptable	Gender Race, ethnic origin Place of birth	Political opinions Sexual orientation

Note: The distinction between acceptable and unacceptable reflects the current values that some disparities are justified if they reflect differences in productivity. The distinction between observable and unobservable is based on what can be seen by the employer or the social scientist, or on the information that one can put on a curriculum vitae.

wages if they do different things. According to the theory of compensating wage differentials, whether a job is dangerous or not, pleasant or unpleasant, and how much responsibility it requires are important determinants of wages. This idea was first expressed over 200 years ago by Adam Smith (1776). To induce workers to do the less desirable jobs, employers must compensate them. For example, jobs in which the probability of dying is high (for example, police work) are paid more than safer jobs (Meng 1989; Meng and Smith 1990; Gunderson and Hyatt 2001). The level of compensation also depends on workers' attitudes toward risk. If some people working in dangerous jobs, such as acrobats, enjoy the risk of doing what they do, the compensation does not need to be as high as for those who do not enjoy the risk.

Work Effort

In the category of acceptable and unobservable factors, differences in the amount of *work effort* and dedication to a job can explain why people with similar characteristics are paid different wages. In any group of people working together, there are always some who work harder than the others, and a few who shirk or are absent regularly. Those who work harder are more likely to get promotions and to be paid more. Work effort is not easy to assess, except by those who observe a person closely.

Innate Talent and Superstars

Innate talent is another key aspect of earnings determination. I have put it in the acceptable category, although it is a bit controversial because it isn't related to what people do. One could argue that it should not be rewarded because it is entirely given. Renowned athletes and artists are examples of individuals who are remunerated for a talent that is highly valued by the public. It is sometimes difficult to distinguish what is due to talent from what is due to hard work. But in the same fields of activity, there are others who work just as hard and never get famous. So, clearly, talent, or perhaps chance, has something to do with it. Nowadays, because of the mass media and the rapidity of communications, superstars tend to receive astronomical amounts of money.

One may wonder whether the high salaries of the bank executives are due to their innate talent in managing financial resources. One argument for paying them high salaries is that if a given bank does not do it, its competitors will. However, this case may be hard to defend when the businesses managed by those executives lose money, which seems to happen frequently.

Discrimination

In Table 3, observable characteristics that are not related to productivity include *gender, race,* and *ethnic origin.* Labour market discrimination against females and visible minorities has been shown to be significant (Gunderson 2006). This discrimination can be due to prejudices on the part of individuals, such as employers, customers, or workers, who do not like to hire, be served by, or work with members of a particular group; this is so even if the members of that group are as productive as workers of other groups (Becker 1957). Discrimination can also be explained by the fact that some groups have less bargaining power than others to secure the best jobs for themselves. If markets were perfectly competitive, such discrimination would not exist in the long run because firms would increase their profits by hiring members of the discriminated group. But that does not appear to be the case, because discrimination persists. Women and visible minorities are still underrepresented and poorly paid in many occupations.

Discrimination can also be related to unobservable characteristics. *Political opinions* and *sexual orientation* are mentioned in Table 3, but there are others as well, such as physical appearance or the way a person dresses. As noted before, though these characteristics are not usually put in a curriculum vitae or seen in data used by social scientists, they can be perceived negatively by those who work with a person every day.

Immigration

Another key observable factor is *place of birth.* In Canada, a group of people that deserves particular attention because of potential discrimination is the group of immigrants. Immigrants now account for about 20 percent of the Canadian population, and they are expected to be between 25 and 28 percent in 2031 (Statistics Canada 2010). When they arrive in their new country, immigrants may not have all the skills they need to work there. For that reason, they earn less than native-born Canadians. However, as they learn new skills, they eventually catch up to Canadians' earnings. It used to be that Canadian immigrants were able to do this in 10 or 15 years. However, for the recent cohorts of immigrants, it takes much longer and they may never be able to reach income equality (Bloom, Grenier, and Gunderson 1995; Aydemir and Skuterud 2005). The determinants of immigrants' integration into the labour market are complex. Some may be related to the transferability of human capital between the home country and Canada, but it is clear that elements of discrimination also exist. Most of the recent immigrants come from the developing world and belong to visible minorities.

Policy Implications

To the extent that some disparities are not based on productivity and are considered unacceptable, something must be done to rectify them. Even if they reflect differences in productivity, the resulting income distribution may still be regarded as too unequal. In this section, I briefly consider some corrective measures.

Taxes and Transfers

All modern societies use a progressive income tax system. Those whose incomes are high pay a larger percentage of it in taxes than those whose incomes are low. Very often, for the lowest incomes, there are no taxes at all. In addition, governments have instituted a wide variety of transfer programs to help people in need. In Canada, those include employment insurance, social assistance, guaranteed income supplement for the old, and many others. Those taxes and transfers attenuate the income differences that result from the market.

However, those programs do not eliminate inequality and they have their limitations. Tax avoidance is a major problem in most countries, leading to huge amounts of money being lost by governments. Work incentives can also be reduced if taxes are too high or if transfer programs are so generous that a person does not find it worthwhile to get a job.

Direct Regulation and Minimum Wages

Instead of letting the market do its job and correcting afterward, governments can act directly on the conditions under which some transactions take place. Minimum wages are an important policy tool that is widely used to ensure that the lowest paid workers enjoy a decent standard of living and are not exploited. Minimum wages have always been controversial and have generated heated debates among social scientists and policy-makers. Some believe they are never high enough, while others think they should not exist because they destroy jobs.

Economists have done a large amount of empirical research to evaluate the impacts of minimum wages on employment. Their approach consists in looking at how variations in minimum wages through time or space affect employment, taking into account other factors, such as economic conditions. Traditionally, studies have found that minimum wages decrease employment among the young (Brown, Gilroy, and Kohen 1982), but some research done in the 1990s revealed that the impact may be lower and more uncertain than what was shown in earlier studies (Card and Krueger 1995; Grenier and Séguin 1991). Now the common wisdom among mainstream economists is that minimum wages are useful in helping low-wage workers, but that they must be kept low enough to prevent employment from decreasing too much. For example, Fortin (2010) suggests that they should be no more than 45 percent of average wages.

The Role of Unions

Unions are a key institution that contributes to the transfer of resources from employers to workers through collective bargaining. Unions are also important political actors that lobby for changes in society. They have a positive impact on the welfare of their members, but their effect on the rest of the labour market is not as clear. On the one hand, the wages of non-unionized workers may be pushed down if those who do not find a job at the higher union wage look for work in the non-unionized sector. On the other hand, non-union employers may fear that their workers will want to organize into a union, which will lead employers to pay a higher wage than they would otherwise.

The importance of unions in a country depends on the policies toward them. In Canada, more than one quarter of the work force is unionized, compared with only one ninth in the United States. That fraction has diminished continuously in the United States since the 1970s, whereas it has increased, then decreased, in Canada. Its level is approximately the same now as it was in 1970 (Cahuc and Zylberberg 2004, Figure 7.2, based on OECD data). This may be because of more sympathetic public opinion toward unions in Canada. The widespread presence of unions can explain to some extent why wage dispersion is lower in Canada than in the United States. Thus it appears that unions are one factor leading to less income inequality in a society.

Conclusion: Does the Market Provide a Correct Distribution of Incomes?

We began by looking at the earnings and at some characteristics of a sample of Canadians. After examining the various factors, are we in a position to explain the disparities and to evaluate the importance of each cause? Perhaps, but a lot remains unknown. Clearly, more research is needed.

To a large extent, our conclusions depend on what we believe about the market. If we believe that the market is intrinsically efficient, then most of the differentials that we observe reflect productivity and are acceptable. Little intervention is necessary. If we believe that the market is inefficient, due to imperfect information and externalities, some economic agents can take advantage of the situation and exploit others. In that case, a lot of intervention may be necessary to transfer resources toward those in need.

The answer is left to the reader. As a mainstream economist, I think that the market is a good instrument to allocate resources, but it needs fine-tuning. Others believe that the market works so badly that governments should control everything: wages, employment, and working conditions. But too many controls lead to distortions. Ultimately, although our values and convictions will always be significant, economic analysis and empirical research must be used to continue to improve our understanding of how the labour market works.

DISCUSSION QUESTIONS

1. Consider the job that you have now (or the most recent job that you had). Do you think that the wage that you receive reflects your productivity? Or do you think that you are underpaid or overpaid for what you do? What are the most important factors that determine your wage?
2. Consider the job that you expect to have 20 years from now. Do you think that you will earn more or less than now? Why? What are the major factors that will determine your wage then?
3. Bank executives in Canada are very highly paid, but those in the United States receive even larger salaries. In contrast, those in China earn a lot less, even when they run very large banks. Is this because the executives in the United States have more talent or work harder than those in other countries?

SUGGESTED READINGS

Benjamin, Dwayne, Morley Gunderson, Thomas Lemieux, and W. Craig Riddell. 2007. *Labour market economics: Theory, evidence and policy in Canada.* 6th ed. Toronto: McGraw-Hill Ryerson.

Ehrenberg, Ronald G., Robert S. Smith, and Richard P. Chaykowki. 2004. *Modern labour economics: Theory and public policy.* Toronto: Pearson Education Canada.

ONLINE RESOURCES

Canadian Census Analyser.
http://datacentre.chass.utoronto.ca.proxy.bib.uottawa.ca/census/.
Statistics Canada, E-Stat.
http://www.statcan.gc.ca.proxy.bib.uottawa.ca/estat/licence-eng.htm.

Note: The above websites provide statistical data on incomes and on a lot of characteristics of Canadians. In accordance with the *Data Liberation Initiative*, free access is granted to students and staff of Canadian universities. The addresses shown are those that I use when I access from the University of Ottawa, but access can be obtained through similar addresses available on the websites of other universities.

REFERENCES

Aydemir, Abdurrahman, and Mikal Skuterud. 2005. Explaining the deteriorating entry earnings of Canada's immigrant cohorts, 1966–2000. *Canadian Journal of Economics* 38 (2): 641–671.

Becker, Gary G. 1957. *The economics of discrimination.* Chicago: University of Chicago Press.

Becker, Gary G. 1964. *Human capital.* New York: National Bureau of Economic Research.

Bloom, David E., Gilles Grenier, and Morley Gunderson. 1995. The changing labour market position of Canadian immigrants. *Canadian Journal of Economics* 28 (4b): 987–1005.

Brown, Charles, Curtis Gilroy, and Andrew Kohen. 1982. The effect of the minimum wage on employment and unemployment. *Journal of Economic Literature* 20 (2): 487–528.

Cahuc, Pierre, and André Zylberberg. 2004. *Labor economics.* Cambridge and London: MIT Press.

Card, David, and Allan Krueger. 1995. *Myth and measurement: The new economics of the minimum wage.* Princeton, NJ: Princeton University Press.

Eder, Steve. Extreme differences in bankers' pay stubs. *National Post.* September 24, 2009. http://www.nationalpost.com/story.html?id=2026194.

Fortin, Pierre. 2010. Unemployment in Canada. In *Introducing macroeconomic analysis: Issues, questions and competing views*, eds. Hassan Bougrine and Mario Seccareccia. Toronto: Emond Montgomery.

Gerlsbeck, Rob. 2009. Inside Stephen Harper's wallet. *MoneySense* (October). http://www.moneysense.ca/2009/10/01/inside-stephen-harpers-wallet/2/.

Grenier, Gilles, and Marc Séguin. 1991. L'incidence du salaire minimum sur le marché du travail des adolescents au Canada: Une reconsidération des résultats économétriques. *L'Actualité économique* 67 (2): 123–143.

Gunderson, Morley. 2006. Viewpoint: Male-female wage differentials: How can that be? *Canadian Journal of Economics* 39 (1): 1–21.

Gunderson, Morley, and Douglas Hyatt. 2001. Workplace risks and wages: Canadian evidence from alternative models. *Canadian Journal of Economics* 34 (2): 377–395.

Meng, Ronald. 1989. Compensating differentials in the Canadian labour market. *Canadian Journal of Economics* 22: 413–424.

Meng, Ronald, and Douglas Smith. 1990. The valuation of risk of death in public sector decision making. *Canadian Public Policy* (16): 137–144.

Mincer, Jacob. 1974. *Schooling, experience and earnings*. New York: Columbia University Press.

Smith, Adam. 1776. *The wealth of nations*. London: Methuen.

Statistics Canada. 2010. *Projections of the diversity of the Canadian population, 2006 to 2031*, Catalogue 91-551-X. http://www.statcan.gc.ca/bsolc/olc-cel/ olc-cel?catno=91-551-x&lang=eng.

Streib, Lauren. June 22, 2009. The year's top-earning musicians. *Forbes*. http://www.forbes.com/2009/06/22/top-eaning-musicians-business-entertainment-musicians.html.

University of Ottawa website. Employees paid $100,000 or more. http://www.hr.uottawa.ca/files/compensation/100000plus_2008.pdf (the six-month salary was multiplied by 2 to get an annual figure).

What Determines Wages? Income Distribution in the Surplus Tradition

Jim Stanford

Introduction: A Leaner, Meaner Labour Market

Explaining distribution, or "who gets what," is one of the most important, and most controversial, subjects in all of economics. The vast majority of Canadians support themselves through paid employment, whereby they perform labour for someone else in return for a wage or salary. So for them, wages are the most important source of income.

However, wage levels in Canada have exhibited a puzzling trend in recent decades. Figure 1 shows the long-run trend in wages and salaries in Canada, going back to 1961. The top line shows all wage and salary income, expressed per hour of employment. The bottom line refers only to wages for hourly-paid workers (who earn less than salaried professionals). Figure 1 is expressed in real dollar terms, with the value of wages and salaries per hour adjusted to reflect the impact of inflation on workers' purchasing power (in this graph, wages are expressed in 2005 dollar terms). Labour income grew quickly during the first decades after the Second World War. In fact, between the end of the Second World War and 1980, average real wages (adjusted for the effects of consumer price inflation) roughly tripled—the most dramatic increase in living standards in Canada's history. This vibrant postwar period, similarly experienced in many other industrial countries, is often called the "Golden Age."

But beginning in the late 1970s and early 1980s, the wage trend dramatically changed. The former strong growth in wages came to a virtual halt. Real wages stagnated for almost two decades. Beginning around the turn of the century, average earnings began to grow slowly again. These modest income gains were concentrated, however, among higher-income salaried workers. For hourly workers, there was no resumption of wage growth. In fact, real hourly wages were still slightly lower in 2008 than they had been 30 years earlier.

Conventional (or "neoclassical") economic theories of distribution are based on the forces of supply and demand, which are assumed to clear markets (both for inputs, or "factors of production," and for produced products). This market-

276

FIGURE 1   Real Wages in Canada 1961–2008, Adjusted for Inflation

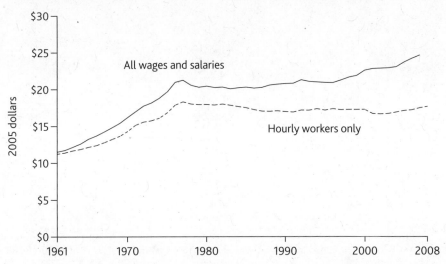

Note: Hourly worker wages from 1961 to 1983 extrapolated on the basis of manufacturing trend.
Sources: Sharpe et al. (2008) and author's calculations from Statistics Canada CANSIM tables 281-0008, 281-0030, and 281-0022.

clearing process supposedly ensures that all factors (including labour) are fully employed in production, and that workers are paid according to their productivity.[1] According to this supply-and-demand model, wages should have continued to grow, because Canadian workers have continued to become more productive. In fact, average hourly productivity by 2010 was more than 40 percent higher than in 1980 (Sharpe et al. 2008). But most workers are not getting paid more, in real terms. Moreover, Canada's economy has continued to accumulate more capital over these decades (through investment in fixed capital and technology). Again, according to supply and demand theories, as a factor becomes relatively "scarce" (that is, complemented in production by larger quantities of other factors), its income should increase. For Canadian labour, however, this has not occurred. As labour became more productive, using larger amounts of capital and technology, its share of output declined markedly. As indicated in Figure 2, labour's share of gross domestic product (GDP) (including all wages, salaries, and supplementary benefits such as pensions and health benefits) has fallen by several percentage points since the late 1970s, to around 50 percent in recent years. The flip side of the coin of labour's falling share of GDP has been a noted growth in profits. Measured as a share of total GDP, corporate profits by the late 2000s had reached the highest levels ever recorded in Canadian economic data.

FIGURE 2   Labour's Share of GDP 1926–2008, All Wages, Salaries, and Benefits

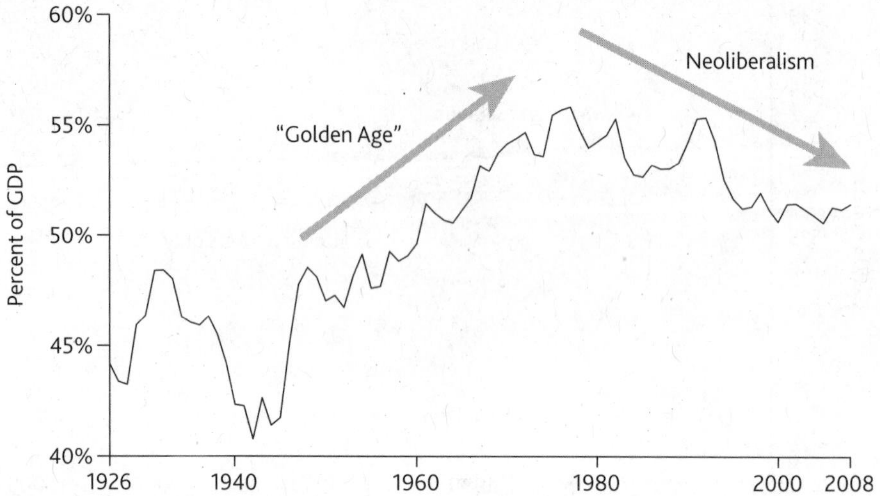

Sources: Author's calculations from Statistics Canada CANSIM tables 380-0016 and 380-0039.

Trends in Minimum Wages and Unionization

Later, this chapter will consider the impact on wages of labour market regulations and institutions like minimum wage laws and collective bargaining. To provide some context for that discussion, Figure 3 illustrates the long-run trend in minimum wages in Canada (once again expressed in real terms, adjusted for inflation). Minimum wages are set separately by each provincial government; Figure 3 illustrates the average minimum wage across the ten Canadian provinces. After peaking in the late 1970s (when governments accepted the idea that higher wages are a good thing), the real value of minimum wages declined sharply in the 1980s and 1990s. Later, in the 2000s, minimum wages experienced a partial resurgence in Canada, recouping over half of the real purchasing power lost by minimum wages in the earlier two decades. It is useful to measure minimum wages relative to the overall level of wages paid in the labour market. As illustrated in Figure 4, minimum wages currently represent about 40 percent of average wages (compared with 50 percent in the 1970s). However, relative to productivity (that is, the amount produced by an average worker in an hour), the value of minimum wages has been eroded continuously since the late 1970s. Today's minimum wage, despite recent improvements, represents only 15 percent of the hourly output of the average Canadian worker (down from 25 percent in the late 1970s).

Like minimum wages, the economic importance of trade unions has also been eroded. Labour law changes in most provinces in recent decades have made it harder for workers to form unions, and harder for unions to win improvement

FIGURE 3   Real Minimum Wages 1965–2009, Unweighted Provincial Average, Inflation-Adjusted

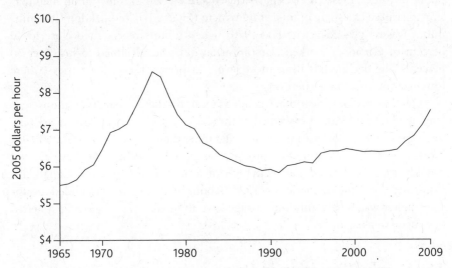

Sources: Author's calculations from HRSDC (2010) and Statistics Canada CANSIM table 326-0021.

FIGURE 4   Minimum Wage Context 1965–2008, Unweighted Provincial Average

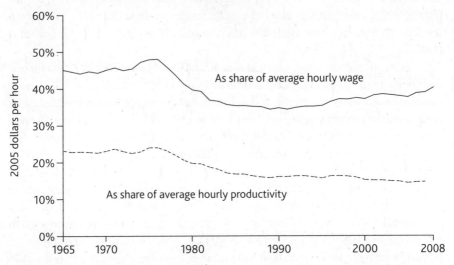

Note: Hourly worker wages from 1961 to 1983 extrapolated on the basis of manufacturing trend.

Sources: Author's calculations from HRSDC (2010), Sharpe et al. (2008), and Statistics Canada CANSIM tables 281-0008, 281-0030, and 281-0022.

for their members. Combined with more intense business competition and shifting public attitudes, these changes have caused a reduction in trade union membership measured as a share of total employment (Figure 5). Unionization (like minimum wages) peaked in the late 1970s, when unions represented close to 40 percent of Canadian workers. Unionization has since declined to just over 30 percent. The decline has been most severe in private sector industries (where unionization is below 20 percent).

Overall, then, it is clear that Canada's labour market has become a more challenging place for workers over the last three decades. Canadian workers are producing more, but most are not getting paid more than they were in the late 1970s. Workers' share of the output they produce has shrunk—and incomes have become notably more polarized between high-income and low-income Canadians. Coincident with the stagnation in wages, labour market policies intended to support higher wages (like minimum wage laws and collective bargaining systems) have been weakened.

The Surplus Tradition in Value and Distribution Theory

How do we explain this puzzling combination of growing productivity, capital accumulation, and technological progress, on one hand, with the stagnation in wage levels and the decline of labour's share of output on the other? Perhaps supply and demand forces, the central explanatory factor in neoclassical theory, do not tell the whole story. In this essay, we will consider income distribution through the lens of an alternative tradition in economic theory known as the "surplus tradition."

The classical economists (such as Adam Smith and David Ricardo) first identified the "virtues" of free markets and trade in the late 18th century—long before modern neoclassical theories were developed. But the classical economists, despite their pro-market bent, never believed that wages and income distribution were determined by markets. On the contrary, the classical tradition emphasized that wages, in general, were determined only by the physiological subsistence needs of workers. How much did capitalists have to pay their workers for a day's labour? The classical writers argued that it was only as much as was necessary to keep those workers alive, and hence able to come back to work the next day. Indeed, the classical economist Thomas Malthus even developed a theory of population growth to explain why wages could not rise above that subsistence level: he argued that workers who had more material abundance than required for sheer survival would simply breed (much like rabbits) until the food supply and other essentials of life limited further population growth. Thus incomes would inevitably return to the

FIGURE 5 Unionization

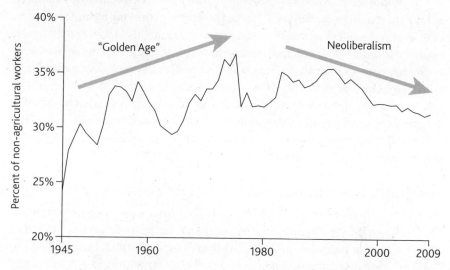

Sources: Author's calculations from Historial Statistics Canada, and Statistics Canada CANSIM tables 279-0026 and 282-0078. Breaks in series 1976 and 1997; 1950 and 1996 data points are interpolated from years before and after.

subsistence level.[2] Meanwhile, profits were interpreted as a "surplus": the production left over after the reproduction requirements of labour were paid for. Since capitalists were the creative driving force of society, and it was assumed that they would reinvest their profits in additional projects, the classical economists supported anything that would increase profits (the surplus). Neoclassical theorists, while also believing in the virtues of markets, have a very different theory of distribution. They argue that every factor (including both labour and capital) is paid a market-clearing rate of pay, reflecting its marginal productivity (that is, the additional output arising from the employment of one additional unit of input). In this view, there is no fundamental difference between how income distribution is determined for workers (wages) and capitalists (profits).

The socialist thinker Karl Marx further developed the classical theory of subsistence wages. Marx agreed that the "cost" of labour was the amount required for its reproduction. But he acknowledged that what was considered to be a bare minimum level of existence was not set in absolute terms. Rather, "subsistence" can vary with history, culture, social attitudes, and even politics. In Marx's view there was an inevitable conflict of interest between workers and employers over the terms of work, and over how to divide the output workers produced on the job. The varying course of this class struggle, reflecting the changing strength and aggressiveness of its two main protagonists, would influence the level of wages.

But unemployment would never disappear, even if wages fluctuated. Capitalism as a system requires a certain level of unemployment in the long term, Marx noted, to maintain discipline among workers and thus ensure profitable conditions for business investment. If unemployment falls too low, the system will recreate unemployment—either by tapping into new pools of wage labour (what Marx called the "reserve army"), and/or by cutting back investment to slow down growth and recreate unemployment. For Marx, too, the level of profits was determined as a residual (or surplus), after wages and other necessary production costs were paid out. No wonder there is a struggle between workers and employers: one's gain, in this understanding, is the other's loss.

Historical, Institutional, and Political Influences

Following from the classicals and Marx, a parallel "heterodox" stream in economic analysis has arisen, maintaining the core idea that wages are determined by structures and institutions, while profits reflect the remaining surplus. Income distribution and wage determination thereby reflect broad structural, institutional, and political factors, which exert their influence in the context of a struggle between competing groups for the control of income and wealth. Various theoretical schools fall within this alternative tradition, including institutional economists (who emphasize the role of cultural norms and institutional inertia in determining work practices and compensation), post-Keynesian thinkers (many of whom treat the wage as a customary or arbitrary benchmark that sets a nominal price level for the whole economy), and structuralist economists (in the tradition of the Polish thinker Michal Kalecki), who have integrated Marxian insights regarding class conflict and production with a Keynesian understanding of the importance of aggregate demand conditions.

What all of these heterodox thinkers share is their insistence that income distribution is not determined by the neutral, impersonal actions of competitive market forces, but, rather, reflects a multidimensional, historical conflict between different social groups, each scrabbling to advance their respective economic interests. It's not market-clearing that determines the division of the pie between wages and profits (and hence relative prices), it's an overarching economic, institutional, and even political tussle between the broad economic constituencies. Wage levels reflect whether workers have been successful in fighting (in the economic, cultural, and political spheres) for a greater share of the pie. Similarly, profits are not a normal market-clearing return to the real productivity of a factor of production called "capital," but the surplus accruing to capitalists after wages (determined by those broader, structural forces) have been paid out. Together, these alternative approaches (stretching from the classical thinkers through to modern structuralists) constitute the "surplus tradition" in the economics of value and distribution.

The classical view that wages are determined by the conditions of physiological subsistence is no longer applicable in modern developed economies, since it is clear that wages are higher than that. However, if subsistence is defined as a relative concept (rather than an absolute one), reflecting evolving cultural norms regarding the requirements of a "basic" life, then the concept of subsistence is still relevant.[3] Alternatively, above-subsistence wages could be interpreted as a reflection of workers' success in capturing a share of the economic surplus for themselves. Either way, it is institutions, social structures, and power that determine income distribution (not the automatic clearing of endowed factor markets). The labour market never "clears" as a normal economic outcome; there is almost always unemployment (and, indeed, the economic system—and the policy-makers, like central bankers, who manage it—will act to *recreate* unemployment whenever labour markets become too tight). Unemployment itself thus becomes a "bargaining chip" in the broad struggle over income distribution, since higher unemployment reduces wage demands. This effect is not experienced through a market-clearing process (because even if workers agree to cut their wages, unemployment never disappears), but because higher unemployment reduces the expectations and bargaining power of workers. This jibes with the observed reality that significant unemployment almost always exists in capitalism.[4] How can wages (and wage differentials between different groups of workers) be determined by a process of market clearing, when the labour market does not actually clear?

In the surplus view, the overall level of employment is not determined by the number of available workers (as in the supply-constrained neoclassical system). Instead, it is limited by the demand for labour from employers, which depends on the amount of production that employers decide to undertake. This in turn is determined by the total amount of expenditure (or aggregate demand). The most important determinants of aggregate demand are the decisions of the leading, dynamic sectors of the economy: primarily business investment, supplemented by export demand and government spending. Spending in these leading sectors, combined with input-output linkages to other sectors and spinoff expenditure effects (including consumer spending by employed workers), determines the overall level of aggregate demand and hence the overall level of employment.

Wages and Wage-Setting Institutions Through a Surplus Lens

This broad alternative understanding of how capitalist economies function is helpful for explaining both the postwar surge in Canadian wages, and their subsequent stagnation and polarization. During the postwar "Golden Age," business investment spending was very strong, driven by high profitability and Canada's structural transformation into a modern, industrialized economy. This vibrant business leadership was reinforced by growing government spending, such as the expansion of welfare state programs and public investment. At the same time, public policy in Canada demonstrated an increasingly "activist" social mission, reflected in various labour market interventions aimed at increasing workers' incomes and promoting more equality among them. Minimum wages increased markedly, and unions grew rapidly (facilitated by union-friendly labour laws, such as the famous 1945 Rand Formula[5]). Social programs such as the 1971 expansion of unemployment insurance provided workers with an additional degree of economic security and independence from their status as wage-earners, thus further reinforcing their bargaining power.

Buttressed by these worker-friendly policies and institutions, wages grew rapidly during the Golden Age, both in absolute terms and as a share of total GDP. Through a surplus lens, this postwar wage growth reflects a mixture of economic, political, and institutional pressures—not the automatic workings of markets. But it was reversed, beginning in the late 1970s and 1980s, through a historic U-turn in economic and social policy. The Golden Age recipe of near-full employment, sustained growth, and a generous "social contract" between labour and capital came unglued. Wealthy investors and business owners were concerned with financial instability, inflation, labour militancy, and geopolitical changes. They pushed hard for a more conservative set of economic and social policies (now known as "neoliberalism"). The causes and components of this historic change in policy direction are too broad to review in detail here,[6] but a focus on dismantling and weakening Golden Age labour market institutions has been a central plank in the overall neoliberal platform from the beginning. Real minimum wages were weakened; labour laws became more hostile to unionization (achieving a desired decline in unionization); and income security programs were reduced, especially those (like unemployment insurance) that support working-age persons.

These changes in labour market policy were reinforced by other policy changes. The former Keynesian commitment to full employment was replaced by a new emphasis on inflation control (in monetary policy) and deficit reduction (in fiscal policy). Both served to undermine (at least initially) aggregate demand conditions and hence employment. Business investment thus, ironically, slowed down (despite the business-friendly tilt to policy), in part because of the contractionary effects of the new "tough-love" stance in macroeconomic policy. Globalization, facilitated by free trade agreements, provided domestic businesses with more international leeway in their investment decisions, and hence more bargaining power with workers.

Facing a much more hostile economic and institutional environment, the wage demands of workers (whether unionized or not) moderated dramatically. Year in and year out, more workers were unemployed; those lucky enough to keep their jobs were less confident about pressing for better compensation. Wages stagnated, despite growing productivity, and labour's share of GDP began to shrink. Again, the explanation for this sea change cannot be found in any model of "natural" or automatic market-clearing forces. Rather, it was a deliberate emphasis on constraining labour compensation, by weakening the structures and institutions underpinning the long postwar rise in wages that had brought about this gritty new labour market regime.

Impacts of Neoliberal Labour Market Policy on Employment

What have been the impacts on employment of this shift in labour market policy? In the standard neoclassical story, labour market interventions aimed at increasing wages cause unemployment, by interfering with the normal market-clearing pressures that would otherwise determine wages. Most neoclassical economists oppose minimum wages and collective bargaining on these grounds; doing away with those interventionist measures should therefore reduce unemployment. Neoclassical interpretations of the low unemployment experienced in the United States in the 1990s and 2000s ascribed this "success" to the relative absence of labour market "distortions" like minimum wages and unions (which are much less powerful in the US than in other countries).

From a surplus perspective, however, there is no inherent reason to expect that higher minimum wages or stronger unions will adversely affect employment (nor, conversely, that weakening these policies will automatically boost employment). To the extent that higher wages translate into significantly lower profits, and to the extent that business investment declines accordingly, then higher wages might indeed lead to lower employment. This does not occur directly via the labour market, but indirectly via the impact of distribution—the division of the pie between wages and profits—on business investment and hence on aggregate demand. However, this chain of causation is by no means certain. If investment depends on factors other than profitability alone—such as interest rates, spending feedback effects (namely, multiplier and accelerator effects), or investor confidence and "animal spirits"—then the negative impact of higher wages on investment is muted. At the same time, higher wages *boost* demand by facilitating more consumer spending. Indeed, under certain conditions, the positive impact of higher wages on aggregate demand might actually outweigh any negative impacts on business investment, in which case higher wages lead to higher employment.[7] Under globalization, it would seem that business investment has become more sensitive to wage levels (since businesses now shift the location of investment, not just its amount, in response to high wages); this could reinforce the relationship between higher wages and lower employment. It is worth stressing that all of these

285

channels depend on the *indirect* impact of distribution on investment, output, and hence employment. Given the various and often countervailing factors that link distribution with employment, the final net impact of labour market interventions (like minimum wages or collective bargaining) on employment depends, unpredictably, on the overall state of investment, aggregate demand, and growth.

Effects of Minimum Wages and Unionization— Comparative Perspectives

In recent years, the impact of minimum wages on employment has received much attention from economists. New research in the 1990s questioned the conventional neoclassical assumption that higher minimum wages reduce employment; most famous was the work of Card and Kruger (1995). Researchers found that the disemployment effect of higher minimum wages in particular enterprises (such as fast food chains) was very small. Moreover, higher minimum wages have other positive impacts, spurring more labour force participation by marginalized groups and resulting in less labour turnover and more job stability in low-wage jobs (Pollin et al. 2008; Fox 2006). This has spurred a rethinking of minimum wage policy, contributing to the recent revitalization of minimum-wage policies in Canada.

There is also a vast economic literature regarding the economic impacts of unions on employment and other variables.[8] The evidence is clear that unions increase wages for their members, and for some non-members, too (via spillover effects, such as the impact of the threat of unionization on wages paid by non-union employers). The amount by which unions increase wages seems to be correlated positively with the proportion of the workforce that is unionized (that is, the higher the unionization rate, the more unions are able to boost wages).[9] Unions reduce wage inequality within workplaces (since union contracts generally limit wage differentials); their impact on inequality in the overall labour market is less clear. Unionization is consistently found to reduce the profitability of unionized firms; unions' impact on productivity is also uncertain. Regarding the impact of unions on employment, the debate remains controversial. Some researchers claim that higher unionization is associated with lower employment and higher unemployment in Canada (for example, Layne-Farrar 2009); others find no evidence of that link (Sran and Stanford 2009). Once again, since employment depends first and foremost on aggregate demand, and since wage-setting institutions (like unions) affect employment decisions only indirectly through a complex chain linking distribution, investment, and expenditure, we would not expect to find any clear link one way or the other between unionization and employment.

Indeed, international experience shows that it is possible to combine high unionization, strong wage protections, and a high degree of income equality with very positive employment outcomes and flexible, innovative workplaces. Several European countries (such as Austria, Denmark, the Netherlands, and Norway) have successfully integrated strong, equity-enhancing labour market interventions and very high unionization with low unemployment, high labour mobility, and high productivity growth. A famous theoretical finding in labour economics suggests that high unionization, if combined with an effective coordination of bargaining and macroeconomic policies, can lead to labour market outcomes that are as efficient as those in unregulated labour markets (Calmfors and Driffil 1988). Research conducted by the Organisation for Economic Co-operation and Development (OECD) (2006) seems to validate this finding; the OECD finds no link between minimum wages, collective bargaining, and unemployment. Meanwhile, the performance of the US labour market, which once seemed to prove the benefits of the "free" market approach (with weak minimum wages, unions, and social protections), has diminished notably. Researchers now suggest that earlier strong US employment had little to do with its uniquely *laissez-faire* labour market structures (Howell 2004), but resulted instead from other factors (such as very low interest rates). And today, despite its "rugged" free-market features, the United States ranks as one of the highest unemployment jurisdictions in the industrialized world.

Similar cross-jurisdictional comparisons can also be made in the Canadian context. Table 1 summarizes long-term unemployment rates in the Canadian provinces. They vary dramatically from 5 percent in Alberta to 15 percent in Newfoundland and Labrador. Minimum wages are more uniform, ranging between $8 and $10 per hour. Large interprovincial variations in employment performance cannot be ascribed to these small interprovincial differences in minimum wages.[10] There are bigger interprovincial differences in trade unionization, mostly reflecting interprovincial differences in labour laws. Alberta, Ontario, and New Brunswick are the least unionized provinces (with unions representing under 30 percent of employees); Newfoundland and Labrador and Quebec are the most unionized (at around 40 percent). Some relatively high-unionization provinces have low unemployment (such as Saskatchewan and Manitoba), while some relatively low-unionization provinces have high unemployment (like New Brunswick); there is no clear correlation one way or the other. Employment, in the surplus tradition, represents the culmination of a complex set of direct and indirect relationships linking income distribution to spending by business and other leading sectors of the economy, mediated by input-output linkages and multiplier effects. From this perspective, it is not surprising that differences in interprovincial labour market structures cannot explain the larger observed divergences in labour market outcomes.

TABLE 1   Minimum Wages, Unionization, and Unemployment, Canadian Provinces

	Minimum wage (Jan. 1, 2010)	Union density (2009)	Average unemployment rate, 2000–2009
Alberta	$8.80	25.0%	4.6%
British Columbia	$8.00	31.0%	6.6%
Manitoba	$9.00	37.0%	4.8%
New Brunswick	$8.25	28.8%	9.5%
Newfoundland and Labrador	$8.75	39.0%	15.4%
Nova Scotia	$8.60	30.6%	8.8%
Ontario	$9.50	27.6%	6.8%
Prince Edward Island	$8.40	31.9%	11.3%
Quebec	$9.00	39.8%	8.3%
Saskatchewan	$9.25	35.8%	5.0%

Sources: HRSDC (2010) and Statistics Canada CANSIM tables 282-0086 and 282-0078.

Conclusion

Neoclassical theory suggests that in a "free" labour market every willing worker can find a job, and will be paid according to his or her marginal productivity. Efforts to boost wages through minimum wages or collective bargaining will backfire by creating unemployment. But this fundamental faith in market-clearing does not match the observed reality of Canada's labour market. Significant unemployment is a normal feature of the labour market, not an exception, and wages have not even remotely kept track with productivity for the last 30 years (in fact, by some measures, real wages haven't grown at all).

A more convincing explanation for the stagnation of wages in Canada (and for their previous vibrant growth during the postwar Golden Age) recognizes the crucial importance of labour market institutions and socio-economic power in determining wages and income distribution. The bargaining field on which income distribution is determined has become notably tilted in favour of employers since the early 1980s—when governments began to adopt a much more business-friendly policy framework, called neoliberalism. This shift in the balance of economic power explains the stagnation and polarization of wages in Canada far better than any reference to automatic "market clearing." And, contrary to the standard prediction of neoclassical models that equity-seeking interventions into labour markets (no matter how well-intentioned) inevitably produce unemployment, Canadian and international evidence suggests that high minimum wages, strong collective bargaining, and other proactive labour market interventions can succeed in boosting and levelling incomes, while still attaining low unemployment and efficient and flexible work practices. But this successful outcome requires a combination of policies aimed at promoting vibrant investment (including by businesses) and innovation, and coordinating income distribution policies with macroeconomic policy. In that manner, the goals of stronger employment and a more desirable income distribution can be pursued simultaneously.

NOTES

1. In conventional economic theory, the determination of wages and incomes is part of an overall theory of value and distribution known as "general equilibrium theory." General equilibrium theory was pioneered in the late 19th century by the founders of the "neoclassical" approach to economics (such as the Swiss economist Léon Walras). This general equilibrium model is still hotly debated, on both theoretical and empirical grounds; see Keen (2001), Cassidy (2009), and Stanford (2008, chaps. 4–6) for accessible discussions of the weaknesses of neoclassical general equilibrium theory.
2. Malthus, of course, had the theory exactly backwards. History has proven that when incomes rise above subsistence, population growth slows (not accelerates), thanks to better education, health, and social security.
3. Two Canadian studies measure the costs of "subsistence" in this broader, relative understanding. They conclude that for a family with two full-time full-year wage earners and two children, an hourly wage of $17 (earned by both wage-earners) just meets those subsistence needs. This is far higher than Canadian minimum wages, and not much less than average hourly wages in Canada (which equalled about $20 in 2009)—so perhaps the concept of "subsistence" is more relevant to modern labour market analysis than is commonly assumed. See Richards et al. (2008) and Mackenzie and Stanford (2009) for details.
4. A situation in which every willing worker has a job is almost never observed (even allowing for a certain amount of labour market "friction," reflecting workers between jobs and other genuinely transitory joblessness). The closest Canada has come to full employment was during the Second World War, when labour demand surged, thanks to a massive government-financed war effort. Over the past 35 years, Canada's official unemployment rate (which excludes some non-employed workers by definition, such as "discouraged workers" and other so-called non-participants in the labour force) has averaged 8.5 percent—not even close to full employment.
5. In 1946, Judge Ivan Rand ended a three-month strike at Ford Canada operations in Windsor by arbitrating a new provision guaranteeing the collection and forwarding of union dues by the employer. By consolidating the financial base of the union, this ruling (emulated in other labour contracts) ushered in a more secure framework for industrial unionism.

6. See Harvey (2005), Klein (2007), and Stanford (2008, Chaps. 2, 3, and 24) for accessible introductions to neoliberalism.
7. In modern structuralist nomenclature, this scenario is termed a "wage-led" or "stagnationist" regime. See Bhaduri (2008) and Bhaduri and Marglin (1990).
8. Freeman and Medoff (1984) and Farber (1987) are classic references; see Addison and Hirsch (1989), Christie (2007), Freeman and Morris (1990), Hirsch (2004), Stewart (1995), and Card et al. (2003) for further examples.
9. In this case, the erosion of unionization has a two-fold negative impact on wages: the share of workers directly receiving higher wages is lower, and the extent to which unions can raise wages (including for non-members) is reduced.
10. In fact, there is a negative correlation between average provincial minimum wages in recent years and long-run provincial unemployment rates, indicating that provinces with higher minimum wages are likely to have lower unemployment rates (the exact opposite of the neoclassical expectation).

DISCUSSION QUESTIONS

1. Think about your past employment experience. Would you feel confident in going to your employer and demanding a higher wage? Why or why not? What do you think would have happened?
2. The share of total GDP received by workers in Canada (in the form of wages, salaries, and non-wage benefits) has declined significantly since the late 1970s. List several factors that, in your view, explain this trend. Do you think it is fair? Do you think it is inevitable that workers are paid less?
3. Neoclassical economic theory believes that all workers are paid according to their productivity. Do you agree that people are paid according to how productive they are? Why or why not? How would you compare the productivity of a financial executive (who works in an office) with a construction worker or a chambermaid?
4. Have you ever belonged to a union? List three costs and three benefits of belonging to a union. In your view, how have Canadians' attitudes toward unions changed in recent years, and why?

FURTHER READING AND WEB RESOURCES

These two works provide readable introductions to trade unions and their economic and social effects in Canada:

diCarlo, Angelo, Chad Johnston, and Jim Stanford. 2010. Canada's labour movement in challenging times: Unions and their role in a changing economy. In *The shifting landscape of work*, eds. Norene Pupo, Dan Glenday, and Ann Duffy. Toronto: Thomson Nelson.

Jackson, Andrew. 2010. *Work and labour in Canada: Critical issues.* 2nd ed. Toronto: Canadian Scholars' Press.

This book provides a short, readable account of a successful campaign by workers and immigrant communities in Ontario to pressure the provincial government to increase the minimum wage to $10:

> Schwartz, Kristin. 2008. *A million reasons: The victory of the $10 minimum wage campaign.* Toronto: Toronto and York Region Labour Council.

This report, available online, discusses the puzzling combination of continued productivity growth and stagnant wages in Canada, which the Centre for the Study of Living Standards (CSLS) concludes was due in part to the erosion of unionization:

> Sharpe, Andrew, Jean-François Arsenault, and Peter Harrison. 2008. *The relationship between labour productivity and real wage growth in Canada and OECD countries.* Ottawa: Centre for the Study of Living Standards, CSLS Research Report.

Human Resources and Skills Development Canada maintains an online database, which is a helpful summary of the historical evolution of minimum wages in Canada:

> http://srv116.services.gc.ca/dimt-wid/sm-mw/menu.aspx?lang=eng.

REFERENCES

Addison, John T., and Barry T. Hirsch. 1989. Union effects on productivity, profits, and growth: Has the long-run arrived? *Journal of Labor Research* 7 (1): 72–105.

Akyeampong, Ernest. 1999. Unionization: An update. *Perspectives on Labour and Income.* Ottawa: Statistics Canada (August).

Bhaduri, Amit. 2008. On the dynamics of profit-led and wage-led growth. *Cambridge Journal of Economics* 32 (1): 147–160.

Bhaduri, Amit, and Stephen Marglin. 1990. Unemployment and the real wage: The economic basis for contesting political ideologies. *Cambridge Journal of Economics* 14 (3): 375–393.

Calmfors, L., and J. Driffil. 1988. Bargaining structure, corporatism and macro-economic performance. *Economic Policy* 6 (April).

Card, David, and Alan B. Krueger. 1995. *Myth and measurement: The new economics of the minimum wage.* Princeton, NJ: Princeton University Press.

Card, David E., Thomas Lemieux, and W. Craig Riddell. 2003. Unionization and wage inequality: A comparative study of the U.S., the U.K., and Canada. NBER Working Paper Series, Vol. 9473.

Cassidy, John. 2009. *How markets fail: The logic of economic calamities.* New York: Farrar, Strauss, and Giroux.

Christie, Virginia. 2007. Union wage effects and the probability of union membership. *Economic Record* 68 (1): 43–56.

Farber, Henry S. 1987. The analysis of union behaviour. In *The handbook of labour economics 2*, eds. Richard Layard and Orley Ashenfelter, 1039–1089. Amsterdam: Elsevier.

Fox, Liana. 2006. *Minimum wage trends: Understanding past and contemporary research.* Briefing Paper #178. Washington, DC: Economic Policy Institute.

Freeman, Richard B., and Morris Kleiner. 1990. The impact of new unionization on wages and working conditions. *Journal of Labor Economics* 8 (1): S8–S25.

Freeman, Richard B., and James L. Medoff. 1984. *What do unions do?* New York: Basic.

Harvey, David. 2005. *A brief history of neoliberalism.* Oxford: Oxford University Press.

Hirsch, Barry T. 2004. What do unions do for economic performance? *Journal of Labor Research* 25 (3): 415–455.

Howell, David R., ed. 2004. *Fighting unemployment: The limits of free-market orthodoxy.* Oxford: Oxford University Press.

Human Resources and Skills Development Canada. 2010. *Minimum wage database.* http://srv116.services.gc.ca/dimt-wid/sm-mw/menu.aspx?lang=eng.

Keen, Steve. 2001. *Debunking economics.* London: Zed.

Klein, Naomi. 2007. *The shock doctrine: The rise of disaster capitalism.* New York: Metropolitan.

Layne-Farrar, Anne. 2009. *An empirical assessment of the employee free choice act: The economic implications.* LECG Consulting (March).

Mackenzie, Hugh, and Jim Stanford. 2009. *A living wage for Toronto.* Ottawa: Canadian Centre for Policy Alternatives.

Organisation for Economic Co-operation and Development (OECD). 1994. *Jobs study.* Paris: OECD.

Organisation for Economic Co-operation and Development (OECD). 2006. Reassessing the role of policies and institutions for labour market performance: A quantitative analysis. *OECD Employment Outlook,* Chap. 7.

Palley, Thomas I. 2006. The causes of high unemployment: Labour market sclerosis versus macroeconomic policy. In *Wages, employment, distribution and growth: International perspectives,* eds. Eckhard Hein, Arne Heise, and Achim Truger. Basingstoke, UK: Palgrave Macmillan.

Pollin, Robert, Mark Brenner, Jeanette Wicks-Lim, and Stephanie Luce. 2008. *A measure of fairness: The economics of living wages and minimum wages in the United States.* Ithaca, NY: Cornell University Press.

Richards, Tim, Marcy Cohen, Seth Klein, and Deborah Littman. 2008. *Working for living wage: Making paid work meet basic family needs in Vancouver and Victoria.* Vancouver: Canadian Centre for Policy Alternatives.

Sharpe, Andrew, Jean-François Arsenault, and Peter Harrison. 2008. *The relationship between labour productivity and real wage growth in Canada and OECD countries.* Ottawa: Centre for the Study of Living Standards, CSLS Research Report.

Sran, Garry, and Jim Stanford. 2009. Further tests of the link between unionization, unemployment, and employment: Findings from Canadian national and provincial data. *Just Labour: A Canadian Journal of Work and Society* 15 (November): 29–77.

Stanford, Jim. 2008. *Economics for everyone: A short guide to the economics of capitalism.* London: Pluto Books.

Statistics Canada. 2008a. *Earnings and incomes of Canadians over the past quarter century, 2006 census.* Ottawa: Statistics Canada. Catalogue 97-563 (May).

Statistics Canada. 2008b. Unionization. *Perspectives on labour and income.* Ottawa: Statistics Canada (August).

Stewart, Mark. 1995. Union wage differentials in an era of declining unionization. *Oxford Bulletin of Economics and Statistics* 57 (2): 143–166.

Is There Labour Market Discrimination? Are Employment Equity Policies Effective?

COMPETING VIEWS

Morley Gunderson, "Pay and Employment Equity Legislation Meets the Market"

Fiona MacPhail, "Labour Market Discrimination: An Institutional Economics View"

Editors' Introduction

Economic discrimination can take on different forms. It can arise at the entry level to an occupation, through the balkanization of labour markets that prevents individuals from entering that particular occupation or sector. Discriminatory hiring thus leads to segregation and the creation of labour market ghettos. It can also arise at the post-entry level, through discriminatory promotion practices and the generation of undesirable labour market income differentials. Such an undesirable outcome in terms of differential economic rewards is said to occur when equivalent individuals receive different remuneration for equal work and equal contribution to output because of differences in age, gender, race/ethnicity, physical disabilities, religion, or sexual orientation.

Economic discrimination may be as old as society itself. However, as modern societies have opened up to integrate traditionally marginalized groups (such as women) into the labour force, and as our societies have become increasingly ethnically diverse through international migration, this discrimination has become universally recognized as a problem that must be eradicated. Economic discrimination is not only morally repugnant, since it violates deeply rooted societal notions of fairness and human rights, but also generates labour market inefficiencies that are costly to society.

Most mainstream economists recognize that discrimination could arise because of gender/ethnic prejudices resulting from employers' "tastes," or because of employer "ignorance," if employers erroneously assume that certain groups with observable gender or ethnic characteristics have lower average productivity. Moreover, it is generally recognized that females and minority groups are often "crowded" or segregated into lower-paying occupations because of entry-level barriers. As Morley Gunderson points out, greater market competition ought to eliminate such differences, especially since ultimately discrimination carries a cost that is borne by those firms that practise discrimination rather than by those that do not discriminate. Hence, the more likely that market pressures would bear on discriminating employers, the greater ought to be the success in eliminating labour market discrimination. Although legislation can help, it can sometimes be counterproductive. In particular, Gunderson argues that "pay equity" policies are far more inefficient and costly to administer than "employment equity" policies, which (notwithstanding their costs) can be more effective.

Developing her analysis from an institutionalist perspective, Fiona MacPhail describes labour market discrimination from the viewpoint of the system as a whole, which relates to norms and practices in society that are oppressive for certain groups and are beneficial for others. The segregation of women and minority groups into what is referred to as the secondary labour market, which serves as a buffer to the primary sector, creates the necessary conditions for the continuation of discrimination that is largely impermeable to competition. According to MacPhail, labour market discrimination is not merely the result of employers' individual choices; it is a systemic reality that imposes itself and cannot be easily eliminated through more pervasive competition in the labour market. While existing employment legislation can help, better support systems for disadvantaged groups, such as greater schooling, better child-care facilities, and more centralized wage bargaining, are also required.

Pay and Employment Equity Legislation Meets the Market

Morley Gunderson

Introduction

Are market forces the worst enemy or the best friend of those who face discrimination? In other words, are market forces part of the solution or part of the problem? These are fundamental questions in the microeconomics of discrimination and they are obviously of immense practical and policy importance, especially for the effectiveness of legislative initiatives to combat discrimination. The purpose of this essay is to use basic principles of microeconomics to address these questions and to illustrate other basic concepts of microeconomics, including the "law of one price," the principle of arbitrage, the "law of unintended consequences," value in use versus value in exchange, and the diamond–water paradox.

The essay begins with a discussion of alternative theories of discrimination and then provides evidence for the issue. It then discusses the main policy initiatives that are in place and how they relate to market forces, concluding—perhaps somewhat controversially—that market forces are a best friend and part of the solution to combat discrimination. The issue is illustrated by gender discrimination; however, the principles apply to all forms of discrimination, such as discrimination by race or colour, religion, physical or mental disability, dependence on alcohol or drugs, age, marital status, national or ethnic origin, and sexual orientation. These are all prohibited grounds of discrimination in the human rights codes of the various jurisdictions in Canada.

Theoretical Perspectives on Discrimination

It is important to have a theoretical understanding of the underlying reasons for or causes of discrimination for a number of reasons. First, without an understanding of the causes, policy initiatives to combat discrimination may simply be dealing with the symptoms and not the causes. Second, understanding the causes is important so as to forecast how the problem may change in the future when the underlying causes themselves change. Third, a causal understanding is important to determine how the private parties themselves may respond to policy initiatives, often "undoing" the effect of well-intended initiatives or leading to unintended impacts—the "law of unintended consequences" in economics.

The starting point for modern economic models of discrimination is generally regarded as Becker's (1957) seminal work, although there were certainly precursors, such as Fawcett (1918) and Edgeworth (1922). Becker's model builds on the notion that people have prejudices against particular groups and favouritism (nepotism) toward others. When firms hire the discriminated-against group, they act as if they are paying a pay premium (a discrimination coefficient) for that group, given their aversion toward hiring them (where the firm's preferences can also embed the preferences of their customers and co-workers). When firms hire their favoured group, they act as if they are paying less than the wage that they pay (a nepotism coefficient), given their preference for that group. Becker uses the analogy of tariffs in international trade to show that, when we impose a tariff, we indicate that we are willing to pay a price premium to consume domestic products rather than cheaper imports. This model yields a situation in which the wages of the group that is discriminated against are less than the value of their marginal product and the wages of the preferred group are greater than the value of their marginal product, in contrast to the competitive model of economics in which wages are equal to the value of the marginal product of labour. Applying that to gender wage differentials suggests that the ratio of female to male wages would be less than the ratio of the value of females' marginal product. A similar implication results from Arrow's (1973) framework: firms are assumed to maximize utility rather than just profits, and their utility is a positive function of profits but also a negative function of the number of the discriminated-against workers and a positive function of the number of preferred workers they employ.

An issue that these models of discrimination have to confront is that firms with such preferences would not survive long under the forces of competition, just as they would not survive long if they paid 20 percent more for a blue machine that was exactly as productive as a red machine. Such firms are essentially forgoing profits by not hiring more of the discriminated-against group, whose wages are less than the value of their marginal product, and less of the favoured group, whose wages exceed the value of their marginal product. Competitive pressures would foster such hiring until the increased demand for the group that is discriminated against would raise their wages, and the reduced demand for the favoured group would lower their wages until equally productive workers were paid the same wage (or, more accurately, the ratio of their wages would equal the ratio of their productivity). In essence, the forces of supply and demand would "arbitrage" or eliminate any price difference for a homogeneous commodity—in this case the services of equally productive workers—until the economic "law of one price" (that is, a uniform price for a uniform product) prevailed. Becker and Arrow recognize this issue—both being Nobel prizewinners!—and emphasize that the forces of competition *would* work to dissipate such discriminatory wage differentials, reducing if not eliminating any discriminatory pay gap. As aptly stated in the early 1920s by Edgeworth (1922, 438): "The best results will presumably be obtained by leaving employers free to compete for male or female labour. Thus equal pay for equal work would be secured in our sense of the term."

Most of the other theoretical perspectives on the economics of discrimination essentially deal with barriers that may inhibit such market forces from dissipating and certainly eliminating discrimination (Gunderson 2006). Using our example of gender discrimination, substantial transactions and adjustment costs may be involved in replacing the more expensive males with the less expensive but equally productive females. For example, substantial quasi-fixed costs tend to be associated with recruiting, hiring, and training new workers. There can also be substantial costs to terminating workers, including severance payments and the possibility of an unjust-dismissal case being brought against the firm. Hence, employers may want to amortize the fixed costs of terminating existing male employees over a longer period of time, rather than immediately replacing them with female workers, thus incurring new fixed costs. In such circumstances, employers would tend to replace male workers with female workers when the male workers leave through normal attrition. Adjustment costs may also occur in the form of conflict with the existing male workforce if male workers discriminate and do not want to work alongside female workers. In essence, market forces would dissipate discrimination, but the adjustment process may take a long time.

Economics emphasizes that when agents make costly mistakes (as when firms fail to maximize profits) they will adjust in a fashion to eliminate the mistakes (in our example, replace males with the less costly females). The perspective of *cognitive dissonance* in psychology (Festinger 1957), however, emphasizes that, rather than eliminate the mistake, individuals will often develop elaborate justifications for their action (for instance, theories of the super-race). To the extent that this occurs, it can certainly serve as a barrier to market forces dissipating discrimination. It does raise the issue, however, of the survival value of such rationalizations in the face of market forces.

The *crowding hypothesis* provides an alternative perspective, arguing that women tend to be crowded into female-dominated occupations because of *segregation* on the part of employers or pressures from family or education institutions that stream females into fields like nursing as opposed to medicine, or fine arts as opposed to engineering and sciences (Sorensen 1990). Segregation can also occur because employers have a degree of *monopsony* power, to the extent that their female workers are less mobile and more tied to their local employer because of family responsibilities (Madden 1972; Manning 2003). Crowding and segregation can also occur to the extent that employers are able to "divide and conquer" their workforce into non-competing groups so that the group that is discriminated against would be unlikely to contemplate applying for the higher-wage jobs or to form a coalition with the higher-paid groups to organize (for example, into a union) so as to raise their wages. Such crowding creates an excess supply of females in those occupations and in local jobs, and this excess supply lowers their productivity (moving down the demand curve for female labour), hence lowering their wage. In such circumstances, females may be paid a wage commensurate with their productivity, but their productivity is lowered by being crowded into female-dominated jobs and excluded from male-dominated jobs. As Edgeworth (1922, 439) stated: "crowding of women into a comparatively few occupations ... is universally recognized as a main factor in the depression of their wages."

While this perspective can explain why market forces may not dissipate such wage discrimination (since females would be paid a wage equal to the value of their depressed marginal product), it does leave open the question of how such segregation can be sustained under competitive market forces. To the extent that females can do the work that males do in the male-dominated jobs, it would pay employers to place them in such jobs given the lower wage they are paid, and to continue doing so until the wage differential is eliminated.

Statistical discrimination can also prevail whereby individuals are judged not on the basis of their individual performance but rather on the basis of the performance of their group, or stereotypes about that performance. While unfair from the perspective of many individuals, such discrimination can persist in the face of competitive market forces because garnering information on individual performance is expensive and basing expectations on group averages may be a low-cost procedure. To the extent that competitive market forces make it more worthwhile to gauge individual performance, however (for instance, in the high-performance workplace, which is growing in importance), then such market forces should dissipate statistical discrimination and put a premium on individual assessments.

Systemic discrimination can also arise as the unintended byproduct of practices that may have served a purpose in the past in the old world of work but are no longer relevant to the new world of work. This can be the case, for example, for strength or height requirements that may have been relevant for carrying out tasks involving physical labour but are now automated. Competitive market forces should dissipate such discrimination, however, to the extent that it is costly to keep such irrelevant requirements and bypass the opportunity to use people who may not meet them.

The previous discussion referred to how competitive market forces should serve to dissipate discrimination. Obviously, from that perspective, *non-competitive factors* can foster the continuation of discriminatory wage differences, since market forces are weakened or non-existent. This can be the case, for example, if market forces are muted by such factors as monopolies, oligopolies, protective tariffs, occupational licensing, wage-fixing legislation, unions, and regulations that inhibit competition. Some of these situations enable wages in general to be paid above the competitive rate, in which case queues of applicants would result that may be rationed, in part on the basis of discrimination. While these forces can mute market pressures that could otherwise dissipate discrimination, they can also embody other pressures that can work toward dissipating discriminatory wage differences. Unions, for example, tend to follow egalitarian pay practices that can compress wages (that is, raise wages at the low end of the wage distribution and lower them at the high end) and therefore disproportionately benefit lower-wage groups. Unions may also monitor and help enforce legislative initiatives that can benefit minorities. Monopolies and public sector employers are often sensitive to their public image and hence may be less prone to discriminate even if they do not face competitive market pressures.

Discrimination *outside the labour market* can also have an effect in the labour market, inhibiting market forces from dissipating discrimination in the labour market. Parents may encourage their daughters to enter fields of education they regard as appropriate for girls and their sons to enter fields they regard as appropriate for boys. Guidance counsellors and educational institutions may do the same. Men may put pressure on their spouses or partners not to take on jobs or promotions that would mean the men would lose their status as "breadwinners." The unequal division of labour within the household means that women typically take on more responsibility for household tasks, including child-raising. This can inhibit their willingness to take on certain jobs or promotions or to travel as part of their work. It can even affect their productivity at work if they are juggling two full-time jobs—one in the household and one in the labour market. As the expression goes: "the household is not an equal opportunity employer."

Evidence for Gender Discrimination

The empirical evidence sheds light on the relative importance of many of the factors cited above that can affect discriminatory wage differentials as well as on the relative importance of market forces in dissipating discrimination. A wide range of empirical procedures have been used to estimate the extent of discrimination, mainly involving different ways of controlling for the effect of factors other than discrimination that can influence wages. Reviews of that extensive literature by Altonji and Blank (1999), Blau (1998), Blau, Ferber, and Winkler (2002), Blau and Kaun (2000, 2003), Gunderson (1989, 2006), Holzer and Neumark (2000), and Jarrell and Stanley (2004) suggest the following generalizations:

- Females earn about 70 percent of what males earn *before* adjusting for the effect of different factors that can influence the gender pay gap.

- The gap tends to be smaller after adjusting for the fact that women tend to work fewer hours, they have less continuous work experience, their education tends to be less labour market-oriented, they tend to work in lower-paying occupations and smaller firms, and they tend to have more household responsibilities. Many of these factors themselves, however, may reflect discrimination.
- The gap is smaller in unionized environments and the public sector, likely reflecting their compressed wage structures and sensitivity to their public image.
- The gap is smaller in countries with centralized bargaining structures, where wage structures tend to be compressed and equal pay issues are incorporated into centralized bargaining.
- It is important to note, given the focus of this paper, that the discriminatory gap is smaller when private sector employers are subject to more competition in their product and service markets, suggesting that "markets may be a women's best friend" and that market forces can be "part of the solution." Evidence on this point is found in Ashenfelter and Hannan (1986), Black and Brainerd (2004), Black and Strahan (2001), Hellerstein, Neumark, and Troske (2002), and Meng (2004).

While the evidence suggests that competitive market forces can help *dissipate* discrimination, the evidence also suggests that at least some of the gender pay gap does reflect discrimination. This conclusion is reached in the various reviews of the literature: Altonji and Blank (1999, 3191), Gunderson (1989, 51), Holzer and Neumark (2000, 499), and Jarrell and Stanley (2004, 828). In a recent review of the literature, Gunderson (2006, 11) concludes: "While zero discrimination cannot be dismissed, a discriminatory wage gap of about 5 to 15 percent seems a more reasonable interpretation of the evidence."

Pay and Employment Equity Initiatives

The fact that at least some of the overall gender pay gap reflects discrimination suggests that there is a role for legislative initiatives to combat discrimination, or at least alleviate some of its symptoms. Even in this area, economics can shed some light on the viability of such initiatives as well as their expected impact and unintended consequences.

Pay Initiatives and Pay Equity

On the pay side, all jurisdictions in Canada have some form of equal pay legislation that requires equal pay for equal work for males and females. In the early legislative initiatives of the 1960s, equal work was strictly defined so that any small difference in work meant it was not equal. This was expanded to allow small differences as long as the work was substantially similar; however, comparisons could only be made within the same occupations within an establishment. Pay equity legislation (termed "comparable worth" in the United States and "equal pay for work of equal value" in Europe) expanded the comparator options further by allowing comparisons between male-dominated and female-dominated occupations within the same establishment, as long as the jobs were of equal value, as determined by a job evaluation scheme. Four steps are involved in determining pay equity. First, the firm must establish its male-dominated and female-dominated jobs based on criteria set out in the legislation, such as 70 percent of either sex in a given job. Second, the firm must establish the "value" of the job based on a gender-neutral job evaluation scheme, typically involving points given for different components of skill, effort, responsibility, and working conditions. Third, the relationship between pay and the job evaluation points must be established, typically by estimating a pay line (that is, a line on a graph that traces the relationship between pay on the vertical axis and job evaluation points on the horizontal axis). Fourth, the pay in the undervalued female-dominated jobs must be adjusted to the pay of the male-dominated jobs of the same value. Pay equity initiatives exist by legislation or administrative rulings in the public sectors of most jurisdictions in Canada, except for Alberta, Saskatchewan, the Northwest Territories, Yukon, and Nunavut. They also exist in the private sectors of Ontario and Quebec.

From an economic perspective, there are a number of concerns with this procedure. For example, it is based on an administrative concept of value, in which value is assigned through a job evaluation procedure, in contrast to the economic concept of value, in which value is determined by demand (what consumers are willing to pay to have a good or service) and supply (what individuals are willing to accept to produce the good or service). The administrative concept is based on value in use, whereas the economic concept is based on value in exchange. For example, the tasks of Spanish and French translator jobs may have the same value in use if they involve the same skill, effort, responsibilities, and working conditions. Spanish translators may be more in demand in the United States, whereas French translators are more in demand in Canada, yet they would have to be paid the same wages according to pay equity principles, as long as they had the same job evaluation points. This is akin to the diamond–water paradox in economics, where water has high value in use but little value in exchange if it is in abundant supply, while diamonds have little value in use but high value in exchange because they are in scarce supply. In economics, value is determined by supply and demand, not by administrative procedures such as job evaluation.

This is part and parcel of the concern in economics that wages or the price of labour services are called upon to serve a myriad of functions, which interferes with their prime economic function of allocating labour to its most valued use and providing the appropriate incentives for human capital formation in such areas as education, training, and labour mobility. In addition to allocating labour and providing the incentives for human capital formation, wages are also called upon to alleviate poverty, to impart social status and self-worth, to curb inflation, and—in the pay equity arena—to correspond to an administrative concept of value. Not surprisingly, serving too many masters can lead to serving none.

The scope of pay equity may be limited by the fact that smaller firms are exempt or difficult to enforce compliance in, since such firms employ the majority of the workforce, especially females (Baker and Fortin 2004). Pay equity can also have other unintended consequences. It can reduce the employment opportunities for women, to the extent that employers reduce their demand for the now higher-priced labour. It can reduce training opportunities by not enabling women to take lower-paying jobs that may have a high training component, which compensates for the lower wage and could lead to higher subsequent wage growth. Most important, by raising wages in female-dominated jobs, pay equity can foster continued segregation by discouraging women from leaving the female-dominated jobs and entering the higher-paying male-dominated jobs—a process that would increase the wages in the female-dominated jobs (given their reduced labour supply), and reduce the wages in the male-dominated jobs (given their increased labour supply).

From a design and implementation perspective, pay equity can be incredibly complex and require expensive job evaluation procedures. Relating job evaluation points to pay also involves procedures whose properties are not well-known. Should pay equity be estimated via pay lines? If so, should they be linear or non-linear? Should a graph of pay lines have an intercept or constant term? Should they have the same slope for male-dominated and female-dominated jobs? Similar questions arise about the procedures for adjusting the undervalued female-dominated jobs to the pay of male-dominated jobs. Should the pay in each female-dominated job be adjusted to the male pay line or to the male job of the nearest value? Or should the female pay line be adjusted to the male pay line? What if there are no male jobs of comparable value? How are establishments to be defined? What is the appropriate measure of compensation? From an economic perspective, these issues require real resources to sort out, involving job evaluators, consultants, and lawyers. These are real resource costs used up in the process of achieving redress; they are not just transfer costs where what one party loses another party gains. As a result, the cost of administering a process can become a large component of the costs associated with achieving redress. This concern of economists has also been emphasized by feminist scholars. As stated by Pat McDermott (1991, 22), "When it comes to implementing pay equity schemes, numerous technical issues usually emerge. Indeed, the very complexity of pay equity is an issue about which pay equity advocates should become concerned." Or, as cynically stated by Debra Lewis

(1991, 225), "That's the final beauty of pay equity as a reform: it simply consumes so many resources that there is little left for anything else."

Employment Initiatives and Employment Equity

The other main strand of policy initiatives deals with discrimination in the various stages of employment, including recruiting, hiring, promotion, and termination. All jurisdictions in Canada have human rights codes that prohibit discrimination in the various aspects of employment. These are designed to provide equal employment *opportunities*. Employment equity legislation (termed "affirmative action" in the United States), however, goes further in that it focuses on *outcomes*, requiring employers to represent specific target groups in their workforce in the same proportion as they exist in the external pool of labour from which employers can be expected to recruit. In Canada, such legislation exists only in the federal jurisdiction, which covers about 6 percent of the workforce, in areas such as banking, transportation, and communication. The federal government also requires employment equity for employers who bid on federal contracts. The specific target groups are women, visible minorities, Aboriginal persons, and disabled persons. Employers are required to do an internal audit to make sure those groups are represented within their establishment. They are then required to match that with their representation in the external pool of available labour from which they are reasonably expected to recruit. If the groups are underrepresented, then the employer must develop a plan and timetable for rectifying this.

Employment equity procedures can also be quite costly to administer. As well, they can have unintended consequences, with people feeling that they received their job or promotion on the basis of their designated status rather than merit. Individuals can be placed "over their heads" and hence suffer from the stress of having to perform at a level beyond their capabilities, or they may fail in the job and hence fuel negative stereotypes. From an economic perspective, however, such policies that work on the employment side should increase the demand for the target groups and this in turn should increase both their wages and employability, in contrast to equal pay or pay equity policies that can reduce employment opportunities because of the higher cost associated with such wage-fixing. Employment equity, for example, can also facilitate women leaving the female-dominated jobs and entering the male-dominated jobs. The supply reduction in the female-dominated jobs raises their pay and the supply influx into the male-dominated jobs lowers their pay, again facilitating equal pay through market forces.

Facilitating Policies

A third line of policy initiatives to deal with gender discrimination makes use of policies that can facilitate the more equal participation of men and women in the labour market. For economists, these can often be appealing since they "grease the wheels" of market adjustments rather than interfering with market forces. Providing information that the monetary returns of acquiring additional education are higher for women than the already high returns for men would be useful, as would the fact that the returns are higher in fields of study that women tend not to enter (Gunderson and Oreopoulos, forthcoming). Providing information to employers, for example, regarding the opportunities that are lost by not hiring groups that are discriminated against, could also help. The same applies to child-care arrangements and parental leave policies, given the disproportionate responsibility that women bear for family responsibilities. An unintended consequence of maternity leave policies, however, is that, given the high cost of such leaves, employers may hire fewer females, or that the cost may be shifted to females in the form of lower compensating wages in return for the leaves. Evidence that such practices exist is found in Ruhm (1998) and Gruber (1994). More liberal divorce policies could also reduce the negative effect of the disproportionate family responsibilities born by females, enabling them to leave, or threaten to leave, oppressive situations. Most important from the perspective of the argument advanced in this paper, fostering competitive market conditions can dissipate discrimination for the reasons outlined. Hence, the conclusion that competitive markets are a woman's best friend— fostering such forces is an important part of the solution to combat discrimination.

DISCUSSION QUESTIONS

1. As an economist, if you were to choose between pay equity and employment equity, how would you choose and why?
2. Indicate why market forces should dissipate discrimination.
3. If market forces should dissipate discrimination, then why does discrimination occur less frequently in the public sector than in the private sector?
4. Discuss the distinction between value in use and value in exchange as applied to job evaluation procedures as used in pay equity.
5. Assume you own a restaurant and you do not have preferences for hiring male or female waiters—you only want to hire the most productive employees relative to their wage. However, as the expression goes in economics, "there is no accounting for tastes," and for whatever reasons your customers prefer to be waited on by male waiters, and your male waiters would prefer not to work with fellow female waiters. What would you do, and what would be the likely outcome of the hiring and pay of female waitresses compared with male waiters?

SUGGESTED READING AND ONLINE RESOURCES

Blau, Francine, and Lawrence Kahn. 2000. Gender differences in pay. *Journal of Economic Perspectives* 14: 75–99.

Gunderson, Morley. 2006. Male–female wage differentials: How can that be? *Canadian Journal of Economics* 39: 1–21.

Holzer, Harry, and David Neumark. 2000. Assessing affirmative action. *Journal of Economic Literature* 38: 483–568.

REFERENCES

Altonji, Joseph, and Rebecca M. Blank. 1999. Race and gender in the labor market. In *Handbook of labor economics 3*, eds. Orley Ashenfelter and David Card. Amsterdam: Elsevier.

Arrow, Kenneth. 1973. Models of job discrimination. In *Racial discrimination in economic life*, ed. Anthony Pascal. Lexington MA: Lexington Books.

Ashenfelter, Orley, and Timothy Hannan. 1986. Sex discrimination and product market competition: The case of the banking industry. *Quarterly Journal of Economics* 101: 149–173.

Baker, Michael, and Nicole Fortin. 2004. Comparable worth in a decentralized labour market: The case of Ontario. *Canadian Journal of Economics* 37: 850–878.

Becker, Gary. 1957. *The economics of discrimination.* Chicago: University of Chicago Press.

Black, Sandra, and Elizabeth Brainerd. 2004. Importing equality? The impact of globalization on gender discrimination. *Industrial and Labor Relations Review* 57: 540–559.

Black, Sandra, and Philip Strahan. 2001. The division of spoils: Rent-sharing and discrimination in a regulated industry. *American Economic Review* 91: 814–831.

Blau, Francine. 1998. Trends in the well-being of American women (1970–1995). *Journal of Economic Literature* 36: 112–165.

Blau, F., A. Ferber, and A. Winkler. 2002. *The economics of women, men and work.* Upper Saddle River, NJ: Prentice Hall.

Blau, Francine, and Lawrence Kahn. 2000. Gender differences in pay. *Journal of Economic Perspectives* 14: 75–99.

Blau, Francine, and Lawrence Kahn. 2003. Understanding international differences in the gender pay gap. *Journal of Labor Economics* 21 (1): 106–144.

Edgeworth, F. 1922. Equal pay to men and women for equal work. *Economic Journal* 32: 431–457.

Fawcett, Millicent. 1918. Equal pay for equal work. *Economic Journal* 28: 1–6.

Festinger, Leo. 1957. *A theory of cognitive dissonance.* Palo Alto, CA: Stanford University Press.

Gruber, Jonathan. 1994. The incidence of mandated maternity benefits. *American Economic Review* 84: 622–624.

Gunderson, Morley. 1989. Male–female wage differentials and policy responses. *Journal of Economic Literature* 27: 46–72.

Gunderson, Morley. 2006. Male–female wage differentials: How can that be? *Canadian Journal of Economics* 39: 1–21.

Gunderson, Morley, and Philip Oreopoulos (forthcoming). Returns to education in developed countries. In *International encyclopedia of education*, 3rd ed., eds. E. Baker, M. McGaw, and P. Peterson. Amsterdam: Elsevier.

Hellerstein, Judith, David Neumark, and Kenneth Troske. 1999. Wages, productivity, and worker characteristics: Evidence from plant-level production functions and wage equations. *Journal of Labor Economics* 17: 409–446.

Hellerstein, Judith, David Neumark, and Kenneth Troske. 2002. Market forces and sex discrimination. *Journal of Human Resources* 37: 353–380.

Holzer, Harry, and David Neumark. 2000. Assessing affirmative action. *Journal of Economic Literature* 38: 483–568.

Jarrell, Stephen, and T.D. Stanley. 2004. Declining bias and gender wage discrimination? A meta-regression analysis. *Journal of Human Resources* 39: 828–838.

Lewis, Debra. 1991. Pay equity and the states agenda. In *Just wages: A feminist assessment of pay equity*, eds. Judy Fudge and Patricia McDermott. Toronto: University of Toronto Press.

Madden, Janice. 1972. *The economics of sex discrimination*. Lexington, MA: Lexington Books.

Manning, Alan. 2003. *Monopsony in motion*. Princeton, NJ: Princeton University Press.

McDermott, Patricia. 1991. Pay equity in Canada. In *Just wages: A feminist assessment of pay equity*, eds. Judy Fudge and Patricia McDermott. Toronto: University of Toronto Press.

Meng, Xin. 2004. Gender earnings gap: The role of firm specific effects. *Labour Economics* 11: 555–573.

Ruhm, Christopher. 1998. The economic consequences of parental leave mandates: Lessons from Europe. *Quarterly Journal of Economics* 113: 285–317.

Sorenson, Elaine. 1990. The crowding hypothesis and comparable worth. *Journal of Human Resources* 25: 55–89.

Labour Market Discrimination: An Institutional Economics View

Fiona MacPhail

Introduction

Labour market discrimination refers to differences in pay, employment, and status that arise from the interaction of economic, social, and political factors in the workplace and family (Figart 2005, 514). Despite increased employment rates among women, gender discrimination in the labour market still exists. The ratio of average annual earnings of women to men rose from 47 to 66 percent between 1976 and 2007, a gender pay gap of 34 percent in 2007.[1] The gender earnings ratio for full-time/full-year workers is 71 percent, a gap of 29 percent.[2] Indicative of racial discrimination, men and women of visible minority groups have lower earnings compared with other men and women.[3]

Although occupational segregation has declined, women and men are still employed in different occupations and industries. For example, in 2008, 53 percent of employed women worked in two broad occupational categories, namely, sales/service and clerical/administrative. Women are also disproportionately employed in caring/health occupations. Forty-seven percent of employed men work in two broad occupational categories, sales/services and trades/transport, and are disproportionately employed in scientific and technical occupations.[4] Further, women tend to be located at lower levels of broad occupation categories, which results in vertical segregation and lower status and pay. Visible minorities are over-represented in low-paid and lower-tier service sector jobs, and recent immigrants are less likely to be working in regulated professions for which they have appropriate qualifications, compared with foreign-born Canadians (Zietsma 2010).

An institutional economics view of the labour market focuses on institutional features that govern the allocation of workers to jobs and determine promotion, pay, and status. Explanations of the variation in labour market outcomes among groups emphasize differences in the jobs to which workers have been allocated. Gender and racial inequalities arise from differences in jobs, rather than differences in individual educational investments (as from the neoclassical perspective).[5]

From an institutional view, discrimination in the labour market arises from norms, practices, and structures that, intentionally or unintentionally, are biased against certain groups. This contrasts with the mainstream view in which discrimination arises from individual employers' preferences or tastes for discrimination, that is, the taste is determined outside the economic system. Another important distinction is that an institutional perspective accommodates the idea that discrimination benefits the employer, whereas from a mainstream view, discriminatory employers should be eliminated by competition. Finally, an institutional view gives priority to explaining changes in occupational segregation and pay gaps over time.

Three institutional explanations of labour market discrimination are examined: gender and racial ideologies, profits and control, and workplace norms and customs. The connection between each explanation and a specific labour market feature or institution and their impacts on racial and gender inequality is outlined. Government intervention to reduce labour discrimination is subsequently analyzed.

Institutional Explanations of Labour Market Discrimination

Gender and Racial Ideologies

Gender ideology refers to the dominant societal view of the appropriate roles, responsibilities, and traits of women and men, which is hierarchical, with male roles being valued more highly and associated with greater power than female roles. Racial ideology in Canadian society accords people of European origin greater power than other racial groups and Aboriginal peoples. The combined gender and racial ideologies in Canadian society place women and non-white people at the bottom of the hierarchy.

The correspondence between female and male traits and key features of occupations has caused certain jobs to be *labelled* or stereotyped as female or male (Anker 1997). The positive female stereotypical traits—being caring, having household-related skills, and being dexterous—have helped women qualify for certain jobs where these characteristics are important, such as nursing, cleaning, typing, kindergarten teaching, and electronic assembling. Negative stereotypes— for example, that women, compared with men, cannot do math, have lower physical strength, are less assertive or aggressive, and avoid danger—have historically reduced women's acceptability for certain occupations, such as engineering, fire-fighting, construction work, mechanics, and law, resulting in these occupations being labelled masculine. Labelling jobs as female or male persists despite behaviours of men and women that differ from the stereotypes; changes in the nature of jobs, such as a decline in physical strength requirements; reduction in gender discrimination at school; and arguments that some skills are not innate but rather learned at home or easily learned in the workplace.

Labelling occupations as feminine or masculine certainly aligns with the occupational segregation data. Over 90 percent of workers in clerical, nursing, and child-care/home support occupations are female and over 90 percent of workers in trades, truck driving, and firefighting occupations are male.[6] Job labelling explains horizontal segregation, that is, that women are more likely to be employed in caring occupations and men in more physical occupations. It also accounts for vertical segregation, with men being more likely to be in positions of authority. The stereotype of women as secondary earners and men as breadwinners aligns with the greater percentage of women, compared with men, who are part-time and temporary workers. In addition to occupational segregation, stereotyping female traits as having less value than male traits results in female-labelled jobs being poorly paid, a pattern sometimes referred to as gender *skill bias*. For example, in 2005, the average annual earnings of a truck driver were $38,400, compared with the average annual earnings of a child-care worker at $16,600.[7]

The allocation of groups of workers to jobs has also been explained as a *queueing* process, which results in occupational segregation. Employers rank groups of workers in accordance with the gender (and racial) hierarchies of society (not according to individual employers' tastes), resulting in the best jobs being allocated to the top group in society (Reskin and Roos 1990, 30). Workers rank jobs in terms of factors such as income, job security, working conditions, and prospects for advancement. Research suggests men and women rank jobs similarly (Reskin and Roos 1990, 38–39) and have the same interest in promotions (Task Force on Barriers to Women in the Public Service 1990, 58).

Changes in occupational segregation arise from changes in the worker queue, changes in the job queue, and changes in the shapes of each queue (for example, number of jobs of each type). Employers change the rankings of groups of workers in response to factors such as changes in the gender gap of education, new information about gender productivity differentials, changes in the nature of work (for example, some jobs take on stereotypical female traits, as described previously, such as being caring and communicative), changes in public tolerance for sex discrimination, and increased regulation. When the number of preferred jobs exceeds the number of preferred workers, employers then start to hire from the less preferred groups. For example, clerical work in the US shifted from men to women in the early part of the 20th century and from white to black women from 1940 to 1990 as a result of a shortage of male labour, technological and organization changes affecting the type of work, and government policy (Reskin and Roos 1990).

Profits and Control

From a labour market segmentation perspective, the labour market is divided into *primary and secondary labour market segments*: jobs in the primary segment are characterized by job security, opportunities for advancement, and good wages, benefits, and work conditions; and jobs in the secondary segment are described in the opposite manner (Doeringer and Piore 1971). Historically, the primary segment emerged after the Second World War as a result of increased market concentration in product markets and automation of production. Under these market and technological conditions, employers have an incentive to develop primary segment jobs to facilitate training and retaining workers. From a radical perspective, employers implement mechanisms to extract the maximum amount of effort from employees and reduce solidarity among workers to increase their control over workers; and bureaucratic and technical controls are more profitable in the primary segment (Gordon et al. 1982).[8]

From both perspectives, discrimination arises because employers use the generally accepted gender and racial hierarchies to allocate different groups of workers to various segments to create and maintain differences among workers. As Bowles and Edwards (1993, 218) state: "racial and sexual divisions are (socially) the most prominent distinctions, so employers seize upon these dimensions to divide workers. Capitalists did not invent racism or sexism, but they have used preexisting prejudices or biases among workers to divide and weaken workers." This division not only affects segregation but has implications for wages. Since women and men from visible minority groups are less likely to be employed in the primary segment, this increases the supply of labour to the secondary segment. This *crowding* into the secondary segment puts downward pressure on wages (Bergmann 1986).

Given these gender and racial ideologies, women and men from visible minorities are more likely to be employed in the secondary segment[9] in which industries are competitive and a simple form of worker control prevails, where a supervisor can easily and directly observe the worker's effort and performance.[10] This segmentation accounts for gender and racial occupational segregation and low wages, with the inferior labour market outcomes occurring because of the competitive product markets, level of technology, and simple types of work control (rather than because the workers are less productive than white men). For example, women are more likely than men to be employed in the highly competitive lower-tier service and manufacturing industries such as retail trade and clothing, rather than in wholesale trade and motor vehicles, where men predominate.[11] In addition, men are more likely to be working as supervisors even in female-dominated industries and occupations, consistent with the power/control perspective in which employers place men in supervisory and managerial positions to monitor and enforce work discipline among women. Women are more likely to have part-time jobs—in 2009, 27 percent of women, compared with 12 percent of men, were employed part-time[12]—and women are slightly more likely to be employed on a temporary contract (especially once seasonal temporary workers are excluded).

In addition to employers' discrimination, some groups of employees (conventionally, white males) may also discriminate against certain groups of workers to reduce *job competition*, increase their own job security and prospects for promotion, and maintain wage differentials (Shulman 1987). Employers may benefit from the discriminatory behaviour of a group of employees if it increases the morale and productivity of the dominant group of workers, provided they can pass the higher wages (net of the productivity gains) on to consumers.[13] For example, in Canada in the 1950s the postal union tried to prevent the hiring of women and did not try to protect the wages and working conditions of the women who were hired part-time (White 1990, chap. 1), although since then the postal union and other unions have been instrumental in raising women's wages. While direct strategies to prevent the entry of women into certain occupations and industries are less likely to be implemented today, more covert strategies, such as sexual harassment, ostracism, and creating a hostile work environment still occur.

Changes in product market competition and technology combined with gender and racial ideology affect segmentation and occupational segregation. Over the period 1900 to 1930, the male-dominated clerical occupation became increasingly feminized, with the female share of clerical workers rising from 21 to 48 percent (Altman and Lamontagne 2003, 1051). Growth in the number of clerical jobs (relative to overall labour force growth) and automation led to the integrated clerical occupation being dismantled into separate jobs, each involving repetitive and routine tasks. These changes led employers to hire women instead of men in the subordinate deskilled jobs, and men became the supervisors. More recently, globalization, increased competition, and decreased unionization have led to a rise in the size of the secondary segment, associated with increased part-time and temporary work. Government deregulation of the labour market facilitates employers' ability to create secondary-segment jobs: for example, deregulation of the labour market in British Columbia after 2001 has been associated with a rise in temporary jobs (MacPhail and Bowles 2008).

Workplace Norms and Customs

Employers establish a workplace institution, known as an *internal labour market*, which describes the wages, job hierarchies, and mechanisms for allocating workers to jobs based on norms and customs. The internal labour market is defined as "an administrative unit, such as a manufacturing plant, within which the pricing and allocation of labor is governed by a set of administrative rules or procedures" (Doeringer and Piore 1971, 2).

The internal labour market comprises a set of job ladders with connections between selected ladders delineating routes to the top. While wages at the bottom of the ladder may be influenced by wage pressures in the external labour market, wages at higher rungs are influenced by norms and customs of acceptable relative wage differentials. Workers tend to be hired from the external labour market for the bottom rung—"ports of entry"—but then move up the job ladder in accordance with rules relating to seniority, performance, and norms of fairness. Various institutional rules and procedures govern the pace of work and the monitoring of workers, promotion procedures, pay structures, and firm-specific training systems. As in the case of the primary labour market segment, employers benefit from the internal labour market because it increases retention of workers, facilitates on-the-job training, and provides a method of control of workers. An internal labour market is associated with a primary labour market segment, most frequently in large corporations and the public sector.

The internal labour market interacts with the gender and racial ideologies to restrict the promotion prospects of women and members of visible minorities. As described above, women are often allocated to "feminine" jobs and to the secondary segment, given perceived congruence with their nurturing, subservient, and secondary-earner roles; and similarly, they are disproportionately allocated to parts of the internal labour market with short job ladders, which further limit their opportunities for promotion. For example, a job ladder for clerical work in the public sector might have only two or three rungs and is not connected to the longer management or professional job ladders; and even with the appropriate credentials it is not possible for women to make the shift between ladders (Task Force 1990, 65). Further, since women are more likely to be working part-time or on a temporary contract, they are less likely to be considered for promotion within any ladder.

The internal labour market may also be constructed to take advantage of the more constrained labour supply of women and perceptions that they have lower career aspirations. For example, an internal labour market in a US grocery chain was constructed so that the job ladder associated with the produce department had the most direct route to store manager, but women were disproportionately employed in the bakery and deli departments (Padavic and Reskin 2002, 110).

Employers alter the internal labour market in response to competitive forces and technological change that may reinforce or modify gender stereotypes. For example, job ladders were adjusted in the banking and insurance sector in the UK to enable female bank employees to sell personal insurance. Previously, men sold both personal and commercial insurance because women were perceived to be insufficiently aggressive to sell insurance. Faced with a need to lower wage costs, banks removed the selling of personal insurance from men's jobs and permitted them to sell only commercial insurance, which was argued to be more difficult and associated with higher commissions (Morgan and Knights 1991).

The internal labour market contributes to the *glass ceiling* for women and visible minorities, preventing them from moving into the top echelons of management. The glass ceiling refers to invisible and artificial barriers, such as the use of stereotypical masculine characteristics to judge management effectiveness, lack of exposure to informal networks, long work hours/weeks required (which reduces women's interest or is perceived to limit women's performance), and sexual harassment (Wirth 2001).[14] In addition to invisible barriers, women may encounter the glass ceiling because their initial job assignment is to a ladder without a path to the top. For example, being director of human resources is not considered to provide the appropriate training to become vice-president, but the job of director of finance is appropriate.

The lack of representation of women in top jobs is indicative of the glass ceiling. Although women account for 75 percent of all clerical and administrative workers, they make up only 37 percent of workers in management occupations and only 22 percent of senior management (Statistics Canada 2006, Table 5.13). Further, in Fortune 500 companies, women comprise only 13.5 percent of executive officers (Catalyst 2009). Direct evidence of the glass ceiling for visible minorities is provided by a Health Canada case study showing that workplace practices reflected systemic racial discrimination and more limited promotions for members of visible minorities. Members of visible minority groups were less likely to be assigned to hiring committees, be given career development and training opportunities, and receive encouragement from supervisors to apply for promotions (Beck et al. 2002).

Does Legislation Reduce Gender and Racial Inequality?

Government intervention to reduce gender and racial inequality has focused on employment equity and pay equity legislation. Employment equity legislation has the potential to reduce the invisible barriers associated with the glass ceiling and internal labour market and to counteract racial and gender stereotypes, thereby reducing occupational segregation and the gender pay gap. Although it has had some success, employment equity legislation is limited because it applies only to the federally regulated sector (about 15 percent of the labour force) and limited enforcement results in low compliance (Agocs and Osborne 2009).

Pay equity legislation and policy are designed to address the wage discrimination in women's jobs arising from the jobs being stereotyped as unskilled. While pay equity wage adjustments have occurred, the legislation is limited because it typically applies only to the public sector and even there, pay equity wage adjustments have been stalled, in part by gender-biased job evaluations and the difficulties of finding appropriate male comparator jobs (Weiner 2002).

The limitations of these two types of legislation, combined with the rise in the secondary labour market segment or "precarious jobs" (see note 9) and the decline in public sector employment, mean that alternative government policies are required to mediate social and market forces and reduce discrimination in the labour market. Indicators of gender inequality in the labour market vary substantially across industrialized countries, suggesting that policy indeed matters!

The broad argument is that countries in which governments implement policies to help women reconcile earning and caring roles, and encourage men to contribute more to the caring of others, have lower gender inequality in the labour market. Evidence for this argument is presented in Table 1, where the main indicator of gender inequality in the labour market is mothers' share of total earnings, since this measure captures participation, hours worked, and wages. Countries are grouped into three categories, following the literature on welfare state regimes, with Canada being included in the liberal regime category, given its emphasis on limited state involvement in the family and the labour market. Social democratic countries (Denmark, Finland, Norway, and Sweden) have lower gender inequality in the labour market (see columns 1 and 2), given greater public support for childcare, more generous maternity and parental leave, restrictions on working time, and more centralized wage-setting institutions.

Child Care

Women provide greater amounts of unpaid time to the care of children (and the elderly), and therefore accessible high-quality and low-cost/subsidized child care is expected to raise women's labour force participation and enhance more equal participation, including making full-time work possible. In Canada, care of children while parents work is viewed as the responsibility of the parents, with very limited government support; care is provided through informal means such as relatives, friends, and neighbours, with only 28 percent of children (infant to five years of age) receiving care in licensed child-care centres (Bushnik 2006). In contrast to other industrialized countries, there is very little public funding in Canada for child care and, as shown in Table 1, only 5 percent of young children (aged between one and two) are in publicly financed care facilities. This compares with 74 percent in Denmark and 48 percent in Sweden.

Employment Policies

Employment policies, such as maternity leave and regulations on working time, help parents reconcile their earning and caring roles. Legislated maternity and paternity leave provide job protection for parents to provide care for newborn and adopted children; such leaves facilitate women's continued participation in the labour market, may increase job tenure in a given workplace, and have positive

TABLE 1 Gender Inequality and Government Support for Balancing the Earning-Caring Responsibilities, Selected Industrialized Countries, Mid-Late 1990s

	Mothers' share of labour market earnings among married or cohabiting parents	Female/male earnings ratio (full-time workers)	% children in publicly financed child care (one to two years of age)	Weeks of paid leave to mothers	Expenditures on maternity leave/per employed woman[a]	Normal work week (hours)[b]	Maximum work time[b]	Statutory vacation time[b]
Social democratic								
Denmark	38	0.71	74	37	594	37	48	25
Finland	37	0.75	22		673	39	40	30
Sweden	34	0.67	48	42	608	38	40	25
Norway	33	0.67	37	42	808	38	40	21
Conservative								
Belgium	32	0.67	42	12	234	39	39	20
France	32	0.71	20	16	431	35	48	25
Netherlands	19	0.50		16	67	37	48	20
Luxembourg	19	0.62	3	16	414	39	48	25
Germany	18	0.54	5	14	465	38	48	20
Liberal								
Canada	31	0.62	5	28	152		No limit	10
United Kingdom	23	0.49	2	5	75	38	48	20
United States	28	0.64	6	0	0		No limit	—

[a] In US dollars, PPP-adjusted.

[b] These are legislated hours. The normal length of the work week may be shorter and vacation time may be longer under the collective agreements.

Source: Data from Gornick and Meyers (2003, figures 3.8, 5.2, and 5.4, and tables 6.1, 6.4, and 7.2).

implications for occupational segregation and the gender pay gap. Canada now provides up to one year of combined maternity and paternity leave with financial benefits of 55 percent of wages, up to a maximum of $413 per week, although not all working mothers (or fathers) qualify for these benefits. Social democratic countries provide the most generous maternity leave in terms of both duration and benefits, typically amounting to 42 weeks of leave on 100 percent pay up to a cap, and policies also encourage fathers to take some of this leave.

Working-time regulations that restrict the length of the work week and the amount of overtime and increase the amount of vacation time can facilitate women's access to full-time employment and increase the amount of time men and women have available for caregiving. Tighter regulation of working time makes it less likely that employers will create a gender-segmented labour market and at the same time levels the playing field among employers. In Canada, key features of work time are a normal work week of 40 hours, no limit on the maximum number of hours worked, and a minimum annual paid vacation of 10 days. In the social democratic countries, the normal work week is shorter, a maximum number of working hours per week is stipulated, and there is a greater amount of paid vacation time.

Industrial Relations

Industrial relations policies that facilitate centralized wage setting through unions and minimum wages reduce wage and gender inequality. In general, the gender earnings gap will be smaller in the countries with lower overall earnings inequality. Thus, in Canada, as in the United States, the gender wage gap is high, compared with countries such as Belgium, Finland, and Sweden, in part because of the high degree of overall earnings inequality (Blau and Kahn 2003).

So is the smaller degree of gender inequality in social democratic countries due to a weaker "taste for discrimination" by employers and greater preferences for paid work of women in these countries, compared with their Canadian counterparts, as the neoclassical explanation would suggest?

It is more likely that the different legislation and policies in social democratic countries compared with Canada affect the institutions of both the labour market and the family, making it easier for women to enter and advance in the labour market. Therefore, women need to have the support of the state; otherwise, labour market dictates, compounded by other problems of stress and provision of child care, will continue to lead to gender inequality in the labour market.

Conclusion

Discrimination against women and people in visible minorities exists in the Canadian labour market, manifesting itself in unequal access to occupations, promotions, pay, and status. Discriminatory methods of allocating workers to jobs build on historical patterns and are recreated as employers respond to increased competition, technological change, and labour market deregulation. Gender and racial ideologies relating to appropriate roles and traits, strategies to enhance profits, and norms and customs give rise to labour market institutions such as job labelling, labour market segments, internal labour markets, and glass ceilings, which perpetuate discrimination against women and certain racial groups.

Legislation and broad social and employment policies mediate discrimination. Employment and pay equity are potentially important for reducing inequality but their limited coverage and the lack of compliance increase the importance of broader policies for reducing gender and racial inequality, particularly in the private sector and secondary labour market segment. Policies such as high-quality, subsidized child-care provision, maternity and parental leave, regulation of working time, and centralized wage-setting institutions (unions, minimum wages), and legislation relating to working conditions are necessary to reduce labour market discrimination.

NOTES

1. Statistics Canada, CANSIM table 202-0102, average female and male earnings, 2007 constant dollars.
2. Statistics Canada, CANSIM table 202-0102, average female and male earnings, 2007 constant dollars.
3. Statistics Canada (2006), table 10.12.
4. Statistics Canada, CANSIM table 282-0010, Labour Force Survey estimates, by National Occupational Classification for Statistics, by sex, annual.
5. On the supply side, attention is given to how the labour market (and broader economic system) influences preferences and constrains behaviour, and preferences are assumed to be changeable and influenced by the system and government regulation.
6. Statistics Canada, *Census 2006*, catalogue no. 97-559-XWE2006011.
7. Statistics Canada, *Census 2006*, catalogue no. 97-563-XWE2006069.
8. *Simple* control occurs when a supervisor, often working in close proximity to employees, can set the pace of work and directly monitor the effort and performance of workers. *Technical* control occurs when the pace of work can be set by technology, such as an assembly line, and the effort can be monitored by the technology; *bureaucratic* control occurs when the pace of work is determined by a set of rules or procedures and typically applies when the nature of work is complex.
9. Recent literature increasingly uses the term "precarious jobs" to refer to jobs which, compared with permanent jobs, have less security as well as lower pay, less access to workplace and statutory benefits, as well as less workplace autonomy (Fuller and Vosko 2008).

319

10. While the data are consistent with women being disproportionately allocated to the secondary segment, jobs in the secondary segment may be skilled and the workforce stable. Further, many jobs in the secondary segment are created explicitly to take account of women's greater willingness to work part time. Thus the demand for labour is not created independently of the supply of labour.
11. Statistics Canada, *Census 2006*, catalogue no. 97-559-XCB2006010.
12. Statistics Canada, CANSIM table 282-0002.
13. As Elson (1999, 620) states: "if the prevailing gender order facilitates building solidarity and team spirit among men on the basis of excluding (and even denigrating) women, then systems of building cooperation in the workplace can mobilize that team spirit by excluding women formally or informally."
14. In the past, firms could advertise jobs explicitly for women or men, professional schools could prohibit women from entry, and firms could refuse to hire married women.

DISCUSSION QUESTIONS

1. Two people graduate from the same university each with the same degree and GPA. A year later they meet again and find out that they earn quite different salaries and benefits, and experience different work conditions and job security. How can this be explained?
2. Suppose two people have the same credentials and job experience. How might an employer decide whom to hire and whom to promote?
3. Institutional explanations of labour market discrimination give rise to features such as job labelling, skill bias, queueing, primary and secondary labour market segments, crowding, job competition, internal labour markets, and glass ceilings. Define each feature and provide an example. If you have experienced any of these features, use your own experience.
4. "Women choose part-time jobs because they are compatible with their family responsibilities and therefore, women's lower earnings and inferior jobs are not a social and economic problem." Critically evaluate this statement.
5. Canada and the United States are economies often characterized as a "male breadwinner/female secondary earner and carer" type, whereas the economies of Nordic countries, such as Sweden and Finland, are characterized as a "dual earner/dual carer" type. What is meant by each type? What type of society and labour market do you want to live in? What policies and legislation would facilitate more equal participation of men and women in earning and caring?

ONLINE RESOURCES

Human Resources and Skills Development Canada. http://www.hrsdc.gc.ca/eng/home.shtml.

International Labour Organization. Women in labour markets: Measuring progress and identifying challenges. http://www.ilo.org/empelm/what/pubs/lang--en/docName--WCMS_123835/index.htm.

International Association for Feminist Economics. Useful links. http://www.iaffe.org/resources/links.php.

National Anti-Racism Council of Canada. http://www.narcc.ca.

Statistics Canada. The Canadian labour market at a glance. http://www.statcan.gc.ca/bsolc/olc-cel/olc-cel?lang=eng&catno=71-222-X.

REFERENCES

Agocs, Carol, and Bob Osborne. 2009. Comparing equity policies in Canada and Northern Ireland: Policy learning in two directions? *Canadian Public Policy* 35 (2): 237–262.

Altman, Morris, and Louise Lamontagne. 2003. On the natural intelligence of women in a world of constrained choice: How the feminization of clerical work contributed to gender pay equality in early twentieth century Canada. *Journal of Economic Issues* 37 (4): 1045–1074.

Anker, Richard. 1997. Theories of occupational segregation by sex: An overview. *International Labour Review* 138 (3): 315–339.

Beck, Helen, Jeffrey Reitz, and Nan Weiner. 2002. Addressing systemic racial discrimination in employment: The Health Canada case and implications of legislative change. *Canadian Public Policy* 28 (3): 373–394.

Bergmann, Barbara. 1986. *The economic emergence of women.* New York: Basic Books.

Blau, Francine, and Lawrence Kahn. 2003. Understanding international differences in the gender pay gap. *Journal of Labor Economics* 21 (1): 106–144.

Bowles, Samuel, and Richard Edwards. 1993. *Understanding capitalism.* 2nd ed. New York: Harper Collins College Publishers.

Bushnik, Tracey. 2006. Child care in Canada. *Children and Youth Research Paper Series*, Statistics Canada. Catalogue no. 89-599-MIE200603.

Catalyst. 2009. Catalyst census of the Fortune 500 reveals women missing from critical business leadership. http://www.catalyst.org.

Doeringer, Peter, and Michael Piore. 1971. *Internal labor markets and manpower analysis.* Lexington, MA: D.C. Heath.

Elson, Diane. 1999. Labor markets as gendered institutions: Equality, efficiency and empowerment issues. *World Development* 27 (3): 611–627.

Figart, Deborah. 2005. Gender as more than a dummy variable: Feminist approaches to discrimination. *Review of Social Economy* 63 (3): 509–536.

Fuller, Sylvia, and Leah Vosko. 2008. Temporary employment and social inequality in Canada: Exploring intersections of gender, race and immigration status. *Social Indicators Research* 88 (1): 31–50.

Gordon, David, Richard Edwards, and Michael Reich. 1982. *Segmented work, divided workers: The historical transformation of labor in the United States.* New York: Cambridge University Press.

Gornick, Janet, and Marcia Meyers. 2003. *Families that work: Policies for reconciling parenthood and employment.* New York: Russell Sage Foundation Publications.

Human Resources and Skills Development Canada. 2009. *Employment equity act: Annual report 2008.* Labour Program. http://www.hrsdc.gc.ca/eng/labour/publications/equality/annual_reports/2008/docs/2008report.pdf.

MacPhail, Fiona, and Paul Bowles. 2008. Temporary work and neoliberal government policy: Evidence from British Columbia, Canada. *International Review of Applied Economics* 22 (5): 545–563.

Morgan, Glenn, and David Knights. 1991. Gendering jobs: Corporate strategy, managerial control and the dynamics of job segmentation. *Work, Employment & Society* 5 (2): 181–200.

Padavic, Irene, and Barbara Reskin. 2002. *Women and men at work.* 2nd ed. Newbury Park, CA: Pine Forge Press.

Reskin, Barbara, and Patricia Roos. 1990. *Job queues, gender queues.* Philadelphia: Temple University Press.

Shulman, Steven. 1987. Discrimination, human capital and black–white unemployment: Evidence from cities. *Journal of Human Resources* 22 (3): 361–376.

Statistics Canada. 2006. *Women in Canada 2005: A gender-based statistical report.* Catalogue no. 89-503-XIE.

Task Force on Barriers to Women in the Public Service. 1990. *Beneath the veneer: The report of the Task Force on Barriers to Women in the Public Service.* Volume 1. Ottawa. Canadian Government Publishing Centre, Supply and Services Canada.

Weiner, Nan. 2002. Effective redress of pay inequities. *Canadian Public Policy* 28 (Supplement 1): S100–S115.

White, Julie. 1990. *Male & female: Women and the Canadian Union of Postal Workers.* Toronto: Thompson Educational Publishing.

Wirth, Linda. 2001. *Breaking through the glass ceiling: Women in management.* 2nd ed. Geneva: International Labour Office.

Zietsma, Danielle. 2010. Immigrants working in regulated occupations. *Perspectives on Labour and Income* 11 (February). Ottawa: Statistics Canada. http://www.statcan.gc.ca/pub/75-001-x/2010102/article/11121-eng.htm.

Would a Guaranteed Annual Income Eliminate Poverty?

COMPETING VIEWS

Derek Hum, "Guaranteed Annual Income and the Cost of Eliminating Poverty in Canada"

Mario Seccareccia, "Employment and Poverty: A Critical Perspective on Guaranteed Income Programs"

Editors' Introduction

Poverty and income inequality appear to be permanent features of our society, both past and present. As humans have progressed technologically, the social organizations within which these tremendous transformations and major leaps in productivity took place have rewarded some. At the same time, they have often excluded a social substratum, the poor, who could not reap as easily the benefits resulting from the remarkable growth in overall income. In commenting on the experience of extensive economic growth during the Industrial Revolution, John Stuart Mill—an established classical economist, defender of economic liberalism, and humanist—advised that priorities for society be reoriented in favour of those who were excluded from economic progress. He remarked: "It is only in the backward countries of the world that increased production is an important object: in those most advanced, what is economically needed is a better distribution."*

Like Mill, many economic thinkers nowadays, from both the left and the right of the political spectrum, continue to ask how we could have reached such a high level of economic affluence and yet could continue to exclude a significant subset of the population whose incomes are insufficient to meet some of their most basic needs, such as food and shelter. To address the fundamental question of income distribution posed by Mill and others, economists and other social thinkers over the ages have advanced various proposals, from the abolition of capitalistic property rights and the

* John Stuart Mill, *Principles of Political Economy, with Some of Their Applications to Social Philosophy* (Toronto: University of Toronto Press, 1965), Book IV, Chapter VI, at 755.

323

establishment of state control of the means of production (Karl Marx), to the achievement of full employment with its accompanying redistribution toward the working poor in conditions of a tight labour market (John Maynard Keynes). However, the most widespread proposal, which remains a preferred policy objective for many all along the political spectrum, is a guaranteed annual income (GAI).

In the tradition of a long list of supporters of GAI programs going back at least to the 1960s, when advocates in both Canada and the United States pressed for such a program as an effective tool in the war on poverty, the two contributors to this chapter agree that a GAI policy is both feasible and desirable, and disagree with those who believe that it would create significant work disincentives. Through its fiscal arm, the government can provide a minimum income transfer to everyone so as to ensure a universal basic income guarantee. As Derek Hum points out, by consolidating existing welfare programs, from old age security benefits to employment insurance transfers, a practical GAI system could be financed that would meet some of the basic objectives of GAI supporters. However, while he agrees that a GAI program would be an important first step in financially addressing the problem of poverty in Canada, Hum suggests that it would not be able to deal with all of its dimensions.

In contrast, Mario Seccareccia points out that a GAI program, while highly desirable, might be counterproductive if it merely promoted low-wage employment without being balanced by an effective full-employment and strong minimum-wage policy. Seccareccia's primary concern is not with the work disincentives that a GAI program can create on the labour supply side, which tend to be the main focus of neoclassical economists, but rather with the undesirable employment incentives that such a program might create on the demand side of the labour market.

Guaranteed Annual Income and the Cost of Eliminating Poverty in Canada

Derek Hum

Introduction

Many lament the lack of progress in our fight against poverty. The Economic Council of Canada (1968) first reported its full extent in this country, and five decades later, much poverty remains. Why haven't we been able to do more? Is a nation as affluent as ours not able to afford it? What can we try next? And many Canadians still ask: would a guaranteed annual income (GAI) eliminate poverty in Canada? In this essay, we address this question, bearing in mind political support for a GAI as well as the financial limits.

The guaranteed income idea is a staple of social policy in Canada. Like the ghost of Hamlet's father, it is a recurring apparition, reminding us of the urgency to end the deprivation that many Canadians endure, as well as the folly of procrastination. Further, Canada is one of the few countries that have studied the guaranteed income in enormous detail, including individual behavioural responses, such as its effect on work effort (Hum and Simpson 1995). These matters are not discussed in the present essay; rather, the focus is on the effectiveness of the guaranteed income in eliminating poverty, and the cost of such programs.

Social Inequality and Income Poverty: Preliminaries

There are many "markers" associated with economic disparities among Canadians. These include: where they live, what kind of work they do, their health status, language, education, gender, age, colour, family situation, and the like.

We might fruitfully consider inequality of opportunity: that is, how some Canadians have good-paying and secure jobs with possibilities for advancement while others must work at minimum wages for long hours just to earn a living. We might talk about inequality of access to essential services such as health care: for example, how residents in urban centres are able to obtain advanced treatment therapies while those in remote areas receive rudimentary medical care. Or we could consider inequality of education, or skill training, or political participation, or access to recreational, informational, and cultural outlets such as playgrounds and national parks, Internet and media events, libraries, theatres, or athletic participation. All these aspects are important in creating and maintaining social and economic inequality.

Canada has a highly sophisticated economy that distributes most of its goods and services through the market. As a result, not having enough money income can reasonably be associated with social inequality; specifically, lack of adequate housing, food and clothing, unstable employment, poor health care, low educational attainment, and even reluctant civic participation. Consequently, the money income "metric" allows for a meaningful discussion of poverty, in the crude sense that someone with income that is below a particular "cut-off" level can be deemed "poor."

Restricting our attention to money income then, suppose we rank all Canadian families according to their income, and then divide them into five equal groups (called quintiles). If incomes were equally distributed, each quintile would receive exactly one-fifth of the total amount. However, the poorest 20 percent, or the bottom quintile, only receives about 4 percent of Canada's total income. On the other hand, Canada's richest 20 percent, or top quintile, receives more than 40 percent of total income. In other words, the top fifth has more than ten times the amount of money to spend as the bottom fifth. And these income shares have been virtually constant during the postwar period.

What Is the Poverty Line in Canada?

Suppose we consider a family to be poor if their total income falls below some predetermined "poverty line." What amount should we adopt as a reasonable poverty line? Canada does not have an official poverty line, although Statistics Canada regularly surveys household spending patterns and publishes a set of measures called the low income cut-offs (LICO). Many non-governmental organizations use this measure as an unofficial poverty line. Families with incomes below the LICO must spend a disproportionate amount on the basic necessities of food, clothing, and shelter. Canadians have a "low income" (or are "poor") if they spend more than about 56 percent of their income on basic necessities. The Statistics Canada LICOs vary by the size and composition of the family as well as by the population of the area of residence. Understandably, a larger family will need more income for necessities. For example, a family of four living in a community with a population of fewer than 30,000 people has a LICO of $31,529 whereas a family of two persons has a LICO of $21,123 (in 2007). Similarly, the cost of necessities, especially housing, will vary depending on the particular city or rural community. The LICO for a family of four living in a city with a population of more than 500,000 people is $40,259 annually. The comparable figure for this family living in a rural area is only $27,214 (National Council of Welfare [NCW] 2008, Appendix C).

A Market Basket Approach to Poverty

Without an official poverty line for policy purposes, and given the difficulties with the way the LICOs are formulated, Human Resources Development Canada (HRDC) has devised an alternative based on a so-called market basket approach. This approach simply calculates the actual cost to a family of purchasing food, shelter, clothing, and other items for comfort, using actual market prices and rents in that family's area of residence. Many prefer this approach because it is more intuitive than the statistical calculation of the LICOs. As well, the market basket avoids regional distortions. For example, high rents in cities such as Vancouver and Toronto would no longer affect housing cost calculations in the poverty line for, say, Winnipeg. This would, of course, affect how poverty rates are determined. For example, adopting the market basket approach suggested by HRDC instead of the LICOs would reduce Quebec's poverty rate from 21.2 percent to 10.8 percent (1996), and Manitoba's rate from 18.8 percent to 11.1 percent (1996). On the other hand, Newfoundland's poverty rate would increase slightly (NCW, 1998–99).

Guaranteeing Income: How to Do It

We need to be specific about what is meant by a "guaranteed income" to assess its potential to eliminate poverty, since the term is used with a wide range of meanings. The traditional understanding of a guaranteed annual income is in terms of a negative income tax mechanism (GAI/NIT). More recently, the notion has been adopted by advocates for a basic income (BI), sometimes termed "citizen's income" or "universal income." The GAI/NIT and BI versions of guaranteed income have different emphases, and their precise relationship to eliminating poverty needs to be made explicit.[1]

The BI Version of Guaranteed Income

The idea of the basic income (BI) is quite simple and easy to describe—everyone would receive an "adequate" income, granted unconditionally and tax-free, from the state as a right of citizenship (see Lerner et al. 1999). The amount of the cash transfer is meant to permit citizens to live "modestly"; therefore, unless the amount is set at the poverty line, the BI cannot eliminate poverty completely. Under the BI formulation, there is no work requirement; receiving the BI is a matter of right. Unfortunately, merely asserting a citizen's right to a BI can ignore the costs of financing the BI plan, and leave unanswered just how much poverty will remain.

No other country has anything close to a BI. Further, the view that generous unconditional transfers should be given to able-bodied persons who choose not to work is highly controversial. This is the vexing issue that the GAI/NIT approach is meant to address.

The GAI/NIT Version

The "traditional" GAI/NIT version has a long history in economics and has been more extensively studied than the BI. The GAI/NIT approach would guarantee some amount of income (G) unconditionally, but escaping poverty would also depend on an individual's earnings.

As originally set out, the GAI/NIT formulation provides a minimum cash benefit (G) to families that have no income whatsoever, but that cash payment is reduced by a "tax-back" or benefit-reduction rate (t) for each dollar of other income received. Since the family can never receive less than the amount G in any case, this is tantamount to guaranteeing the family a minimum payment, hence the term guaranteed (annual) income. Advocates of the GAI/NIT emphasize the system's lack of discretion in determining eligibility and benefits, and its avoidance of stigma, qualities also present in the BI. However, the GAI/NIT also claims efficiency in targeting payments to the low-income population, and the possibility of integrating the GAI/NIT into the positive income tax system. One of its most feared drawbacks, however, is its effect on work incentives. Clearly, the more generous the GAI program, as depicted by high support levels (G) or low tax-back rates (t), the larger the program costs will be. This will result because non-workers will receive larger payments, low-income earners will keep a larger fraction of their earnings, and a larger proportion of the population will be recipients since high guarantees and low tax-back rates have the effect of raising the eligibility threshold of the program (see the next section).

Advocates for the GAI/NIT plan base their arguments on its superiority over existing welfare programs, including preserving work incentives, rather than grounding a rights claim through universal entitlement.

Payment Formulas of BI, GAI, and Poverty Elimination

All guaranteed income proposals give some amount of unconditional support, G, to those with zero income. Typically, GAI/NIT plans set G below the poverty line (PL), while simultaneously reducing payments by some tax-back rate on earnings. This tax-back rate (t) is kept below 100 percent so that individuals will always be financially better off working than not working at all. At some income threshold (labelled the break-even level $[B = G/t]$), cash payments will cease.

There are many ways to combine the grant (G) and the tax-back rate (t). Since the BI is unconditional, and requires no obligation to work, the grant amount under a BI would have to be set at the nation's poverty line to eliminate poverty for everyone. If the *G* amount under the GAI/NIT were also set at the poverty line, then the BI and GAI plans would be identical in terms of their claim in eliminating poverty.

On the other hand, one could set *G* at some level so that poverty is eliminated only by working a certain number of hours, with these earnings taxed at a "negative" rate. In that case, the GAI/NIT ensures that poverty is eliminated, by combining the support amount *G* with a given level of earnings.

The payment formulas for the BI and GAI/NIT given below, demonstrate the close resemblance between both proposals if specific values are selected, as well as their relationship to the poverty line (*PL*). In particular, the BI could be regarded as a GAI/NIT with a zero tax-back rate (*t* = 0); alternatively, the GAI/NIT could be viewed as a BI with an income tax applied to other income (*Y*).

Basic Income: $\$ = BI = G (= PL?)$ PL = Poverty line

Guaranteed Income: $\$ = G - (t \times Y)$ $B = G/t$ = Poverty line

The GAI/NIT typically provides a smaller unconditional income grant than a BI plan. In other words, it would not eradicate poverty with one single transfer but requires additional earnings to do so.

The Cost of Eliminating Poverty in Canada

How much would it cost to eliminate poverty with a guaranteed annual income? Even when armed with a specific poverty line, we need to know how many Canadians have incomes below that line (the head count ratio), as well as the total amount of dollars required to bring the income of each person below the poverty line up to the level of the poverty line. This is known as the poverty gap. Finally, we need to decide on the type of guaranteed income program—whether it is a BI design or a NIT design—and what the support level (*G*) and tax-back rate (*t**) will be. There are many possibilities.

Plans That Completely Eliminate Income Poverty

Table 1 shows the extent of poverty in Canada, recent government expenditures on major income transfer programs, and the estimated costs of various guaranteed income proposals.

The top two rows of Table 1 show the amount of poverty in Canada in 2000, excluding and including existing government transfer payments to families (child tax benefits, old age security/guaranteed income supplement, employment insurance, social assistance, goods and services tax credits, Canada/Quebec Pension Plan, and worker's compensation). We use two definitions of poverty: (1) the low

329

TABLE 1   Estimates of the Extent of Poverty and the Cost of Basic Income and Guaranteed Income Plans for Canada

Transfer program	Low income measure of poverty (LIM)			Market basket measure of poverty (MBM)		
	Cost ($b)	Poverty incidence	Poverty gap ($b)	Cost ($b)	Poverty incidence	Poverty gap ($b)
No transfers	0.0	28.8%	40.2	0.0	26.3%	31.5
Current transfers	75.8	15.3%	11.6	75.8	11.9%	7.7
BI = *PL*	251.7	0.0%	0.0	217.1	0.0%	0.0
GI: *G* = *t** *PL*						
t = 30%	12.1	28.8%	28.2	9.4	26.0%	22.0
t = 50%	20.1	28.8%	20.1	15.7	26.0%	15.7
t = 70%	28.2	28.8%	12.1	22.0	26.0%	9.4

Notes:

[a] The basic income (BI) proposal gives every economic family in Canada an amount equal to the poverty line (PL = LIM or MBM) to replace existing transfers to families.

[b] The guaranteed income (GI) proposal provides a guaranteed income equal to the negative tax rate times the poverty line ($G = t^*$ times PL) and taxes earnings (only) at the negative tax rate (30, 50, or 70 percent).

[c] All cost and poverty gap (poverty depth) estimates are in billions of Canadian dollars.

Source: Hum and Simpson (2005). Calculations using SLID Public File 2000, weighted to reflect the population of economic families in Canada.

income measure (LIM), and (2) the market basket measure (MBM). The first row portrays the situation without existing government transfers. We estimate that 28.8 percent of families lived below the LIM poverty line in 2000, compared with 26.3 percent of families using the MBM poverty line. The lower MBM poverty rate reflects the lower amount of the MBM. The poverty gap is $40.2 billion using the LIM, and $31.5 billion using the MBM. These figures establish an initial benchmark for discussion, that is, a perfectly targeted antipoverty transfer program could eliminate poverty in Canada for $40.2 billion under the LIM definition, and $31.5 billion under the MBM definition, ignoring any adverse behavioural consequences of the transfers in terms of labour market disincentive effects on the working poor.

The second row of Table 1 shows the effect of existing government transfers, which amount to $75.8 billion. Transfer payments leave 15.3 percent of families below the LIM poverty line and 11.9 percent of families below the MBM poverty line. Transfers reduce the poverty gap to $11.6 billion using the LIM and $7.7 billion using the MBM. Therefore, a second benchmark can be useful for discussion, namely, what the current system is accomplishing at a cost of $75.8 billion, and what remains to be done to reduce poverty.

Given the above poverty gaps, let us now consider a BI that eliminates poverty. The third row of Table 1 provides an estimate of the cost of a BI that replaces existing government transfer payments to households. Since we are using the LIM and MBM definitions of poverty, we adopt their equivalence scale in designing a BI; that is, citizens would receive a BI that would vary according to their household size in the same fashion as the LIM or MBM measure of poverty. At the poverty line established by the LIM, the BI would cost $251.7 billion; at the MBM poverty line, the cost would be $217.1 billion. With transfer savings of $75.8 billion from present programs, this implies that the net cost of a BI would be $175.9 using the LIM and $141.3 billion using the MBM. This represents an additional expenditure of about 16.4 percent of GDP under the LIM and 13.1 percent under the MBM— both considerable sums.

The above BI plans would eliminate poverty, but the transfers would not be "targeted." Since the BI is universal, it provides the same cash benefit to families above the poverty line as well as to families below the poverty line, regardless of the depth of their poverty. Even among poor families, circumstances differ considerably between the working poor, who may have significant earnings, and other poor families. Indeed, half of all poor families have some income from employment. These families work an average of 814 hours per year and earn an average of $3,719 (using the LIM definition); or they work 783 hours and earn $3,134 (using the MBM measure). For a family of four, these earnings represent about 15 percent of the LIM.

More modest transfers to the poor are involved with a GAI/NIT, which allows the poor to retain only a portion of their earnings in determining their ultimate transfer amount.

The final three rows of Table 1 present GI plans that are perfectly targeted at the poor by setting the break-even level (B) at the poverty line (PL); that is, $B = G/t = PL$ or $G = t \times PL$. For the LIM and a tax rate of 30 percent, a GI plan costs $12.1 billion; the cost rises to $20.1 billion with a tax rate of 50 percent, and to $28.2 billion with a tax rate of 70 percent. All these estimates are well below the current transfer budget of $75.8 billion because only the poor would receive payments. As a result, there is no reduction in poverty below the 28.8 percent level of incidence established by pre-transfer incomes. Note that the effect of a higher tax-back rate (t) is to raise the guarantee relative to the poverty level and tax back more of all income received; it both raises and flattens the income profile for the poor. This increases transfers to the poor, and the cost of the GI plan, but reduces the poverty gap. Thus, for a tax rate of 70 percent, the poverty gap is reduced to $12.1 billion, only slightly higher than the $11.6 billion poverty gap under the existing system. For the MBM, the cost of the GI plans is more modest, since there is less poverty to begin with: $9.4 billion for a tax rate of 30 percent, $15.7 billion for a tax rate of 50 percent, and $22.0 billion for a tax rate of 70 percent. Again, the 70 percent tax rate provides a poverty gap of $9.4 billion for a cost of $22.0 billion, only slightly higher than the gap of $7.7 billion under the current transfer system that costs $75.8 billion, although the incidence of poverty is 26.0 percent compared with 11.9 percent using existing transfers. Thus, these plans provide a modest level of expenditure from which to consider improvements in the circumstances of the poor.

Plans That Reduce but Do Not Eliminate Income Poverty

Table 2 examines a set of intermediate plans: BI plans less generous than the BI plans in Table 1 that eliminated poverty entirely, as well as GAI/NIT plans more generous than those in Table 1 directed only at poor families. These "compromise" plans might be more politically and socially acceptable in terms of both their cost and their effectiveness in reducing poverty.

Although the LIM and MBM poverty lines are both widely used, they are not without controversy. Sarlo (1996) argues for more modest lines based on basic needs. These lines are about 70 percent of the MBM for a family of four (Tsoukalas and MacKenzie 2003). Since we calculate that working poor families generate, on average, earnings equal to 15 percent of the poverty line, we use 85 percent of the MBM or LIM poverty line as yet another benchmark. In other words, the plan is designed to ensure that the working poor will escape poverty under a guaranteed income. These plans are presented in Table 2.

The BI plans are presented in the top two rows of Table 2. Reducing the cash transfer to 70 percent of the poverty line reduces costs to $176.2 billion using the LIM definition of poverty and to $152.0 billion using the MBM definition. The incidence of poverty is 14.2 percent using the LIM, and 13.4 percent using the MBM, while the poverty gap is $7.1 billion and $5.9 billion, respectively. Note that these results for poverty incidence are about as good as those from the existing system, albeit at some additional cost. A BI set at 85 percent of the poverty line would cost $213.9 billion under the LIM and result in poverty incidence of 11.4 percent and a poverty gap of $3.1 billion; the corresponding figures using the MBM are $184.5 billion, 11.0 percent, and $2.6 billion. This BI plan clearly does a better job of fighting poverty than the existing transfer program, although at considerable additional cost.

The GAI/NIT plans are presented at the bottom of Table 2. We again use plans with guarantees of 70 percent and 85 percent of the poverty line and a tax-back rate of 50 percent. The 50 percent rate is consistent with both the top positive tax rates in Canada and the flat tax rate that would be necessary to harmonize negative and positive taxes (Hum and Simpson 1995, Table 13.2). These NIT plans are more

TABLE 2   Intermediate Basic Income and Guaranteed Income Plans for Canada

Transfer program	Low income measure of poverty (LIM)			Market basket measure of poverty (MBM)		
	Cost ($b)	Poverty incidence	Poverty gap ($b)	Cost ($b)	Poverty incidence	Poverty gap ($b)
BI = 0.70*PL*	176.2	14.2%	7.1	152.0	13.4%	5.9
BI = 0.85*PL*	213.9	11.4%	3.1	184.5	11.0%	2.6
GI: *t* = 50%			•			
G = 0.70*PL*	35.2	20.6%	9.1	27.1	18.9%	7.3
G = 0.85*PL*	49.4	14.2%	3.6	37.8	13.4%	2.9

Source: Hum and Simpson (2005). Calculations use SLID Public File 2000, weighted to reflect the population of economic families in Canada.

generous than those considered earlier in Table 1 because they involve break-even levels of 1.4 and 1.7 times the poverty line, thereby transferring more income to both poor and non-poor families. Setting the income guarantee at 70 percent of the poverty line and a tax rate of 50 percent, costs are $35.2 billion, and we get a poverty rate of 20.6 percent and a poverty gap of $9.1 billion using the LIM; the corresponding figures using the MBM are $27.1 billion, 18.9 percent, and $7.3 billion. This plan reduces the poverty gap compared with current programs, but leaves poverty incidence higher. At a guarantee set at 85 percent of the poverty line, poverty using the LIM definition is reduced to 14.2 percent (less than the current poverty rate), the poverty gap is reduced to $3.6 billion, and the total cost of the program would be $49.4 billion. Under the MBM definition, poverty incidence is 13.4 percent (slightly above the current level), although the poverty gap is much lower ($2.9 billion) under this plan than the current poverty gap ($37.8 billion). Notice that this guaranteed income (GI) plan does better than the BI plan at 70 percent of the poverty line in the first row of Table 2. The GI plan generates the same poverty incidence but lower poverty gaps at less than one-third the cost.

One final plan might be considered to illustrate the cost reduction from adopting a GAI/NIT plan with a clawback rate. Consider a guarantee set at 100 percent of the poverty line and a negative tax rate of 50 percent. By definition, this would eliminate poverty in Canada. The cost of the plan would be $66.2 billion under the LIM definition of poverty and $50.3 billion under the MBM definition. These represent significant savings and a significantly improved chance of political acceptance, compared with the BI plan. At the same time, they represent a reduction in what Canadians pay (and receive) under current transfer arrangements.

Concluding Remarks

Income poverty may be reduced by various means, including some form of guaranteed income. Government could give all individuals an identical amount, tax-free (universal BI), and raise the necessary funds by implementing a progressive income tax. On the other hand, government might give a guaranteed sum to everyone but alter the payments based on employment and other income available to individual recipients of the income transfer. This would be a negative income tax (NIT) version of guaranteed annual income (GAI).

The discussions in Canada concerning guaranteed income have centred on certain behavioural issues (regarding the disincentive effects of a guaranteed income program) as much as poverty reduction and financial costs. But we should not be blind to the fact that Canada already enjoys limited forms of both NIT and BI programs. The refundable tax credit—first introduced with the 1979 refundable child tax credit—is an unabashed step toward a GAI/NIT, since, formally, there is no distinction.

The notion of a guaranteed annual income continues to have a firm hold on Canada's imagination. For advocates who prefer a BI type of delivery, the old age security benefit (OAS) might be a prototype. Others will want a NIT system. Canada, to this point, has neatly deferred the delivery design question between BI and NIT by having both: a demogrant[2] system (OAS for the elderly) as well as a refundable tax credit system (for families with children).

Poverty status is marked by many and diverse deprivations beyond the bare necessities to stave off hunger, cold, and homelessness—it also involves a lack of marketable job skills, a sense of insecurity, low self-esteem, a sparse support system, a shorter lifespan with poor health, and more important, a sense of despair that there is no hope of future improvement. A guaranteed annual income can only directly address the money requirements of alleviating poverty, and even then, only in "the short run," as economists are wont to qualify. But perhaps that is enough as a long-overdue first step—simply to make the lives of poor Canadians less nasty, brutish, and short.

NOTES

1. Young and Mulvale (2009) provide a good discussion of the ways in which the term guaranteed income is used to mean different things.
2. A demogrant is an income transfer or grant based purely on demographic characteristics, such as age and gender, and does not vary with income.

DISCUSSION QUESTIONS

1. Everyone in Canada over 65 years of age receives a cash payment from the government called the old age security (OAS). All workers in Canada must also pay into the Canada Pension Plan (CPP) but will receive that pension when they retire. Finally, Canada gives an income supplement to those receiving the OAS whose income falls below a certain amount. Find out the details of these programs and decide whether you think Canada already has a guaranteed income for elderly Canadians. Is it a BI? Or is it a GAI/NIT?

2. Suppose a person has a lot of "money wealth" (say, $250,000 in a trust fund or a $500,000 house with no mortgage) but their income is below the guaranteed level. Should they receive the guaranteed income? If yes, why? And if not, why not?

3. Should teenagers be eligible for the guaranteed income on their own if they choose to leave home and live by themselves? At what age should this be allowed?

4. If the guarantee level is set below the poverty line, how would persons with disabilities who cannot work or earn additional income escape poverty? Should they receive an extra guaranteed supplement? Are there other groups in Canada that you think should also get an extra supplement? Would this violate the spirit of a guaranteed income?

5. If Canada were to bring in a guaranteed income program, should newly landed immigrants to Canada be eligible to receive it? What conditions do you think immigrants should have to satisfy before becoming eligible to receive the guaranteed income?

6. Do you think a guaranteed income would strengthen marriages (by alleviating potential financial stress)? Or might it cause marriages to break up (since couples need not stay together simply for economic reasons because each would be entitled to a guaranteed income on their own)? (See Choudhry and Hum 1995 in Suggested Readings.)

7. How would a guaranteed income program handle self-employed business owners who do not have a wage-paying job? Or seasonal occupations like fishers and farmers?

8. Do you think a guaranteed income in Canada should be delivered by the federal government? Or would it be better to let each province design its own program? What are some of the problems with federal delivery? Provincial delivery? What, if anything, does the Canadian Constitution have to say about this?

SUGGESTED READINGS

Basilevsky, Alexander, and Derek Hum. 1984. *Experimental social programs and analytic methods: An evaluation of the U.S. income maintenance projects.* New York: Academic Press.

Choudhry, Saud, and Derek Hum. 1995. Graduated work incentives and how they affect marital stability: The Canadian evidence. *Applied Economic Letters* 2: 367–371.

Hum, Derek. 1985. Social security reform in Canada during the 1970s. In *Canadian social welfare policy: Federal and provincial dimensions,* ed. J.S. Ismael. Toronto: Institute for Public Administration in Canada.

Hum, D., and W. Simpson. 1993. Whatever happened to Canada's guaranteed income project? *Canadian Public Administration /Administration publique du Canada* 36 (3): 442–450.

ONLINE RESOURCES

Canadian Social Research Links: http://www.canadiansocialresearch.net.

Human Resources and Skills Development Canada: http://www.hrsdc.gc.ca.

National Council of Welfare: http://www.ncwcnbes.net.

REFERENCES

Canadian Council on Social Development (CCSD). 2003.

Economic Council of Canada. 1968. The problem of poverty. *Fifth Annual Review.* Ottawa: Economic Council of Canada.

Hum, D., and W. Simpson. 1995. Reducing spending and increasing equity: How far can refundable tax credits take us? *Canadian Public Administration* 38: 598–612.

Hum, D., and W. Simpson. 2005. The cost of eliminating poverty in Canada: Basic income with an income test twist. In *The ethics and economics of basic incomes,* eds. M. Lewis, S. Pressman, and K. Widerquist, 282–292. Burlington, VT: Ashgate.

Lerner, S., C. Clark, and W. Needham. 1999. *Basic income: Economic security for all Canadians.* Toronto: Between the Lines Press.

National Council of Welfare (NCW). 1998–99. *A new poverty line: Yes, no or maybe?* Ottawa: National Council of Welfare.

National Council of Welfare (NCW). 2008. *Welfare incomes, 2006 and 2007.* Ottawa: National Council of Welfare.

Sarlo, C. 1996. *Poverty in Canada.* 2nd ed. Vancouver: The Fraser Institute.

Tsoukalas, Spyridoula, and Andrew MacKenzie. 2003. *Personal security index 2003.* Ottawa: Canadian Council on Social Development.

Young, M., and J. Mulvale. 2009. *Possibilities and prospects: The debate over a guaranteed income.* Ottawa: Canadian Centre for Policy Alternatives.

Employment and Poverty: A Critical Perspective on Guaranteed Income Programs

Mario Seccareccia

Introduction

The idea of a guaranteed income (GI) keeps resurfacing in policy circles and has attained incredible heights of intellectual popularity over the last half century. Its success can be measured by the regularity of its appearance in the anti-poverty policy menu of both celebrated conservative and left-leaning economists and policy-makers. Even in the classic writings of such diametrically opposed economists as Milton Friedman and John Kenneth Galbraith, a GI program is often depicted as a comprehensive and coherent alternative to the status quo—the latter consisting of a patchwork quilt of segmented income-support programs, such as old age security, employment insurance, and provincial social welfare programs. GI is a proposal that is frequently alluded to in mainstream economic policy circles and is a key instrument in the limited arsenal of policy options that are normally found in chapters of economics textbooks that discuss poverty and its possible solutions.

In its most general form, a GI policy is simply a government-funded income support program that would insure a minimum basic income to either individuals or households regardless of their labour market status in society. While actual proposals differ from each other because of such particularities as the basic benefit levels that they would guarantee, broadly speaking GI programs are mainly distinguished according to whether they are means-tested or fully universal programs. For instance, the unconditional basic income (UBI), as advocated by Philippe van Parijs (1995) in Europe and by Sally Lerner, Charles Clark, and Robert Needham (1999) in Canada, is the most broadly based GI program. It would unconditionally grant an income on an *ex ante* basis (that is, paid "in advance" at regular intervals during a given year) to all citizens without either a means test or a work requirement.

The UBI is different from other popular GI programs, namely the guaranteed annual income *cum* negative income tax (GAI/NIT) program of the type proposed by Milton Friedman (1962), as well as by an extensive number of private sector organizations and official government commissions in Canada. Indeed, the GAI/NIT has been advocated historically, for instance, by groups as disparate as employers' associations, such as the Canadian Manufacturers' Association (now called the Canadian Manufacturers and Exporters) since the 1980s, and anti-poverty organizations such as the Canadian Council on Social Development (CCSD). Important government commissions have also recommended variants of a GAI/NIT program, perhaps the most path-breaking one being the Croll Report of the Special Senate Committee on Poverty in 1971. Others include such heavyweights as the 1985 report of the Macdonald Commission (the Royal Commission on the Economic Union and Development Prospects for Canada), and numerous provincial commissions over the last 40 years, for example, the Newfoundland Income Supplementation Proposal of the Newfoundland Economic Recovery Commission in 1993. Last but not least, Conservative Senator Hugh Segal (2008) has pressured the Harper government to institute a GAI/NIT scheme. Unlike the UBI proposal, a GAI/NIT program would involve both a minimum guaranteed income and a program-specific tax-back, which would grant a supplement through *ex post* transfers to the working poor (that is, paid out "after the fact" when market income has been earned and the information made available to the fiscal authorities, such as the Canada Revenue Agency, at income tax time). Although the minimum benefits could vary a great deal among the various proposals, the objective of the two main types of GI programs would nevertheless be the same, providing those entitled to them with at least a minimum subsistence income. The only difference would be whether individuals receive the transfer *ex ante* (in which case it is not means-tested but universal) or *ex post* (in which case the transfer would be provided only when an individual's employment income is accounted for and is below the thresholds recognized by the fiscal authorities). It is noteworthy that, despite its broad appeal, neither the *ex ante* nor the *ex post* types has ever been fully implemented, either internationally or across Canada, although historically some local experiments have taken place.

In addition to the perennial moral dilemma with which societies have struggled over millennia, about whether the poor are "deserving" or "undeserving" of social support (often, in the past, with a political penchant for the latter), the reason, in part, for the dearth of such GI programs is that there is no general consensus on which programs such schemes should actually replace if implemented. For example, the original GAI/NIT idea put forth by conservative Chicago economists George Stigler and Milton Friedman was to *replace* all other existing transfers, such as those arising from provincial welfare and federal employment insurance programs, thereby simplifying the administration of income support, and removing all institutional obstacles to labour market flexibility, including minimum wage legislation. In contrast, proponents of the UBI, such as left-leaning Belgian economist Philippe van Parijs, would *retain* all other programs, such as old age security benefits, employment insurance benefits, and so on because the latter are deemed to serve social functions other than merely income support.

In part, however, perhaps these programs don't exist because there is also no strong agreement on what the guaranteed basic income to alleviate poverty ought to be. For instance, in Canada there is no official definition of poverty and Statistics Canada refers only to what is normally called the low-income cut-off (LICO) definition.[1] In fact, even in countries that have an official definition of poverty (such as the United States and many European countries), the concept of a poverty level has proven to be very elusive when identifying a subsistence income, whether in absolute or relative terms. For this reason, various minimum basic income levels have been floated around by proponents. Some of these proposed levels have only a tenuous relationship with prevailing unofficial estimates of the poverty line and are usually well below Statistics Canada's LICO measure. However, before commenting on the problems with the implementation of GI programs, let us first analyze more carefully the mechanics of such an income support program.

The Mechanics of a GI Supplementation Scheme

One of the earliest hybrid forms of GI programs was actually first introduced in England during the late 18th century under the Speenhamland system, which behaved somewhat like its modern variant by providing a floor under the Poor Laws relief system for individuals who were unable to work or could not find a job. At the same time it also provided a subsidy for those holding a job below the income floor, thereby serving as an income support or an "aid-in-wage" (to use Karl Polanyi's expression) for low-wage employment along the lines of the GAI/NIT schemes. Ironically, while the less-than-universal systems that had been instituted under the English Poor Laws in the local parishes were conceived of as means-tested schemes to deal with growing numbers of unemployed (or unemployable) people during the Industrial Revolution, those who first began to theorize about GI programs, such as the 18th-century American revolutionary Thomas Paine, believed in an equitable universal GI system. In conceiving of the earth as the common property of humanity, Paine recommended a UBI that would distribute the rent from the land equitably across the entire population, much as Henry George envisaged land rent a century later in the United States. These hypothetical universal systems could take different forms, including a "credit" income tax, which, in the case of Canada during the late 1930s under William Aberhart's Social Credit government (in the province of Alberta), for instance, was distributed as a "national dividend" paid out to provincial households, much as a national UBI would be. In contrast, the post–Second World War GI proposals advocated by mainstream neoclassical economists such as Milton Friedman, and the various federal and provincial committee reports, were universal in coverage but adopted some of the structural design features of the old Speenhamland system.

The basic design features of these mid-to-late-20th-century models of the GAI/NIT variety are: (1) an income floor, G_0, that is a subsistence income level households would be guaranteed regardless of the labour market status of their members, (2) a rate at which the subsidy is eliminated (the so-called tax-back, or benefit-reduction, rate, t), whose purpose would be to create incentives to take up employment, and (3) a break-even level of income at which the subsidy from the GI program eventually becomes zero. For instance, if we assume that individual households should be guaranteed a minimum subsistence income of, say, $15,000 annually and that the household income should reach a break-even LICO level of $30,000 before paying income taxes, it follows that any additional employment income between zero and $30,000 ought to be taxed back at 50 percent. From the above, we could conclude that the total or gross income accruing to the household eligible for GI support would be the sum of employment income plus the GI transfer, that is:

$$Y_T = Y_E + S \tag{1}$$

where Y_T is total income, Y_E is employment income, and S is the subsidy from the GI program, with the subsidy being equal to $G_0 - tY_E$. Hence, the subsidy portion would be the minimum income G_0 at $15,000 less the portion of the employment income tY_E that would be taxed back at 50 percent and would serve as income supplement to the basic income. From the above, we thus get that total income is:

$$Y_T = Y_E + G_0 - tY_E \tag{2}$$

Hence, from the above formula for the income supplement S, when $Y_E = 0$ and $t = 0.5$, $S = G_0 = \$15,000$; on the other hand, when Y_E is $30,000, $S = 0$. If employment income were to be between zero and $30,000, total income would continue to exceed the employment income because of the income support $G_0 - tY_E$. For instance, with Y_E at $15,000, the plan would generate Y_T of $22,500, and so on as Y_E varies. All of this is depicted graphically in Figure 1, with total income Y_T measured on the y-axis and employment income Y_E on the x-axis and with the subsidy from the income supplementation program depicted in the shaded area as the gap between Y_T and Y_E above G_0. Also shown in the graph, Y_E above $30,000 would eventually be subject to an income tax, with Y_T being less than Y_E.

The difference between the above GAI/NIT scheme and UBI programs is that the latter would probably provide a basic income level that would be considerably higher and thus closer to the $30,000 threshold income level under a strong

FIGURE 1   A Hypothetical GI Earnings Supplementation Scheme

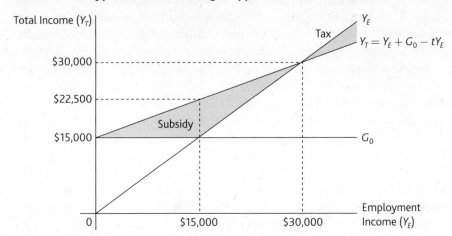

progressive income tax system. However, for both schemes the basic income would be an "aid-in-wages" or add-on to any employment income that households can earn. Indeed, this is one of the critical reasons for the support for GI plans. Under traditional social assistance programs, the choice is either work *or* welfare. Welfare recipients would be able to improve their net income position only if they accept jobs whose employment income is above the welfare level, because earnings below this level would normally be subject to a 100 percent tax-back rate—one could either be working or receiving welfare, but not both. Instead, with GAI/NIT and UBI proposals, they would be able to hold a job while receiving the income support from the GI program.

Traditional Critics of GI Programs

While many mainstream economists subscribe to GI programs, albeit mostly the means-tested GAI/NIT variety, neoclassical economists are deeply divided on their merits. For instance, some conservative neoclassical economists have been strongly critical of such programs, largely because of the disincentive effects that are alleged to result from the implementation of a GI program. Starting from the questionable presupposition that poverty is primarily a choice, they assume that rational individuals would trade off more "leisure" for less "work," and would therefore willingly fall into poverty as long as the government subsidizes those individuals who most want leisure. As Anderson and Block (1993) argue, there are "able-bodied adults who rationally prefer leisure to labor and receive a government subsidy for this preference" (1993, S353). They continue: "Rational individuals sometimes choose to remain poor because they perceive themselves to be better off as a result. Labor is onerous and produces disutility. ... It is only by lucky happenstance that individuals sometimes find pleasure in pursuing activities that also produce marketable output and, hence, income" (1993, S358–S359). From this hedonistic perspective on human behaviour, it would follow that any type of income support (whether a GI program, welfare programs, or, say, employment insurance) would necessarily encourage a significant number of individuals to choose leisure instead of work. Hence, an anti-poverty program would merely create more poor who would deliberately drop out of the labour force because of the disincentive effects that the program would generate. All of this, of course, hinges on the view that work is a "bad" while leisure is a "good," an assumption that may not square well with the facts: that individuals generally value the holding of a job vis-à-vis more leisure (see Bellemare and Poulin-Simon 1983). In particular, although an insignificant substratum of individuals who could fit the Anderson/Block stereotype might legitimately exist, this view ignores the non-pecuniary returns to working and also fails to recognize the significant social stigma that is generally attached to being without a job and living on government support, thereby making such a group quite inconsequential to the overall effects of the GI program.

In fact, most neoclassical economists would recognize that the introduction of a GI program could lead to an increased demand for "leisure," but mainstream neoclassical supporters of such programs have argued that these effects are not strong enough to lead to significant negative labour supply response (that is, individuals either reducing their hours of work or withdrawing altogether from the labour force). For instance, in their thorough review of the data collected from the five controlled experiments in GI programs in North America from the late 1960s to the late 1970s in New Jersey, Gary (Indiana), Seattle (Washington), Denver (Colorado), and the Mincome experiment in Dauphin/Winnipeg (Manitoba), Hum and Simpson (1993) concluded that the evidence tended to corroborate what was already generally known from non-experimental studies that found relatively low negative responsiveness of labour supply variables to the introduction of such income supplementation schemes. This would mean that the numbers of people who dropped out of the labour market because of their strong preference for leisure would be small as a result of the GI transfers. More important, however, the whole defence of a GAI/NIT program, going back to Friedman and Stigler, was not to encourage those individuals already employed to leave their jobs and live off the GI support but just the opposite, that is, to induce individual welfare recipients who are prevented from working by the current institutional structure of welfare programs (because they would lose 100 percent of their welfare transfers) to actually take up employment! Indeed, as we shall see below, it is with respect to the latter that much of the heterodox critique of GI programs has been formulated.

Heterodox Critique of GI Programs

Most of the controversy among mainstream economists has been centred on the behaviour of labour supply and the disincentive effects of GI programs, and therefore remains stuck in the traditional debate over whether the poor are deserving or undeserving of the income support, because of the presumed strength of their labour supply response. Not only do heterodox economists argue that such labour supply effects are insignificant, thereby strongly supporting the income transfers, but they point to the primarily negative effects of such programs, at both the industry and macroeconomic levels, on the demand for labour and on the behaviour of individuals already employed. While recognizing that a GI policy could allow the poor greater opportunities to work their way out of poverty and welfare traps, and also prevent them from slipping through the existing safety net patchwork (Clark and Kavanagh 1996), some heterodox economists have argued that, in the absence of other wage and employment policies, a GI system could have the effect of inducing wage deflation and the proliferation of low-wage jobs.

As Friedman (1962) pointed out, unlike minimum wages and other similar income support programs such as employment insurance that would be eliminated under a comprehensive GAI/NIT, a GI system would not much "distort the market or impede its functioning" (1962, 191). This is because a GI policy would create incentives for individuals to offer their services in the labour market, while at the same time providing a basic income that would not hinder wage flexibility in response to labour market demand and would actually reduce workers' resistance to wage and employment adjustment. Indeed, an earnings supplementation scheme, such as the GAI/NIT that Friedman had defended, could seriously affect wages and industrial structure over time. This is because the income support constitutes a subsidy to workers holding jobs with earnings below the break-even level of income defined by the program (in our example in Figure 1, it was $30,000)—that is, at the level where S is zero. To understand the effective incidence of the earnings subsidy, one must consider the passage of time following the introduction of a GI scheme. In the very short run, the income supplement would boost the net income of the low-wage workers by the full amount of the GI transfer. However, over the medium term, firms and GI-subsidized workers would be adjusting their wage-bargaining behaviour to the new labour market environment and this would spawn downward wage pressures.

As was argued elsewhere (see Iacobacci and Seccareccia 1989, 153–160), the subsidy effect could operate through a number of different channels or mechanisms in this new flexible labour market environment. The first of these mechanisms arises from the operation of the guaranteed level, G_0, and the tax-back rate, t, of the income supplementation, which can be dubbed the "compensation effect." In an economy characterized by substantial unemployment, this effect would serve to reduce workers' resistance to a cut in gross earnings because the GI supplement would automatically rise to partially compensate the wage cut, thus having a mitigating effect on net earnings. In other words, a cut in wages for the working poor under a GI scheme would generate a less than proportional reduction in net earnings. Second, one would expect a positive labour supply response from previous welfare recipients, who would now be able to obtain employment income as a result of the income supplementation. While empirical studies have shown this labour supply response to be not very significant, it has often been defended as the *raison d'être* of a GI program. Thus one cannot altogether rule out the importance of this effect. Third, downward wage flexibility could arise from the incentive effect on firms to fragment full-time jobs into part-time ones so that these jobs could qualify for the earnings supplementation.

If these microeconomic effects are significant, the implementation of such a GI policy in a demand-constrained labour market in which substantial unemployment exists would intensify the downward pressure on wages and would activate forces pushing for a low-wage/part-time economy. A generous employment insurance support and an active minimum wage policy could serve as partial checks against the proliferation of low-wage jobs, but the job fragmentation mechanism would be prevented only in the unlikely case that the minimum wage policy also included a floor on weekly or monthly earnings. Much as was the case with the archaic Speenhamland wage-supplementation system, such a GI program could thus create incentives for firms to increase the proportion of jobs that would qualify for the "working poor" subsidy, thereby working somewhat against the very people it is supposed to help.

At the macroeconomic level, the adoption of a GI supplement would affect the responsiveness of wages to the business cycle. During a recession, the number of workers willing to accept lower-paying jobs or a cut in their wages could rise even more than would have been the case in the absence of the compensation effects of the GI program. In the case of growing cyclical unemployment, the share of part-time and low-wage employment would increase, culminating in a greater downward movement in both the average level of wages and the total flow of earnings. This could thus somewhat revive the neoclassical mechanism of downward wage flexibility; but, as Keynes and post-Keynesians argue, flexible labour costs do not necessarily move the economy closer to full employment—they could actually exacerbate the problem of effective demand at the macroeconomic level (Seccareccia 1991).[2]

Concluding Remarks

GI programs, regardless of whether they are UBI or GAI/NIT types, can be an important tool to address some of the negative consequences of the existing welfare system and can be efficient in eliminating some of the current institutional obstacles that prevent welfare recipients from taking up jobs in the labour market. However, these benefits would materialize only in a world in which full employment was the norm. In the absence of a full-employment commitment of the type discussed, for instance, by Wray (2010) and also in the absence of other floors to wage deflation, such as a comprehensive minimum wage system and employment insurance, an income supplementation scheme of the GAI/NIT variety would merely be a mechanism to spread low-wage employment, even while guaranteeing a basic income. This could therefore hurt some of the very people that it is supposed to assist through its income supplementation. The challenge for governments is how to commit themselves to achieving the twin goals of full employment *and* a universal basic income. Interestingly, this was also largely the opinion expressed by the 1971 Croll Report of the Special Senate Committee on Poverty, which pointed out that, while a long-term solution to poverty must rely on a dynamic labour market to generate good jobs that would tap into the income-generating potential of the poor themselves as the economy reaches full employment, a comprehensive income supplementation scheme was still necessary to prevent working people from falling into abject poverty.

NOTES

1. According to Statistics Canada (2009), "the LICO is the after-tax income below which most Canadians spend at least 20 percentage points more than the average on food, shelter and clothing." Estimates for 2007 are found in Zhang (2009). For instance, for a family of four residing in a Canadian urban area of 500,000 residents or more, the LICO was $33,946 in 2007.

2. The destabilizing effect is further reinforced because of the way most of these proposals would finance a GI program. Programs that have traditionally been proposed normally tend to assume deficit neutrality, which means that (1) whatever is currently being spent on other social programs should be regrouped to finance the GI program; and (2) if there is a deficit, say in times of recession, the GI fund should be balanced (which would entail raising revenues and/or cutting spending elsewhere). In fact, in Iacobacci and Seccareccia (1989), the impact of a wage cut in the low-wage sector was actually simulated using the Conference Board large-scale econometric model of the Canadian economy at the time, and there were estimated significant negative macroeconomic effects on overall real GDP both for the short and medium term of up to five years. Without deficit neutrality, however, these destabilizing macroeconomic effects would be somewhat attenuated.

DISCUSSION QUESTIONS

1. Does the nature of the guaranteed income program—that is, whether it is an *ex ante* or universal basic income or an *ex post* or means-tested guaranteed annual income program—matter in assessing the possible effects of guaranteed income policies?
2. Why do you think that research on the disincentive effects of income implementations shows that these effects are weak or insignificant?
3. What is the "compensation effect" of an income supplementation scheme?
4. Why would a guaranteed annual income policy, in the absence of strong minimum wage legislation and a full-employment policy, reinforce a tendency toward lower wages and part-time employment?

SUGGESTED READINGS AND ONLINE RESOURCES

Canadian Social Research Network. 2010. Canadian Social Research links: Guaranteed annual income. http://www.canadiansocialresearch.net/gai.htm.

Human Resources Development Canada (HRDC). 1994. *Improving social security in Canada, guaranteed income: A supplementary paper*. Ottawa: HRDC. http://www.canadiansocialresearch.net/GAIpaper.pdf.

National Council of Welfare. 1976. *Guide to the guaranteed income*. Ottawa: National Council of Welfare.

Special Senate Committee on Poverty. 1971. *Report of the Special Senate Committee on Poverty* (Croll Report). Ottawa: Information Canada.

Widerquist, Karl, Michael Anthony Lewis, and Steven Pressman, eds. 2005. *The ethics and economics of the basic income guarantee*. Aldershot, UK: Ashgate.

Young, Margot, and James P. Mulvale. 2009. *Possibilities and prospects: The debate over a guaranteed income* (An Economic Security Project Report). Ottawa: Canadian Centre for Policy Alternatives. http://www.policyalternatives.ca/publications/reports/possibilities-and-prospects.

REFERENCES

Anderson, Gary M., and Walter Block. 1993. Comment on Hum and Simpson. *Journal of Labor Economics* 11 (1, pt. 2): S348–S363.

Bellemare, Diane, and Lise Poulin-Simon.1983. *Le plein emploi: Pourquoi?* Montréal: Les Presses de l'Université du Québec.

Clark, Charles M.A., and Catherine Kavanagh. 1996. Basic income, inequality, and unemployment: Rethinking the linkage between work and welfare. *Journal of Economic Issues* 30 (2) (June): 399–406.

Friedman, Milton. 1962. *Capitalism and freedom* (in collaboration with Rose Friedman). Chicago: University of Chicago Press.

Hum, Derek, and Wayne Simpson. 1993. Economic response to a guaranteed annual income: Experience from Canada and the United States. *Journal of Labor Economics* 11 (1, pt. 2): S263–296.

Iacobacci, Mario, and Mario Seccareccia. 1989. Full employment versus income maintenance: Some reflections on the macroeconomic and structural implications of a guaranteed income program for Canada. *Studies in Political Economy* 28 (Spring): 137–173.

Lerner, Sally, Charles M.A. Clark, and W. Robert Needham. 1999. *Basic income: Economic security for all Canadians.* Toronto: Between the Lines.

Parijs, Philippe van. 1995. *Real freedom for all: What (if anything) can justify capitalism.* Oxford: Clarendon Press.

Seccareccia, Mario. 1991. An alternative to labour-market orthodoxy: The post-Keynesian/institutionalist policy view. *Review of Political Economy* 3 (1) (January): 43–61.

Segal, Hugh. 2008. Guaranteed annual income: Why Milton Friedman and Bob Stanfield were right. *Policy Options* (April): 45–51.

Statistics Canada. 2009. Income of Canadians. *The Daily.* June 3. http://www.statcan.gc.ca/daily-quotidien/090603/dq090603a-eng.htm.

Wray, L. Randall. 2010. The social and economic importance of full employment. In *Introducing macroeconomic analysis: Issues, questions, and competing views,* eds. Hassan Bougrine and Mario Seccareccia, 219–228. Toronto: Emond Montgomery.

Zhang, Xuelin. 2009. *Low income measurements at Statistics Canada.* August 4. Statistics Canada. http://www.oeb.gov.on.ca/OEB/_Documents/ EB-2008-0150/FAWG_StatsCan_meeting4.pdf.

Do Equalization Payments Solve the Problem of Regional Inequality?

Editors' Introduction

The unequal distribution of national income and wealth in capitalist societies is a thorny issue that well-intentioned and even well-designed policies have failed to resolve. Some would argue that the most encouraging results are those that accompanied the rise of the welfare state in advanced economies after the Second World War. Within the general Keynesian interventionist policy framework of the era, policy-makers in these jurisdictions recognized the necessity of helping low-income workers and the unemployed, and instituted policies in support of universal health care, education, and the provision of basic physical and social infrastructures to the general population. However, no matter how well-intentioned these policies were, as the Canadian experience shows, public investment—for example, in schools, hospitals, and roads—is not uniformly distributed over the entire national territory. Some regions within the country (historically referred to as the hinterland) receive less than others (the heartland) in terms of public services or public investment. In addition, people living in particular regions tend to suffer long-term structural unemployment, earn low wages, and often work in low-skilled or seasonal occupations. At the same time, those living in more dynamic regions or centres tend to have higher-paying and more stable jobs.

Disparities among regions do not represent a serious concern for neoclassical economists, simply because they assume that any differences (in regional incomes, for example) will disappear over time through the working of the market mechanism.

Thus, in the absence of any impediments such as government support, the unemployed and low-wage earners would migrate to regions where wages are high and employment opportunities are better. As labour becomes abundant in the receiving regions, wages will tend to fall. At the same time, wages are pushed up in the sending regions as labour becomes scarce. A convergence or equalization of incomes is thus achieved through the *automatic* adjustment process envisaged in this model. Hence, most neoclassical economists oppose government attempts to correct regional disparities, and argue that such attempts can only delay the ineluctable progress toward regional convergence. They recommend that policy-makers pursue *laissez-faire* policies by abolishing government income-support programs that would prevent the market from achieving its primary allocative function of equalizing income differences. The essay by Fred McMahon represents this view well, arguing that the post-1970 experience with Canadian regional development policy in Atlantic Canada wasted financial resources that could have been better spent. Regional development programs reduce mobility and market adjustment, and they have done more harm than good by preventing the market from achieving convergence.

An alternative view, expressed by Brian K. MacLean and Michael Bradfield, argues that government intervention (in the form of equalization programs and other transfers) aids regional convergence precisely because these programs affect public investment in areas such as education and health care, thereby improving the economic performance of regions. By ensuring that all regions in the country receive funding to provide the needed education and health services, policy-makers give equal opportunities to all citizens to improve their health, skills, and knowledge and increase their productivity, which prepares them to compete for jobs in other parts of the country. Equalization payments have not impeded interregional labour migration, as predicted by the neoclassical model.

Their general conclusion is that since the free-market mechanism cannot bring about the long-awaited convergence, redistribution through government programs is necessary. For MacLean and Bradfield, the fundamental issue really concerns social programs. Those on the political left want well-funded social programs; those on the political right want less funding for social programs, because the latter interfere with the functioning of the private market economy. MacLean and Bradfield argue that if the right were to succeed in undermining equalization, it would strengthen tax competition among provinces and thereby weaken social programs.

The Many Failures of Regional Development Policy

Fred McMahon

[D]evelopment economics were too often used [as] justification for policies that in retrospect impeded growth rather than helping it.

Nobel laureate Paul Krugman (1995, 24)

Introduction

In the early 1970s, Ottawa launched ambitious and costly regional development programs to increase prosperity in Atlantic Canada. This essay looks at the results of, the theories behind, and the problems with regional development programs. As this essay will detail, the 1970s was the heyday of regional policies and the damage from them was most evident in that period, which is why it is a good case study of what goes wrong with regional policies. However, as we shall see, damage from regional development programs continues to this day.

Nothing like the great Atlantic Canadian regional development experiment had been tried before in Canadian history, and there are few, if any, examples of such an effort elsewhere in the world. The European Union's regional programs typically transfer a few percentage points of the recipient nation's gross domestic product. Canadian net federal transfers—the difference between what the federal government raises in revenue in Atlantic Canada and what it spends—often reached a third or more of the GDP of the region (McMahon 2000a). This massive flow of wealth distorted virtually all aspects of the Atlantic economy. It is a stark object lesson in the failure of regional development policy.

Regional development in Canada racked up an impressive number of unintended consequences. Roughly speaking, regional development policy was intended to:

- combat regional unemployment;
- spark regional development;
- attract new private sector investment;
- generate entrepreneurship; and
- develop economic independence.

Instead, through the 1970s,

- unemployment soared, from around 5 percent at the beginning of the decade to well into the double digits at the end of the decade;
- growth tanked, from a faster rate than the rest of Canada to a slower rate for much of the decade;
- private sector investment was suppressed, from close to parity with the Canadian average to about $2,400 less than the Canadian average per capita by the end of the decade;
- *grant*repreneurship pushed out entrepreneurship, as per capita business subsidies rose from about $225 to about triple that, not counting petroleum related subsidies;
- Atlantic Canada became more government-dependent, as government spending increased from about 50 percent of regional GDP to about 70 percent.

Some will object to the claim that regional policy was the cause, and will finger other villains. But that hardly supports the idea that regional policy accomplished its goals. In other words, the best defence of regional policy is that the hundreds of billions of dollars spent did no damage. This is not a particularly impressive defence, but it is still generous since the negative consequences described above actually happened.

Success was largely achieved in one area, however: bringing government services in Atlantic Canada up to national levels. This essay takes little issue with this goal and the relatively modest sums spent on equalization and shared-cost programs. It is critical, instead, of the heroic regional development programs designed to boost growth.

Regional Development

Regional development theories come in changing flavours and names: resource scarcity, growth poles, balanced growth, planned structural change, and basic needs. These shifts in fashion appear to reflect the failures of experience. When efforts arising out of one development theory collapse, regional theorists dream up another idea that wraps the old cry for government intervention in a new covering.

A key idea in many of these theories is that investors in poor regions do not have the means to invest and/or are denied the means because of financing imperfections. At the same time, outside investors ignore or are ignorant of investment opportunities in peripheral regions, and this lack of investment dooms regions to slow growth.

However, lagging and isolated countries have become prosperous without the benefit of great subsidies. A prime example is the so-called Asian tigers: South Korea, Taiwan, Hong Kong, and Singapore. In the last couple of decades, they have been joined by a number of other Asian nations and countries like Chile and Botswana. The key is good economic policy, not regional development subsidies (Barro and Sala-i-Martin 1995).

Catch-up growth is due in part to "convergence"—the fact that poorer nations tend to grow faster than rich nations. Convergence has two main engines, lower costs and technology. Costs are lower in lagging regions. Businesses invest there to take advantage of the lower costs, particularly labour costs. Investment brings modern technology. The increase in investment and technology pushes up wages and reduces poverty. (See, for example, McMahon 2000b and Sala-i-Martin 2005; Barro and Sala-i-Martin 1995 explore growth theory, convergence, and the empirical evidence in technical detail.)

This analysis also applies to lagging regions within nations. Barro and Sala-i-Martin (1995) show that for the period they studied, lagging regions in Europe, the United States, and Japan closed the gap with advanced regions by 2 or 3 percent per year. This is a faster rate of catch-up than that experienced by the heavily subsidized Atlantic Canada region. Had Atlantic Canada closed the gap with the rest of Canada at the lower end of that speed between 1961 and 1997, GDP in the region would have been nearly $2,000 higher per capita (McMahon 2000a, 145).

In other words, it would seem that market failure was introduced by Canadian regional development policies, not by the market. Much of this follows from Nobel laureate James Buchanan's seminal work on public choice, in which he and others argued that civil servants and elected officials act as self-interested agents and that government spending and programs are thus all too often aligned with their interest in benefiting powerful groups and existing economic structures, even while those structures are declining and require massive support (see Buchanan 2003). Meanwhile, as we shall see, future economic activities can be frustrated because government supports old structures and creates politically popular distortions in the employment market.

Equalization

Buchanan himself made the classic fairness case for equalization in a 1950 essay. He argued that low revenues in lagging regions meant governments would not be able to provide national-standard services, and suggested equalization payments as a solution. Buchanan has since qualified his views and suggests that it might be impossible in practice, due to politicization and game-playing, to develop an efficient system of equalization—a conclusion derived from his work on public choice (Buchanan 2003). Design problems abound: How is the size of the payments determined? How do you ensure the money goes to help people, rather than reward powerful local interests (similar to the problem with foreign aid)? How can accountability be created when the link between taxation and spending is broken (that is, equalization is paid by taxpayers outside the receiving region, while regional politicians unaccountable to these taxpayers spend the money)? Fairness is undermined if poor people in a rich region subsidize rich people in a poor region, and, because the provincial government controls equalization resources, it is likely that resources will be directed to privileged groups that favour the ruling party.

Formulas for equalization transfer payments have changed frequently, because each formula has been found to contain perverse incentives and/or assumptions that failed to accurately reflect the economic situation of the provinces (see Clemens and Veldhuis 2007 for a review).

Sensible arguments can be made for modest equalization. However, the equity and efficiency goals of equalization would likely be better served by directing resources to poor people rather than to poor regions, and by an equitable system of cost-sharing for government services.[1]

Regional Development Programs

The 1960s were a period of economic hope in Atlantic Canada. It was the time of "the Atlantic Revolution." Prosperity grew and equality with the rest of Canada seemed in sight. Despite breakneck economic growth across Canada, Atlantic Canada's economy grew at an even faster rate than the rest of Canada's (see Figure 1).

Throughout the 1960s, even the region's most painful malaise, high unemployment, seemed to be loosening its grip. By 1970, unemployment levels in Atlantic Canada and the rest of Canada were virtually identical. Only Newfoundland had an unemployment rate significantly above the national average (see Figures 2a and 2b).

Private sector investment soared—from about $1,550 per capita in 1961 to about $3,900 per capita in 1971, almost the same level it was nationally. (All dollars are in constant 2002 values.)

Then catastrophe hit. The turnaround was so great that an outsider might have assumed the region had suffered a civil war, an invasion, or a natural disaster. Atlantic Canada's catch-up with the rest of the nation slowed in 1970 and then went into reverse. Unemployment soared. The gap with the rest of Canada went from virtually zero in 1971 to 4 percentage points by 1976.

The gap between investment in Atlantic Canada and the rest of Canada grew from almost zero in 1971 to an average of about $1,400 per capita throughout the 1970s, reaching nearly $2,400 by the end of the decade, according to Statistics Canada, Business Investment data (see Table 1). What happened? Two things: the federal

FIGURE 1   Atlantic Canada GDP per Capita as a Percent of the National Average

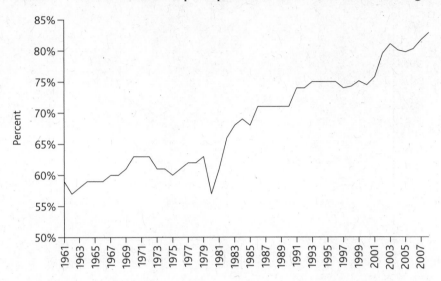

Source: Statistics Canada, Provincial Economic Accounts; calculations by author, series breaks between 1980 and 1981.

FIGURE 2a   Unemployment Rates: Canada, Newfoundland, and PEI

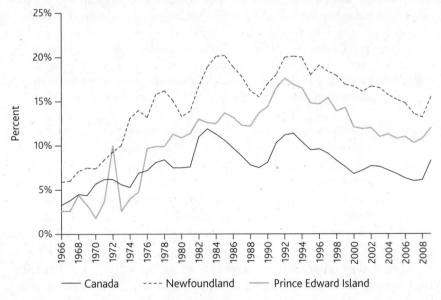

Source: Statistics Canada, Labour Force Survey; series breaks between 1980 and 1981.

FIGURE 2b   Unemployment Rates: Canada, Nova Scotia, and New Brunswick

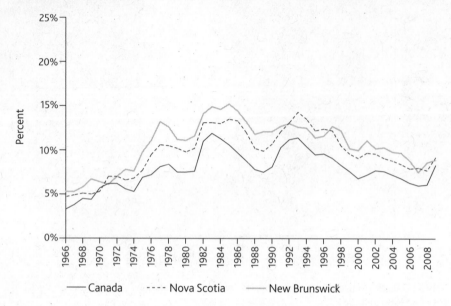

—— Canada   ---- Nova Scotia   —— New Brunswick

Source: Statistics Canada, Labour Force Survey; series breaks between 1980 and 1981.

government had launched its heroic regional development program and the successes of the 1960s had fed into the demand for increased government action:

> Far from attenuating the demands of Atlantic Canada for a greater national commitment to reducing regional disparities in the country, the general prosperity of the 1960s made the idea of regional development seem a more obtainable goal. (Bickerton 1990, 175)

An accounting problem now occurs. Canada's regional programs didn't fall under one heading with a clear accounting stream. Instead, a myriad of programs was involved—regionally extended unemployment insurance (now employment insurance); various economic development programs; subsidies for fading industries, such as the Cape Breton coal mines; program transfers; equalization; and various ad hoc measures, particularly make-work projects. It was this toxic mix, not simply equalization (which is a defensible program), that comprised regional development policy.

The only way to appreciate the magnitude of the regional development effort is to examine the total wealth transfer into Atlantic Canada. This can be measured by the difference between federal expenditures in the region and federal revenues, although accurate measurement is difficult. For example, in times of deficit, Canada

TABLE 1 Difference Between per Capita Business Investment: Canadian Average Minus Atlantic Canadian Average (2002 constant dollars)

1961	$920
1970	$209
1971	$72
1980	$2,373
1981	$2,405
1991	$1,510
2001	$2,192
2008	$1,656

Note: The series starts in 1961, so years ending in 1 are shown, except for 1970 and 1980, to show the data at the start and end of the sample decade and 2008 for recent data.

Source: Statistics Canada, "Business Investment."

as a whole will have higher expenditures than revenues. In addition, there is a discontinuity in Statistics Canada's data series between 1980 and 1981, hence the data are not fully comparable.

The data should therefore be treated as an approximation. However, the changes are so enormous that the information contained in these estimates is unmistakable (see Figure 3). The great boost in wealth transfers to the region was accompanied by a falling off of Atlantic Canada's catch-up with the rest of Canada.

Two arguments—the oil crisis and declining economic conditions—try to deny the relevance of the skyrocketing net transfers to the sudden weakening of regional growth. Some observers claim that the oil crisis of the early 1970s caused both the spike of federal net transfers through oil subsidies and the regional retreat from growth.

The problem is that the oil crisis didn't begin until October 1973. Atlantic Canada's growth relative to the rest of Canada slowed in 1970 and was in reverse by 1973. Net transfers to the region began growing in 1970, and while it is true they rose rapidly after 1973, only a small part of that rise reflected petroleum subsidies—typically around $1,000 out of about the $6,000 per capita net transfers in the mid-1970s to early 1980s—before being phased out in the late 1980s. (See McMahon 2000a, 16–20 for a full discussion.)

The other argument is that net transfers to the region rose because of declining economic conditions. This argument fails on two grounds: (1) it is possible to mark off the new programs and how they affected spending (see McMahon 2000a), and (2) the soaring expenditures began before the economic decline.

FIGURE 3   Federal Net Transfers to Atlantic Canada per Capita (2002 constant dollars)

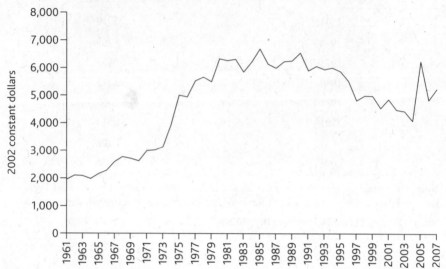

Source: Statistics Canada, Provincial Economic Accounts; calculations by author. A new series was introduced in 1981. Data from the first series is used up to 1997, when it was eliminated. Data from the new series used after that. The jump in transfers in 2005 is due to a spike in transfers to Newfoundland.

Nor was there doubt in Atlantic Canada that the inflow of money was due to regional programs. For example, in July 1974, the Atlantic Provinces Economic Council's (APEC) *Atlantic Report* stated that "government employment and transfer payments [had become the] chief underpinnings" of the Atlantic economy (2). Looking back at that period later, APEC made the same point. "Regional policy hit its stride during the 1970s" (APEC 1993, 8).

We now turn to the negative effects of these regional programs.

Employment

Regionally extended unemployment insurance (UI—now employment insurance, or EI) was meant to aid low- and seasonal-employment regions by providing extra benefits. Initially, UI offered 42 weeks of benefits for 10 weeks of work. It quickly became known as Lotto 10-42, named after the national Lotto 6/49. Work patterns across Atlantic Canada adjusted to stretches of 10 weeks of work followed by 42 weeks of unemployment with benefits.

Private companies were forced to parcel out work in 10-week packages. Government pitched in with 10-week make-work projects. Quits and layoffs after 10 weeks of employment soared. When the number of qualifying weeks changed, as they did during periodic reforms of UI, quits and layoffs soared at the end of the *new* qualifying period (see Green and Riddell 1995).

Perverse incentives discouraged workers from seeking employment while collecting UI. UI benefits were based on an average of earnings while employed. Because seasonal work was often highly paid whereas off-season work offered lower wages, thus reducing UI payments, the best strategy for the highest possible income was to work 10 weeks in a well-paid seasonal job and collect UI for the rest of the year.

As a result, labour shortages spread across the region despite double-digit unemployment, with strongly negative results for business development and growth. As the *Atlantic Report* said:

> Somewhat surprisingly, in view of the high unemployment levels, constant complaints of shortage of workers are heard and reports of the forest, fishing, and farming industries being unable to obtain sufficient workers are common. (APEC October 1973, 6)

In many winter months throughout the 1970s and 1980s, the number of people in Atlantic Canada collecting UI was almost double the number officially unemployed. Unemployment rates were calculated based on a survey of people actively seeking work, but many collecting UI were not seeking work and, in fact, didn't consider themselves unemployed. It was thus possible for the number of people collecting UI to easily exceed the number that were officially unemployed (Statistics Canada, Labour Force Survey).

The problems were highlighted by a pilot project in 1999 offering subsidies to seasonal workers to make up for income losses they would suffer by taking a low-paying off-season job. Two-fifths of the workers approached refused even to register. Ultimately, only 2 percent of the workers approached found and accepted work. The take-up was so small, even in cities with low levels of unemployment like Moncton and Halifax, that researchers cancelled the program (Tattrie 1999).

These effects still plague the region. Crowley and McIver (2004) find labour shortages throughout the region. Busby (2008) shows that regional imbalances of unemployment remain, which he attributes largely to distortions caused by regionally extended EI. This regional program has caused immense damage.

Business Environment

Government, pumped up by federal transfers, became the biggest subsidizer and customer of businesses, one relatively unconcerned about quality and cost. Instead of creating entrepreneurship, a "grantrepreneur" mentality was fostered.

To compare the competitiveness of firms in Nova Scotia and New England, the Atlantic Canada Opportunities Agency and the Nova Scotia Department of Industry Trade and Technology contracted P.N. O'Farrell, at the Heriot-Watt Business School.

O'Farrell found that regional programs undermined competitiveness—businesses became content on a rich diet of government subsidies and contracts and put little effort into quality, productivity improvement, or sound management. Instead, they focused on obtaining government contracts, which seldom had stringent cost or quality controls.

> *The more modern machinery found everywhere in Nova Scotian firms seems to be related to the more generous levels of assistance available rather than to commercial success. The "grantrepreneur" mentality ... appears to be widespread* [emphasis in the original]. *... As one precision engineer in Bristol stated succinctly when I showed him the U.S. and Canadian samples, "[I]f you can't compete without grants, you won't compete with them."* (O'Farrell 1990, 16)

Despite newer machinery—New England firms often purchased secondhand machinery from subsidized Nova Scotia firms—and lower wage costs, Nova Scotia prices were 20 to 30 percent higher than New England prices and the quality of Nova Scotia goods was sub-par. O'Farrell blames regional policy, "grants, subsidies and preferential [government] purchasing, thereby reducing the incentive to change" (24). O'Farrell also noted how government involvement in economic decisions had politicized the economy, particularly the labour market, further distorting and complicating business decisions and the market. Mintz and Smart (2003) continued to find poorly targeted, politicized business subsidies and argued that tax reductions would be more effective and politically impartial.

Business Investment

As noted earlier, in 1971 the difference between business investment in Atlantic Canada and the rest of Canada was virtually zero. The gap soon grew to around $1,400 per capita. What caused this?

Costs were on the rise, making the region less attractive for private investment. Government bid against private sector employers for resources, in particular workers, raising costs and making Atlantic businesses less competitive.

Throughout the 1960s, wages in the Atlantic provinces fell compared with the rest of Canada. This made the region more attractive to investors and was a key factor in the economic success of the region in that decade. By the late 1960s, average hourly earnings were less than 85 percent of the national average (Statistics Canada, Labour Force Survey). Low wages are a driving force of convergence. They attract investment, which, over the long term, boosts productivity and thus wage growth. In Atlantic Canada, however, factors unrelated to productivity started driving wage growth.

Although wages were growing rapidly across Canada during the 1970s, growth in Atlantic Canada exceeded national growth. By the late 1970s, hourly wage rates soared to above 90 percent of the Canadian average, and over 95 percent in Nova Scotia. The negative impact on investment was evident early. The *Atlantic Report* noted "[n]arrowing profit margins caused by escalating costs of labour" were the major factor that had "forced dramatic cut-backs in the optimistic capital spending plans of the business sector in 1970 in the Atlantic region" (January 1971, 9).

Employers had to compete with generous government salaries and make-work projects. Even worse, they had to compete against generous UI payments, in what was actually a tight labour market, with so many UI/EI recipients unwilling to work.

Soaring labour costs and difficulty in even attracting workers reduced the competitiveness of the region and thus its attractiveness as a place to invest. This has become a long-term problem. "Wage rate and other forms of government competition" continued into at least the 1990s, weakening Atlantic Canada's ability to compete, according to a report prepared for Industry Canada (DRM Advisory Group 1994, 12). This loss of competitiveness is a further negative effect of regional policy spending because rising costs force out sustainable private sector economic activity.

Government Attitudes

Government spending became increasingly politicized by regional policies. Schools, hospitals, and roads came to be seen more as make-work projects than as investments in education, health care, or infrastructure, and this attitude persisted. Of a $340 million school project in the Pictou, Nova Scotia region, *Halifax Herald* columnist Jim Meek said, "[The school] board treats the schools as an economic development opportunity without understanding or much caring about the effects on the quality of education" (Meek 1999, B1).

Regional programs also changed attitudes to government spending. Usually, a clear relationship exists between spending and taxes, creating pressure on the government to be transparent. In Atlantic Canada, so much money came from outside the region that demands for accountability were weakened. As an Atlantic Canada Opportunity Agency (ACOA) study noted: "Regional governments scored low on transparency: citizens and business find it hard to follow how and why decisions are made" (McNiven and Plumstead 1996, 47–48).

Government spending seemed like a free good. Loss-making industries and inefficient economic activities were frozen into place by rich subsidies. A prime example was in Cape Breton, where a coal-mining industry—uneconomical since 1924, when subsidies for it began—and an antiquated steel-making industry were supported with billions of dollars of government money (McMahon 2000a, 57).

Rural Economics

The fisheries suffered the worst damage, ecologically and economically, from regional policies. Officially, fisheries policy was motivated to help economic viability and preserve traditional ways of life. It did neither.

Economic and ecological sustainability were undermined by a vast subsidized fisheries expansion. This had nothing to do with a traditional way of life. By the late 1980s, fish plants employed nearly two-and-a-half times as many people as in 1961 (McMahon 2000a, chap. 7). Numerous researchers reported that the bloating of the industry went beyond either traditional levels or any expansion justified by the extension of the 200-mile limit in 1977:

> Ottawa was expected to make turkeys fly. Regardless of how inefficient an operation might be, it was always a major political issue to close a plant. ... Subsidies were paid to open new plants and then paid again whenever overexpansion threatened to close them. There was 50 per cent overcapacity in frozen fish plants in Newfoundland, 45 percent in the Maritimes [Nova Scotia, PEI, and New Brunswick]. (Harris 1998, 87)

There is not enough space here to discuss the consequences for northern cod and other overfished species, but there is little doubt that the vast expansion had devastating consequences.

Conclusion

Economic research shows unambiguously that moderate taxes, well-functioning labour markets, a depoliticized economy, and modest regulations spark growth (see McMahon 2000b; Sobel, Clark, and Lee 2007; and Karabegović and McMahon 2008). In contrast, regional programs promoted high taxes (to pay for the programs), government subsidies (to pick winners), a distorted labour market, political interference, and increased costs throughout the economy—all of which damage economic growth.

Regional development programs benefited powerful existing interests and politically powerful groups, such as voters who benefited from unemployment/employment insurance programs. This endemic flaw in regional development programs follows directly from public choice theory and is reinforced because government-sponsored activities leave less room for sustainable private sector activity, which benefits the region in the long run.

Thus, regional unemployment programs end up subsidizing unemployment and leaving less space for other economic activities; business subsidy programs and high levels of government spending become politically directed to support powerful interests, outmoded industries, and voting blocs, rather than the economic activity of the future; and dependence on high levels of government spending becomes entrenched. As noted, the damage done by regional policies continues to affect both employment and business attitudes. Mintz and Smart (2003) show that the politicization of business subsidies continues; Tattrie (1999) shows how employment insurance continues to create negative attitudes toward work while regional unemployment remains high (Figures 2a and 2b); and federal transfers and dependence on them remain powerful (Figure 3).

> It is not by planting trees in a desert or subsidizing tree planting in a desert created by politicians that government can promote … industry, but by refraining from measures that create a desert environment.
>
> *Assar Lindbeck, long-time chair of the Nobel Prize in Economics selection committee, speaking about Sweden's economic-development policy*
> *(The Economist, March 3, 1990)*

NOTE

1. The functional word is "equitable." In the early 20th century, the maritime provinces were often too poor to participate in federal shared-cost programs. Since richer provinces were able to participate and collect federal funding, these programs were a form of "reverse equalization."

DISCUSSION QUESTIONS

1. How can increased government spending politicize the economy and reduce both entrepreneurship and market incentives to improve quality and reduce price?
2. Why would unemployment insurance (now employment insurance) increase levels of unemployment?
3. Should government endeavour to maintain rural, traditional, and outdated modes of economic activity even if it results in high levels of unemployment, dependence on government, and ecological damage?
4. How do the insights from public choice theory affect our view of regional development programs?

SUGGESTED READINGS AND ONLINE RESOURCES

Buchanan, James M. 2003. *Public choice: The origins and development of a research program.* Center for Study of Public Choice. Fairfax, VA: George Mason University. http://sb.cofc.edu/pv_obj_cache/pv_obj_id_
C75D512B1781A110978C02C20FADB6A32CE10700/filename/Public%20
Choice%20Origins%20Buchanan.pdf.

Clemens, Jason, and Niels Veldhuis, eds. 2007. *Beyond equalization: Examining fiscal transfers in a broader context.* Vancouver: The Fraser Institute.

Karabegović, Amela, and Fred McMahon. 2008. *Economic freedom of North America: 2008 annual report.* Vancouver: The Fraser Institute.

McMahon, Fred. 2000. *Retreat from growth: Atlantic Canada and the negative sum economy.* Halifax: Atlantic Institute for Market Studies.

McMahon, Fred. 2000. *Road to growth: How lagging economies become prosperous.* Halifax: Atlantic Institute for Market Studies.

Mintz, Jack M., and Michael Smart. 2003. *Brooking no favours: A new approach to regional development in Atlantic Canada.* C.D. Howe Institute Commentary (December) 192. Toronto: C.D. Howe Institute.

REFERENCES

Atlantic Entrepreneurial Institute. 1992. *Small business in Canada: A human resource perspective.* St. John's, NF: The Institute. Reference taken from DRI Canada, APEC, and Canmac Economics 1994.

Atlantic Provinces Economic Council (APEC). 1993. *Atlantic Canada: Facing the challenge of change: Task 1, A preliminary report on the economic history and current state of the Atlantic economy.* Halifax: Atlantic Canada Opportunities Agency.

Atlantic Provinces Economic Council (APEC). *Atlantic Report.* Various issues.

Barro, Robert J., and Xavier Sala-i-Martin. 1995. *Technological diffusion, convergence, and growth.* NBER Working Papers 5151. Cambridge, MA: National Bureau of Economic Research. http://www.nber.org/papers/w5151.

Bickerton, J.P. 1990. *Nova Scotia, Ottawa and the politics of regional development.* Toronto: University of Toronto Press.

Biswal, B.P. 1997. *Federal transfers in Canada: A multivariate cointegration and convergence analysis across Canadian provinces.* A paper presented to the meeting of the Canadian Economics Association.

Brubaker, Elizabeth. 1995. *Making the oceans safe for fish.* Halifax: Atlantic Institute for Market Studies.

Buchanan, James M. 1950. Federalism and fiscal equity. *The American Economic Review* 40 (4): 583–599. http://web.cenet.org.cn/upfile/100523.pdf.

Buchanan, James M. 2003. *Public choice: The origins and development of a research program.* Center for Study of Public Choice, Fairfax, VA: George Mason University. http://sb.cofc.edu/pv_obj_cache/pv_obj_id_ C75D512B1781A110978C02C20FADB6A32CE10700/filename/Public%20 Choice%20Origins%20Buchanan.pdf.

Buchanan, James. 2005. Posted interview with the Frontier Institute, Winnipeg (October). http://www.fcpp.org/publication.php/236.

Busby, Colin. 2008. *Fixing a persistent problem: Canada's regional pockets of unemployment.* CD Howe, e-brief (October 23). http://www.cdhowe.org/pdf/ ebrief_66.pdf.

Clemens, Jason, and Niels Veldhuis, eds. 2007. *Beyond equalization: Examining fiscal transfers in a broader context.* Vancouver: The Fraser Institute.

Crowley, Brian Lee, and Don McIver. 2004. *You can get there from here: How Ottawa can put Atlantic Canada on the road to prosperity.* Halifax: Atlantic Institute for Market Studies.

DRM Advisory Group. 1994. *Creating value for export: Success factors, obstacles and challenges in the development of innovative export firms in Nova Scotia and PEI—Summary.* Halifax: Industry Canada.

Green, David A., and W. Craig Riddell. 1995. *Qualifying for unemployment insurance: An empirical analysis of Canada.* Ottawa: Human Resources Development Canada. http://www.hrsdc.gc.ca/eng/cs/sp/hrsdc/edd/reports/1995-000322/ rep17.pdf.

Harris, Michael. 1998. *Lament for an ocean: The collapse of the Atlantic cod fishery: A true crime story.* Toronto: McClelland & Stewart.

Karabegović, Amela, and Fred McMahon. 2008. *Economic freedom of North America: 2008 annual report.* Vancouver: The Fraser Institute.

Krugman, Paul R. 1995. *Development, geography, and economic theory.* Cambridge, MA: MIT Press.

Lindbeck, Assar. March 3, 1990. Quoted in *The Economist.*

Mathias, Philip. 1971. *Forced growth: Five studies of government involvement in the development of Canada.* Toronto: James, Lewis, and Samuel.

McMahon, Fred. 2000a. *Retreat from growth: Atlantic Canada and the negative sum economy.* Halifax: Atlantic Institute for Market Studies.

McMahon, Fred. 2000b. *Road to growth: How lagging economies become prosperous.* Halifax: Atlantic Institute for Market Studies.

McNiven, J.D., and Janice Plumstead. 1996. *Atlantic Canada and the world: A development comparison.* Halifax and Moncton, NB: North American Policy Studies Group and the Atlantic Canada Opportunities Agency.

Meek, Jim. 1999. *The Halifax Chronicle Herald.* December 11, B1.

Mintz, Jack M., and Michael Smart. 2003. *Brooking no favourites: A new approach to regional development in Atlantic Canada.* C.D. Howe Institute Commentary (December) 192. Toronto: C.D. Howe Institute.

O'Farrell, P.N. 1990. *Small manufacturing competitiveness and performance: An analysis of matched pairs in Nova Scotia and New England.* Halifax: In association with Gardner Pinfold Consultants, for the Nova Scotia Department of Industry, Trade and Technology and the Atlantic Canada Opportunities Agency.

Rotstein, Abraham. 1971. Introduction. In Philip Mathias, ed., *Forced growth: Five studies of government involvement in the development of Canada.* Toronto: James, Lewis, and Samuel.

Sala-i-Martin, Xavier. 2005. The world distribution of income: Falling poverty and ... convergence, period(*). Draft (October 9). http://www.columbia.edu/~xs23/papers/pdfs/World_Income_Distribution_QJE.pdf.

Sobel, Russell, J.R. Clark, and Dwight R. Lee. 2007. Freedom, barriers to entry, entrepreneurship, and economic progress. *The Review of Austrian Economics* 20 (4): 221–236.

Tattrie, Doug. 1999. *A financial incentive to encourage employment among repeat users of employment insurance: The earnings supplement project.* Ottawa: Social Research and Demonstration Corporation for Human Resource Development Canada.

Becoming a Trained Observer of Canada's Equalization Program

Brian K. MacLean and Michael Bradfield[1]

Introduction

When Canada's system of equalization payments[2] is the subject of newspaper headlines, the situation reveals much about equalization in Canada to the trained observer. The purpose of this chapter is to help you become a trained observer.

In February 2010, headlines such as "Equalization gives best public services to have-not provinces" (*Ottawa Citizen*) appeared in papers of the Canwest chain and also in the *Toronto Star* and *The Globe and Mail*. The headlines were triggered by a media release promoting *The Real Have-Nots in Confederation: Ontario, Alberta and British Columbia*, a public policy institute's latest report on equalization.[3]

The release recognizes that the "well-intentioned" equalization program of federal government transfers to provincial governments allows provinces to provide reasonably comparable public services. But it warns that the program has "adverse, unintended consequences," such as providing "an incentive for have-not provinces to spend more freely on government programs than they would if taxpayers elsewhere were not being forced to pick up part of the tab." It says British Columbia, Alberta, and Ontario now have lower levels of services than the so-called "have-not" provinces. Examples cited include:

- Nova Scotia and Quebec have more doctors per 100,000 people than British Columbia, Alberta, and Ontario do;
- New Brunswick, Prince Edward Island, Nova Scotia, Manitoba, and Quebec have more nurses per 100,000 people than Ontario, Alberta, and British Columbia do;
- Prince Edward Island, New Brunswick, Manitoba, and Nova Scotia have more long-term residential care beds per 100,000 people than Ontario, Alberta, and British Columbia do.

The media release declares that equalization "damages the entire country because it transfers excessive amounts from high productivity jurisdictions to those with lower levels." It recommends freezing equalization spending in the short term and that "all provinces should urge an end to transfers in return for GST revenue and other tax room as necessary in order to facilitate an end to the equalization program."

These claims were duly repeated in newspaper stories and columns, citing the "independent" Frontier Centre for Public Policy. Some gave the release a local twist: the *Toronto Star*, for example, carried the headline "Ontario loses in wealth-sharing plan."

It seems reporters and editors found the claims of the Frontier Centre sufficiently plausible that they did not investigate them. Judging from the comments sections of the online editions of the newspapers that ran stories, the typical reader took the claims of the Centre report at face value. But how would a trained observer evaluate these claims?

To the trained observer, this Frontier Centre report appears deceptive, seeking to undermine Canada's system of equalization. It is but one in a long line of misleading publications over the past two decades by a connected set of politically motivated policy institutes that dominate coverage and analysis of equalization in Canada's news media.[4]

To become a trained observer of equalization—someone not easily deceived by publications such as the Frontier Centre report—you need to arm yourself with the knowledge of relevant theories, history, institutions, and data.

We begin by situating the equalization program in Canadian history. In the second section we present evidence of the likely impact of equalization on interprovincial labour migration and convergence of provincial output per capita. The third section considers the economics of equalization. In the final section we consider the issue of which provinces receive equalization payments and whether they actually have higher levels of public services than other provinces.

Equalization in Historical Context

Canada's system of equalization has deep historical roots. When the country was established, the economy was based upon agriculture, forestry, and fisheries, and government focused on nation-building. The main responsibilities of the state were defence, immigration (naturalization of citizens), Indian affairs, interprovincial transportation (mainly interprovincial railways and canals), and international trade. These were assigned to the federal government by the *British North America Act*, along with sources of revenue to support its responsibilities through its authority for the "raising of Money by any Mode or System of Taxation."[5] The federal (Dominion) government relied heavily on indirect taxes: "For more than 50 years customs and excise duties provided the bulk of Dominion revenues; by 1913 they constituted over 90% of the total."[6]

The provinces were assigned limited responsibilities, including education, hospitals, and the "Management and Sale of the Public Lands belonging to the Province and of the Timber and Wood thereon." The permitted revenue sources of the provinces included direct taxation (then insignificant), various licences and fines, and borrowing. With time, and changes in the economy, it became clear that the revenue sources of the provinces were inadequate to their responsibilities (known in federal–provincial discussions as "vertical imbalance"), and that the provinces had substantially unequal abilities to raise revenue (known as "horizontal imbalance"). One solution was to have the federal government assume some of the responsibilities of the provinces. This occurred, for example, with various *British North America Acts*—one in 1940, by which the federal government acquired jurisdiction over unemployment insurance; one in 1951, which enabled the federal government to pass the *Old Age Security Act*; and one in 1964, which permitted the creation of the Canada Pension Plan.[7] This trend to a greater role for the federal government, however, has been reversed since the mid-1990s, with the federal government downloading responsibilities to the provinces. This is indicated by the decline of federal program expenses as a percentage of GDP, from an average of almost 18 percent over the 1970–1995 period to just under 13 percent over the 1995–2009 period.[8]

An alternative to a greater role for the federal government, represented early in the 20th century by the *British North America Act* of 1907, was for the federal government to transfer a portion of federal tax dollars to the provincial governments.[9] This was important during the Great Depression when some of the poorer provinces, including Saskatchewan and Alberta, were on the verge of bankruptcy, and ad hoc transfers from the federal government kept them afloat.[10]

Since the Great Depression, the transfer of federal tax dollars to provincial governments has been more systematic. Currently, there are three major federal transfer programs for the provinces: the Canada health transfer (CHT), the Canada social transfer (CST), and equalization. The CHT and CST support specific provincial expenditures such as health care and post-secondary education. Equalization payments are unconditional (they can be spent as the provinces see fit). For 2010–2011, total federal transfers to the provinces and territories will come to about $65 billion, of which about $14 billion will be equalization payments.[11]

The federal government created the equalization program in 1957 when it agreed to transfer shares of the personal income tax, the corporate income tax, and succession duties (inheritance taxes) to the provinces. As Courchene (2007, 23) has explained:

> these transfers were on a derivation basis, i.e., in line with what was actually collected in the various provinces; this meant that the richer provinces would receive larger per capita transfers. The federal solution to this resulting revenue

inequality was to launch Canada's formal Equalization Program, which, in its inaugural version, guaranteed that all provinces' revenues from these shares of the standard taxes would be brought up to the per capita level of the average of the richest two provinces.

The equalization program does not equalize up and down to a standard, but only equalizes up. A formula, which has changed from time to time, is used by the federal government to determine the per capita payment to each province. The formula takes into account the province's fiscal capacity—its ability to raise revenue. Roughly speaking, the per capita payment is lower the greater the fiscal capacity of the province relative to a measure of average fiscal capacity, currently the average fiscal capacity of all provinces. Provinces with the greatest fiscal capacity do not receive equalization payments but do receive the CHT and CST transfers, which are considerably larger in total than equalization payments.

The equalization formula is related to the commitment in section 36(2) of the *Constitution Act, 1982*: "Parliament and the government of Canada are committed to the principle of making equalization payments to ensure that provincial governments have sufficient revenues to provide reasonably comparable levels of public services at reasonably comparable levels of taxation."[12]

With this background, the trained observer can evaluate the suggestion in reports such as *The Real Have-Nots in Confederation* that the equalization program should be replaced by giving the provinces "GST revenue and other tax room." Providing the provinces with more tax room today would, as in 1957, generate larger per capita gains for provinces with higher per capita incomes. It would increase the horizontal imbalance among provincial governments that equalization is designed to address. It would not permit the provision of comparable levels of public services at comparable levels of taxation. Moreover, the transfer of tax room to the provinces fails to address the insurance function that the equalization provides—that is, the formula-based assistance that all provinces have been able to draw upon if their situation warrants it.

Trends in Provincial Net Migration and Provincial Output per Person

Reports such as *The Real Have-Nots in Confederation* suggest that Canada's equalization program impedes the convergence of output per worker and output per person to a common standard across provinces. These reports assume that differences in output per worker and output per person across regions (and even countries) should naturally erode over time through the operation of markets. If the evidence shows that they do not erode over time, then by assumption the evidence is not evidence of the failure of markets. By assumption, there must be something such as a government equalization program impeding the operation of markets.

An associated suggestion is that equalization prevents convergence by preventing labour migration from provinces with low output per worker (labour productivity) to regions with high output per worker.

The trained observer can evaluate such suggestions in light of three key facts about output per person and net migration across Canadian provinces.[13]

First, although reports such as *The Real Have-Nots in Confederation* create the impression that equalization results in little migration between Canadian provinces, actual migration flows are substantial. For example, in some years as a have-not province, Newfoundland (NL) lost a full percentage point of its population (see, for example, Table 1). Conversely, in its many years as a have province Alberta (AB) welcomed net migration from other provinces equalling or exceeding a full percentage point of Alberta's population (see, for example, Table 1). The long-term trend is that "have-not" provinces lost population to other provinces as the "have" provinces gained population from other provinces. There is also a cyclical element to net migration—for example, during the energy industry downturn of the early 1980s, Alberta experienced negative net migration when in-migrants from the previous boom returned home as opportunities dried up in Alberta.

Second, since 1957 there has been considerable convergence of per capita output across Canada's provinces. For example, in 1961 GDP per capita in the Atlantic provinces (Newfoundland, Prince Edward Island, New Brunswick, and Nova Scotia) was less than half that of Ontario, which was then the province with the highest GDP per capita.[14] By 2004, the GDP per capita of the Atlantic provinces was almost 79 percent of that of Ontario, as shown in Table 2.

TABLE 1 Provincial Net Migration Relative to Population, Canadian Provinces, 1981–1985 Versus 2004–2008

Year	NL	PE	NS	NB	QC	ON	MB	SK	AB	BC
1981	−0.99	−0.69	−0.23	−0.40	−0.39	−0.06	−0.25	−0.03	1.60	0.31
1982	0.32	0.51	0.44	0.50	−0.38	0.26	0.24	0.36	−0.49	−0.05
1983	−0.35	0.64	0.44	0.25	−0.26	0.40	0.03	0.21	−1.34	0.23
1984	−0.59	0.20	0.29	−0.09	−0.12	0.37	−0.06	−0.14	−0.87	−0.07
1985	−0.99	−0.06	−0.15	−0.26	−0.08	0.36	−0.21	−0.68	−0.16	−0.15
2004	−0.72	−0.10	−0.32	−0.28	−0.07	−0.09	−0.62	−0.95	1.06	0.20
2005	−0.84	−0.46	−0.32	−0.47	−0.12	−0.14	−0.67	−0.71	1.38	0.21
2006	−0.80	−0.62	−0.44	−0.35	−0.17	−0.16	−0.46	0.16	0.99	0.35
2007	−0.10	−0.21	−0.19	−0.12	−0.15	−0.12	−0.31	0.42	0.44	0.34
2008	0.46	−0.40	−0.13	−0.07	−0.14	−0.14	−0.13	0.41	0.64	0.11

Source: Adapted from Statistics Canada series on net migration from CANSIM table 510018 and population from table 051-0001. Minus signs indicate net population outflows.

TABLE 2   Evidence of Convergence of GDP per Capita Across Canadian Regions

Region/province	GDP per capita as percentage of Ontario GDP per capita	
	1961	2004
Atlantic	49.7	78.6
Quebec	74.4	84.8
Manitoba-Saskatchewan	70.5	89.2

Note: Comparisons across jurisdictions between two points in time do not give a completely accurate picture of convergence because of the statistical phenomenon of "regression toward the mean." See, for example, Smith (1998).

Source: Steven Gordon 2005, "Convergence in Canada," *Worthwhile Canadian Initiative* blog, November 11, http://worthwhile.typepad.com/worthwhile_canadian_initi/2005/11/convergence_in_.html.

Table 3 provides the Atlantic provinces' GDP per capita as a percentage of the Canadian average for 1981–1985 and for 2004–2008. In each of the four provinces, GDP per capita rose relative to the Canadian average.[15]

Third, provinces have also moved from "have-not" to "have" status and vice versa. Every Canadian province has been a "have-not" province at one time. British Columbia received equalization payments from 1957 to 1962 and again in 1999 to 2007.[16] Historically, Alberta received equalization payments when the equalization program was established in 1957. By the mid-1960s, with the development of its energy resources and help from the National Oil Policy, Alberta had graduated to "have" status. More recently, Newfoundland and Saskatchewan graduated to "have" status, again thanks to non-renewable natural resources. But the resources boom, of which the energy boom is the main component, produced a very strong Canadian dollar.[17] In recent years, Ontario has had a "difficult time with its manufacturing industry because of the rising value of the Canadian dollar."[18] For this and other reasons, Ontario moved to "have-not" status and qualified for almost $1 billion in equalization payments in fiscal year 2010–2011.[19]

These are three facts about labour migration and changes in provincial output per capita known by a trained observer. They do not suggest that the equalization program has impeded labour migration across provinces or hindered the convergence of GDP per capita among provinces.

Before proceeding to the next section, we should address a claim by critics of equalization that out-migration from lower-income regions is good, and the more of it the better. There is a standard economic model that points to gains from labour migration both to regions that lose population and those that gain. The model is based on the assumption of competitive labour markets in both regions.

But, as is often the case in lagging regions, when employers have market power in the labour market, the standard model leads to different conclusions. When

TABLE 3 **Provincial GDP per Capita as a Percentage of the Canadian Average, Atlantic Provinces, 1981–1985 Versus 2004–2008**

	Newfoundland	PEI	Nova Scotia	New Brunswick
1981	61.7	59.5	64.2	61.9
1982	64.6	61.7	70.7	65.9
1983	63.8	66.8	73.6	69.4
1984	62.6	62.5	74.2	69.7
1985	61.1	60.2	74.4	68.9
2004	92.8	71.6	78.6	78.2
2005	100.2	69.6	78.1	77.6
2006	114.8	69.3	76.1	78.0
2007	124.0	69.8	75.6	77.8
2008	128.6	69.1	76.0	76.3

Source: Adapted from Statistics Canada CANSIM table 3840001 on GDP and table 051-0001 on population.

employers have market power (the extreme case of a single buyer of labour is called monopsony) wages are depressed below the worker's productivity. Under this condition, migration to higher-paying regions can decrease overall productivity since it means that workers are migrating to jobs where their productivity will be lower than it was in the jobs they left.[20] Moreover, the standard model does not take into account the psychic costs associated with the separation from families and friends that goes along with migration.

The Economics of Equalization

Two major theories predict that Canada's equalization program should foster economic growth, and one questionable model suggests that equalization may impair growth. To the extent that they touch upon the economics of equalization, reports such as *The Real Have-Nots in Confederation* tend to draw only on the questionable model and to ignore the two major theories that support equalization.

Roughly speaking, the questionable model is one in which the objective of each province is to maximize its revenue, but if a province receives equalization payments its incentive to develop its economy and thereby increase its own-source revenue is weakened. The argument is that the incentives facing the provincial government are perverse because an increase in the province's own-source revenue will be offset by a reduction in equalization payments.

Even granting the assumption that provincial governments are focused on their revenue, the model neglects the fact that equalization payments are calculated on a per capita basis. A province concerned with revenue maximization will be concerned with economic growth because economic growth enables a province to attract more population, and more population, even without more revenue per capita, means more total revenue.[21]

The major logical problem with the model, however, is that provincial governments do not seek to maximize revenue. Governments seek to be re-elected, and voters care about incomes and jobs, not just about the revenues that make public services possible. The other major problem with the model is empirical—statistical testing suggests that the model has no practical relevance.[22]

One major theory that Canada's equalization program fosters economic growth is based on the idea that "reasonably comparable levels of public services at reasonably comparable levels of taxation" work to ensure that interprovincial migration occurs in search of genuine economic opportunities. For example, migration tends to occur in search of higher-paying, higher-productivity jobs rather than in search of lower-paying, lower-productivity jobs in a province that offers lower taxes and/or more generous public services that more than offset the lower pay. The seminal model (Boadway and Flatters 1982) supporting this theory is summarized as: "[Under equalization] economic migration, moving to follow opportunity, is encouraged, but fiscal migration, moving to find a government with deeper fiscal pockets, is not."[23] Wilson (2003) finds support for the Boadway and Flatters model in the form of a benefit–cost ratio of 1.6 for the equalization program.[24]

The other major theory relating to equalization and growth, probably the more important one, is based on the fact that provinces are responsible, among other things, for expenditures on education, health, and provincial infrastructure, all of which are important for productivity levels and growth. A properly functioning equalization program ensures that there are no areas of the country where these productivity-enhancing expenditures are seriously underfunded. Education is particularly important for productivity, and the years in which the equalization program has been in place have seen dramatic improvements in, and greater equality of, educational attainment across all provinces.[25]

Equalization, Provincial Services, and Taxation

Reports opposing equalization argue that Canada's equalization program is unfair. The innovation of *The Real Have-Nots in Confederation* is to use indicators of provincial services, particularly on health care, to claim that equalization allows residents of "have-not" provinces to have public services that are superior to the "have" provinces of Ontario, Alberta, and British Columbia.

There are at least four problems with this claim. First, although Alberta has been a "have" province since the mid-1960s, Ontario is currently a "have-not" province, British Columbia was a "have-not" province as recently as 1999–2007, and both Newfoundland and Saskatchewan are currently "have" provinces. The provinces compared are not really "have" versus "have-not" provinces but two groups: Alberta, British Columbia, and Ontario as one group versus Quebec, Manitoba, and the Maritimes as the other group.

Second, health-care spending very much depends on the demographic composition of a province. Provinces with a higher percentage of older residents tend to have higher health-care spending, and the two groups of provinces have different demographic compositions. For example, to take extremes, 46.3 percent of Nova Scotia's population was 45 years and over in 2009 compared with only 36.2 percent of Alberta's population. The correlation is not perfect, but provinces that tend to experience net population outflow to other provinces also tend to have a higher proportion of older residents.

Third, the proper way to compare public services across provinces is not to pick and choose indicators in accordance with the point one would like to prove, but to use aggregate statistics on program expenditure by provinces.[26] As Figure 1 shows, program expenditures per capita are not highest in "have-not" provinces—Quebec, for example, ranks ninth among the ten provinces. Program expenditures per capita tend to be highest in high-income provinces with substantial revenues from non-renewable resources—Newfoundland, Alberta, and Saskatchewan are among the top four spenders. Alberta drew upon non-renewable resource revenue

FIGURE 1 Program Expenditures per Capita, Canadian Provinces, 2008–9

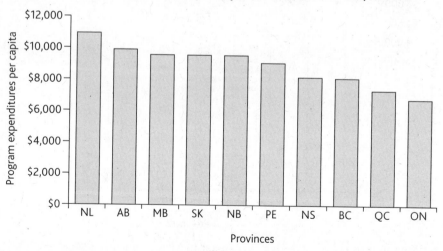

Source: Population data from CANSIM table 051-0001; program expenditures from Department of Finance Canada, Fiscal Reference Tables, Provincial and Territorial Governments Public Accounts, tables 17 to 26, http://www.fin.gc.ca/frt-trf/2009/frt0904-eng.asp.

for $12 billion of its $36 billion total revenue for 2008–9, a particularly good year for resource revenue.[27] Saskatchewan received $4.6 billion of non-renewable resource revenue out of $12.1 billion of total revenue,[28] and Newfoundland received offshore royalties equal to $2.5 billion of its $8.1 billion total revenue.[29]

Fourth, public services provided by provinces are supported not just by equalization payments or other federal payments, but by own-source revenues (including revenues from non-renewable resources). Therefore, to understand the level of public services provided by a province, we have to look at its own-source revenues. Figure 2, based on Alberta government data in its 2007 budget, indicates that Alberta, BC, and Ontario have the lowest taxes, and Quebec has the highest. This fits the facts about income taxes and sales taxes across provinces. Alberta has the lowest provincial income tax rate—a flat tax of 10 percent; Ontario's highest marginal rate for provincial income tax is 11.2 percent; and BC's top rate is 14.7 percent. The rest of the provinces have top marginal rates of 15 percent or more, with Quebec's top marginal rate being 24 percent.[30] Sales taxes are more equal across most provinces but range from 5 percent combined (0 percent provincial; 5 percent federal) in Alberta to 15.5 percent combined in Prince Edward Island.

Some people, who would rather not pay taxes, seem to think of taxes as always being wasted. But taxes are the basis for program expenditures, including at the provincial level, at least for governments that cannot function on the basis of non-renewable resource revenue.

FIGURE 2   Canadian Provincial Taxes per Capita Relative to Alberta, 2007

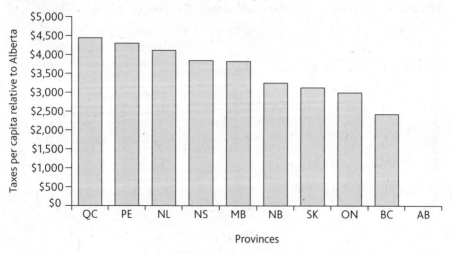

Note: For all provinces except Quebec, the rates can be found at http://www.cra-arc.gc.ca/tx/ndvdls/fq/txrts-eng.html. For Quebec, the rates can be found at http://www.revenu.gouv.qc.ca/en/ministere/default.aspx.

Conclusion

There are problems with Canada's equalization system and the broader system of federal–provincial fiscal relations. Many problems arise because non-renewable resources, especially oil and gas, are not significantly controlled by the federal government, as is the case in many federal countries.[31] One of these problems, destined to grow in importance, involves dealing with greenhouse gas emissions on a national basis.[32] Another problem is that, as the country has become extremely decentralized, major provinces engage in competition to have the lowest income tax rates (Ontario, British Columbia, and Alberta) and royalty competition (Alberta, Saskatchewan) that benefits corporations, including oil and gas producers, at the expense of other taxpayers.[33]

In Canada, there are research institutes that contribute to our understanding of the equalization program and the broader system of federal–provincial fiscal relations, notably, the Institute for Research on Public Policy (IRPP) and the Canadian Centre for Policy Alternatives (CCPA).

But the news media pay far greater attention to the barrage of misleading but well-marketed material issued by a set of corporate-funded policy institutes, which includes the Frontier Centre for Public Policy and the Atlantic Institute for Market Studies.[34] We hope this chapter arms you with the knowledge you need to avoid being deceived by such institutions.

NOTES

1. We would like to thank Hassan Bougrine, Kathleen Stokes, and Erin Weir for valuable feedback on this chapter and Sudbury mayor and former MP John Rodriguez for kindly answering questions on intergovernmental fiscal relations. We are fully responsible for any remaining errors.
2. There is a counterpart program involving Yukon, the Northwest Territories, and Nunavut called territorial formula financing (TFF). The per capita transfers to the territories under TFF are large multiples of the highest per capita transfers to provinces, but the 2009 total population of the territories was only about 109,300, or a third of a percentage point of Canada's total population. For a description of TFF, see http://www.fin.gc.ca/fedprov/tff-eng.asp.
3. The media release can be found at http://www.fcpp.org/publication.php/3197.
4. The institutes are the Atlantic Institute for Market Studies (AIMS) (Nova Scotia), the Montreal Economic Institute (Quebec), the C.D. Howe Institute (Ontario), the Frontier Centre for Public Policy (Manitoba, Saskatchewan, and Alberta, but often presented as Winnipeg-based), the Canada West Foundation (Alberta, with staff in all four western provinces), and the Fraser Institute (British Columbia). They are funded by corporations, the Donner Canadian Foundation, and the Max Bell Foundation. The C.D. Howe Institute,

the Canada West Foundation, and the Fraser Institute are the more established of the six. The C.D. Howe Institute, though it shares the goals of the others, produces higher-quality research, and it and the Canada West Foundation are not as obviously ideological as the others. The others interact with the Canadian Taxpayers Federation and the Alliance wing of the Conservative Party (including current Prime Minister Stephen Harper, co-author of the infamous "firewall letter" and critic of the "culture of defeat"). A key function of AIMS, the Montreal Economic Institute, and the Frontier Centre is to create the misleading impression of local experts in have-not provinces who oppose equalization and the supposedly wasteful social programs it facilitates. AIMS has a list of like-minded institutes at http://www.aims.ca/inside. asp?cmPageID=309. We have previously critiqued material on equalization from these institutes in Bradfield (1997) and MacLean (2001).

5. See http://thecanadianencyclopedia.com/index.cfm?PgNm=TCE&Params=A1 ARTA001001.

6. George Carter. Taxation. *The Canadian Encyclopedia,* http://www.thecanadianencyclopedia.com/index.cfm?PgNm=TCE&Params =A1ARTA0007883.

7. See http://en.wikipedia.org/wiki/British_North_America_Acts.

8. See http://www.fin.gc.ca/frt-trf/2009/frt0901-eng.asp#tbl2. Many provinces, in turn, downloaded responsibilities to their municipalities.

9. A corresponding system operates within each province—the provincial governments provide transfers to their respective local governments. For example, Ontario has a municipal partnership fund (http://www.fin.gov.on.ca/ en/budget/ompf/2010/techguide.html#i2) with an explicit equalization component and Alberta has a municipal grants program (http://www.municipalaffairs.alberta.ca/mc_municipal_grants.cfm).

10. See Belanger (2001).

11. See http://www.fin.gc.ca/fedprov/mtp-eng.asp.

12. The equalization program was never intended to be sufficient to eliminate regional disparities in Canada. Section 36(1) of the *Constitution Act, 1982* implies that the reduction of regional disparities requires programs beyond equalization. For more on this issue, see Ryan (2002).

13. Output per person is typically measured by GDP/population. Output per worker is measured as GDP/employment. The connection between the two measures is that GDP/population = (GDP/employment)*(employment/ population). That is, for a given employment/population ratio, changes in GDP/population will equal changes in GDP/employment.

14. The year 1961 is used rather than 1957 because the GDP series from the current version of Statistics Canada's CANSIM database only goes back to 1961.

15. The most significant exception to the pattern of convergence is that with higher oil prices Alberta has been pulling away from the rest of the provinces, reaching a level of GDP per capita in 2008 almost 70 percent above the Canadian average.

16. For example, British Columbia received $590 million in 2005–6 and $459 million in 2006–7. See http://www.fin.gc.ca/fedprov/mtp-eng.asp#BritishColumbia.

17. See, for example, Stanford (2009).

18. CTV.ca News Staff. 2008. Historic first: Ontario in, N.L. out of equalization. November 3, http://www.ctv.ca/servlet/ArticleNews/story/CTVNews/20081103/Flaherty_ministers_081103/20081103/.

19. Ontario's equalization payments for 2010–11 are given at: http://www.fin.gc.ca/fedprov/eqp-eng.asp.

20. See Bradfield (1990). For an empirical demonstration of the relevance of employer power in the labour markets of lagging regions, see Hirsch et al. (2009).

21. This argument is presented in a paper by Annette Ryan cited by Cavlovic and Day (2003).

22. See Cavlovic and Day (2003).

23. Ryan (2002, 11).

24. Wilson's paper re-examines the migration data employed in a previously influential paper that had mistakenly arrived at a much lower benefit-cost ratio for the equalization program in the 1970s.

25. For a comparison of educational attainment across provinces from the most recent census, see http://www40.statcan.gc.ca/l01/cst01/educ41a-eng.htm. For statistics on the dramatic increase in educational attainment in Newfoundland over the period from 1976 (when more than 70 percent of the Newfoundland population had not completed high school) to 1996, see http://www.ed.gov.nl.ca/edu/publications/archives/indicators98/CHAPT3.PDF.

26. See also the comparison of provincial government health expenditures per capita in Government of Alberta, *Budget 2007 fiscal plan*, http://www.finance.alberta.ca/publications/budget/budget2007/fiscal.pdf, 18, which ranks Alberta the highest and Prince Edward Island and Quebec the lowest.

27. See Government of Alberta, *Budget 2010, 2010–2013 fiscal plan revenue outlook*, http://www.finance.alberta.ca/publications/budget/budget2010/fiscal-plan-revenue.pdf.

28. See Government of Saskatchewan, *Saskatchewan provincial budget, 09–10*, http://www.finance.gov.sk.ca/budget2009-10/Budget200910Estimates.pdf, 14.

29. Government of Newfoundland and Labrador, *Estimates of the program expenditure and revenue of the consolidated revenue fund 2009–10*, http://www.budget.gov.nl.ca/budget2009/estimates/estimates2009.pdf.

30. Erin Weir has kindly pointed out to us that Ontario has a personal income surtax that effectively makes the top marginal income tax rate more like 15 percent.

31. Derived from Government of Alberta, *Budget 2007 fiscal plan*, 30, http://www.finance.alberta.ca/publications/budget/budget2007/fiscal.pdf.

32. See, for example, http://www.forumfed.org/en/global/thematic/Oil_Gas_Template.pdf.

33. See Courchene (2008, especially 13–15) for a discussion of key issues.
34. The latest development is Alberta's reversal of its increase in conventional oil and gas royalties. See, for example, Weir (2010).

DISCUSSION QUESTIONS

1. What do the terms "horizontal imbalance" and "vertical imbalance" mean in the context of federal–provincial fiscal relations? Does the transfer of "tax room" to the provinces deal with "horizontal imbalance"?

2. In what sense does Canada's equalization program perform an insurance function for provincial governments?

3. Explain two reasons or theories why an equalization program could contribute to the economic growth of a country.

4. Give at least two reasons why it is misleading to claim that equalization gives the best public services to "have-not" provinces.

5. Discuss how the following quotation (from Black and Silver 2004, 13) relates to Canada's equalization program: "Disproportionate numbers of interprovincial migrants tend to be in the age range most likely to be employed. Provinces losing such people through migration incur two main costs. First, such individuals are likely to be paying more in taxes than they receive in benefits. Second, the province is likely to have made significant investments in their education and training. When these individuals leave the province, the expected return from that investment in the form of increased productivity and earnings is lost. The provinces to which they move reap that gain, at no cost."

6. Mcnutt and Marchildon (2009, 229–231) examine website traffic and links to analyze the impact of various policy institutes on equalization policy debates in Canada, and find that, even compared with debates on other policy issues, the impact of what the authors label as "free market," "conservative," or "right-wing" institutes is especially large compared with centrist or left-wing ones. (What the authors have in mind as right-wing institutes corresponds closely to the list of institutes mentioned in note 4.) Mcnutt and Marchildon recognize that the greater attention that the right-wing institutes devote to equalization is difficult to explain in terms of ideology and is not completely explained by the greater attention that the right-wing institutes typically devote to economic issues. Why do right-wing institutes such as the Atlantic Institute for Market Studies, the Frontier Centre for Public Policy, and the Fraser Institute devote so much attention to Canada's equalization program?

SUGGESTED READINGS

Black, Errol, and Jim Silver. 2004. *Equalization: Financing Canadians' commitment to sharing and social solidarity.* Canadian Centre for Policy Alternatives, http://www.policyalternatives.ca/sites/default/files/uploads/publications/Nova_Scotia_Pubs/NSequalization.pdf.

Courchene, Thomas J. 2007. A short history of equalization. *Policy Options* (March) 22–29. http://www.irpp.org/po/archive/mar07/courchene.pdf.

Osberg, Lars. 2005. Equalization—A family history. *Halifax Chronicle Herald*, April 6. Posted by Marc Lee, Progressive Economics Forum blog, http://www.progressive-economics.ca/2006/06/09/equalization---a-family-history/.

Ryan, Annette. 2002. Equalization: Neither welfare trap nor helping hand. Conference paper (April). http://www.aims.ca/library/welfare.pdf.

ONLINE RESOURCES

A very brief, up-to-date description of the equalization program from the federal government perspective can be found on the Finance Canada website at http://www.fin.gc.ca/fedprov/eqp-eng.asp.

For blog posts dating from mid-2006 to the present on equalization issues from a social democratic perspective, see posts tagged with "equalization" (http://www.progressive-economics.ca/category/equalization/) and "fiscal imbalance" (http://www.progressive-economics.ca/category/fiscal-imbalance/) on the Progressive Economics Forum blog.

The Expert Panel on Equalization and Territorial Formula Financing produced the O'Brien report in 2006. The research commissioned by the panel and the report itself are available on the panel's website at http://www.eqtff-pfft.ca/english/index.asp. The website includes a detailed listing of Canadian research papers on equalization up to about 2006: see http://www.eqtff-pfft.ca/english/EQTreasury/bibliography.asp.

Research papers on equalization from the Institute for Research on Public Policy are listed under "Canadian federalism" at http://www.irpp.org/research/re_fed.asp.

REFERENCES

Bélanger, Claude. 2001. The Rowell-Sirois report and Canadian federalism during the Great Depression (1929–1939), http://faculty.marianopolis.edu/c.belanger/quebechistory/federal/rowell.htm.

Boadway, Robin W., and Frank R. Flatters. 1982. Efficiency and equalization payments in a federal system of government: A synthesis and extension of recent results. *Canadian Journal of Economics* 15: 613–633.

Bradfield, Michael. 1990. Long-run equilibrium under pure monopsony. *Canadian Journal of Economics* 23 (3): 700–704.

Bradfield, Michael. 1997. Review of *Looking the gift horse in the mouth: The impact of federal transfers on Atlantic Canada* by Fred McMahon. *Canadian Journal of Regional Science* 20 (3): 435. http://www.lib.unb.ca/Texts/CJRS/bin/get.cgi?dir ectory=Fall97/&filename=Bradfield.htm.

Cavlovic, Ann, and Kathleen Day. 2003. Equalization and the incentives for growth: An empirical investigation of the "tax-back" effect. Department of Finance Canada, Working Paper 2003: 23.

Courchene, Thomas. 2008. Climate change, competitiveness, and environmental federalism: The case for a carbon tax. June 3: 1–22. http://www.irpp.org/ miscpubs/archive/tjc_canada2020.pdf.

Eisen, Ben, and Mark Milke. 2010. *The real have-nots in confederation: Ontario, Alberta and British Columbia.* Frontier Centre for Public Policy Series 83, February. http://www.fcpp.org/files/1/10-02-24-Equalization%20FINAL.pdf.

Hirsch, Boris, Marion König, and Joachim Möller. 2009. *Is there a gap in the gap?* Institute for the Study of Labour Discussion Paper Series. IZA DP No. 4231. June: 1–29.

MacLean, Brian K. 2001. Equalization's predictably distorted image. *National Post.* June 11: C19.

Mcnutt, Kathleen, and Gregory Marchildon. 2009. Think tanks and the web: Measuring visibility and influence. *Canadian Public Policy* 35 (2): 219–237.

Ryan, Annette. 2002. Equalization: Neither welfare trap nor helping hand. Conference paper (April). http://www.aims.ca/library/welfare.pdf.

Smith, Gary. 1998. *Introduction to statistical reasoning.* Boston: WCB McGraw Hill.

Stanford, Jim, 2009. Loonie out of control. Progressive Economics Forum blog. October 13. http://www.progressive-economics.ca/2009/10/13/ loonie-out-of-control/.

Weir, Erin. 2010. Goofy oil-industry advocacy. Progressive Economics Forum blog. March 13. http://www.progressive-economics.ca/2010/03/13/ goofy-oil-industry-advocacy/.

Wilson, L.S. 2003. Equalization, efficiency and migration: Watson revisited. *Canadian Public Policy* 29 (4): 385–396.

Glossary

Access to information
The right of citizens to obtain information from the government regarding its activities, unless public release of the information is not in the public interest or may constitute a threat to national security. The objective of access to information legislation is to increase the accountability of government and the transparency of its operations, although on "national security" or other grounds governments have often attempted to prevent the release of information that might prove embarrassing to the government.

Affirmative action
Legislation enacted to limit the effects of discrimination in the labour market against certain groups such as women and people of colour by increasing access for them to jobs in which they are generally under-represented.

Antitrust laws
See *Competition policy*.

Big government
A term used, often pejoratively, to describe a situation in which the government plays a significant direct role in the economy, through the provision of public services such as health, education, and public infrastructure; redistribution of income to support the poor and the unemployed; and regulation of private industry.

Capital controversy
A theoretical debate focused on the neoclassical concept of capital, particularly the marginal productivity theory of distribution, initiated in the late 1950s by the critical analyses of economists including Joan Robinson and Piero Sraffa of Cambridge University, in which the neoclassical concept was defended and refined by economists such as Paul Samuelson and Robert Solow at MIT in Cambridge, Massachusetts.

Capital formation
Another term for investment; the creation of new productive equipment, buildings, and infrastructure, sometimes extended to include education and skills training as "human capital" formation.

Causal analysis
An attempt to explain why specified events occur, in terms of a model that assumes that changes in one or more variables will result in determinate changes in other variables (linear causality) or that changes in two or more variables are mutually conditioned by their interaction (dialectical causality).

Classical economics

The school of economics—associated with writers like Adam Smith, Thomas Malthus, and David Ricardo—that flourished in the 18th and 19th centuries, and provided much of the foundation for modern neoclassical economics. Classical economists focused on the sources of economic growth, the determination of the relative value of commodities in exchange, and the distribution of income among social-economic classes.

Competition policy

Government acts and regulations—of which the most important in Canada is the *Competition Act*—designed to prevent excessive industrial concentration and anti-competitive practices on the part of firms, and to ensure that consumers are provided by firms with accurate information regarding the composition and characteristics of marketed commodities.

Competitive conditions

The model of *perfect competition* in a market assumes that there is a standardized or homogeneous product, that buyers and sellers are price-takers, that there is free entry into and exit from the market, and there is *perfect information* on the part of buyers and sellers. These conditions are never completely met in real-world markets, but the term is often used to describe markets that roughly fulfill these definitional criteria.

Conspicuous consumption

A term coined by the critical economist Thorstein Veblen to describe individuals' ostentatious use of luxury items, not for their intrinsic want-satisfying characteristics but in order to gain status by showing that one is wealthy enough to consume them. Veblen also argued that *conspicuous leisure* and *conspicuous waste* performed a similar function.

Consumer's free choice

The view that consumers are never forced to purchase anything in an exchange relationship, because they always have the freedom simply to refuse a proposed exchange that does not benefit them.

Consumption externalities

In contrast to the strict rational self-interest model of economic behaviour, such externalities occur when one person's level of consumption affects the utility or level of satisfaction of another person. Examples include *positive* externalities—as with altruism, where one person makes an unrequited gift to another person in need because improving the other's welfare makes the first person happier—and *negative* externalities, as with envy, where greater consumption by one person makes another, envious, person less satisfied. As well, one person's cigarette smoking can cause negative consumption externalities for those in the person's vicinity, while another's passion for her gardening hobby results in positive consumption externalities and pleasure for a whole neighbourhood.

Cumulative causation

Process whereby an initial change in one variable results in a change in another variable that results in a further change in the first variable that changes the second variable, and so on. Examples include multiplier processes, arms races, "vicious cycles," and "virtuous cycles." In regional economics, the cumulative causation theory maintains that once regional economic disparities emerge, they tend to be self-perpetuating because they lead to reactions that intensify the initial inequalities.

Debt instruments
Written promises to repay a debt—normally the principal (the original amount of the loan) plus interest—including government and corporate bonds, treasury bills, and certificates of deposit.

Deregulation
Reduction or elimination of government laws, regulations, and controls on industry, in the belief that the resultant "streamlining" will improve economic efficiency and that competitive market forces will provide sufficient discipline on firms.

Ecological debt
Has two main senses: (1) the accumulated global deficit, in resource depletion and environmental degradation, relative to a *sustainable* growth path; (2) the net difference between the ecological damage caused *by* a given country and the ecological damage caused *to it* by its actions and those of other countries. In the second sense, a country that causes more damage than it sustains is an ecological *debtor*; if the reverse is true, it is an ecological *creditor*. It has been estimated that the *ecological* debt of the industrialized nations to the less-developed countries (LDCs) exceeds the total *financial* debt of LDCs to the industrialized world.

Economic cost
A concept of production cost that takes account not only of accounting costs (costs reflected in monetary flows) but also of the *opportunity cost* of resources used in production. For example, if a self-employed businesswoman could earn $50,000 in another, equally satisfying job, if she pays herself no salary, and if her business shows an accounting profit of $40,000, then she is actually making an *economic loss* of $10,000.

Economic efficiency
A condition in which, with given prices, output is produced at minimum cost; the incremental (or marginal) cost of each output is equal to its price for all commodities; and for each consumer the ratio of the satisfaction provided by the last unit of each commodity consumed to its price is equal.

Economic rent
In neoclassical theory, the difference between the payment received by the owner of a productive input in exchange for its use and the minimum amount of money for which the owner would willingly have provided it.

Economies of scale
Refers to increases in productivity and cost-saving opportunities, with corresponding reductions in cost per unit, as the level of a firm's output increases.

Elasticity of the demand curve
A measure of the degree of responsiveness of the quantity demanded to changes in the determinants of demand, such as the good's own price (own-price elasticity), the consumer's income (income elasticity), and the prices of other goods (cross-price elasticity). Measured as a ratio of the percentage change in quantity demanded to the percentage change in the relevant determinant, holding other determinants constant.

Emissions permits
A means of controlling the total volume of pollution (emissions) produced by an industry or industries. Firms are required to have permits equal to the quantity of pollutants they emit. The permits may be allocated by assignment or sold by the government at competitive auctions. In some cases, the permits may be transferred or traded among firms.

Environment
The natural—geological, climatic, and resource—basis of human activity.

Environmental externalities
Effects of human production activity on the environment not reflected in market prices, leading to a divergence between the *private* cost of the outputs produced (their market price) and their *social* cost (their market price *plus* the non-priced pollution cost per unit).

Equity
A share in the ownership of an enterprise—for example, in the form of stocks—as distinct from *debt*, which is incurred as the result of a loan to the enterprise.

Ex post
"After the fact," *actual* values of a variable, as distinct from *ex ante* ("before the fact"), *anticipated* values of the variable.

Externalities
See *Consumption externalities, Environmental externalities,* and *Production externalities.*

Fiscal federalism
A system of government finance involving taxation and expenditure at federal, provincial, and municipal levels and coordinated transfers of funds between governmental levels.

Forecasting
Estimation of the future values and behaviour of particular variables such as the rate of interest, the value of the dollar, or the price of a commodity, using business and consumer surveys, focus groups, or formal economic models and econometric techniques.

Foreign ownership
Refers to corporations that are wholly or partially owned by foreign investors.

Free enterprise
An approach to business that emphasizes the freedom of private individuals or firms to operate with minimal government regulation or control.

Full cost pricing
Determining the price of a firm's output by adding an allowance for overhead costs and a profit margin to the direct costs per unit of output, typically allowing for less than maximum (full-capacity) production over the period. Sometimes referred to as "markup pricing."

Globalization
The process of increasing economic and social integration among countries, usually through trade and investment, leading to the emergence of a single global market.

Government regulation of foreign investment
Policies whereby acquisition of ownership or control of domestic firms by foreign-based firms is subject to government restrictions and conditions, sometimes involving a formal review process before acquisitions are approved.

Growth maximization
An alternative to the hypothesis that firms aim at profit-maximization; according to growth maximization theory, firms characterized by a separation between owners (shareholders) and managers aim to maximize the rate of growth of the firm's sales revenue.

Historical growth of government
From the late 1800s to about 1990 in Canada, the share of gross domestic product accounted for by the total expenditures of all levels of government followed a generally upward trend. In recent decades, however, there has been a significant relative contraction of the government sector.

Informational property rights (or Intellectual property rights)
Government protection—through means such as patents, copyright, and trademark registration—afforded to the creator of intangible property (or to an entity, such as a corporation, to which the rights have been transferred), which entitles the owner to determine the conditions under which it may be legally used and to receive remuneration for its use.

Interdependent utility functions
Utility functions in which individuals' levels of satisfaction are determined not exclusively by their own consumption of goods but also by the consumption or the utility levels of others (as in cases of altruism or envy).

Kyoto Protocol
An agreement to combat global warming adopted in Kyoto, Japan in December 1997, which came into force in February 2005, setting supposedly legally binding targets for reduction of greenhouse gas emissions by the European Economic Community and other industrialized nations. Emissions were to decrease on average by about 5 percent of their 1990 levels by 2008–2012.

Labour market
The market in which those seeking employment by firms, households, and individuals offer to provide their labour services in exchange for wages, salaries, and other benefits. The term is used in relation to particular geographical markets (for example, the Sudbury labour market), particular occupations (the market for electricians), and for the aggregate of all such particular labour markets (the Canadian labour market).

Laissez-faire
The economic doctrine that advocates limited government involvement in the economy and stresses the importance of economic freedom (free market and free enterprise) in achieving the best social outcome.

Lexicographic preference ordering
A decision rule that (in the case of two goods, X and Y) says "If a bundle A has more X than all other bundles, choose bundle A, regardless of how much Y any other bundle has. If two or more bundles have the same amount of X, then choose the bundle with the greatest amount of Y." The rule can also be extended to the case of more than two goods.

Logic
The study of the principles or rules of deductive reasoning, and the application of such rules.

Managerial decision making
If the owners of a firm make decisions on broad policy objectives and hire managers to implement these decisions, then managerial decision making relates to implementation of the *owners'* plans. If there is a degree of separation between owners and managers and the interests of managers and owners do not completely coincide, then managerial decisions may be taken to achieve the *managers'* objectives, rather than those of the owners.

Marginal cost
The cost of the last unit of output produced. With marginal cost pricing in competitive markets, products are sold at their marginal cost.

Marginal productivity
The increase in a firm's output that results from adding one additional unit of a particular type of input, holding all other inputs constant. Marginal productivity theory claims that with perfect competition in all markets, workers are paid according to their marginal productivity.

Marginal utility of consumption
The additional utility or satisfaction received by consuming one additional unit of a given good or service.

Market as a rationing device
The hypothesis that—given an initial distribution of resources among economic agents—the interaction between supply and demand will allocate commodities efficiently, so that those who are willing to pay the most to acquire a commodity are the ones who do acquire it.

Market efficiency
See *Economic efficiency.*

Market failure
A situation in which markets fail to produce economically efficient results. Causes of market failure include ignorance or imperfect information, monopoly or collusive behaviour among firms, the existence of public goods, and positive and negative consumption and production externalities.

Market structure
A method of categorizing markets in terms of the number and behaviour of buyers and sellers and the ease of entry into and exit from the market. On the supply side of the market, the following four types are normally identified: monopoly (single, price-setting seller), oligopoly (few, strategically interdependent sellers); monopolistic competition (larger number of differentiated sellers, each with some price-setting power); and perfect competition (large number of price-taking firms). On the demand side, the three types commonly identified are monopsony, oligopsony, and perfect competition.

Markup pricing
See *Full cost pricing.*

Mathematical modelling
The use of formal quantitative models for purposes of hypothesis testing and prediction, often using econometric techniques.

Mercantilism
A school of economic thought prominent from the 16th to the 18th century, which emphasized the importance of a "favourable" balance of trade (a surplus of exports over imports), and the acquisition of colonies as markets and sources of raw materials.

Minimum wage
By law, the lowest amount of money an employer can pay to an employee for one hour of work. In Canada, it is set by each provincial government for its province.

Monopoly
A market structure dominated by a single supplier.

Natural monopolies (see also *Monopoly*)
These arise in industries where there are increasing returns to scale, so that the long-run cost per unit of output declines continuously as output increases, and provision of the commodity to the market by more than one firm would therefore raise the cost per unit and result in an inefficient use of resources. Because of the lack of effective competition, such industries are usually government-regulated.

Negative income tax
Within a comprehensive progressive tax/transfer system, this provides an after-tax transfer in some proportion to income for those individuals or households earning an income below the poverty line. The objective is to ensure that all individuals receive a minimum after-tax income, while creating labour-market incentives to work.

Neoclassical economics
Also known as "marginalist" economics, currently the orthodox or mainstream variety of economic theory; it originated in the 1870s, with the work of economists like Stanley Jevons, Léon Walras, Carl Menger, and Alfred Marshall. It treats economics as the study of rational decision making in the allocation of scarce resources among alternative and competing objectives, and focuses on optimizing or maximizing behaviour, assuming the objective of all economic agents in decision making is to maximize their net benefit.

New Economy
A term popularized during the 1990s, at a time during which the high-tech industry had been spearheading growth. It refers to an economy in which a knowledge-based service sector has replaced the traditional manufacturing sector as the primary source of economic growth.

Opportunity cost
The value of a resource in its next-best alternative use, when individuals face a choice in allocating their time and other resources.

Optimality
The best possible outcome, normally taking into account some limits or constraints, such as finite and scarce resources.

Overhead costs
Ongoing expenses incurred by a firm that do not vary with the level of production, such as insurance, rent and utilities, and in some cases, start-up costs. They are sometimes referred to as fixed costs.

Perfect competition
A market structure characterized by the existence of a standardized product produced by a large number of price-taking firms, perfect information on the part of firms and consumers, free entry to and exit from the market, and perfect long-run mobility of factors of production.

Perfect information
A situation in which individual participants in a market costlessly have complete knowledge of the prices, want-satisfying characteristics, and quality of all products.

Physiocracy
The doctrine of a group of 18th-century economists, among whom Jacques Turgot and François Quesnay were the principal figures, which held that agriculture is the foundation of economic society, and which is credited with the first model of the circular flow of the economy, Quesnay's *Tableau économique*.

Piracy
The illegal use or reproduction, for personal or commercial use, of copyright or patented material, such as computer software, video and music files, and published material.

Poverty line
The minimum level of income estimated to be required to provide an adequate basic standard of living in a country.

Predatory pricing
Setting the price of a firm's output below cost in order to drive competitors out of the market or as a barrier to entry, to discourage firms from entering the market. Predatory pricing is illegal in Canada and in most other countries.

Prediction
Anticipating a future outcome through inference based on either a theoretical model or an empirically based statistical model.

Prime cost pricing
The process of setting prices in the short run on the basis of those costs that vary directly with production, such as labour and material costs.

Privatization
The sale to private investors of publicly owned corporations and other assets, and the increased use of private suppliers rather than government employees to provide public services.

Production externalities
Costs or benefits of production activities that are experienced by individuals other than producers or purchasers—for example, effluent from a factory that pollutes an adjacent river (*negative* externality) or a beekeeping operation that has the indirect effect of pollinating the trees in a nearby apple orchard (*positive* externality).

Profit maximization
The hypothesis that firms' primary concern is to maximize the difference between total revenues and total costs, by choosing output levels consistent with that goal.

Profit satisficing
A business strategy of choosing price and output levels that meet adequacy requirements, in terms of a firm's need to cover its expenses and to grow at a reasonable rate, instead of a policy of achieving the maximum possible flow of profit.

Public good
A good whose private consumption by one individual does not reduce its availability for others and for which it is very difficult or impossible to exclude those who do not pay for the good from consuming it.

Rationality
Behaviour involving the use of logical thought processes, normally associated in economics with decisions regarding the use of scarce resources to achieve one's objectives, where individuals are assumed to weigh the benefits against the costs of pursuing an action so as to maximize their net advantage.

Regional convergence
A theory that assumes that with the unconstrained operation of market processes, regional disparities will disappear over time as incomes, productivity, and growth rates are equalized.

Regional disparity
Inequality of living standards and of economic opportunities among regions.

Regional divergence
A theory that assumes that the inequality gap among regions tends to widen over time.

Regulation
A form of government intervention designed to influence the behaviour of firms and individuals in the private sector. Regulation can be aimed at narrowing choices and eliminating the effects of market imperfections in certain areas, including regulating prices (for example, the setting of minimum wages, telephone rates), supply (broadcasting licences, agricultural production quotas), or disclosure of information (food content labelling).

Role of ideology
An ideology is a comprehensive vision of the world that may often motivate individual research. There is an ongoing debate about whether researchers' value judgments in economics may bias their theory and interpretation of empirical evidence.

Sales maximization
A view according to which firms are more concerned with maximizing their sales than maximizing their profits. In particular, maximizing total sales revenue may not be consistent with maximizing profits. In imperfectly competitive industries, however, if greater sales—and hence greater market share—result in more market power for a firm, then short-run sales maximization may be consistent with long-run profit maximization.

Small government
The view that government's role should be reduced to the minimal functions associated with classical liberalism, such as national defence and the establishment of a legal system based on private property rights.

Statistical discrimination
Differential treatment of individuals based on their membership in a particular identifiable group rather than on their own individual characteristics. For example, notwithstanding human rights legislation, Canadian insurance companies are legally able to charge a male under 25 years of age higher car insurance premiums than a female in the same age group even if he is accident-free and she has been in an accident, because she belongs to a group that has lower claims per policyholder. Similarly, income inequity can arise if an individual's characteristics in terms of age, race, and gender are associated with group-specific productivity. An individual can then be stereotyped and discriminated against, especially in the hiring process, on the basis of these statistical mean values, even if they are completely inappropriate for the specific individual in question.

Subsidies
Payments from the government to certain producers to help them cover part of their costs in an effort to enable them to remain profitable or to achieve a desired level of production.

Technology transfer
Assistance in providing or in teaching how to use and/or produce a particular technology. This is usually considered the major contribution by transnational corporations from highly industrialized countries to the less-developed world.

Trade union
A group constituting a legal bargaining unit that negotiates with employers to achieve advantages in the workplace—wages and salaries; benefits; health, safety, and general working conditions; satisfaction of worker grievances; hours of work; and employment—in accordance with existing labour relations legislation.

Transnational corporations
Corporate business enterprises that undertake production and delivery of goods and services in more than one country and across national borders. They are also referred to as *multinational corporations*.

Universal basic income
A system of welfare provision that guarantees to all citizens regardless of their employment and property income a minimum transfer to meet each individual's basic needs without means testing or any other discriminatory mechanism for allocating the income transfer.

Utility curve (or function)
A relation, graphically depicted in two-dimensional space, that associates the amount of satisfaction (or utility) that an individual derives from the consumption of varying quantities of a good. Utility functions involving two or three goods may be depicted using indifference maps, but with more than three goods, diagrammatic representation is not possible.

Utility maximization
A theory of economic behaviour which assumes that consumers consciously seek to maximize the satisfaction (or utility) they get from purchasing goods and services by consuming each good up to the point where the additional utility derived from the last unit of the good purchased is equal to the additional cost of acquiring it.

Views of science
There are competing views regarding the correct norms for scientific research and regarding the boundaries between what is and is not a science. Over time there has been a shift away from a prescriptive approach to correct scientific method and toward a situation in which there is more fluidity in defining the boundaries of science.

Wage setting
The process of determining the price of labour services in the labour market can take different institutional forms, from highly atomistic or decentralized systems, to highly centralized systems where wages are negotiated by employer associations and large trade union bodies through industry-wide bargaining. Sometimes, wages in an industry can be set by government decree, or by a tripartite process involving government, labour unions, and employers.

Welfare maximization
Normally associated with the concept of *social* welfare, typically (in neoclassical theory) imbedded in a *social welfare function* that attaches weights to the consumption of each individual in society.

Index

D

E

N